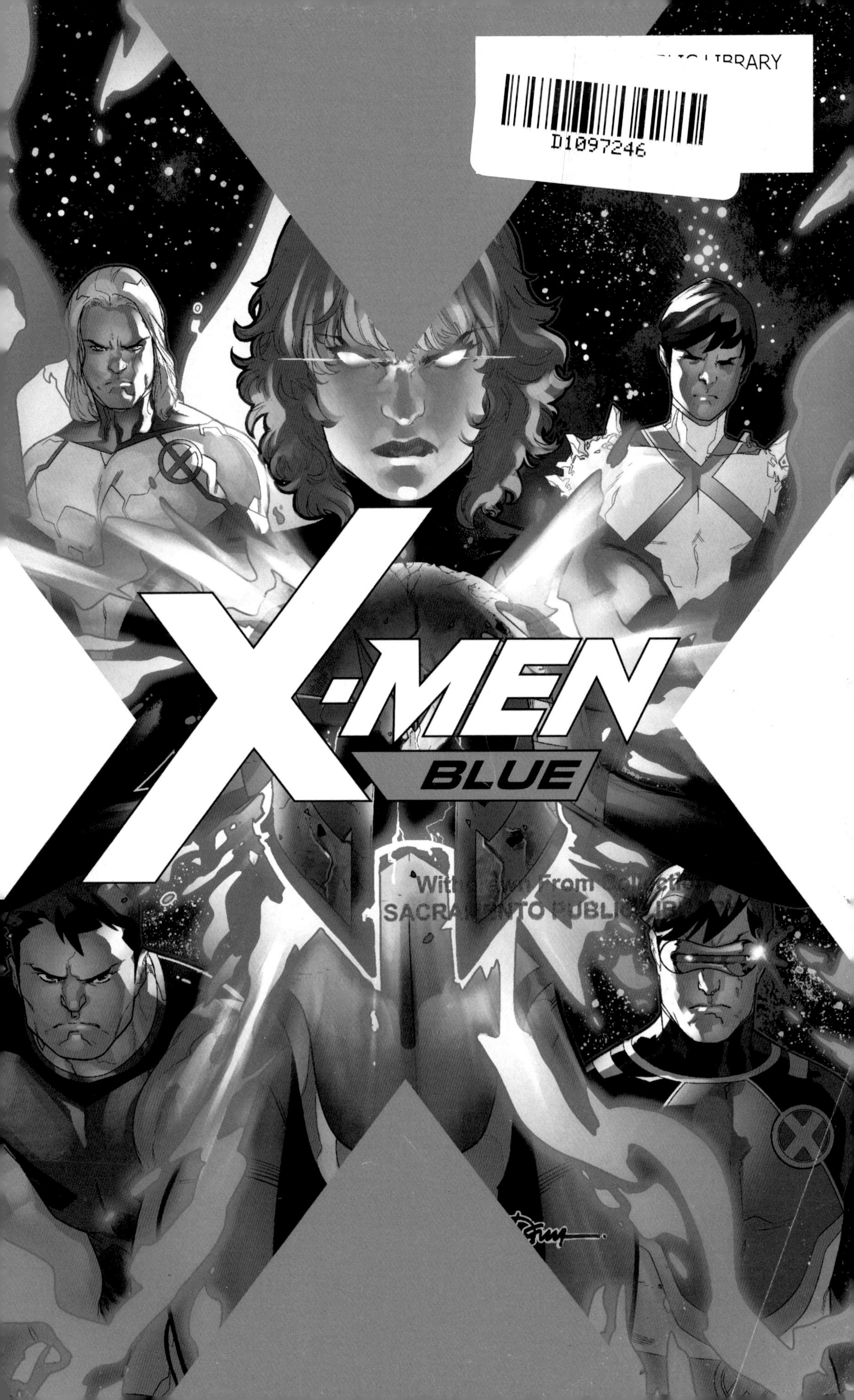
X-MEN
BLUE

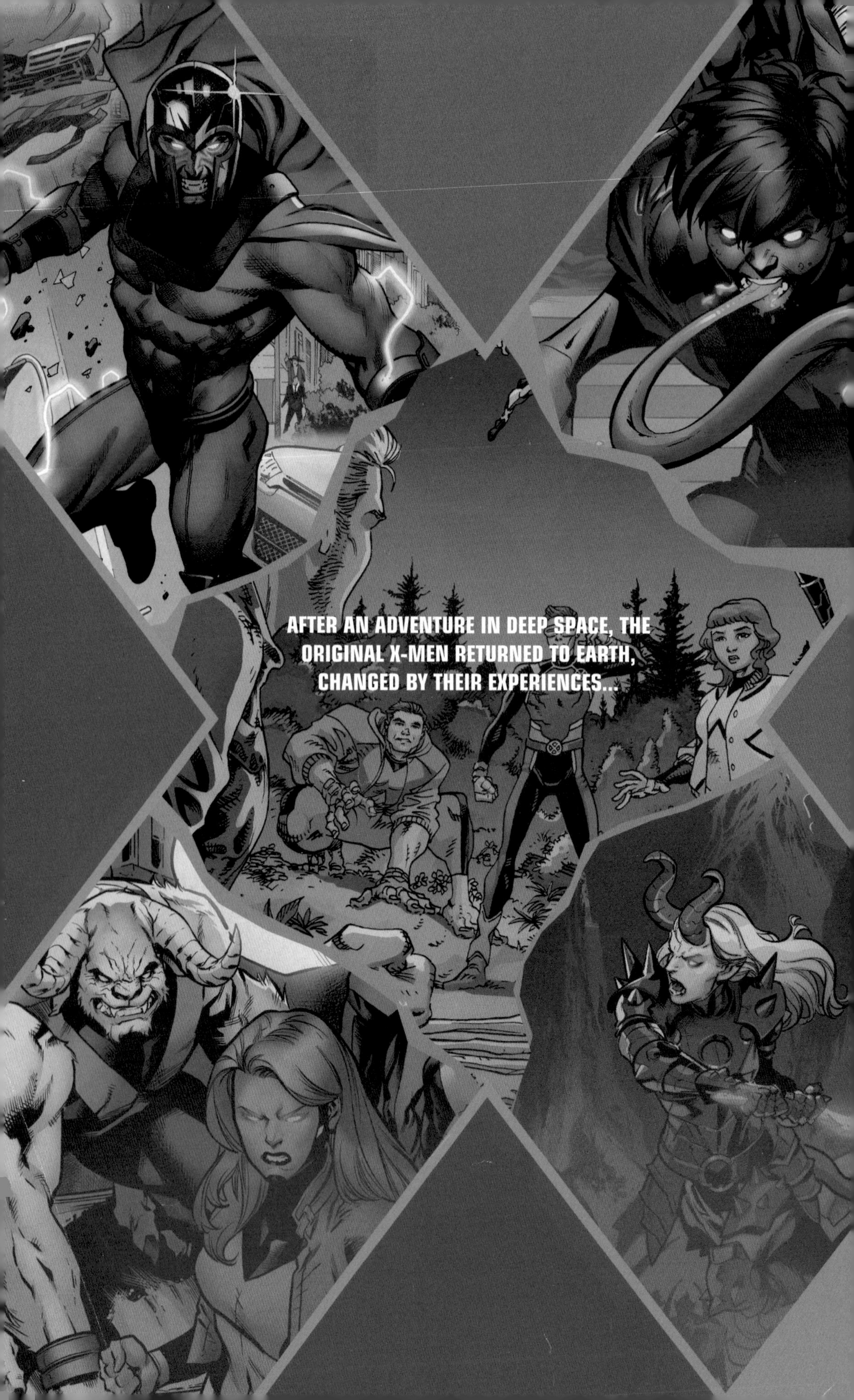
AFTER AN ADVENTURE IN DEEP SPACE, THE ORIGINAL X-MEN RETURNED TO EARTH, CHANGED BY THEIR EXPERIENCES...

# X-MEN BLUE

# SURVIVING THE EXPERIENCE

Writer/**CULLEN BUNN**
Artists/**NATHAN STOCKMAN** (#29-30),
**JORGE MOLINA** (#31),
**ANDRÉS GENOLET** (#32)
& **MARCUS TO** (#33-36)
Color Artist/**MATT MILLA**
Letterer/**VC's JOE CARAMAGNA**
Cover Art/**R.B. SILVA** with
**RAIN BEREDO** (#29-34)
& **MATT MILLA** (#35-36)

Assistant Editor/**CHRIS ROBINSON**
Editor/**DARREN SHAN**
X-Men Group Editors/**MARK PANICCIA** & **JORDAN D. WHITE**

X-MEN CREATED BY **STAN LEE** & **JACK KIRBY**

Collection Editor/**JENNIFER GRÜNWALD** • Assistant Editor/**CAITLIN O'CONNELL**
Associate Managing Editor/**KATERI WOODY** • Editor, Special Projects/**MARK D. BEAZLEY**
VP Production & Special Projects/**JEFF YOUNGQUIST** • SVP Print, Sales & Marketing/**DAVID GABRIEL**
Book Designer/**JAY BOWEN**

Editor in Chief/**C.B. CEBULSKI** • Chief Creative Officer/**JOE QUESADA**
President/**DAN BUCKLEY** • Executive Producer/**ALAN FINE**

**X-MEN BLUE VOL. 5: SURVIVING THE EXPERIENCE.** Contains material originally published in magazine form as X-MEN BLUE #29-36. First printing 2018. ISBN 978-1-302-90980-2. Published by MARVEL WORLDWIDE, INC., a subsidiary of MARVEL ENTERTAINMENT, LLC. OFFICE OF PUBLICATION: 135 West 50th Street, New York, NY 10020.  **Printed in the U.S.A.** DAN BUCKLEY, President, Marvel Entertainment; JOHN NEE, Publisher; JOE QUESADA, Chief Creative Officer; TOM BREVOORT, SVP of Publishing; DAVID BOGART, SVP of Business Affairs & Operations, Publishing & Partnership; DAVID GABRIEL, SVP of Sales & Marketing, Publishing; JEFF YOUNGQUIST, VP of Production & Special Projects; DAN CARR, Executive Director of Publishing Technology; ALEX MORALES, Director of Publishing Operations; DAN EDINGTON, Managing Editor; SUSAN CRESPI, Production Manager; STAN LEE, Chairman Emeritus. For information regarding advertising in Marvel Comics or on Marvel.com, please contact Vit DeBellis, Custom Solutions & Integrated Advertising Manager, at vdebellis@marvel.com. For Marvel subscription inquiries, please call 888-511-5480. **Manufactured between 9/7/2018 and 10/9/2018 by LSC COMMUNICATIONS INC., KENDALLVILLE, IN, USA.**

10 9 8 7 6 5 4 3 2 1

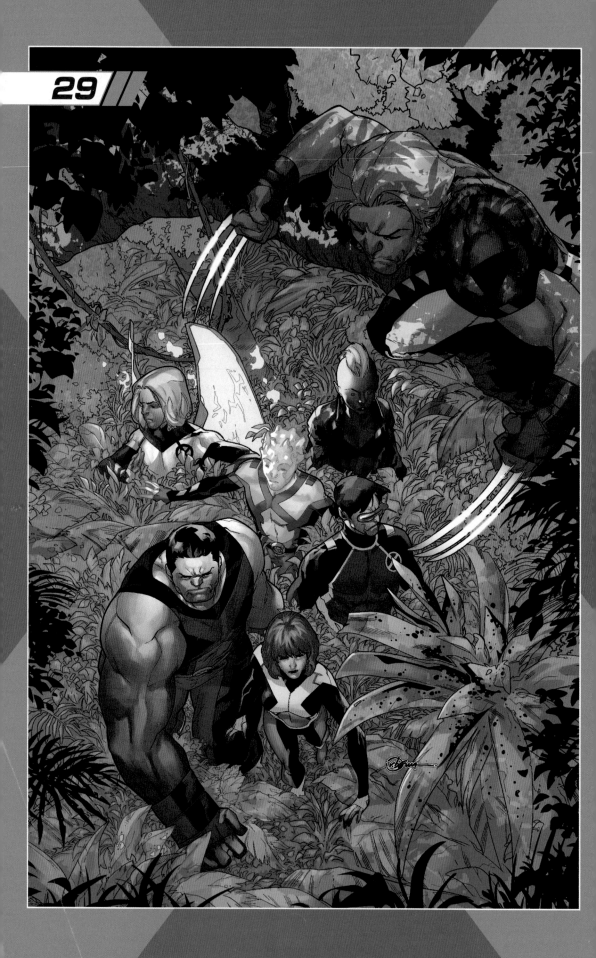

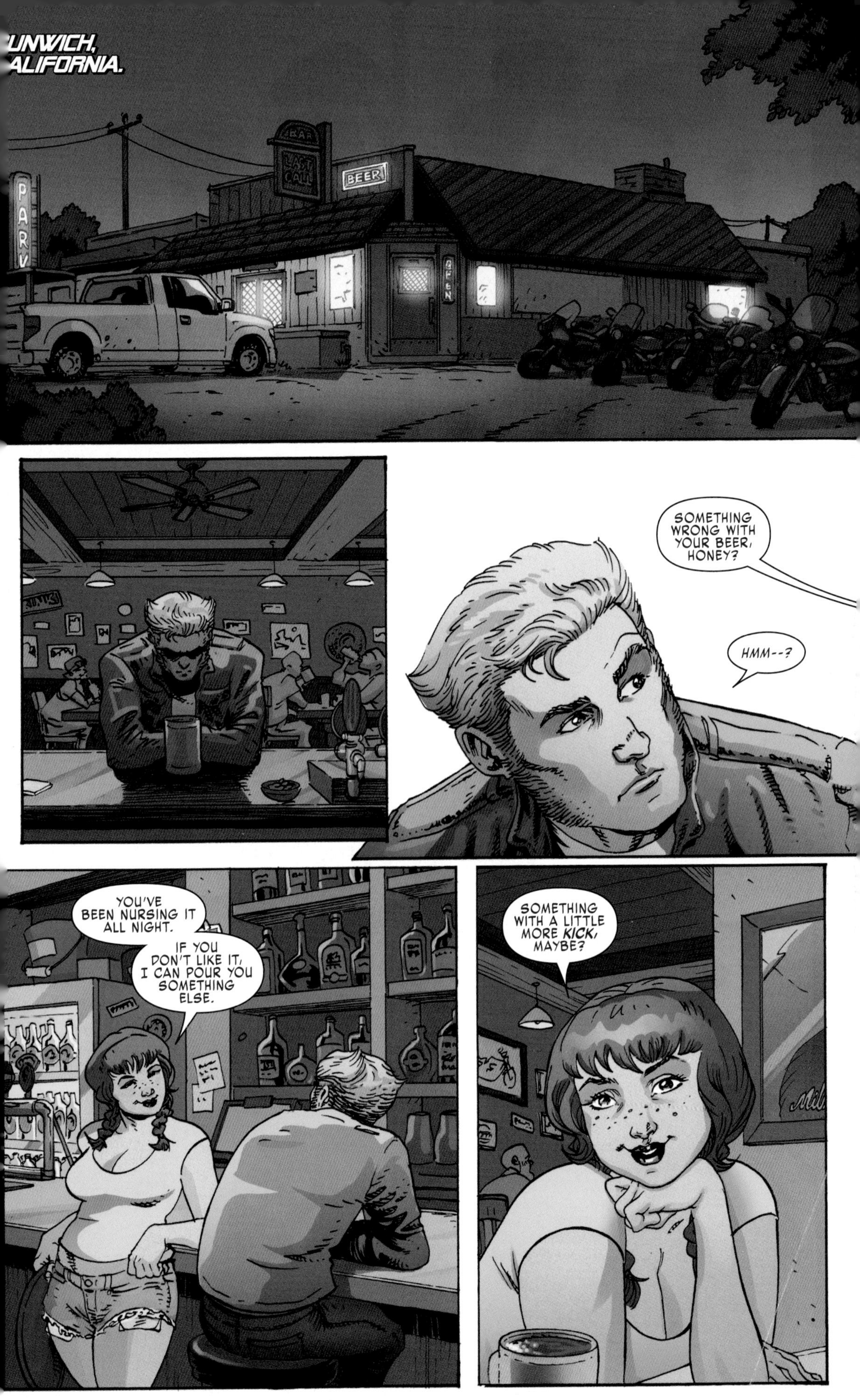
UNWICH,
ALIFORNIA.
BAR
LAST CALL
BEER
OPEN
SOMETHING WRONG WITH YOUR BEER, HONEY?
HMM--?
YOU'VE BEEN NURSING IT ALL NIGHT.
IF YOU DON'T LIKE IT, I CAN POUR YOU SOMETHING ELSE.
SOMETHING WITH A LITTLE MORE KICK, MAYBE?

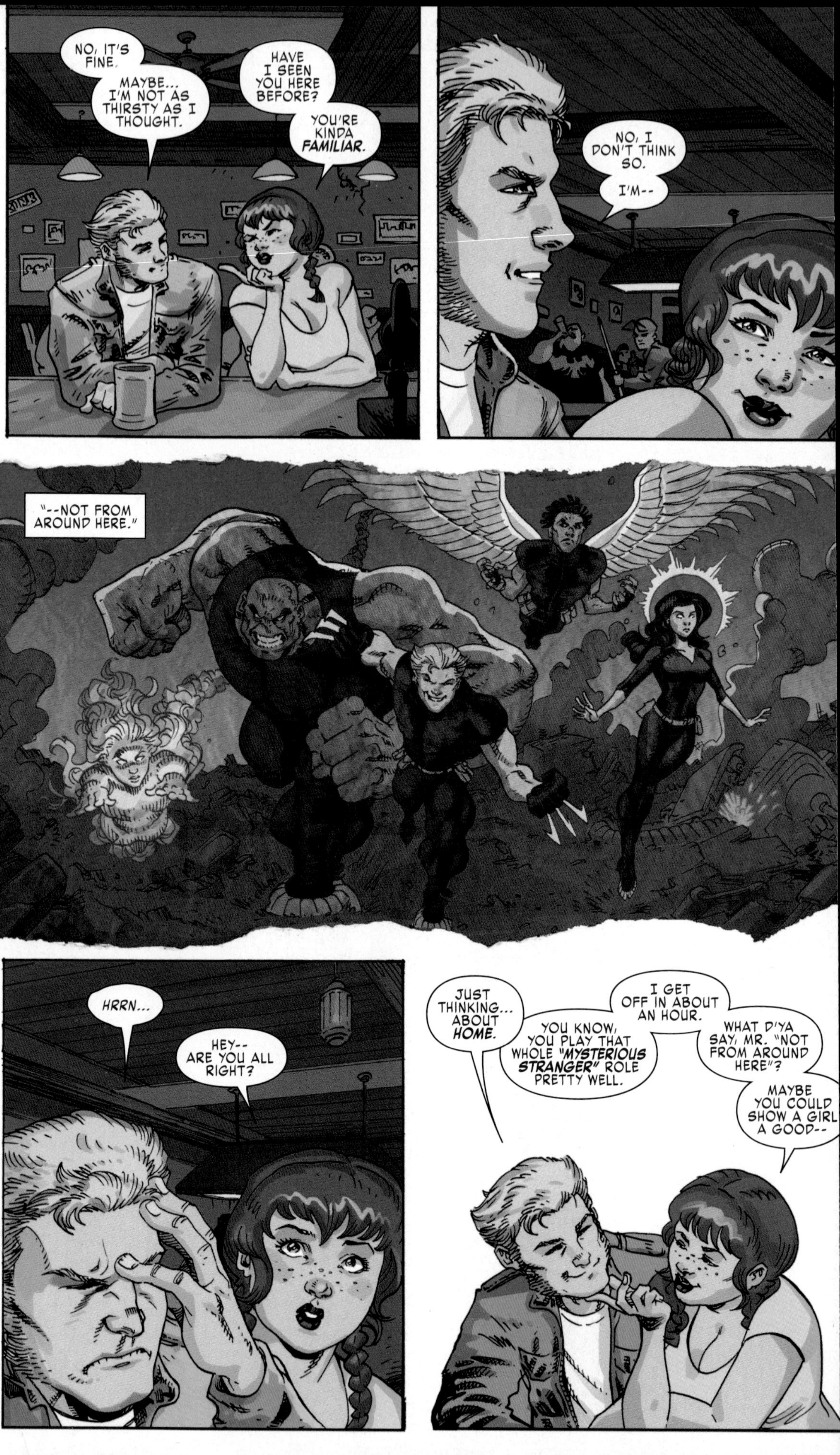
NO, IT'S FINE.
MAYBE... I'M NOT AS THIRSTY AS I THOUGHT.
HAVE I SEEN YOU HERE BEFORE?
YOU'RE KINDA FAMILIAR.
NO, I DON'T THINK SO.
I'M--
"--NOT FROM AROUND HERE."
HRRN...
HEY-- ARE YOU ALL RIGHT?
JUST THINKING... ABOUT HOME.
YOU KNOW, YOU PLAY THAT WHOLE "MYSTERIOUS STRANGER" ROLE PRETTY WELL.
I GET OFF IN ABOUT AN HOUR.
WHAT D'YA SAY, MR. "NOT FROM AROUND HERE"?
MAYBE YOU COULD SHOW A GIRL A GOOD--

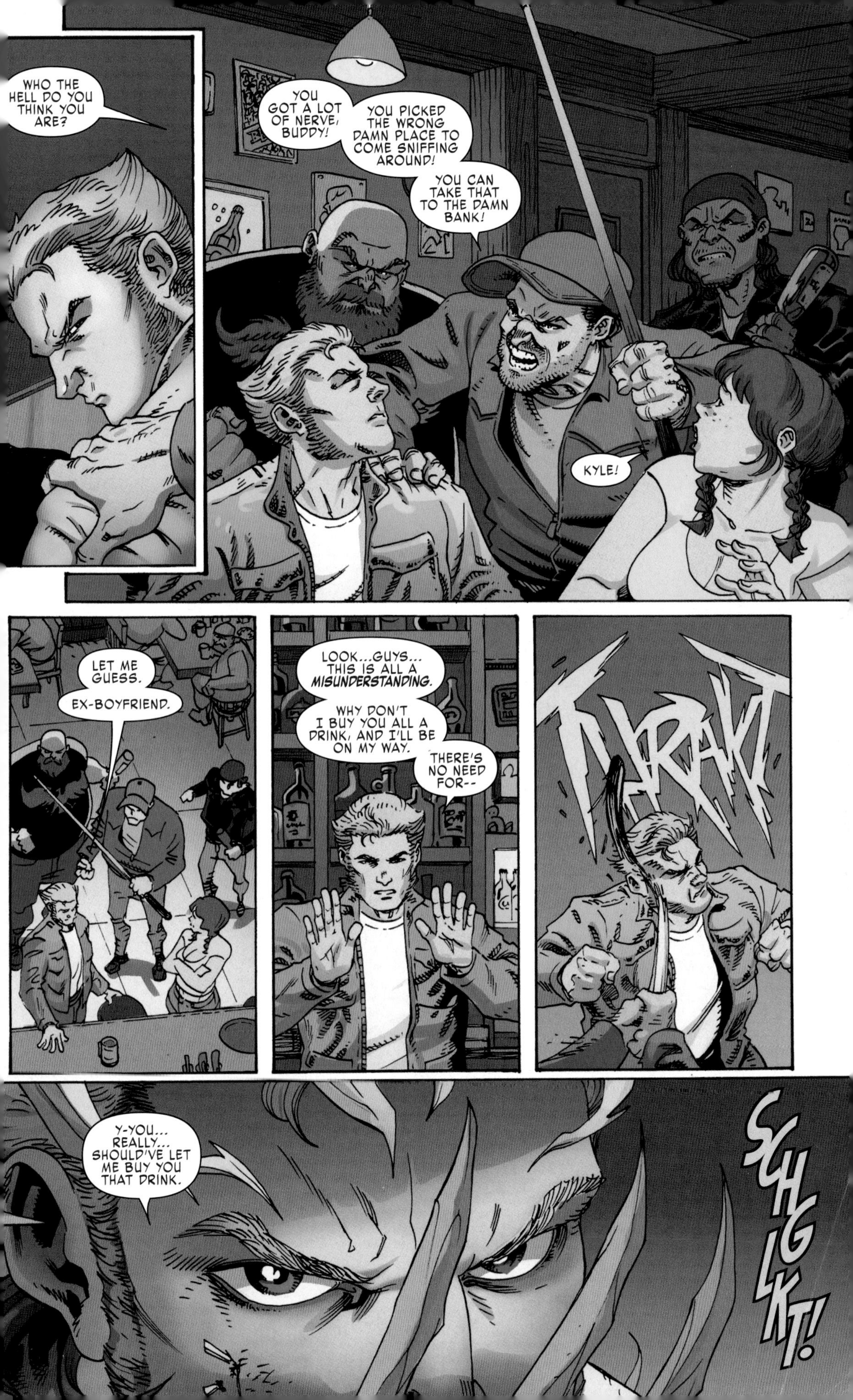
WHO THE HELL DO YOU THINK YOU ARE?
YOU GOT A LOT OF NERVE, BUDDY!
YOU PICKED THE WRONG DAMN PLACE TO COME SNIFFING AROUND!
YOU CAN TAKE THAT TO THE DAMN BANK!
KYLE!
LET ME GUESS.
EX-BOYFRIEND.
LOOK...GUYS... THIS IS ALL A MISUNDERSTANDING.
WHY DON'T I BUY YOU ALL A DRINK, AND I'LL BE ON MY WAY.
THERE'S NO NEED FOR--
THRAKT
Y-YOU... REALLY... SHOULD'VE LET ME BUY YOU THAT DRINK.
SCHGLKT!

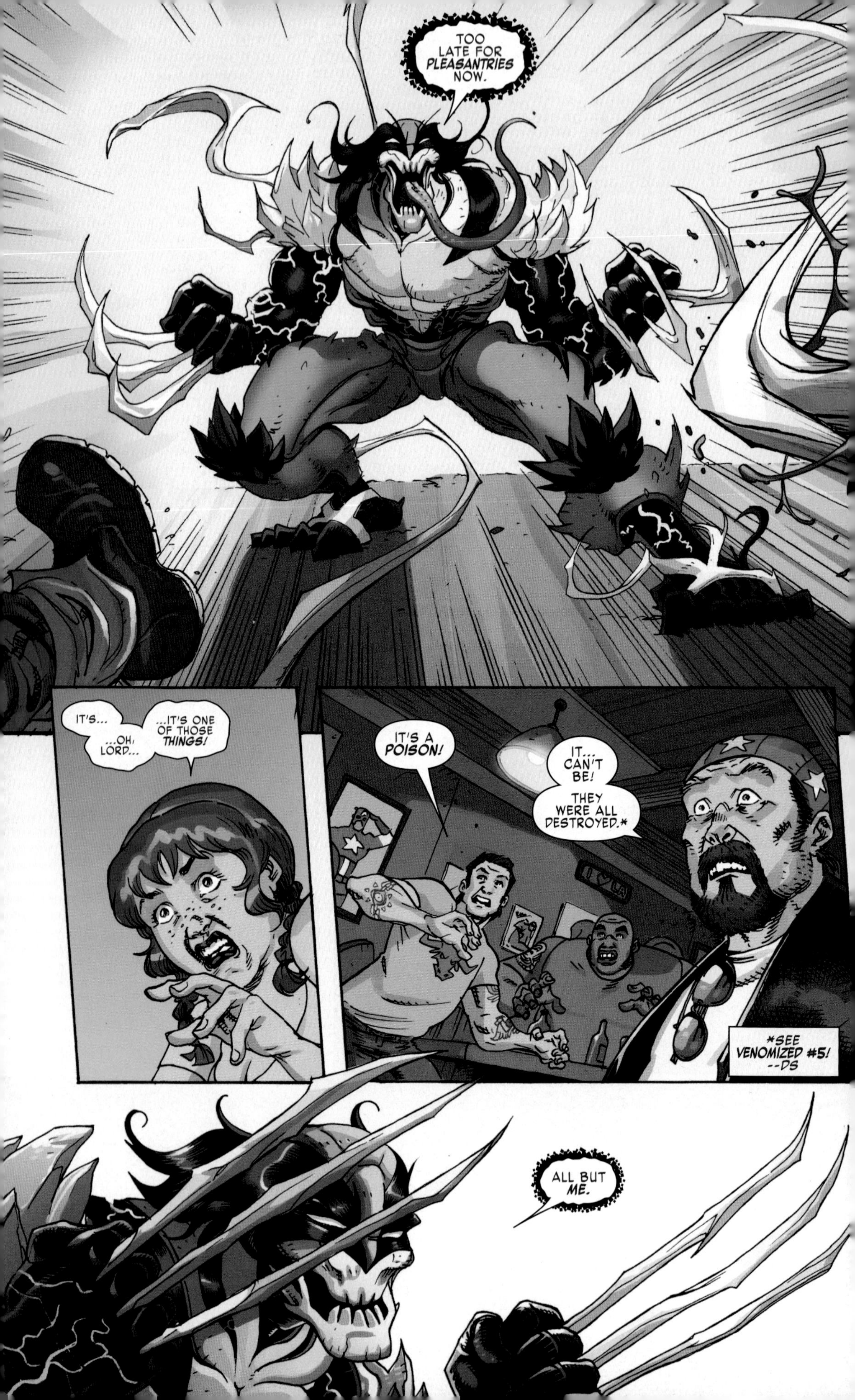
TOO LATE FOR PLEASANTRIES NOW.
IT'S...
...OH, LORD...
...IT'S ONE OF THOSE THINGS!
IT'S A POISON!
IT... CAN'T BE!
THEY WERE ALL DESTROYED.*
*SEE VENOMIZED #5! --DS
ALL BUT ME.

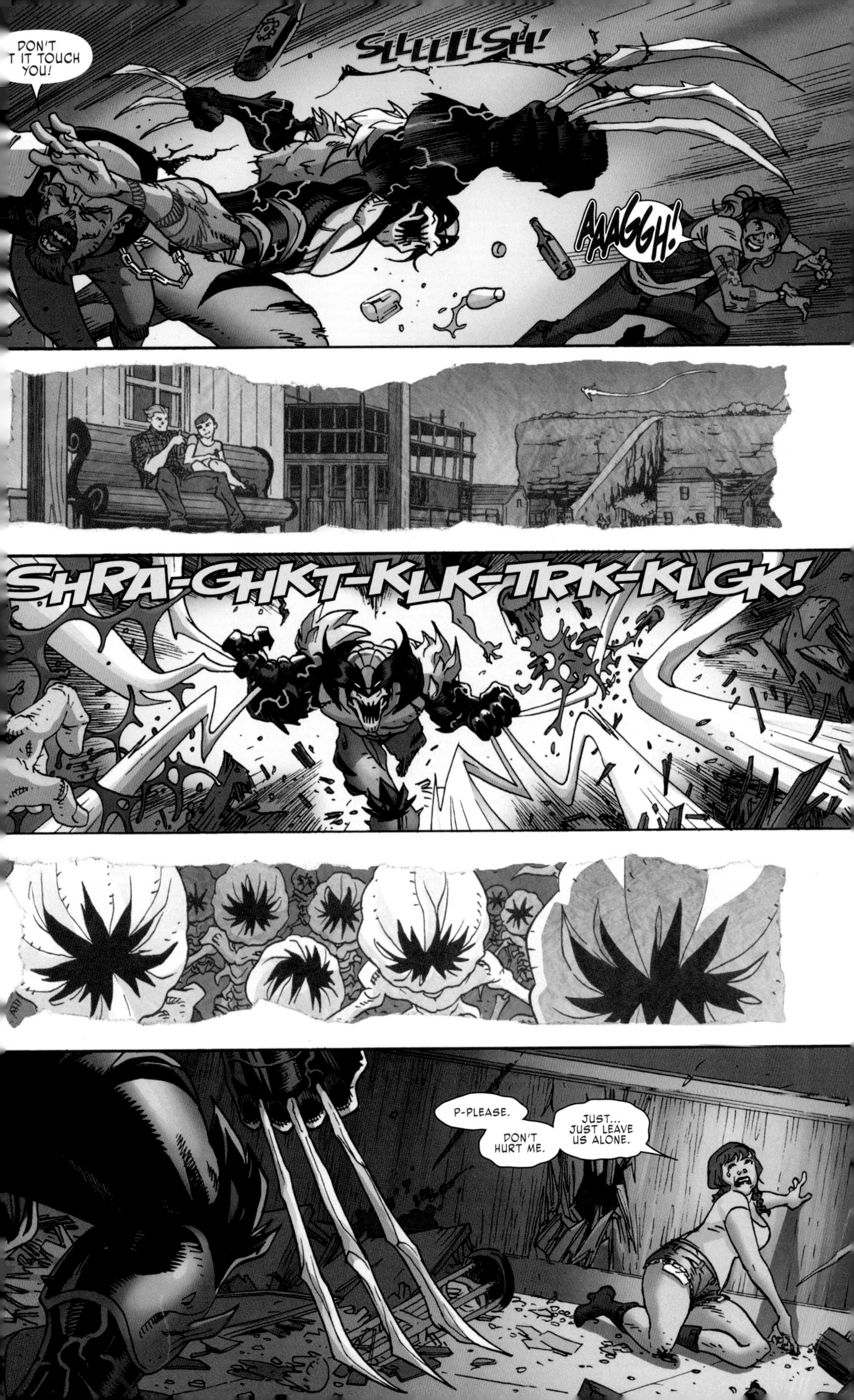
DON'T
T IT TOUCH
YOU!
SLLLLLISH!
AAAGGH!
SHRA-GHKT-KLK-TRK-KLGK!
P-PLEASE.
DON'T
HURT ME.
JUST...
JUST LEAVE
US ALONE.

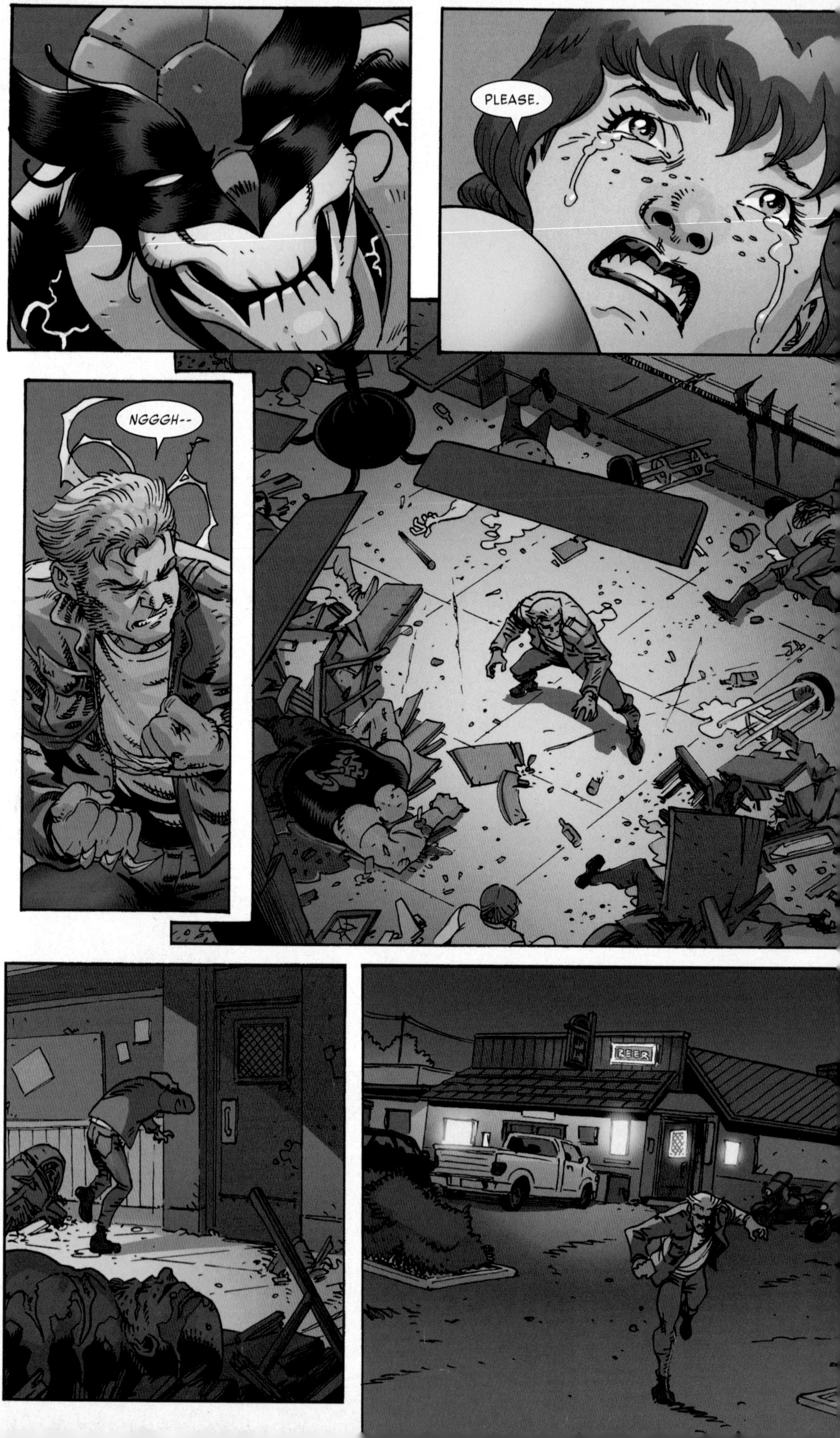
PLEASE.
NGGGH--
BEER

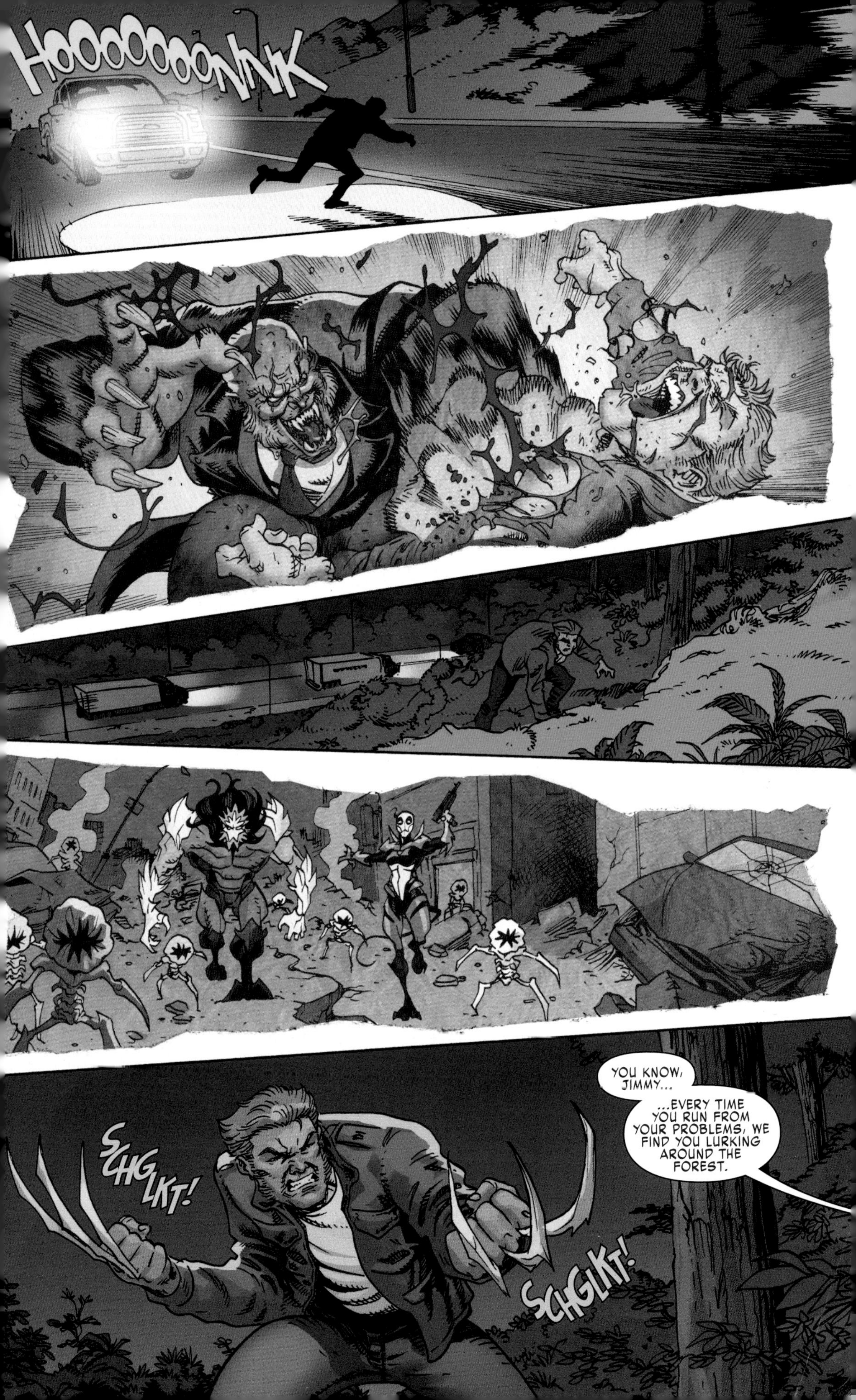
HOOOOOOONNK
YOU KNOW, JIMMY...
...EVERY TIME YOU RUN FROM YOUR PROBLEMS, WE FIND YOU LURKING AROUND THE FOREST.
SCHGLKT!
SCHGLKT!

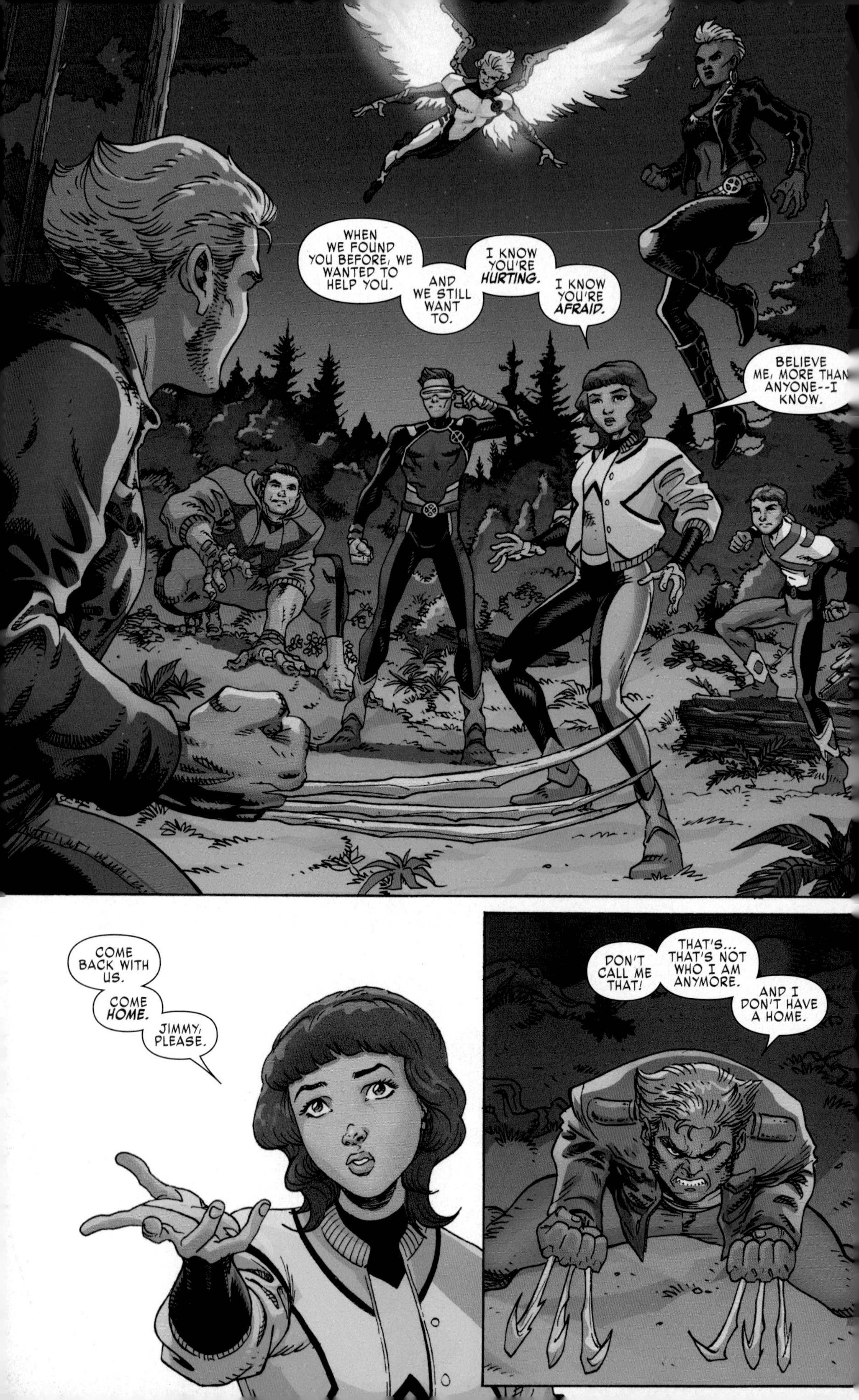
WHEN WE FOUND YOU BEFORE, WE WANTED TO HELP YOU.
AND WE STILL WANT TO.
I KNOW YOU'RE HURTING.
I KNOW YOU'RE AFRAID.
BELIEVE ME, MORE THAN ANYONE--I KNOW.
COME BACK WITH US.
COME HOME.
JIMMY, PLEASE.
DON'T CALL ME THAT!
THAT'S... THAT'S NOT WHO I AM ANYMORE.
AND I DON'T HAVE A HOME.

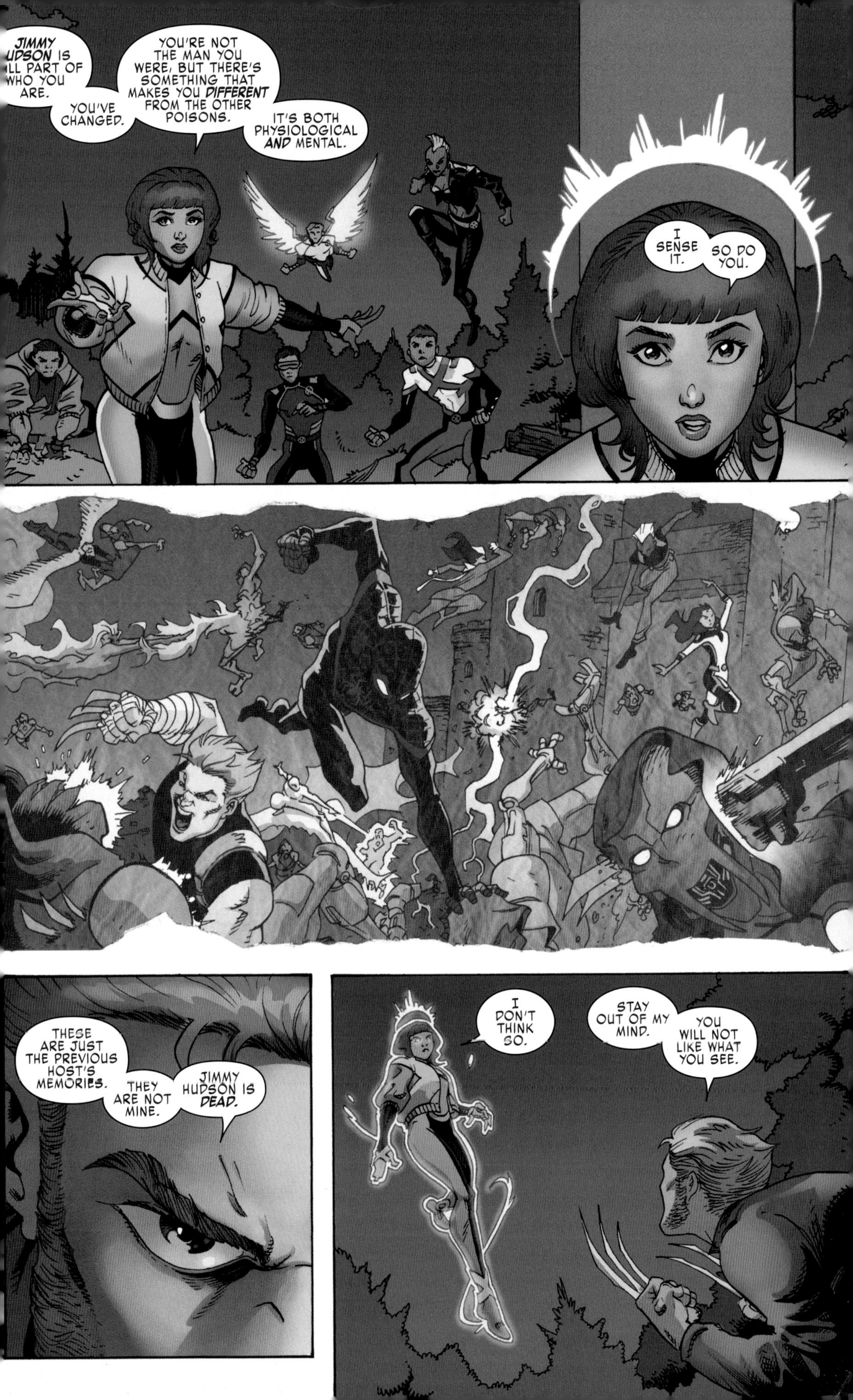
JIMMY HUDSON IS ...ILL PART OF WHO YOU ARE.
YOU'VE CHANGED.
YOU'RE NOT THE MAN YOU WERE, BUT THERE'S SOMETHING THAT MAKES YOU DIFFERENT FROM THE OTHER POISONS.
IT'S BOTH PHYSIOLOGICAL AND MENTAL.
I SENSE IT.
SO DO YOU.
THESE ARE JUST THE PREVIOUS HOST'S MEMORIES.
THEY ARE NOT MINE.
JIMMY HUDSON IS DEAD.
I DON'T THINK SO.
STAY OUT OF MY MIND.
YOU WILL NOT LIKE WHAT YOU SEE.

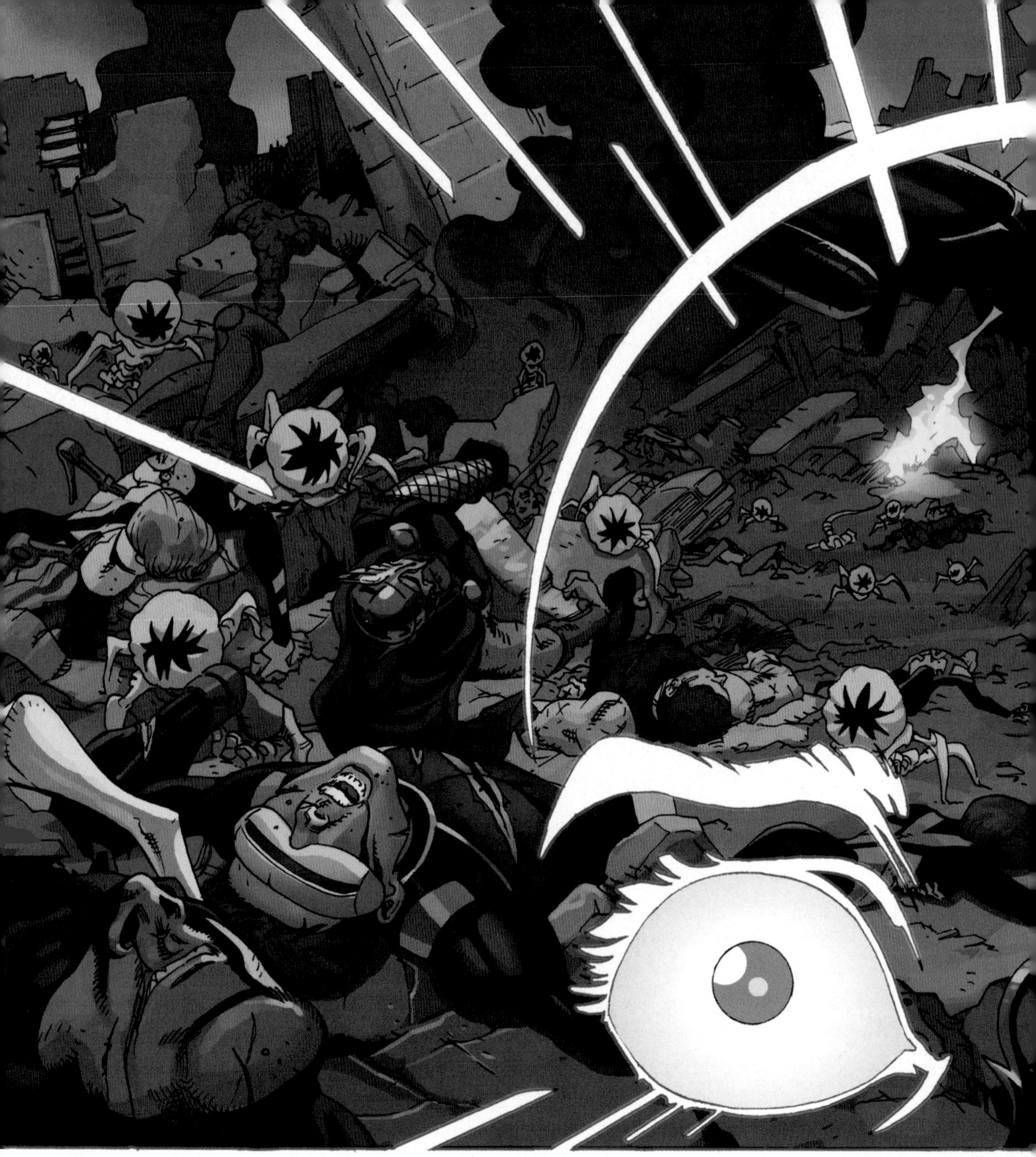

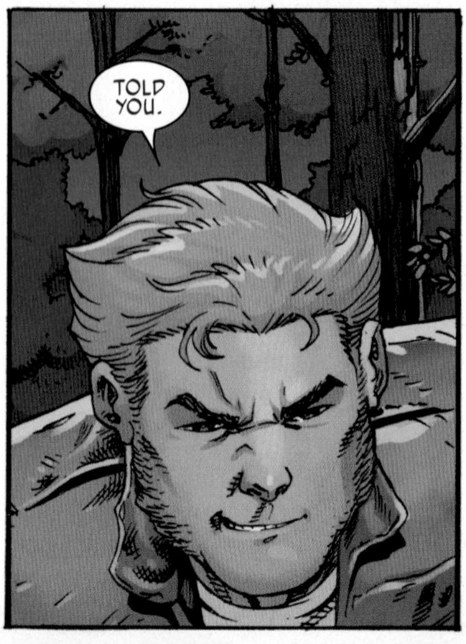
TOLD YOU.

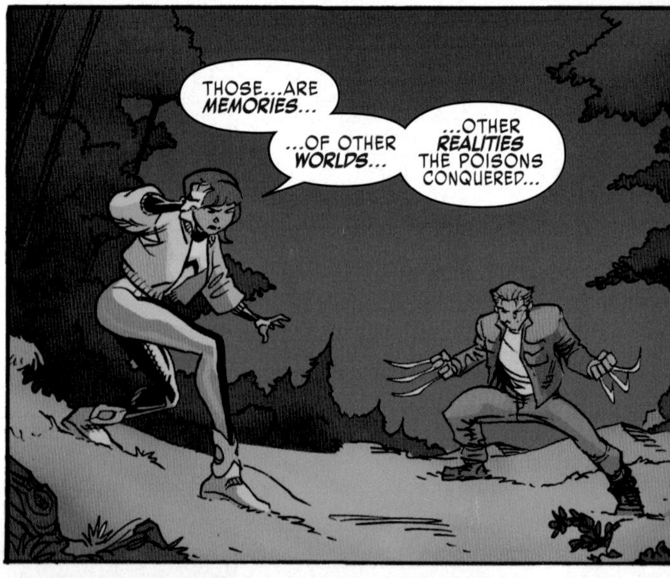
THOSE...ARE MEMORIES...
...OF OTHER WORLDS...
...OTHER REALITIES THE POISONS CONQUERED...

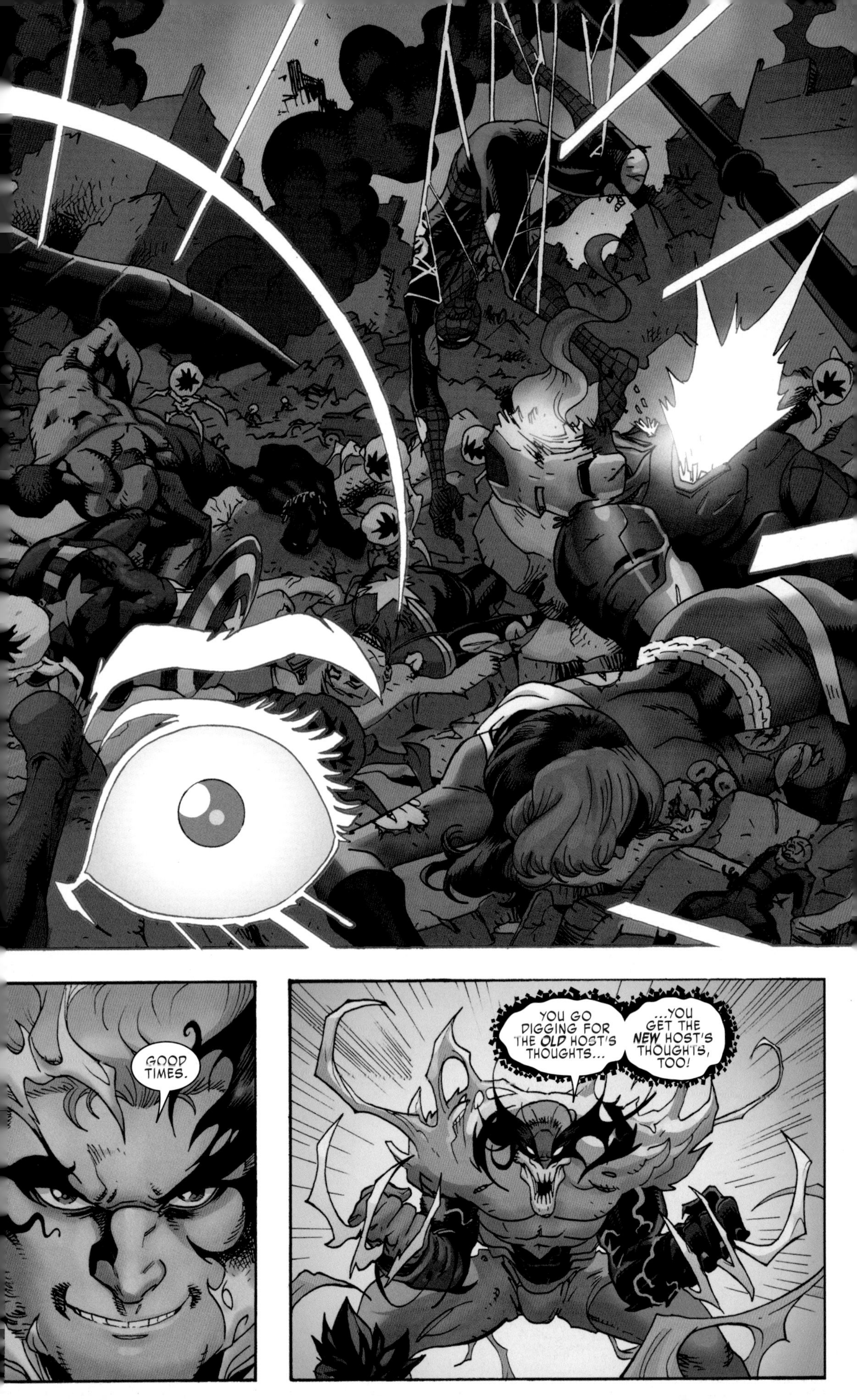
GOOD TIMES.
YOU GO DIGGING FOR THE OLD HOST'S THOUGHTS...
...YOU GET THE NEW HOST'S THOUGHTS, TOO!

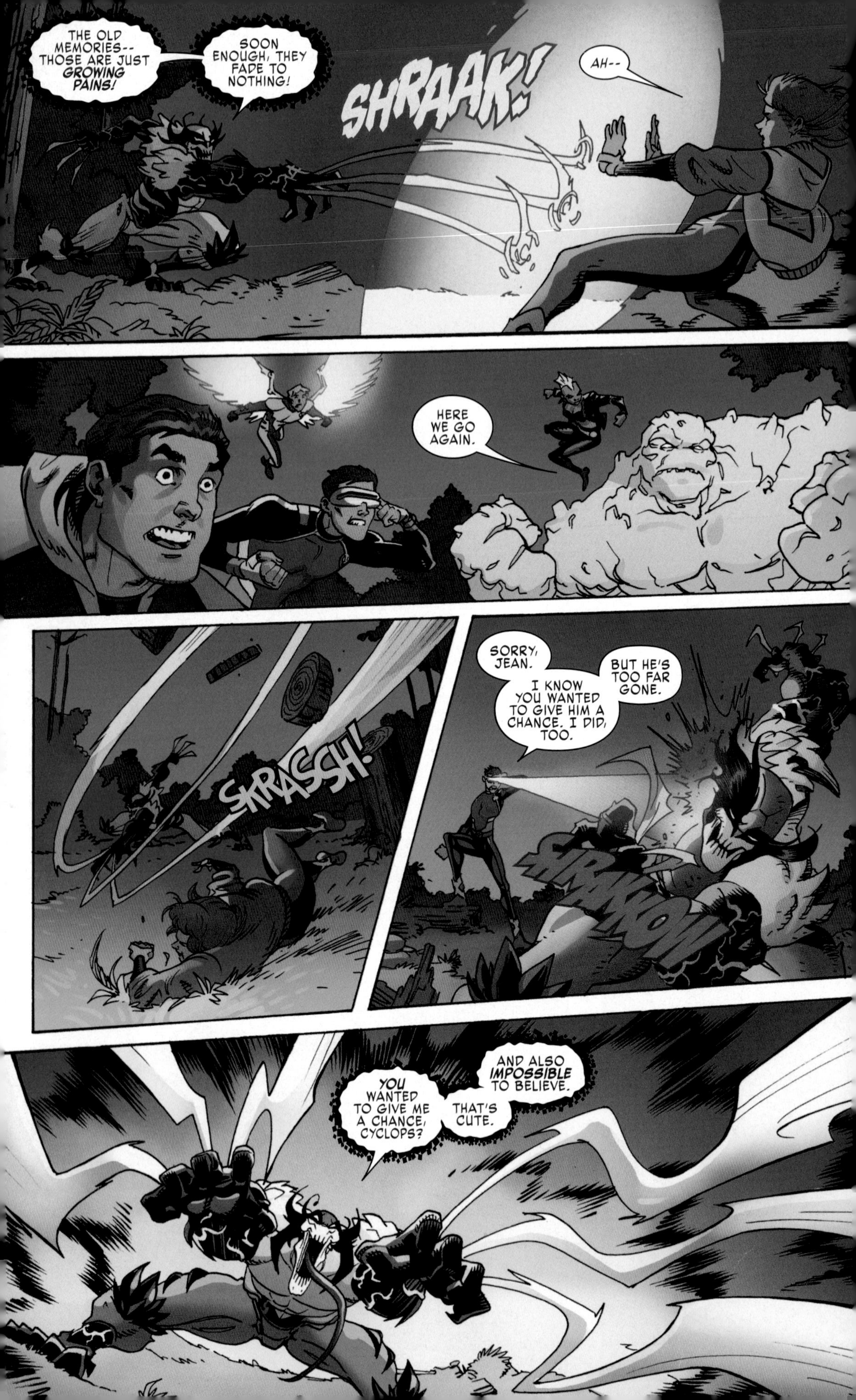
THE OLD MEMORIES-- THOSE ARE JUST GROWING PAINS!
SOON ENOUGH, THEY FADE TO NOTHING!
SHRAAK!
AH--
HERE WE GO AGAIN.
SKRASSH!
SORRY, JEAN.
I KNOW YOU WANTED TO GIVE HIM A CHANCE. I DID, TOO.
BUT HE'S TOO FAR GONE.
YOU WANTED TO GIVE ME A CHANCE, CYCLOPS?
THAT'S CUTE.
AND ALSO IMPOSSIBLE TO BELIEVE.

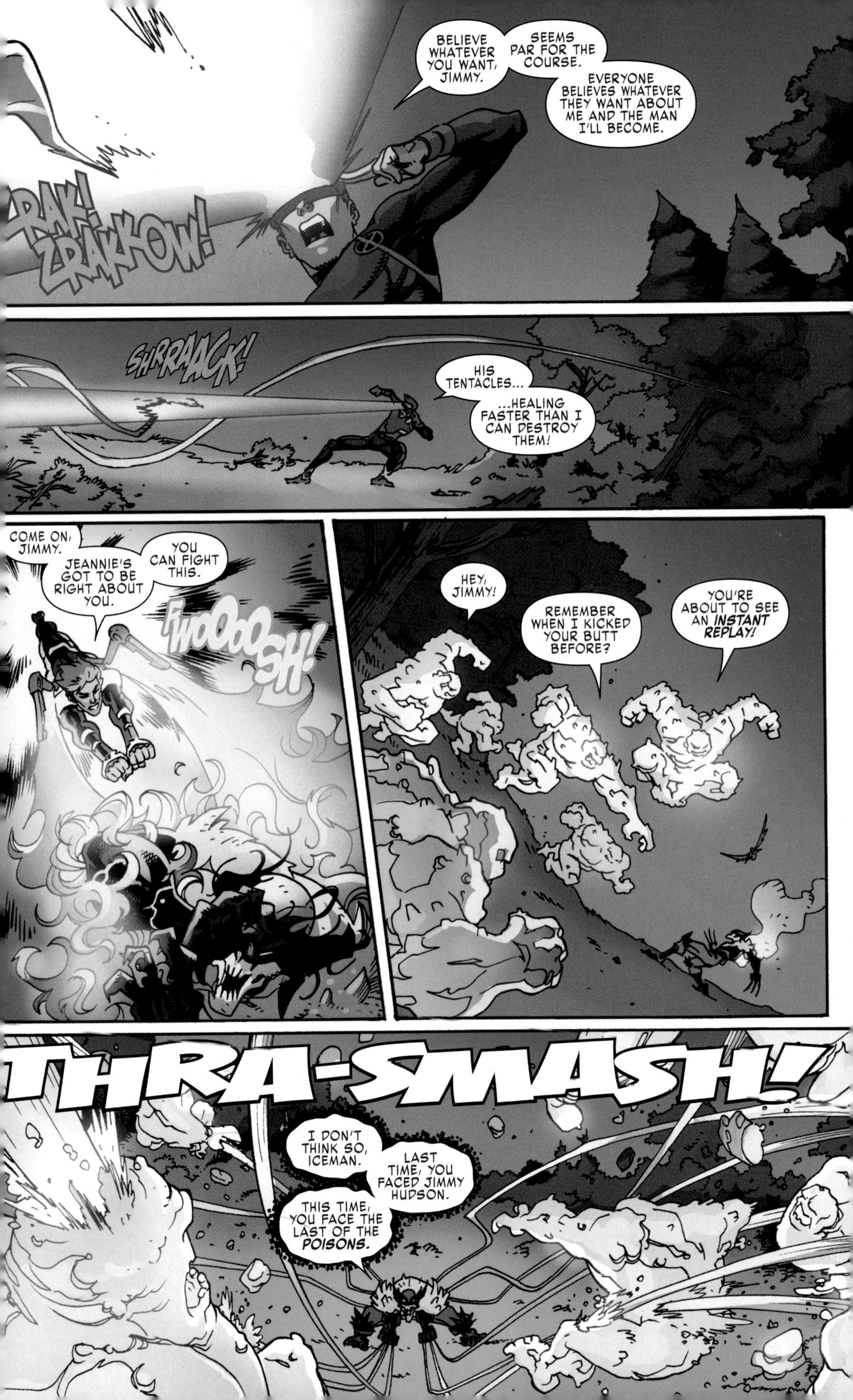
BELIEVE WHATEVER YOU WANT, JIMMY.
SEEMS PAR FOR THE COURSE.
EVERYONE BELIEVES WHATEVER THEY WANT ABOUT ME AND THE MAN I'LL BECOME.
ZRAK! ZRAKKOW!
SHRRAACK!
HIS TENTACLES...
...HEALING FASTER THAN I CAN DESTROY THEM!
COME ON, JIMMY.
JEANNIE'S GOT TO BE RIGHT ABOUT YOU.
YOU CAN FIGHT THIS.
FWOOOOOSH!
HEY, JIMMY!
REMEMBER WHEN I KICKED YOUR BUTT BEFORE?
YOU'RE ABOUT TO SEE AN INSTANT REPLAY!
THRA-SMASH!
I DON'T THINK SO, ICEMAN.
LAST TIME, YOU FACED JIMMY HUDSON.
THIS TIME, YOU FACE THE LAST OF THE POISONS.

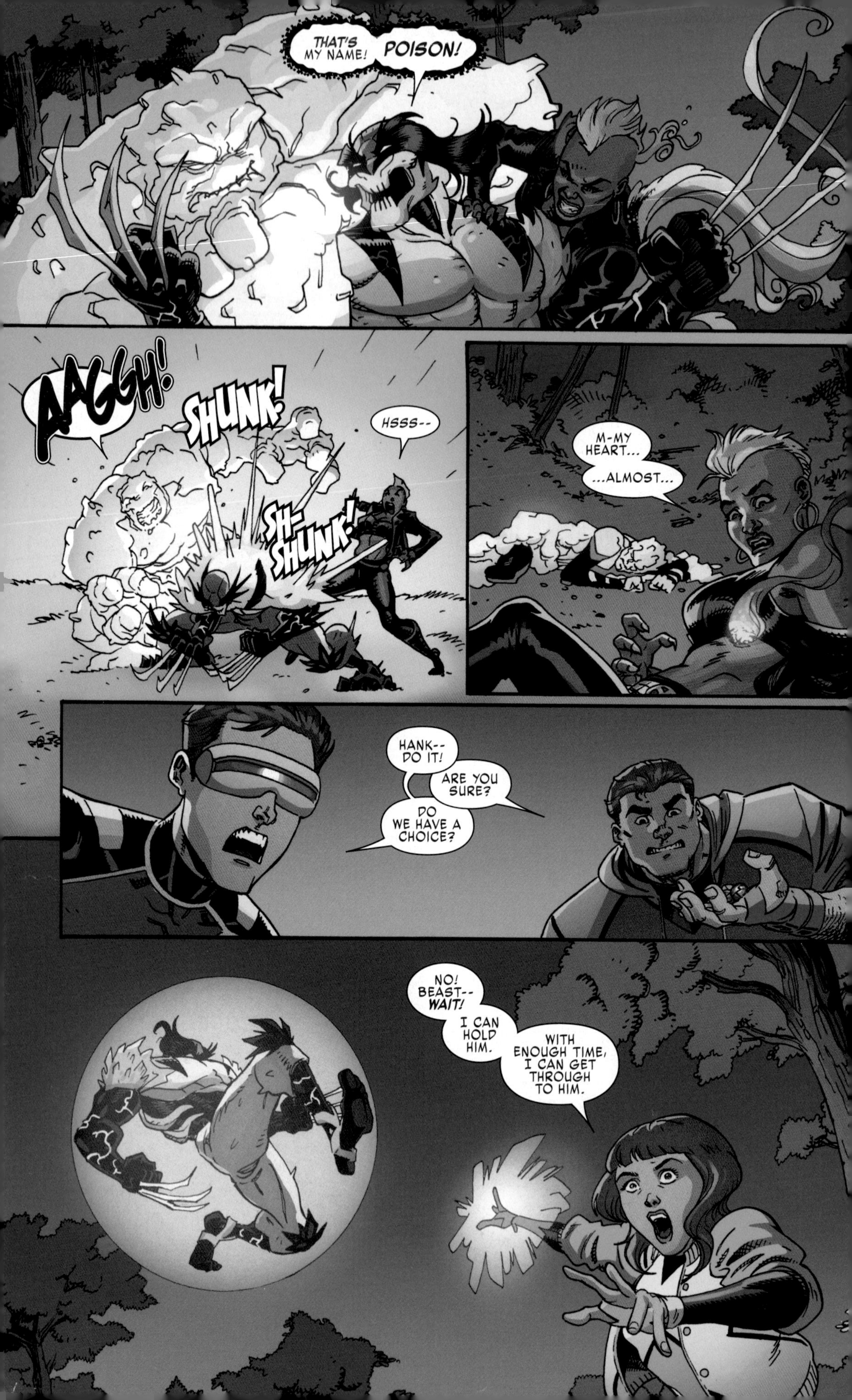
THAT'S MY NAME! POISON!
AAGGH!
SHUNK!
HSSS--
SH-SHUNK!
M-MY HEART...
...ALMOST...
HANK-- DO IT!
ARE YOU SURE?
DO WE HAVE A CHOICE?
NO! BEAST-- WAIT!
I CAN HOLD HIM.
WITH ENOUGH TIME, I CAN GET THROUGH TO HIM.

SH-CHUNK!

SH-CHUNK!

THK!

THRASH!

THRASH!

AAGGH!

SLLLSH!

SGLK!

JEAN!

JEAN GREY WOULD **DESTROY** ME.

SHE WOULD KILL THE **LAST** OF MY KIND.

JUST AS SHE KILLED THE **FIRST.**

SHE **DESERVES** TO DIE.

I CAN'T WAIT ANY LONGER.

I'M **ACTIVATING** THESE REMOTE **ANTI-VENOM** MODULES.

THEY'LL KILL HIM ON **CONTACT.**

I'M **SORRY,** JIMMY.

SO **SORRY.**

BUT YOU GIVE ME NO **CHOICE.**

ARE YOU **SURE,** BEAST?

I'M BETTING I'M **FASTER** THAN YOU THINK.

DROP THEM.

TH-THUMP

LET HER GO, JIMMY.

CALL ME BY MY *TRUE* NAME.

ALL RIGHT...*POISON*... WHATEVER YOU WANT TO BE CALLED.

YOU CAN GO, ALL RIGHT?

I GIVE YOU MY WORD.

LET JEAN GO, AND WE'LL LEAVE YOU BE.

BUT JEAN GREY STILL HAS *HOPE* FOR THE PREVIOUS HOST.

AND SHE IS ONE OF THE ONLY PEOPLE TO RESIST OUR INFLUENCE.

I'D BE BETTER OFF KILLING--

WE'LL FIGURE THIS OUT.
I HOPE YOU REALIZE NOW THAT WE'RE **FRIENDS,** JIMMY.
IF YOU COME WITH US, WE MIGHT BE ABLE TO HELP YOU.
J-JEAN?
SCOTT...
...WARREN...
...WHAT'S **HAPPENING** TO ME?
I KNEW IT.
I KNEW JEAN WAS RIGHT.
OH...
...OH, LORD...
...I DIDN'T MEAN IT...
...I WOULD NEVER HURT YOU...

I THINK...
I THINK SHE'LL BE ALL RIGHT.

I CAN'T HELP MYSELF.

IT'S LIKE I HAVE...I DUNNO...TWO SETS OF THOUGHTS... TWO SETS OF MEMORIES...IN MY HEAD.

AND THEY'RE TRYING TO KILL EACH OTHER.

DUDE.

WE WANT TO HELP.

BUT YOU KNOW I HAVE TO ICE YOU UP OR SOMETHING, RIGHT?

DON'T BOTHER, BOBBY.

SHGGGKT

DAKEN?
GUESSED IT IN ONE!
I'VE BEEN TRAILING YOU FOR A WHILE NOW.
WANTED TO SEE IF YOU HAD THE STONES TO DO WHAT NEEDED TO BE DONE.
AND SINCE YOU DON'T... WELL...
...MAGNETO SENDS HIS REGARDS.

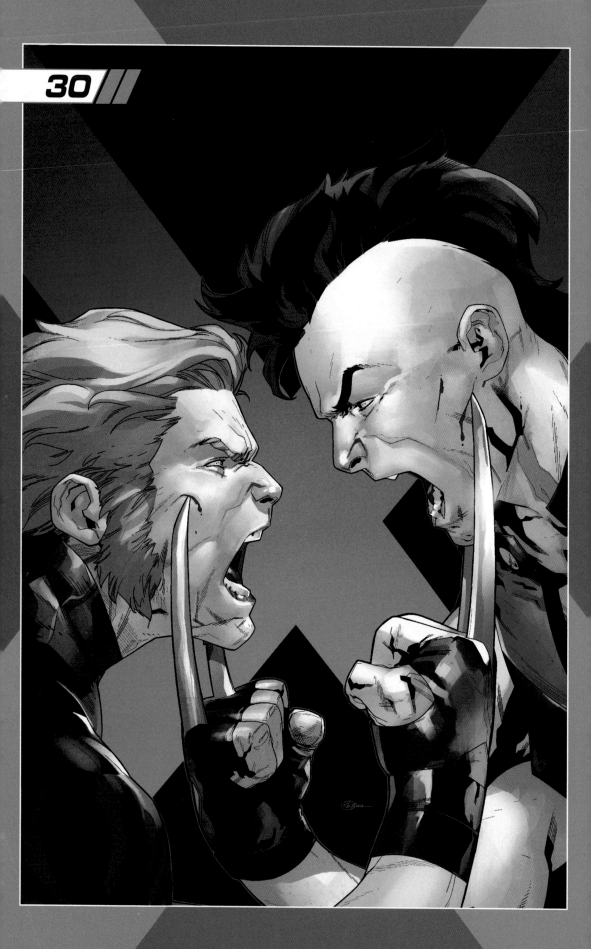

DAKEN--? WHAT DO YOU THINK YOU'RE DOING?

CALL IT AN ASSASSINATION, CYCLOPS.

CALL IT A MERCY KILLING.

CALL IT SIBLING RIVALRY.

THE END RESULT'S THE SAME...

...JIMMY HUDSON DIES TODAY.

D-DON'T CALL ME THAT. THAT'S NOT MY NAME. NOT ANYMORE.

POISON. I'M THE LAST... POISON.

IN A FEW SECONDS, IT WON'T MATTER WHAT I CALL YOU, "BROTHER."

UNLESS, OF COURSE, SOMEONE SPRINGS FOR A TOMBSTONE.

STAY BACK!

WE'RE NOT GOING TO LET YOU HURT HIM!

WOOOOSSSH!

YOU... STUBBORN DAMN *KIDS.*

NNN--

JIMMY HUDSON DIED WHEN THE POISONS TOOK HIM.

WHO... DO YOU THINK THAT IS?

HE'S AN X-MAN.

SHRAKKOW!

BLOODSTORM!

I AM SORRY ABOUT THIS, DAKEN.

JIMMY HUDSON STRUGGLES AGAINST A TERRIBLE DARKNESS.

THIS IS SOMETHING I UNDERSTAND.

SOMETHING I INTEND TO HELP HIM FACE.

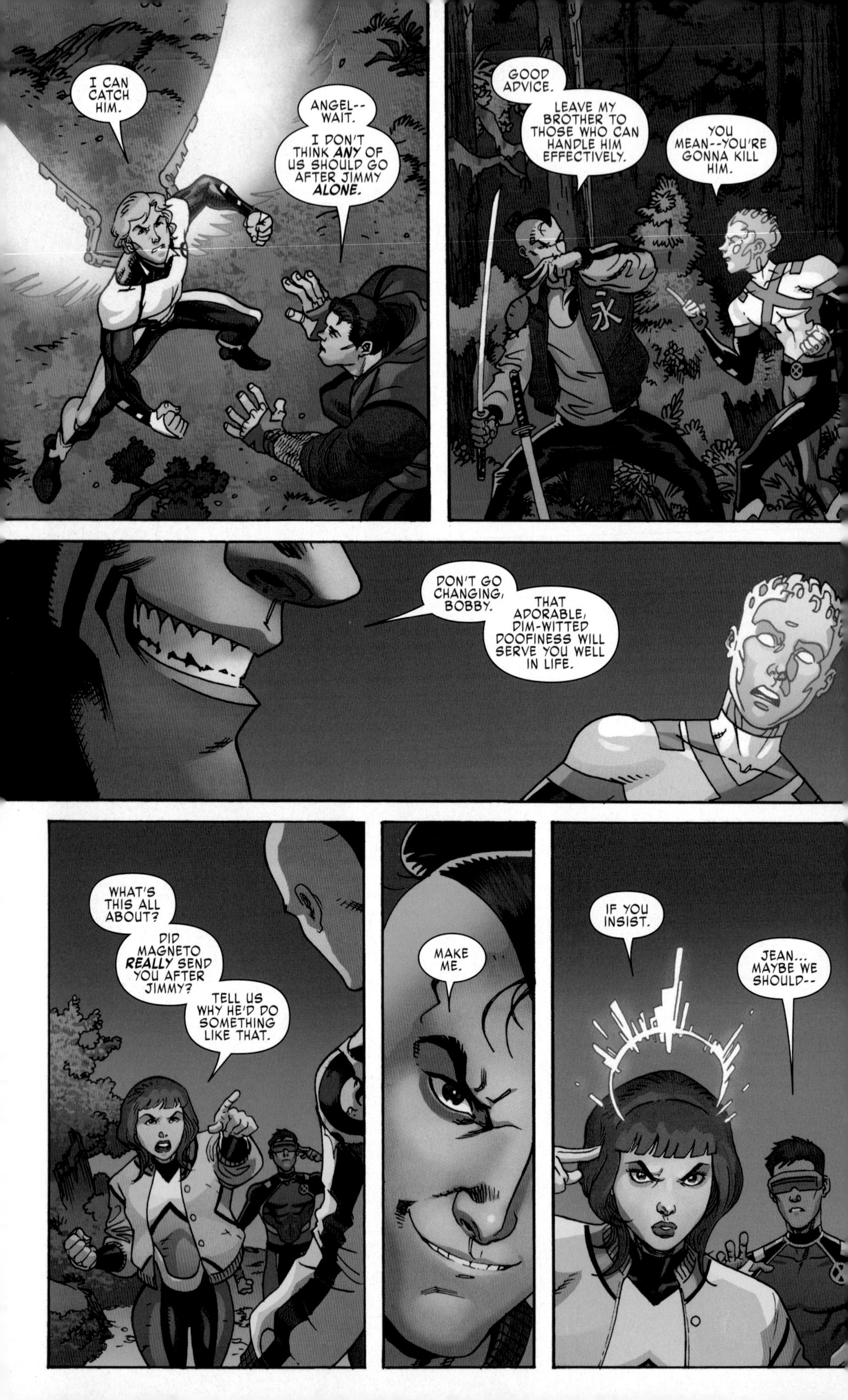
I CAN CATCH HIM.
ANGEL-- WAIT.
I DON'T THINK ANY OF US SHOULD GO AFTER JIMMY ALONE.
GOOD ADVICE.
LEAVE MY BROTHER TO THOSE WHO CAN HANDLE HIM EFFECTIVELY.
YOU MEAN--YOU'RE GONNA KILL HIM.
永
DON'T GO CHANGING, BOBBY.
THAT ADORABLE, DIM-WITTED DOOFINESS WILL SERVE YOU WELL IN LIFE.
WHAT'S THIS ALL ABOUT?
DID MAGNETO REALLY SEND YOU AFTER JIMMY?
TELL US WHY HE'D DO SOMETHING LIKE THAT.
MAKE ME.
IF YOU INSIST.
JEAN... MAYBE WE SHOULD--

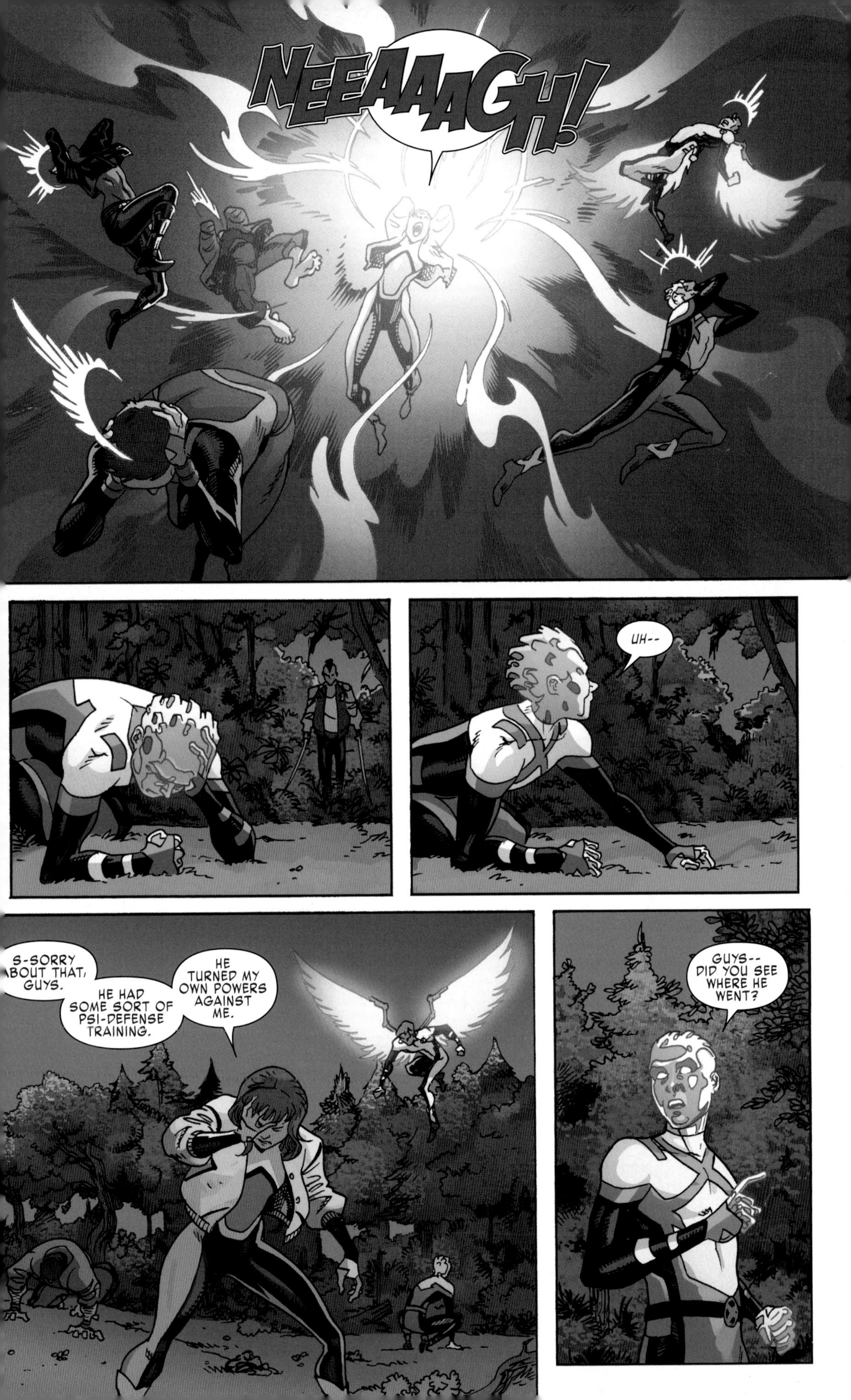

NEEAAAAGH!
UH--
S-SORRY ABOUT THAT, GUYS.
HE HAD SOME SORT OF PSI-DEFENSE TRAINING.
HE TURNED MY OWN POWERS AGAINST ME.
GUYS-- DID YOU SEE WHERE HE WENT?

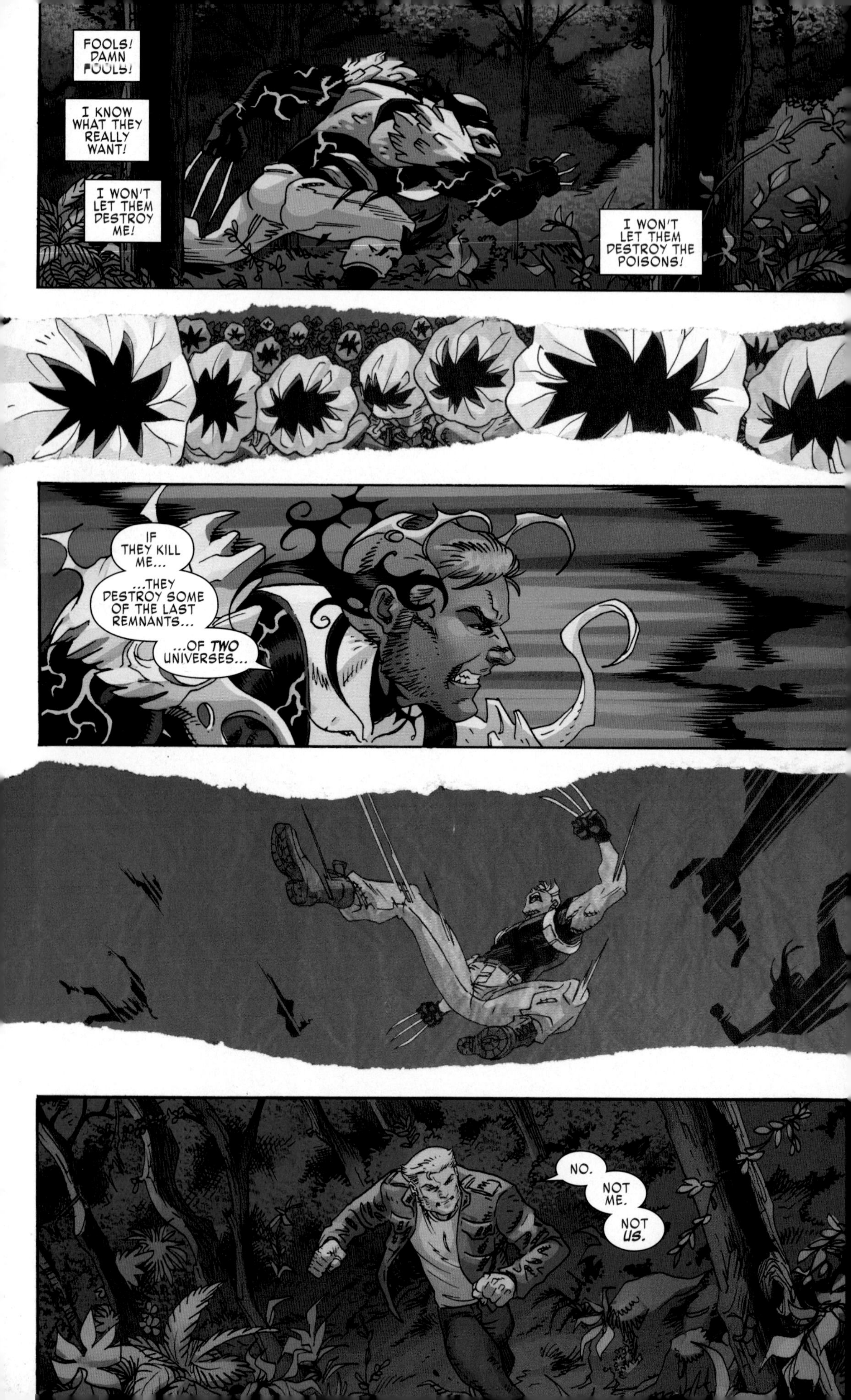
FOOLS! DAMN FOOLS!
I KNOW WHAT THEY REALLY WANT!
I WON'T LET THEM DESTROY ME!
I WON'T LET THEM DESTROY THE POISONS!
IF THEY KILL ME...
...THEY DESTROY SOME OF THE LAST REMNANTS...
...OF TWO UNIVERSES...
NO.
NOT ME.
NOT US.

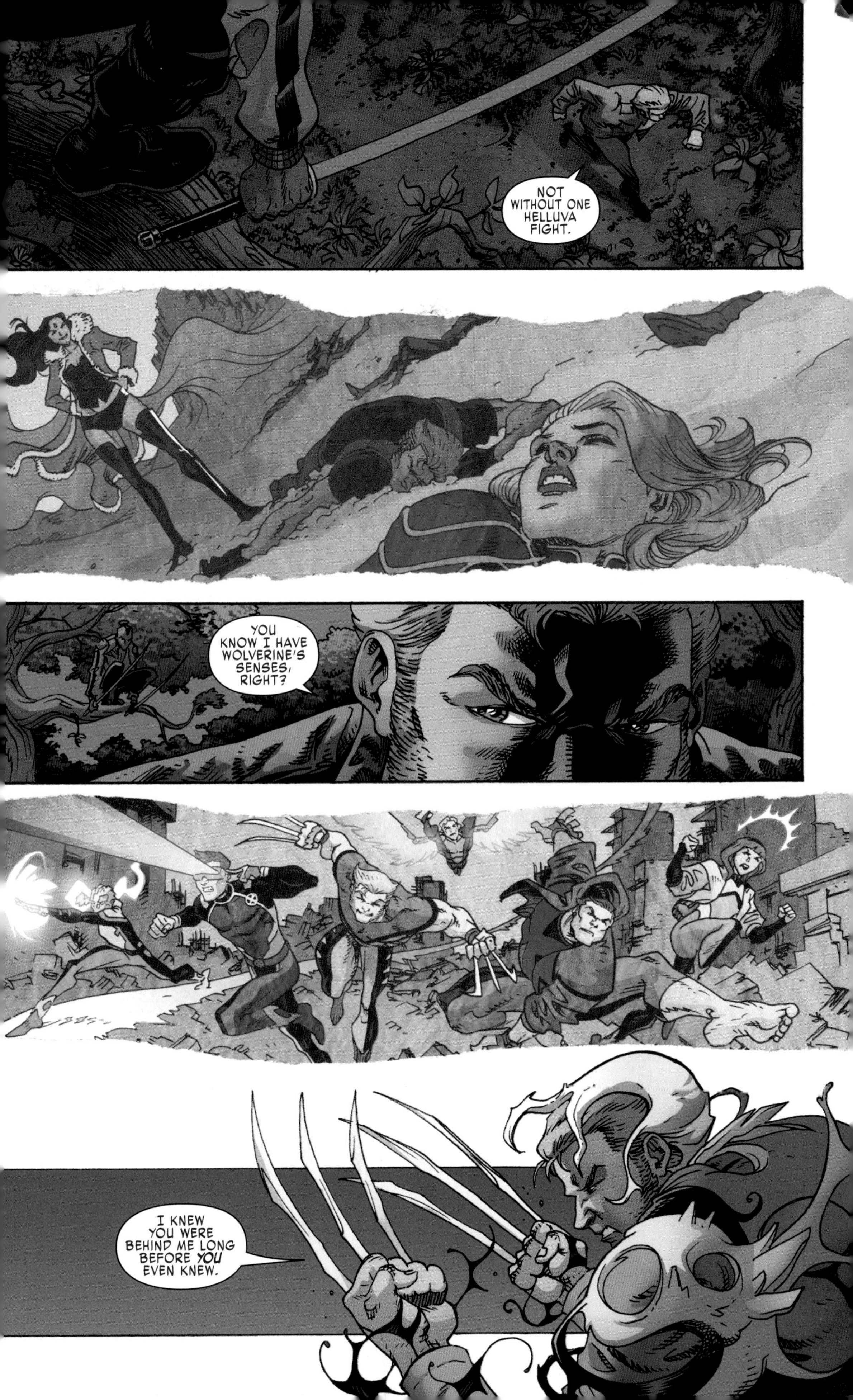
NOT WITHOUT ONE HELLUVA FIGHT.
YOU KNOW I HAVE WOLVERINE'S SENSES, RIGHT?
I KNEW YOU WERE BEHIND ME LONG BEFORE *YOU* EVEN KNEW.

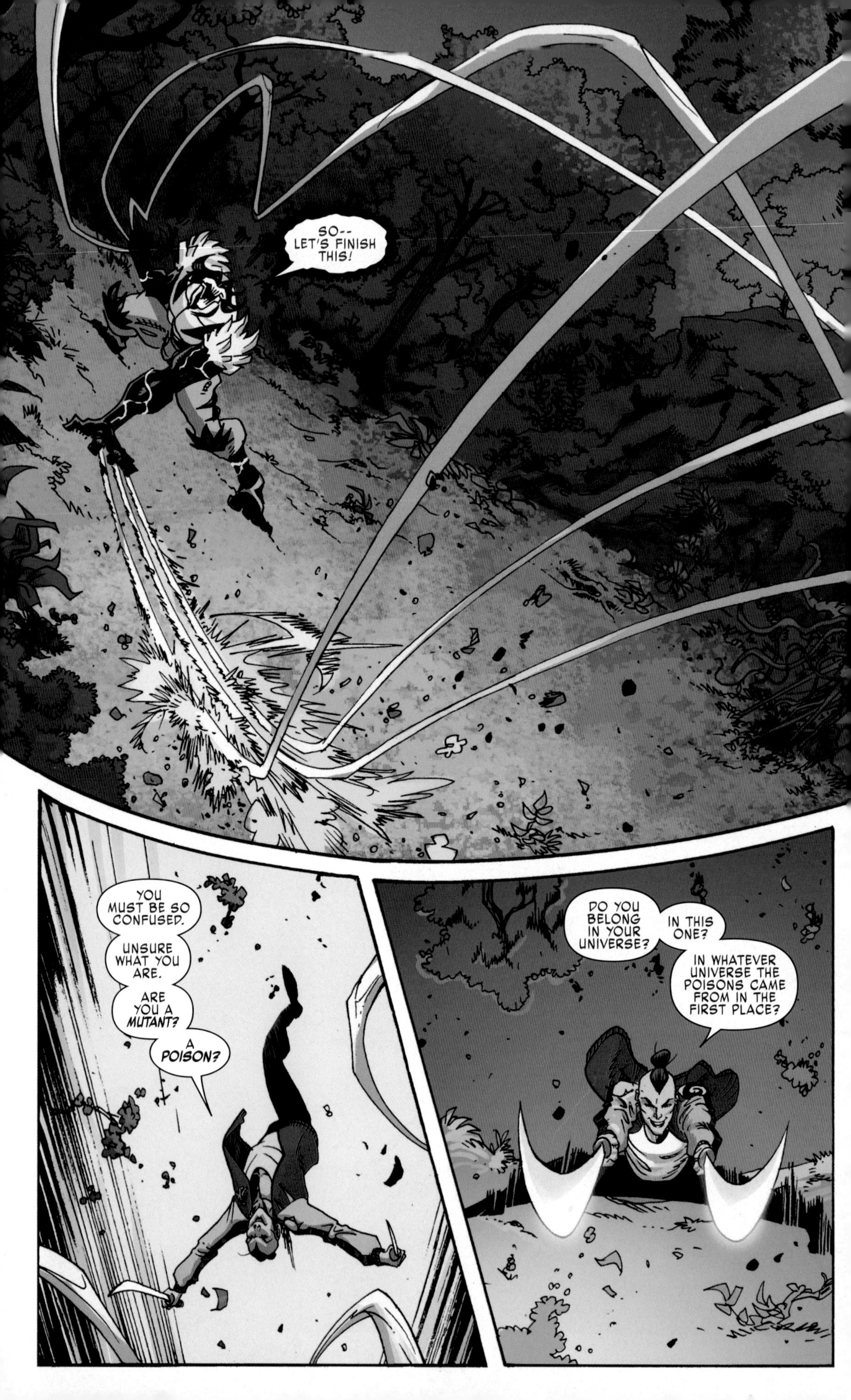
SO-- LET'S FINISH THIS!
YOU MUST BE SO CONFUSED.
UNSURE WHAT YOU ARE.
ARE YOU A MUTANT?
A POISON?
DO YOU BELONG IN YOUR UNIVERSE?
IN THIS ONE?
IN WHATEVER UNIVERSE THE POISONS CAME FROM IN THE FIRST PLACE?

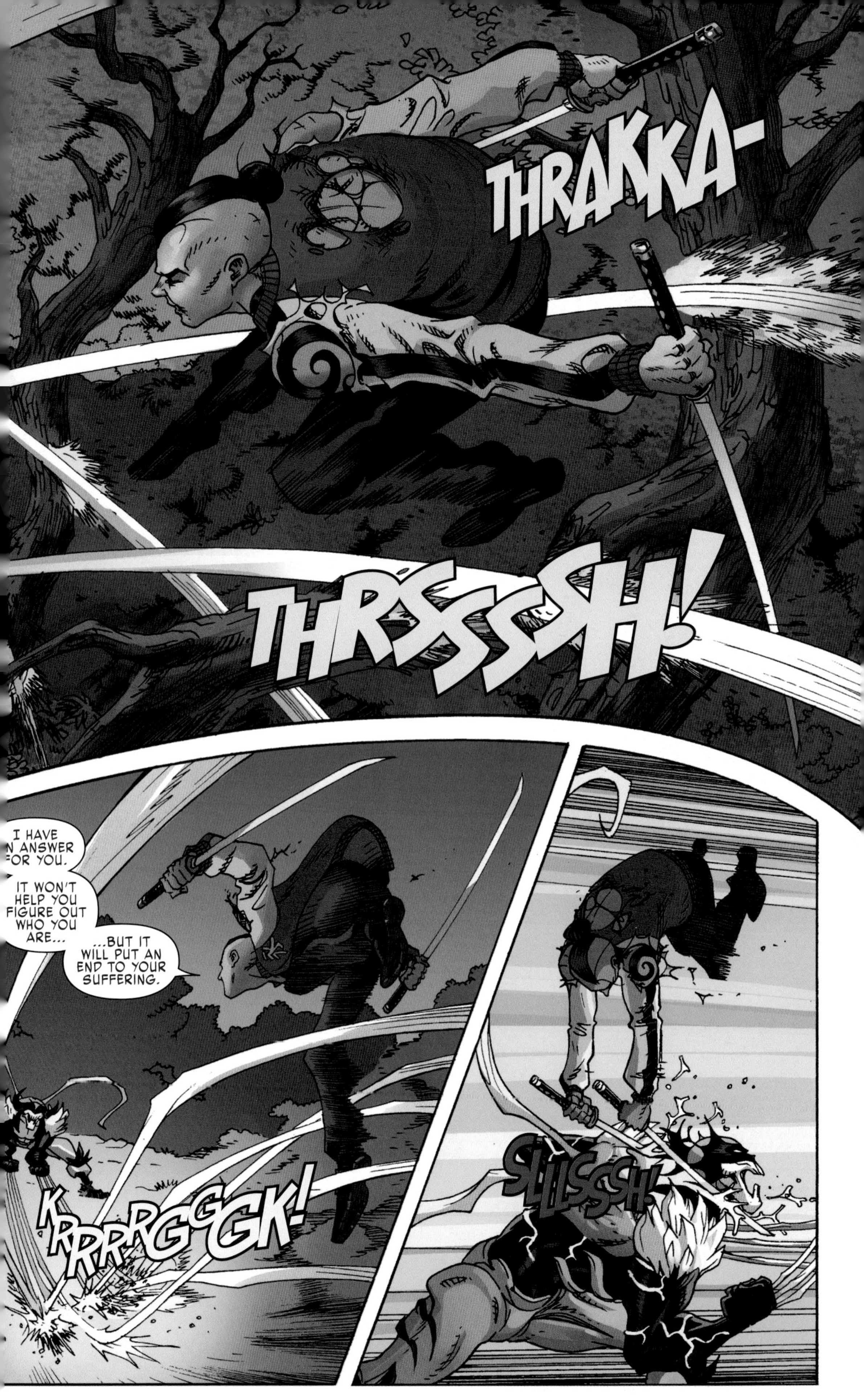
THRAKKA-
THRSSSSH!
I HAVE N ANSWER OR YOU.
IT WON'T HELP YOU FIGURE OUT WHO YOU ARE...
...BUT IT WILL PUT AN END TO YOUR SUFFERING.
KRRRRGGGK!
SLLLSSSH!

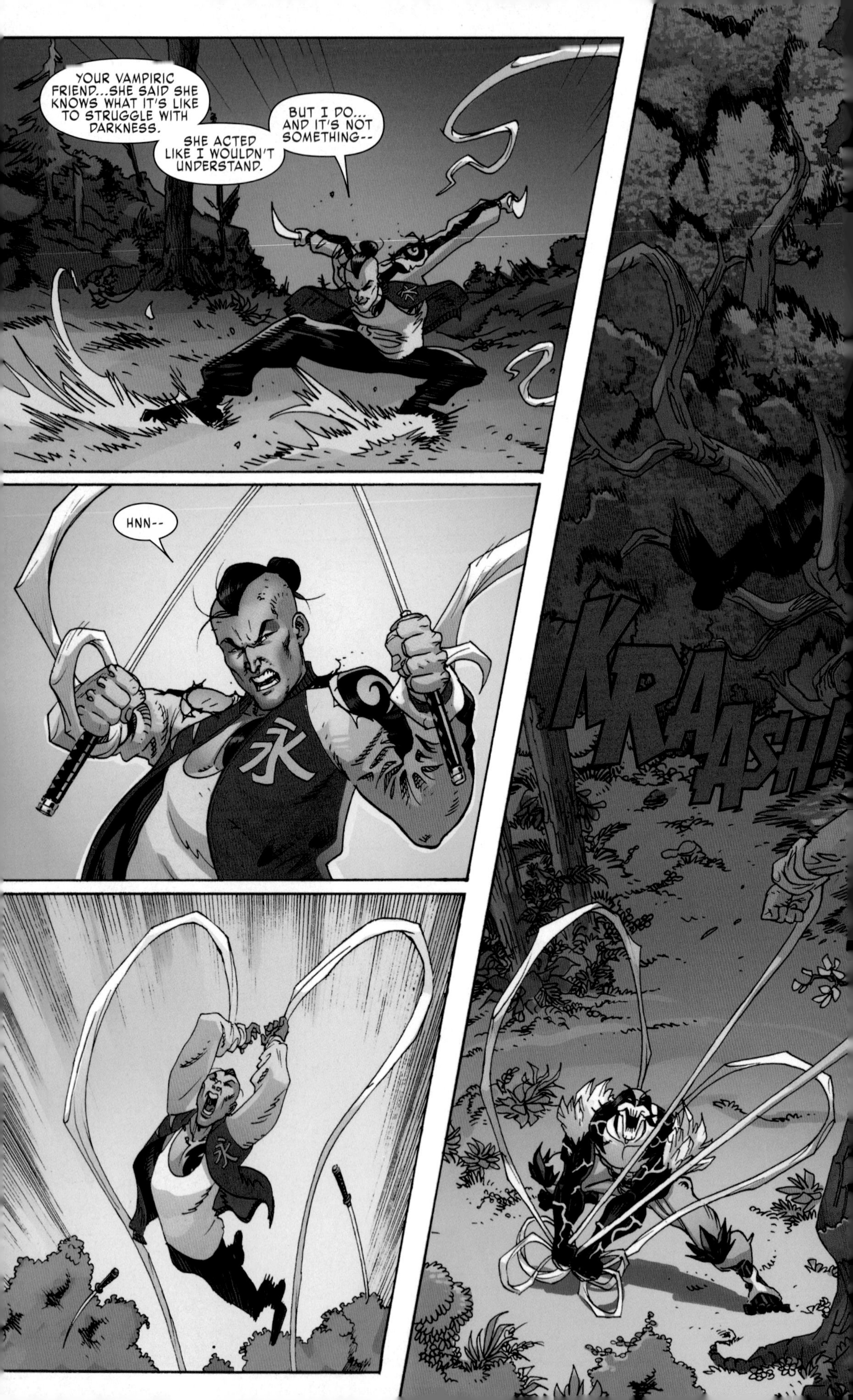
YOUR VAMPIRIC FRIEND...SHE SAID SHE KNOWS WHAT IT'S LIKE TO STRUGGLE WITH DARKNESS.
SHE ACTED LIKE I WOULDN'T UNDERSTAND.
BUT I DO... AND IT'S NOT SOMETHING--
HNN--
KRAASH!

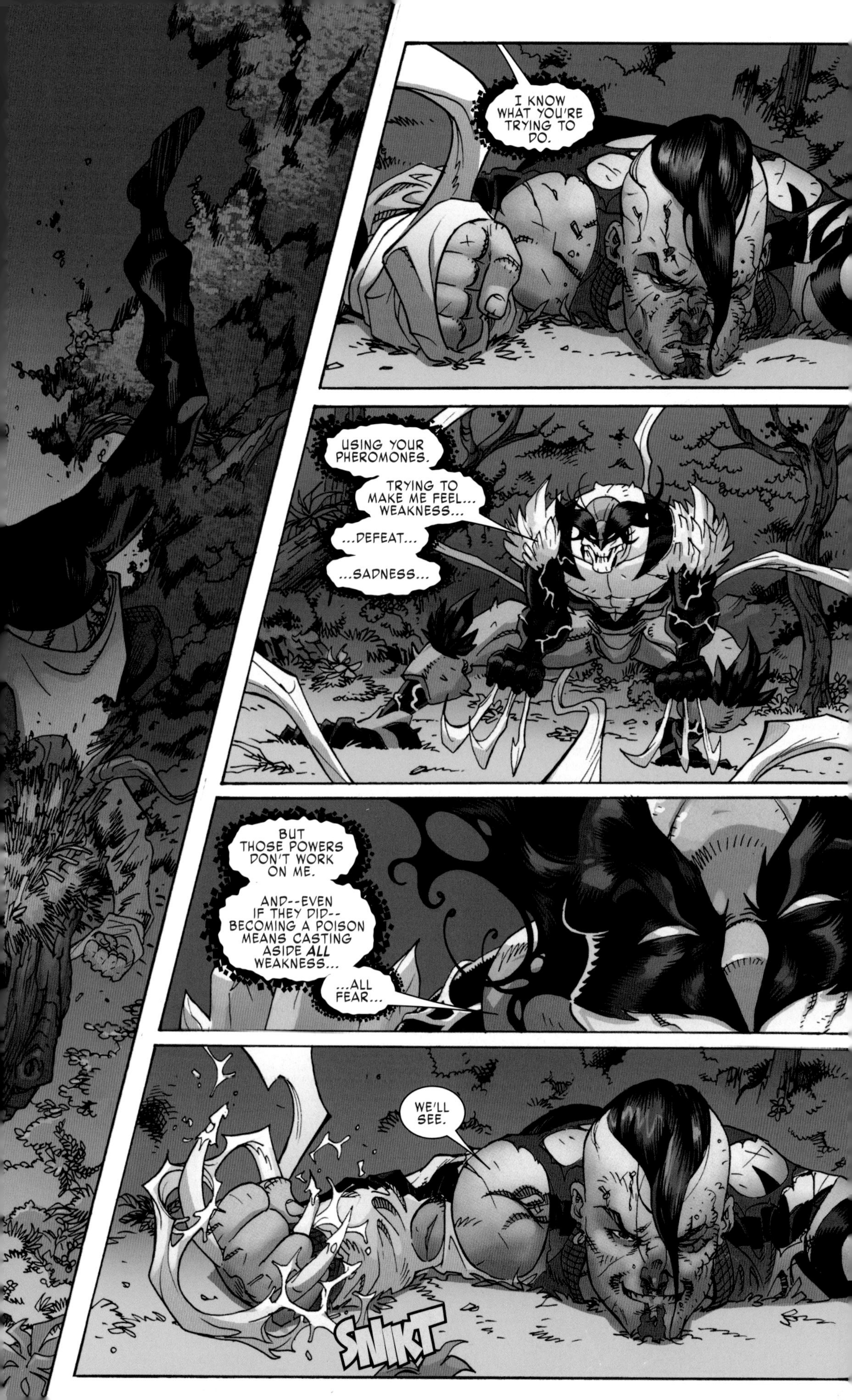

I KNOW WHAT YOU'RE TRYING TO DO.
USING YOUR PHEROMONES.
TRYING TO MAKE ME FEEL... WEAKNESS...
...DEFEAT...
...SADNESS...
BUT THOSE POWERS DON'T WORK ON ME.
AND--EVEN IF THEY DID--BECOMING A POISON MEANS CASTING ASIDE *ALL* WEAKNESS...
...ALL FEAR...
WE'LL SEE.
SNIKT

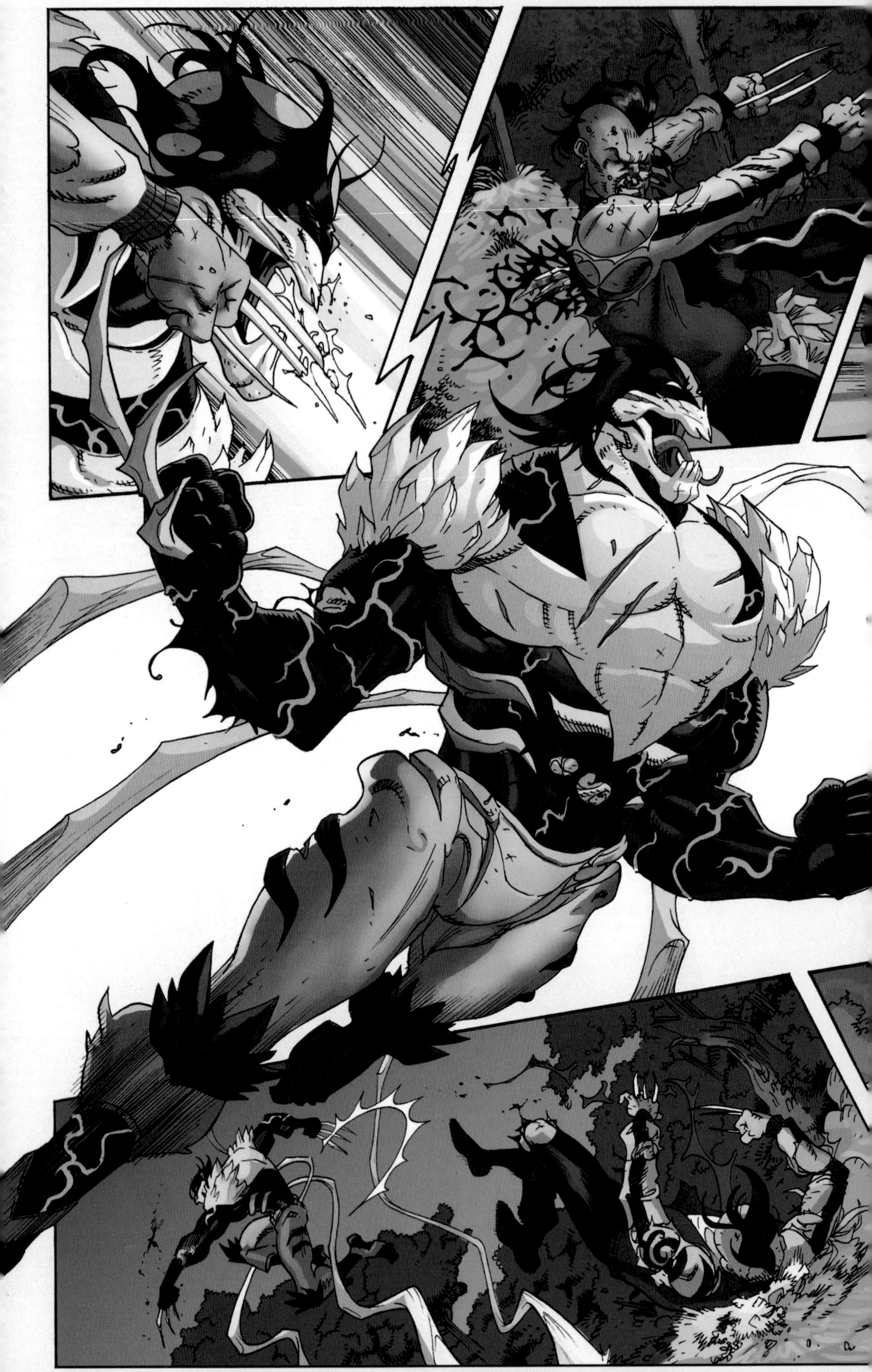

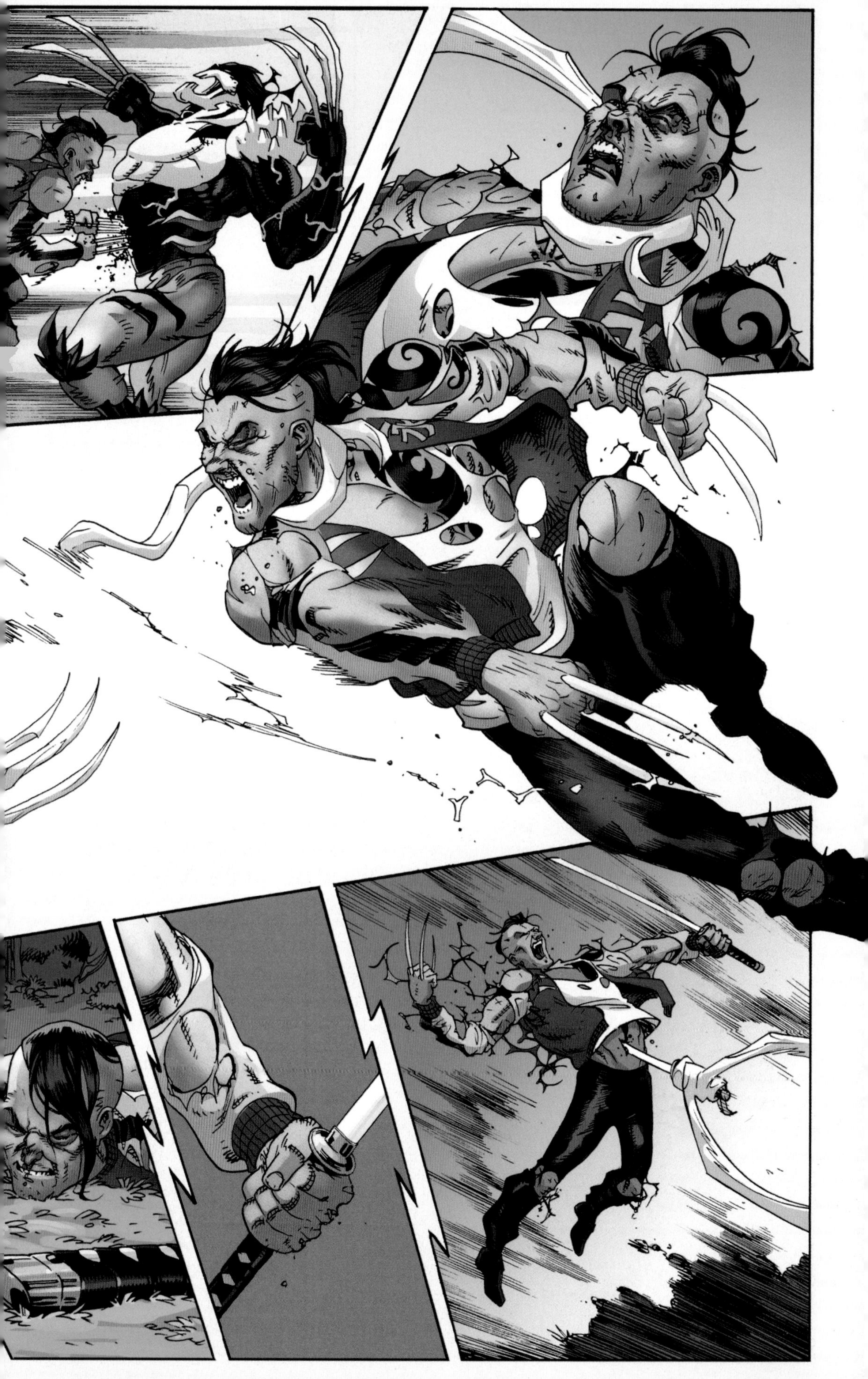

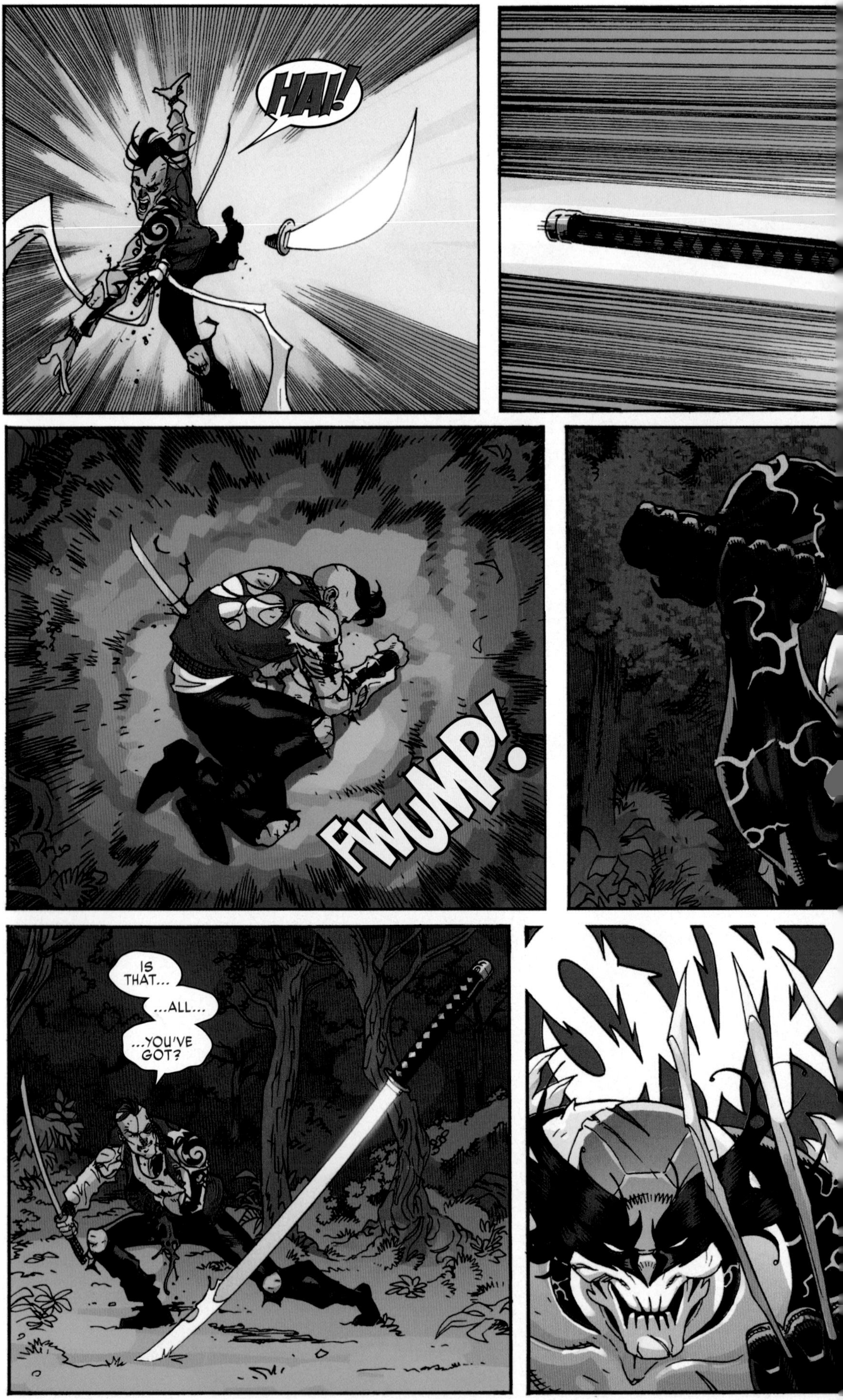
HAI!
FWUMP!
IS THAT...
...ALL...
...YOU'VE GOT?

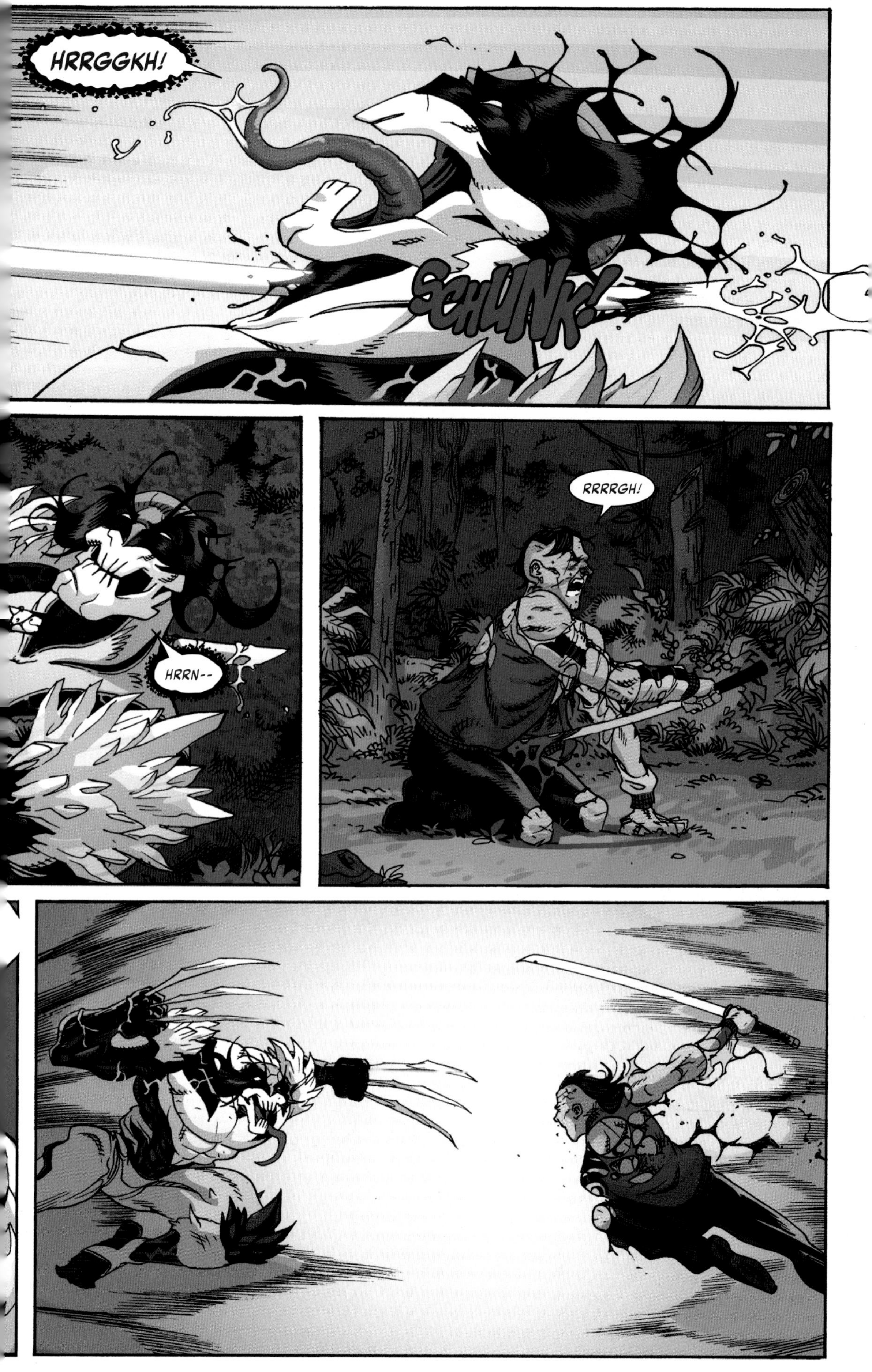
HRRGGKH!
SCHUNK!
HRRN--
RRRRGH!

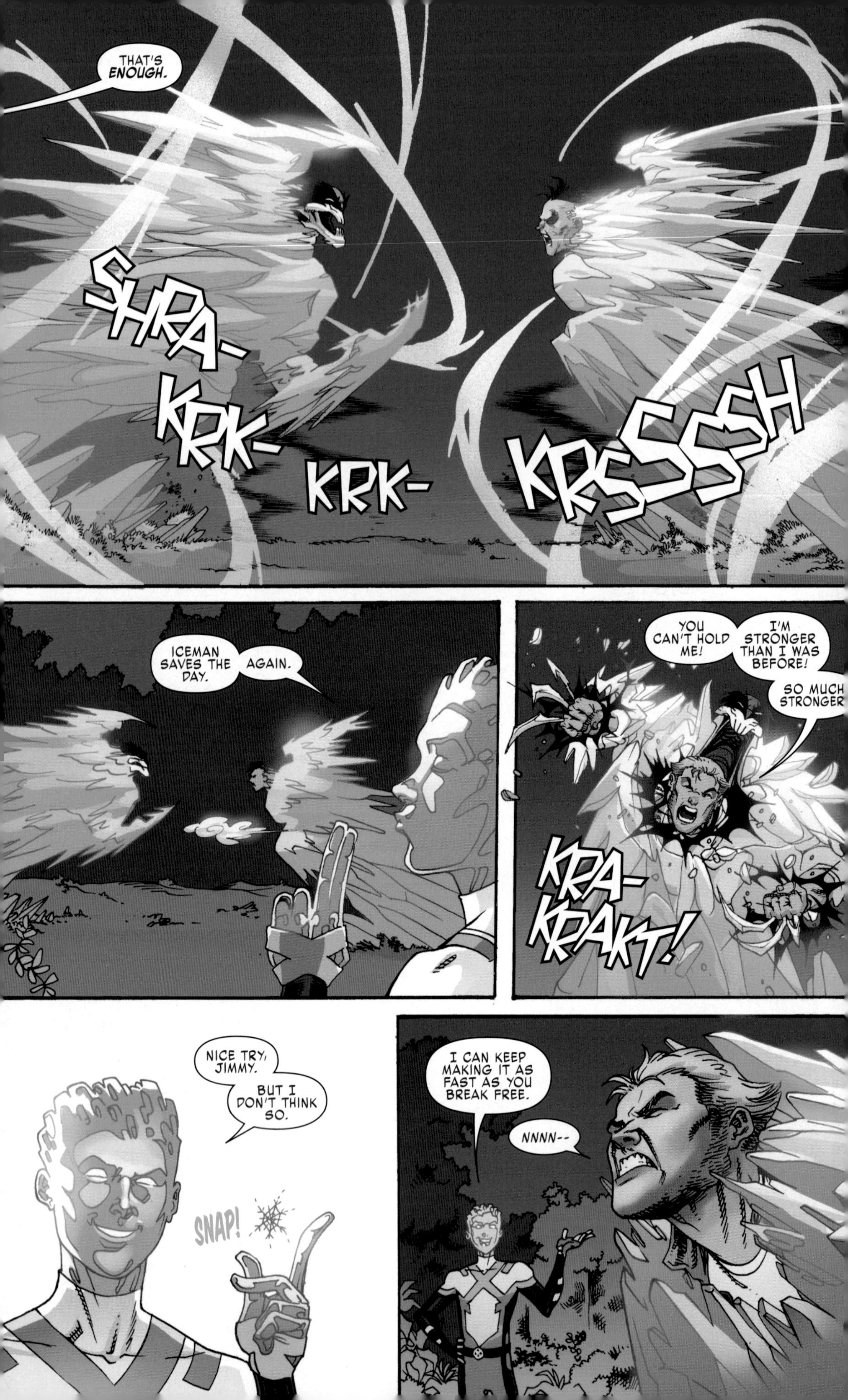
THAT'S ENOUGH.
SHRA-KRK-KRK-KRSSSSH
ICEMAN SAVES THE DAY.
AGAIN.
YOU CAN'T HOLD ME!
I'M STRONGER THAN I WAS BEFORE!
SO MUCH STRONGER
KRA-KRAKT!
NICE TRY, JIMMY.
BUT I DON'T THINK SO.
SNAP!
I CAN KEEP MAKING IT AS FAST AS YOU BREAK FREE.
NNNN--

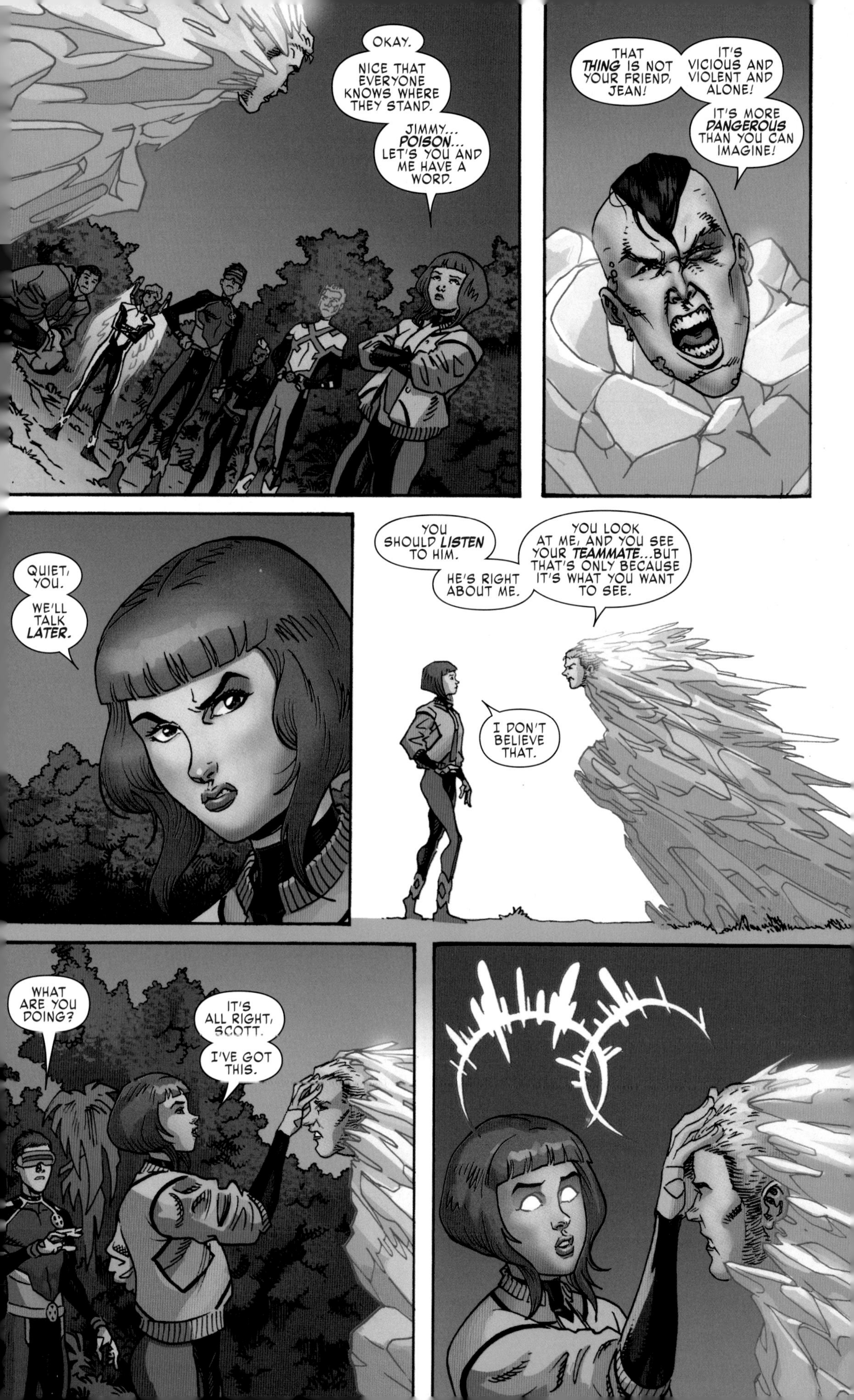
OKAY.
NICE THAT EVERYONE KNOWS WHERE THEY STAND.
JIMMY... POISON... LET'S YOU AND ME HAVE A WORD.
THAT THING IS NOT YOUR FRIEND, JEAN!
IT'S VICIOUS AND VIOLENT AND ALONE!
IT'S MORE DANGEROUS THAN YOU CAN IMAGINE!
QUIET, YOU.
WE'LL TALK LATER.
YOU SHOULD LISTEN TO HIM.
HE'S RIGHT ABOUT ME.
YOU LOOK AT ME, AND YOU SEE YOUR TEAMMATE...BUT THAT'S ONLY BECAUSE IT'S WHAT YOU WANT TO SEE.
I DON'T BELIEVE THAT.
WHAT ARE YOU DOING?
IT'S ALL RIGHT, SCOTT.
I'VE GOT THIS.

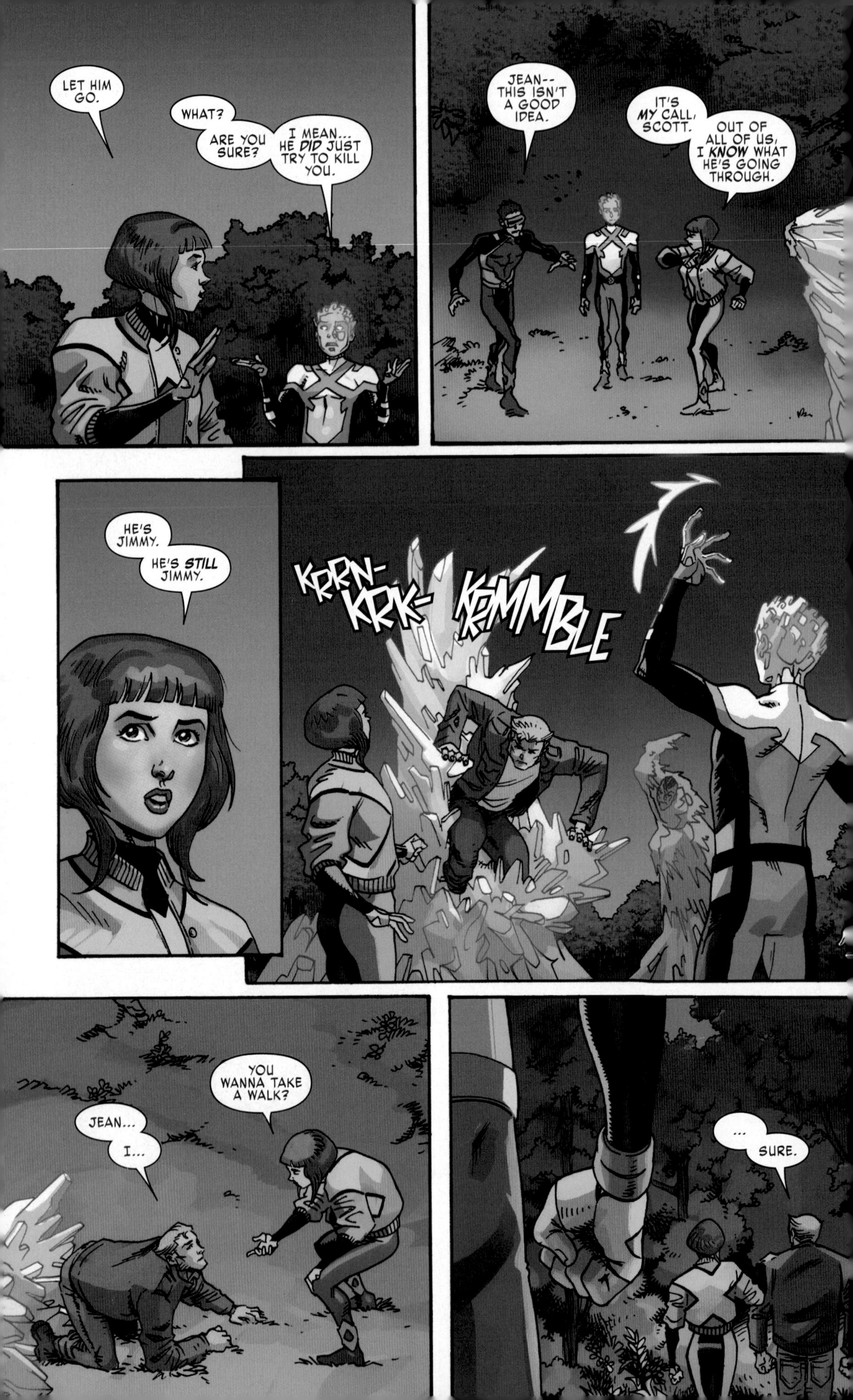
LET HIM GO.
WHAT?
ARE YOU SURE?
I MEAN... HE DID JUST TRY TO KILL YOU.
JEAN-- THIS ISN'T A GOOD IDEA.
IT'S MY CALL, SCOTT.
OUT OF ALL OF US, I KNOW WHAT HE'S GOING THROUGH.
HE'S JIMMY.
HE'S STILL JIMMY.
KRRN-KRK-KRMMBLE
JEAN... I...
YOU WANNA TAKE A WALK?
... SURE.

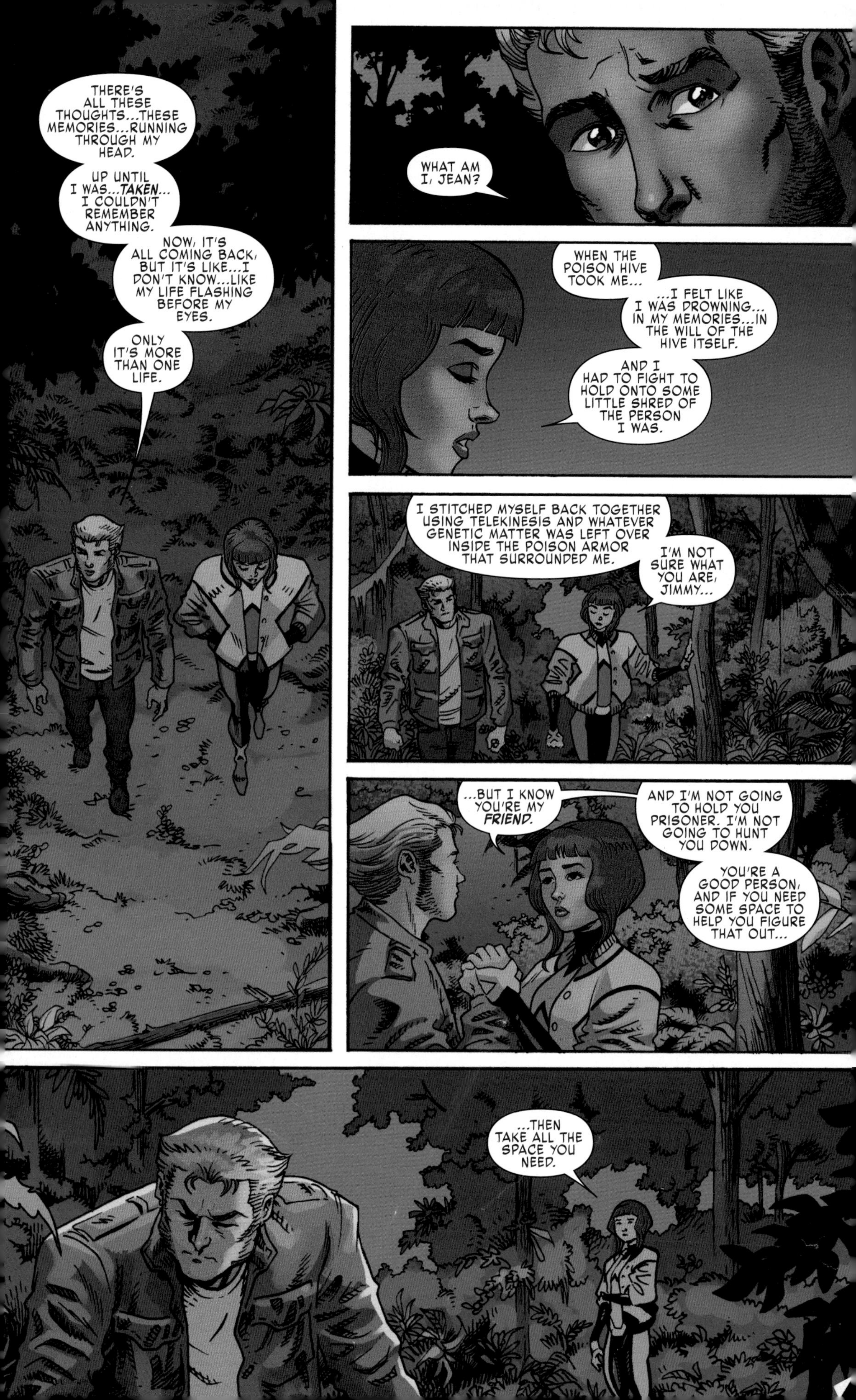
THERE'S ALL THESE THOUGHTS...THESE MEMORIES...RUNNING THROUGH MY HEAD.
UP UNTIL I WAS...*TAKEN*... I COULDN'T REMEMBER ANYTHING.
NOW, IT'S ALL COMING BACK, BUT IT'S LIKE...I DON'T KNOW...LIKE MY LIFE FLASHING BEFORE MY EYES.
ONLY IT'S MORE THAN ONE LIFE.
WHAT AM I, JEAN?
WHEN THE POISON HIVE TOOK ME...
...I FELT LIKE I WAS DROWNING... IN MY MEMORIES...IN THE WILL OF THE HIVE ITSELF.
AND I HAD TO FIGHT TO HOLD ONTO SOME LITTLE SHRED OF THE PERSON I WAS.
I STITCHED MYSELF BACK TOGETHER USING TELEKINESIS AND WHATEVER GENETIC MATTER WAS LEFT OVER INSIDE THE POISON ARMOR THAT SURROUNDED ME.
I'M NOT SURE WHAT YOU ARE, JIMMY...
...BUT I KNOW YOU'RE MY *FRIEND*.
AND I'M NOT GOING TO HOLD YOU PRISONER. I'M NOT GOING TO HUNT YOU DOWN.
YOU'RE A GOOD PERSON, AND IF YOU NEED SOME SPACE TO HELP YOU FIGURE THAT OUT...
...THEN TAKE ALL THE SPACE YOU NEED.

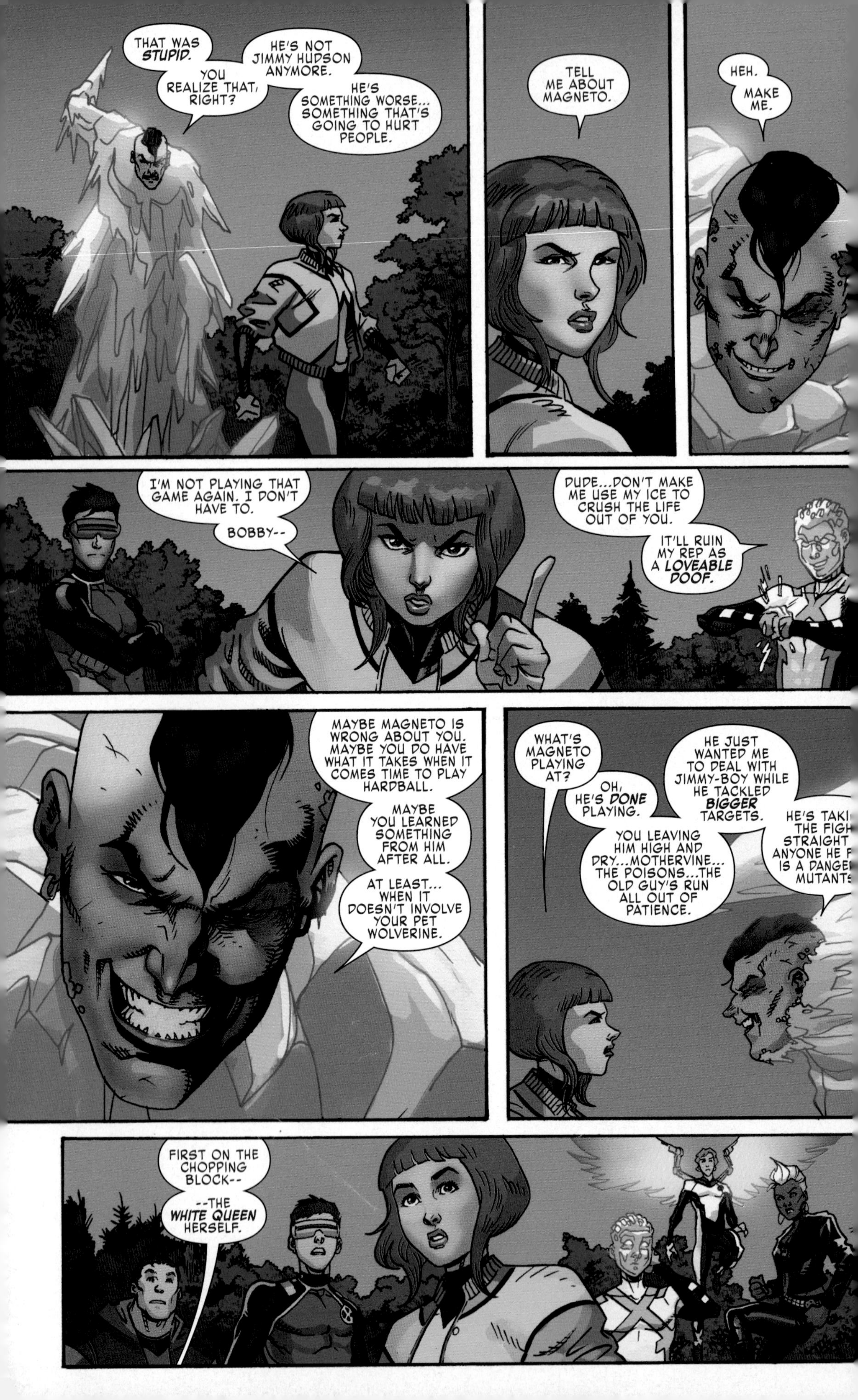
THAT WAS STUPID.
YOU REALIZE THAT, RIGHT?
HE'S NOT JIMMY HUDSON ANYMORE.
HE'S SOMETHING WORSE... SOMETHING THAT'S GOING TO HURT PEOPLE.
TELL ME ABOUT MAGNETO.
HEH.
MAKE ME.
I'M NOT PLAYING THAT GAME AGAIN. I DON'T HAVE TO.
BOBBY--
DUDE...DON'T MAKE ME USE MY ICE TO CRUSH THE LIFE OUT OF YOU.
IT'LL RUIN MY REP AS A LOVEABLE DOOF.
MAYBE MAGNETO IS WRONG ABOUT YOU. MAYBE YOU DO HAVE WHAT IT TAKES WHEN IT COMES TIME TO PLAY HARDBALL.
MAYBE YOU LEARNED SOMETHING FROM HIM AFTER ALL.
AT LEAST... WHEN IT DOESN'T INVOLVE YOUR PET WOLVERINE.
WHAT'S MAGNETO PLAYING AT?
OH, HE'S DONE PLAYING.
HE JUST WANTED ME TO DEAL WITH JIMMY-BOY WHILE HE TACKLED BIGGER TARGETS.
YOU LEAVING HIM HIGH AND DRY...MOTHERVINE... THE POISONS...THE OLD GUY'S RUN ALL OUT OF PATIENCE.
HE'S TAKI THE FIGH STRAIGHT ANYONE HE P IS A DANGE MUTANTS
FIRST ON THE CHOPPING BLOCK--
--THE WHITE QUEEN HERSELF.

31

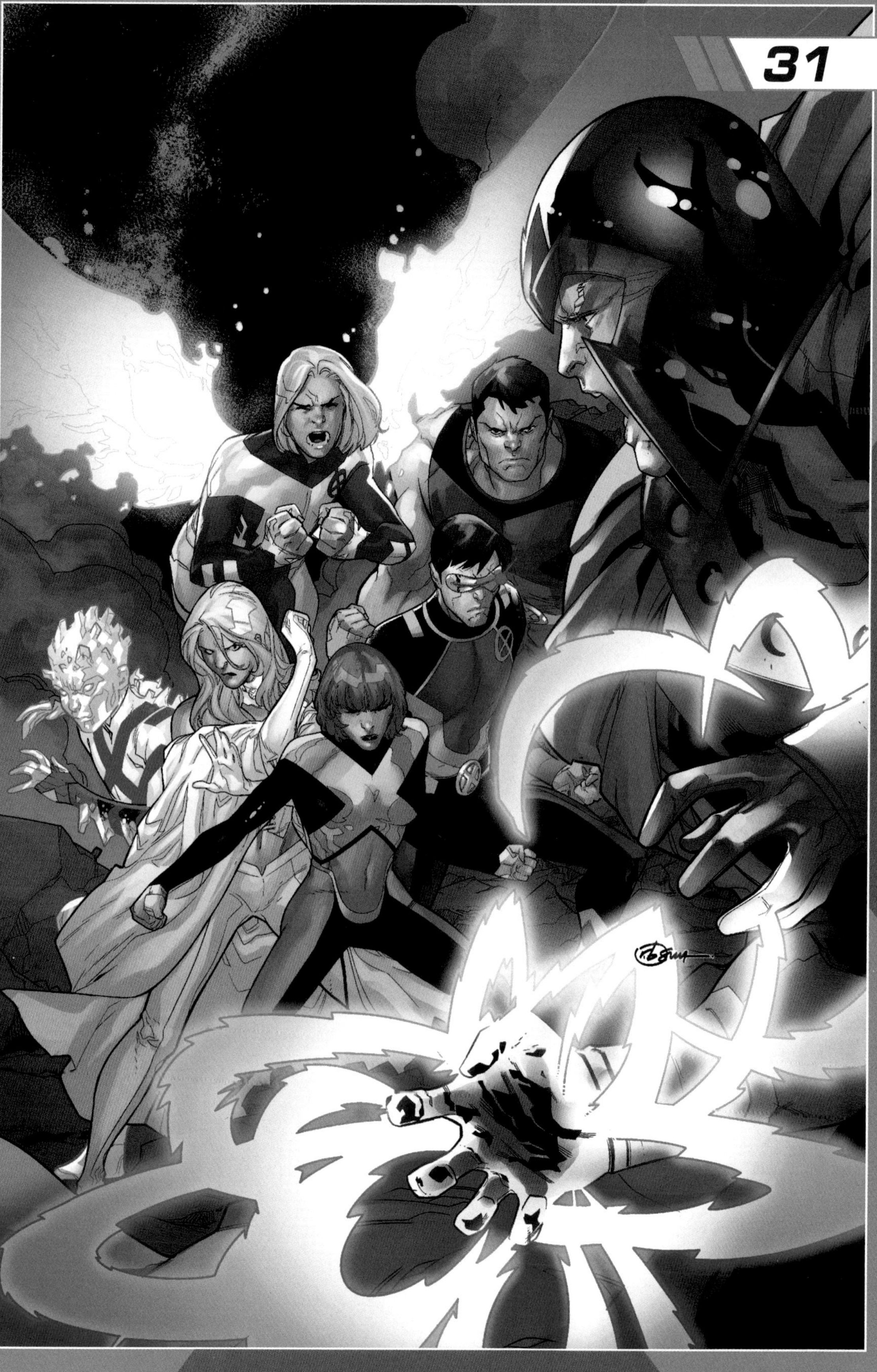

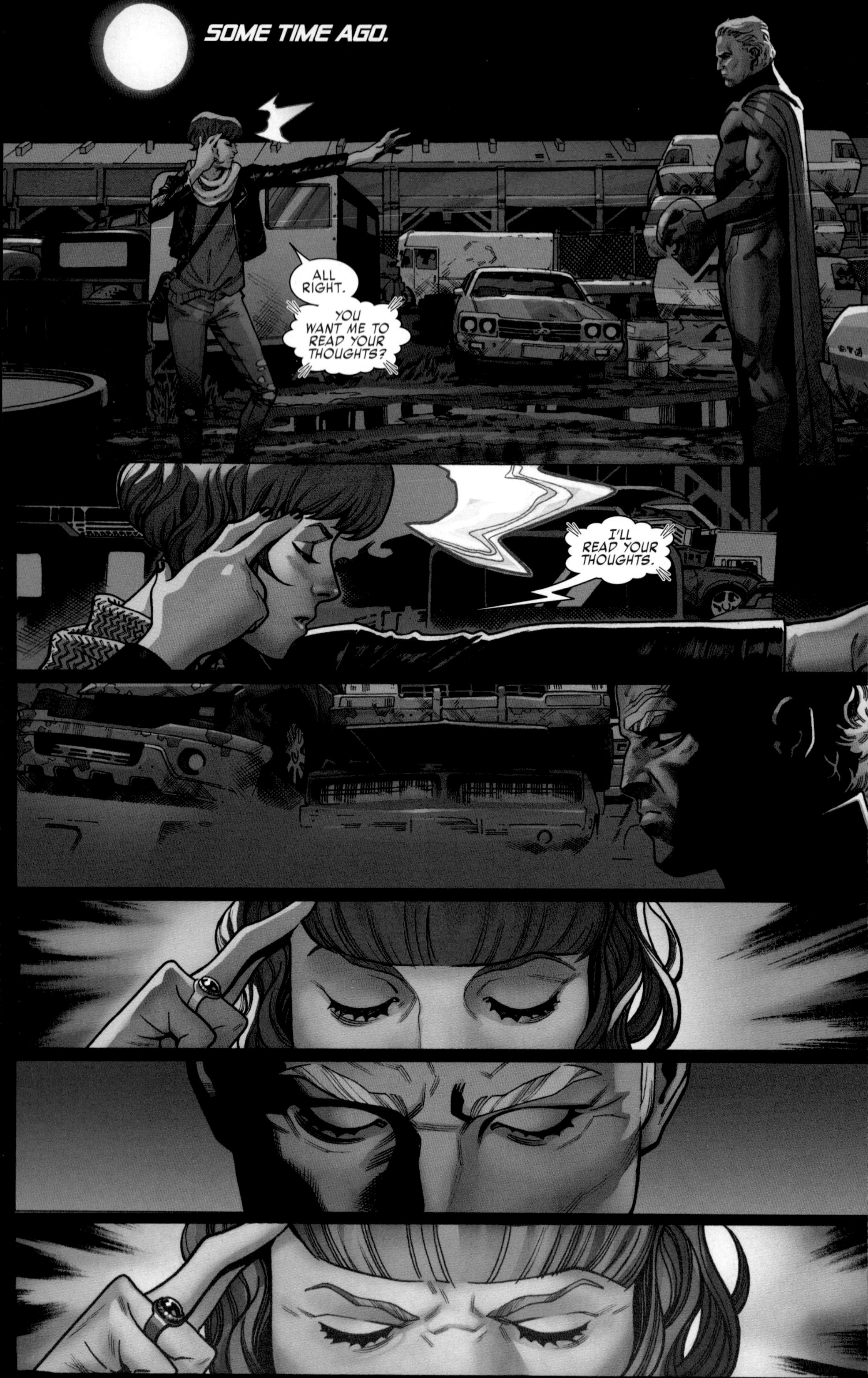
SOME TIME AGO.
ALL RIGHT.
YOU WANT ME TO READ YOUR THOUGHTS?
I'LL READ YOUR THOUGHTS.

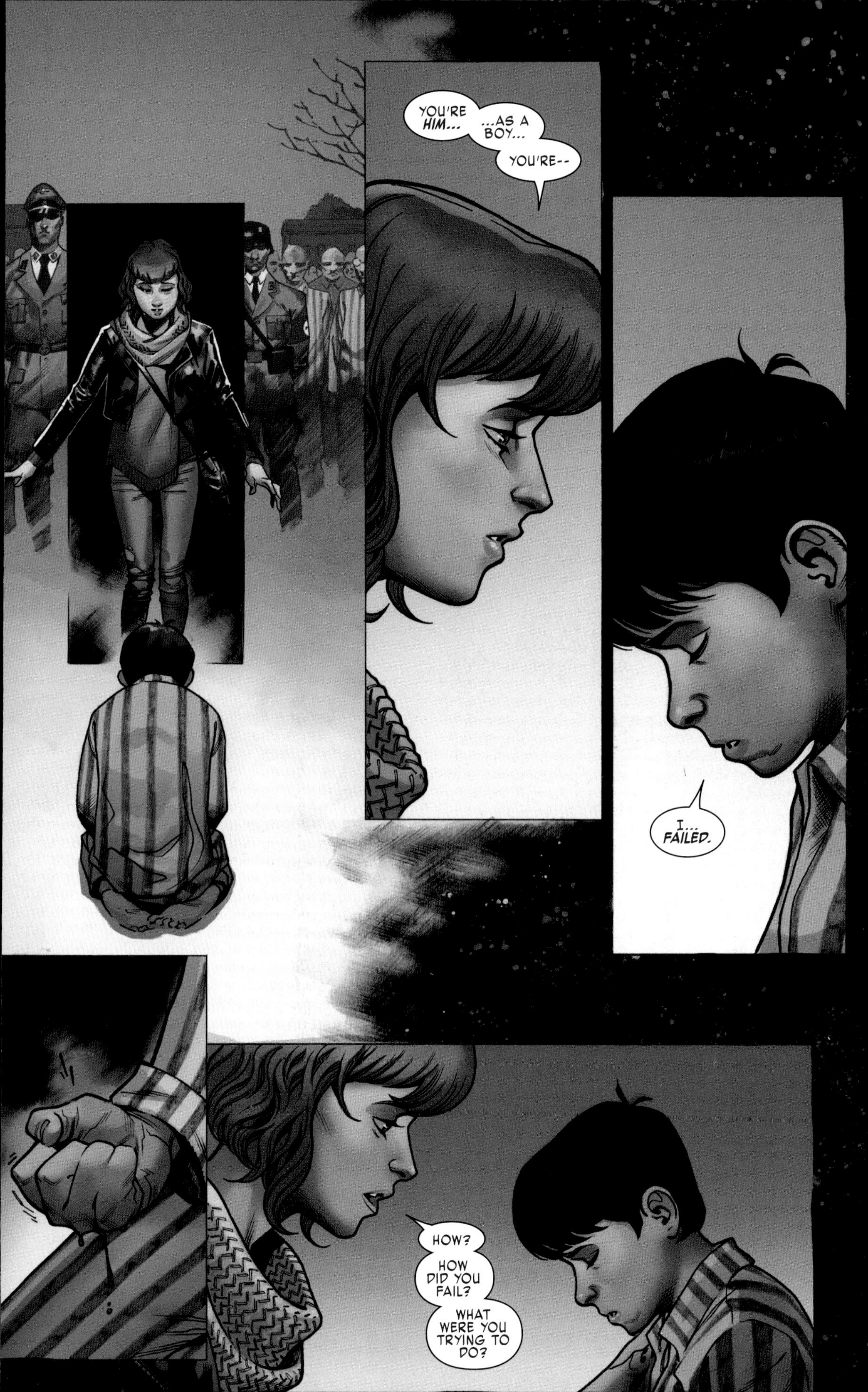
YOU'RE HIM...
...AS A BOY...
YOU'RE--
I... FAILED.
HOW?
HOW DID YOU FAIL?
WHAT WERE YOU TRYING TO DO?

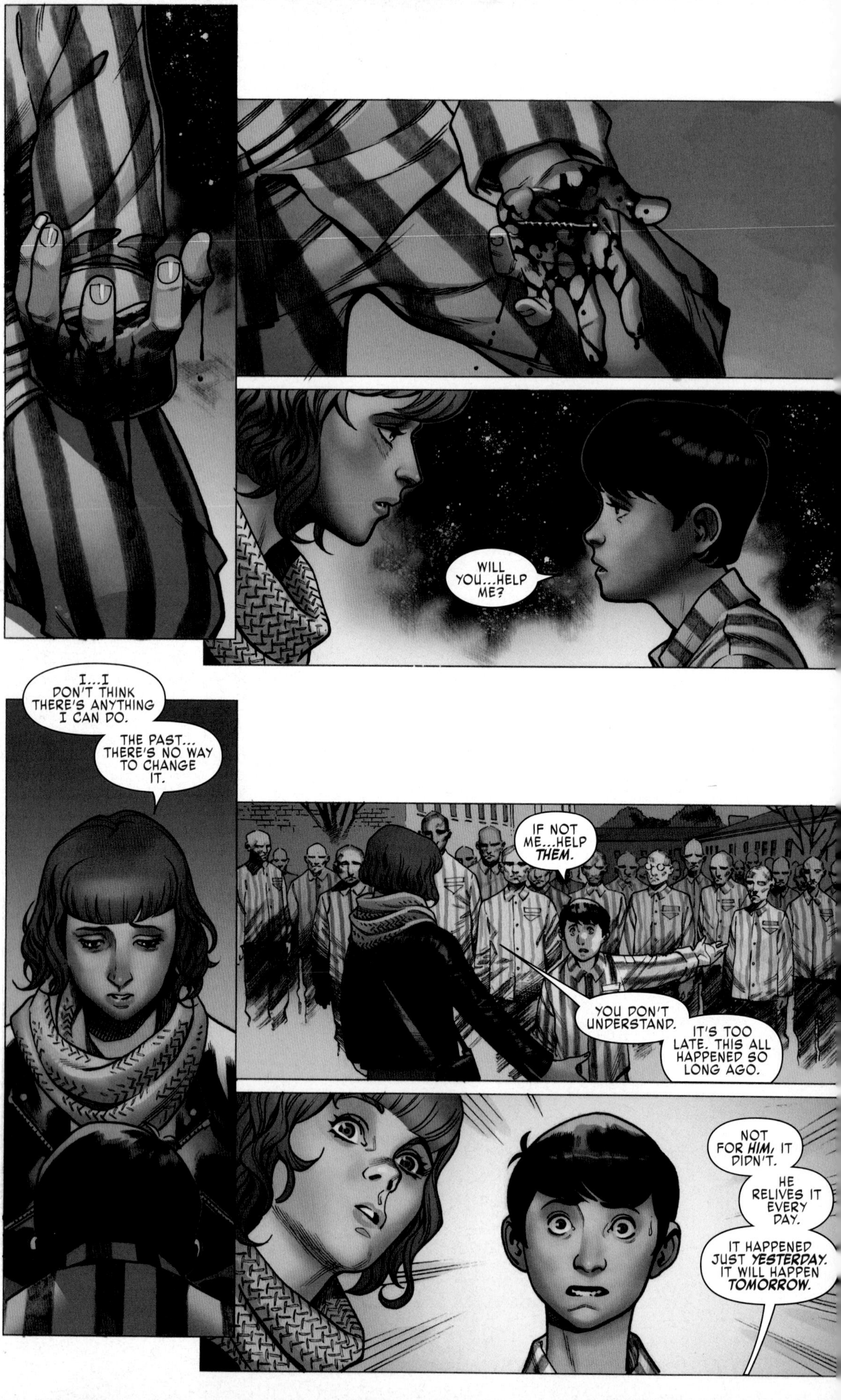
WILL YOU...HELP ME?
I...I DON'T THINK THERE'S ANYTHING I CAN DO.
THE PAST... THERE'S NO WAY TO CHANGE IT.
IF NOT ME...HELP *THEM*.
YOU DON'T UNDERSTAND.
IT'S TOO LATE. THIS ALL HAPPENED SO LONG AGO.
NOT FOR *HIM*, IT DIDN'T.
HE RELIVES IT EVERY DAY.
IT HAPPENED JUST *YESTERDAY*. IT WILL HAPPEN *TOMORROW*.

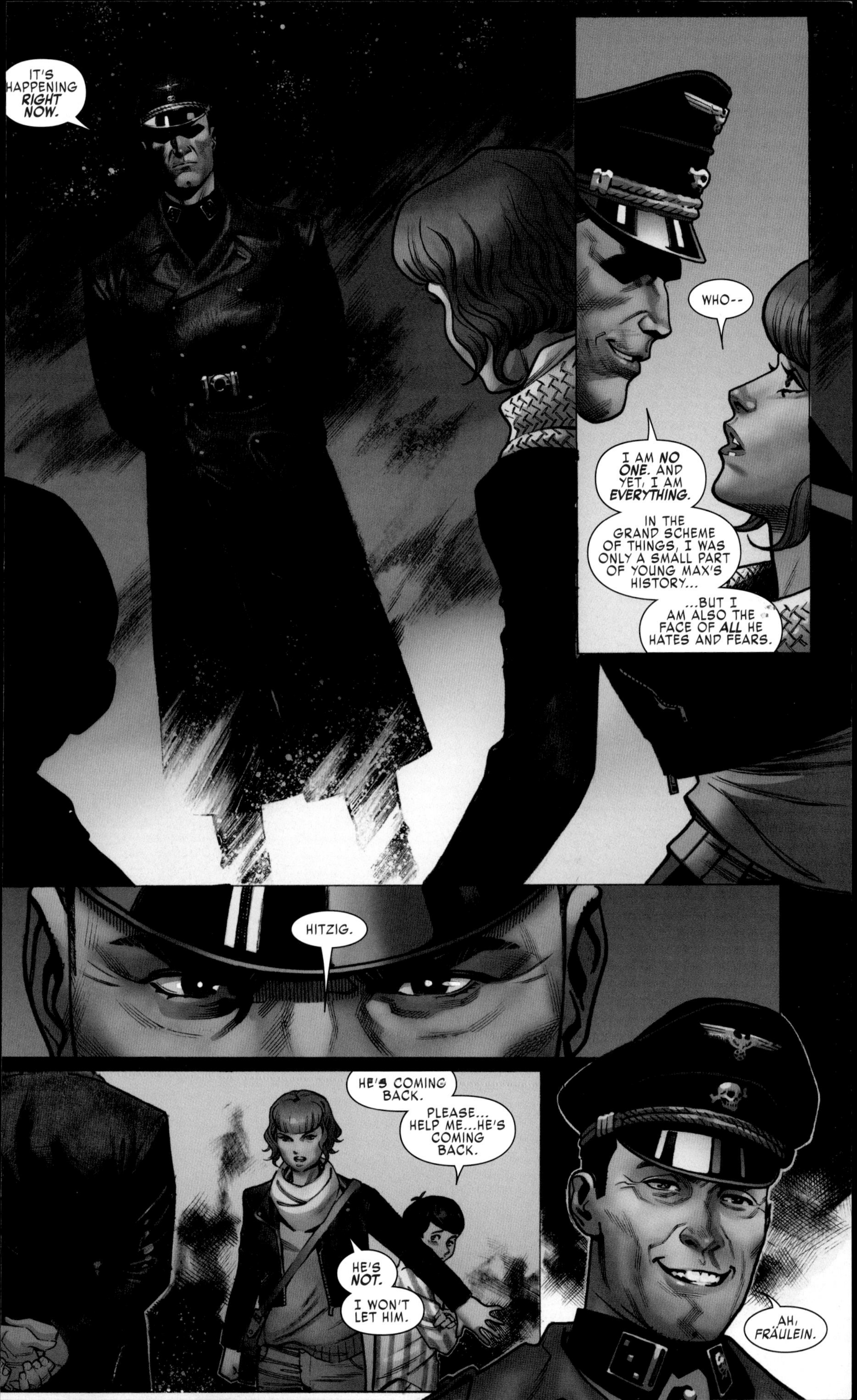
IT'S HAPPENING RIGHT NOW.
WHO--
I AM NO ONE. AND YET, I AM EVERYTHING.
IN THE GRAND SCHEME OF THINGS, I WAS ONLY A SMALL PART OF YOUNG MAX'S HISTORY...
...BUT I AM ALSO THE FACE OF ALL HE HATES AND FEARS.
HITZIG.
HE'S COMING BACK.
PLEASE... HELP ME...HE'S COMING BACK.
HE'S NOT.
I WON'T LET HIM.
AH, FRÄULEIN.

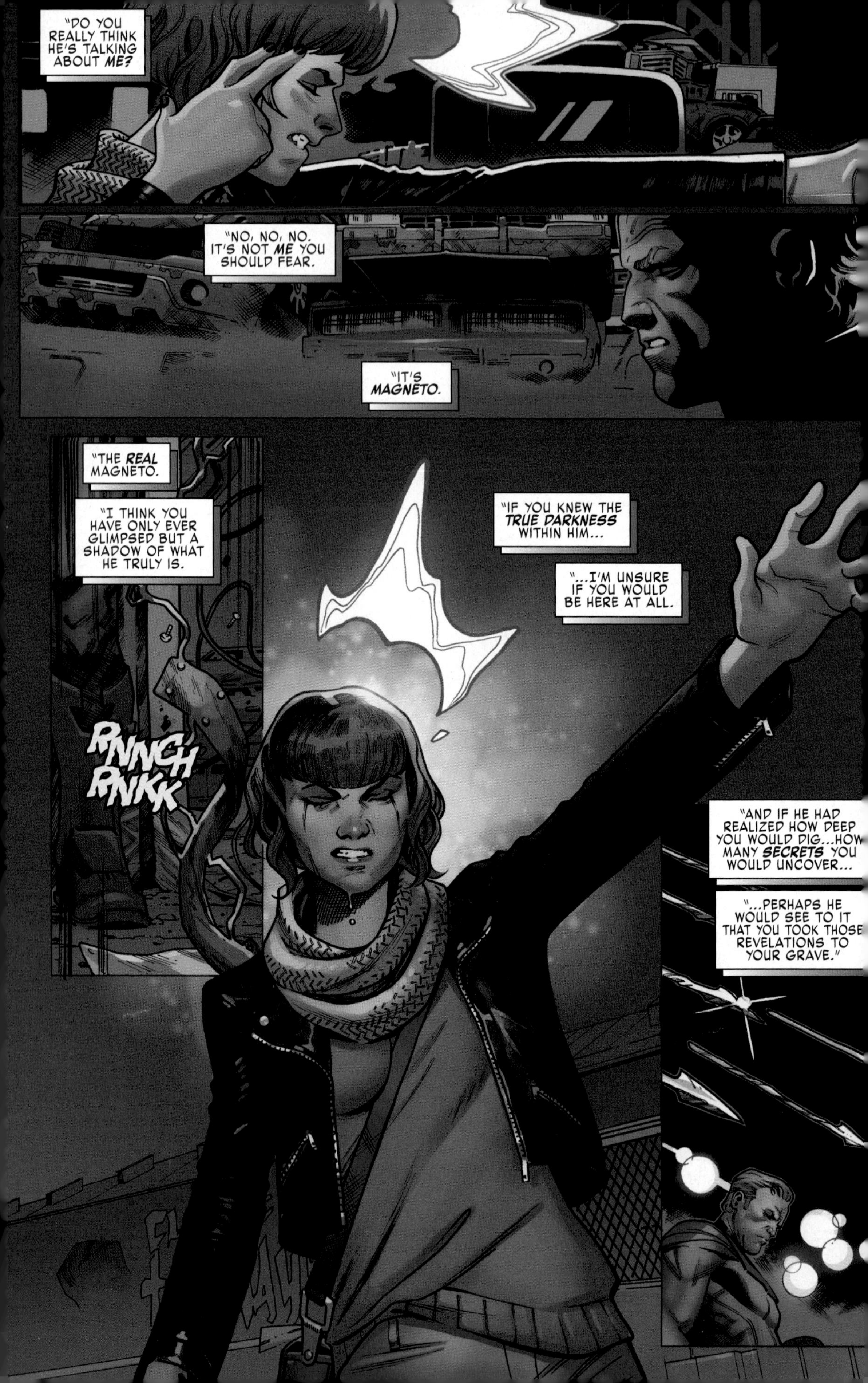
"DO YOU REALLY THINK HE'S TALKING ABOUT ME?
"NO, NO, NO. IT'S NOT ME YOU SHOULD FEAR.
"IT'S MAGNETO.
"THE REAL MAGNETO.
"I THINK YOU HAVE ONLY EVER GLIMPSED BUT A SHADOW OF WHAT HE TRULY IS.
"IF YOU KNEW THE TRUE DARKNESS WITHIN HIM...
"...I'M UNSURE IF YOU WOULD BE HERE AT ALL.
RNNCH RNKK
"AND IF HE HAD REALIZED HOW DEEP YOU WOULD DIG...HOW MANY SECRETS YOU WOULD UNCOVER...
"...PERHAPS HE WOULD SEE TO IT THAT YOU TOOK THOSE REVELATIONS TO YOUR GRAVE."

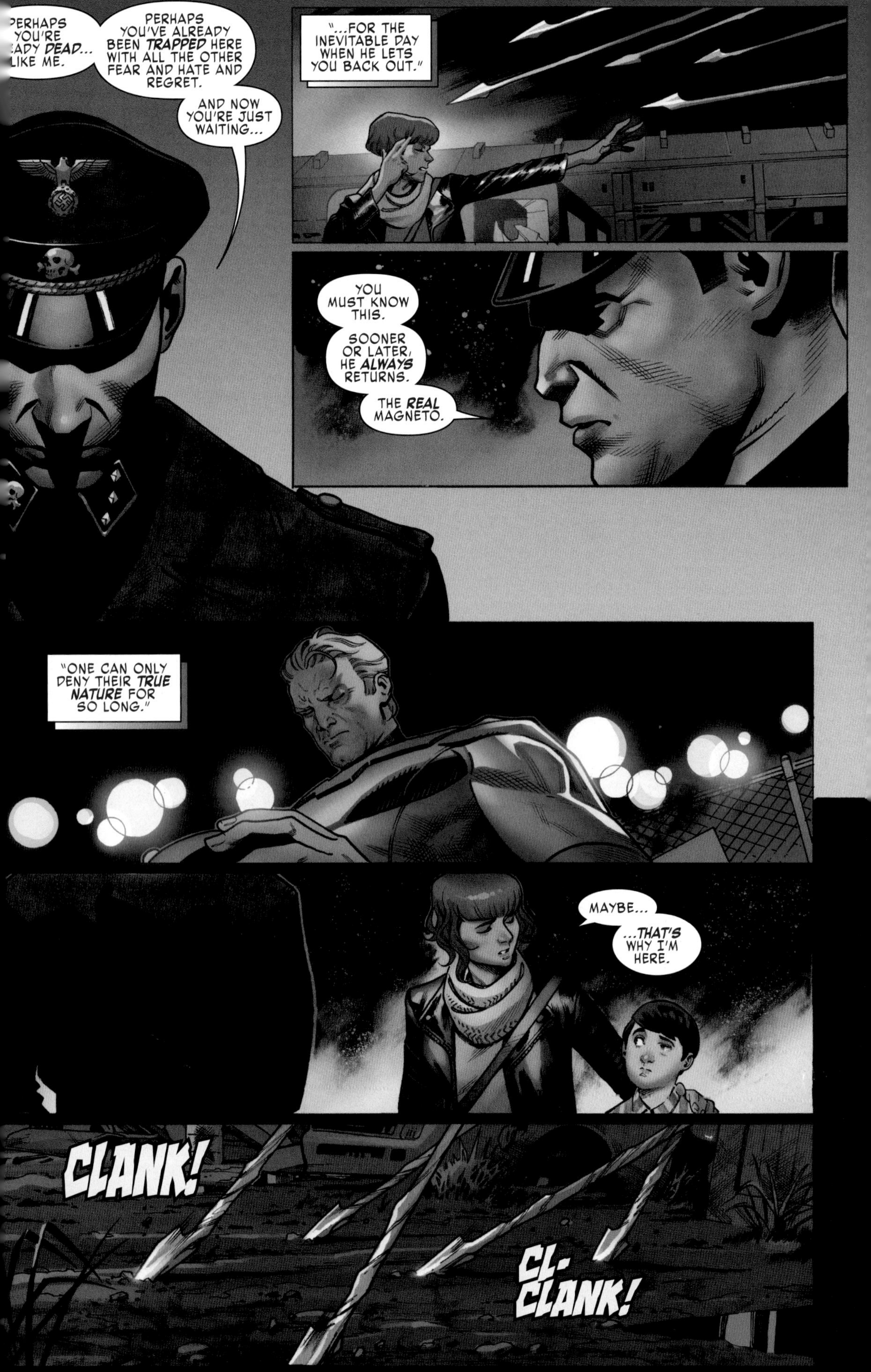

PERHAPS YOU'RE ...EADY DEAD... LIKE ME.
PERHAPS YOU'VE ALREADY BEEN TRAPPED HERE WITH ALL THE OTHER FEAR AND HATE AND REGRET.
AND NOW YOU'RE JUST WAITING...
"...FOR THE INEVITABLE DAY WHEN HE LETS YOU BACK OUT."
YOU MUST KNOW THIS.
SOONER OR LATER, HE ALWAYS RETURNS.
THE REAL MAGNETO.
"ONE CAN ONLY DENY THEIR TRUE NATURE FOR SO LONG."
MAYBE...
...THAT'S WHY I'M HERE.
CLANK!
CL-CLANK!

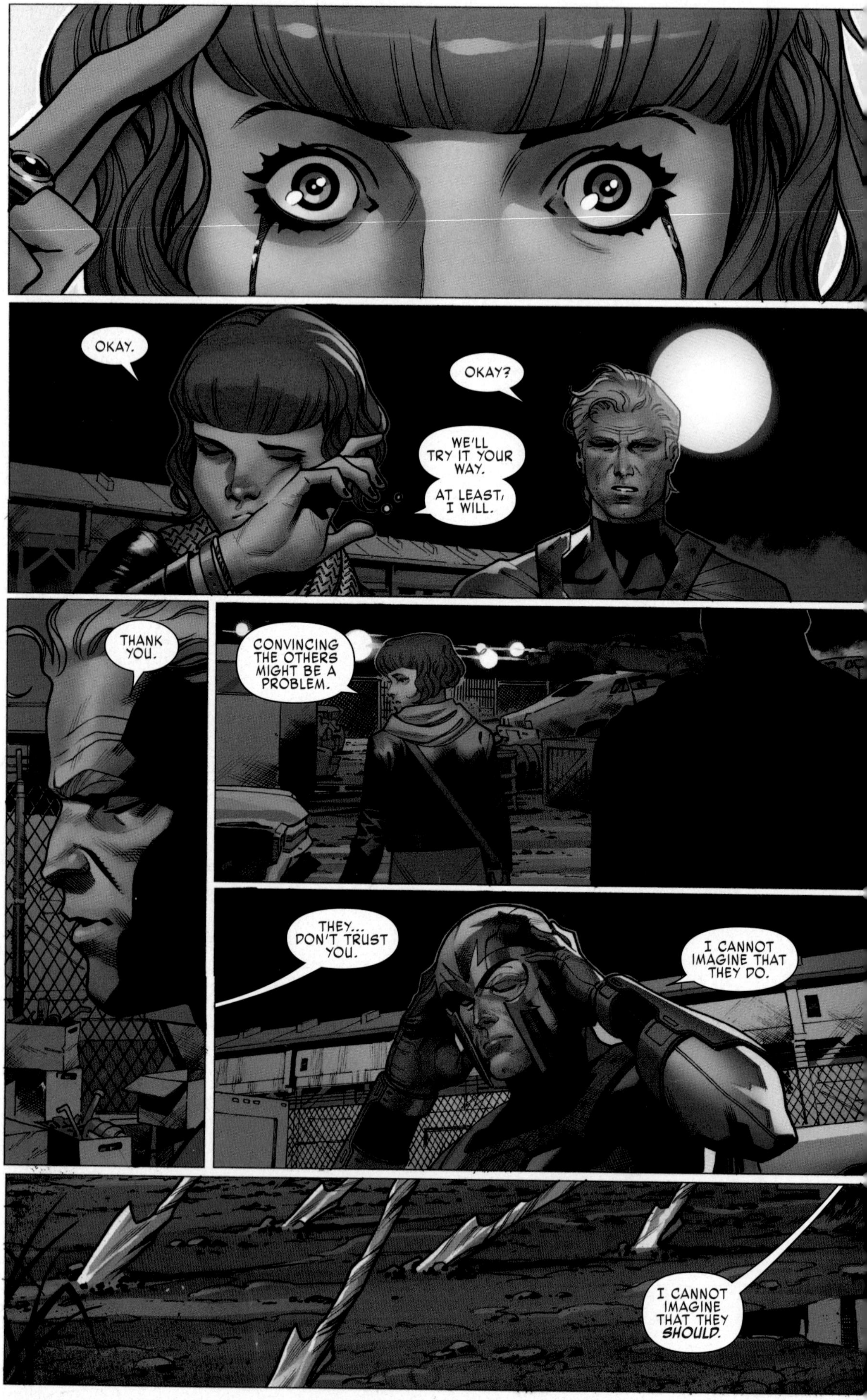
OKAY.
OKAY?
WE'LL TRY IT YOUR WAY.
AT LEAST, I WILL.
THANK YOU.
CONVINCING THE OTHERS MIGHT BE A PROBLEM.
THEY... DON'T TRUST YOU.
I CANNOT IMAGINE THAT THEY DO.
I CANNOT IMAGINE THAT THEY *SHOULD*.

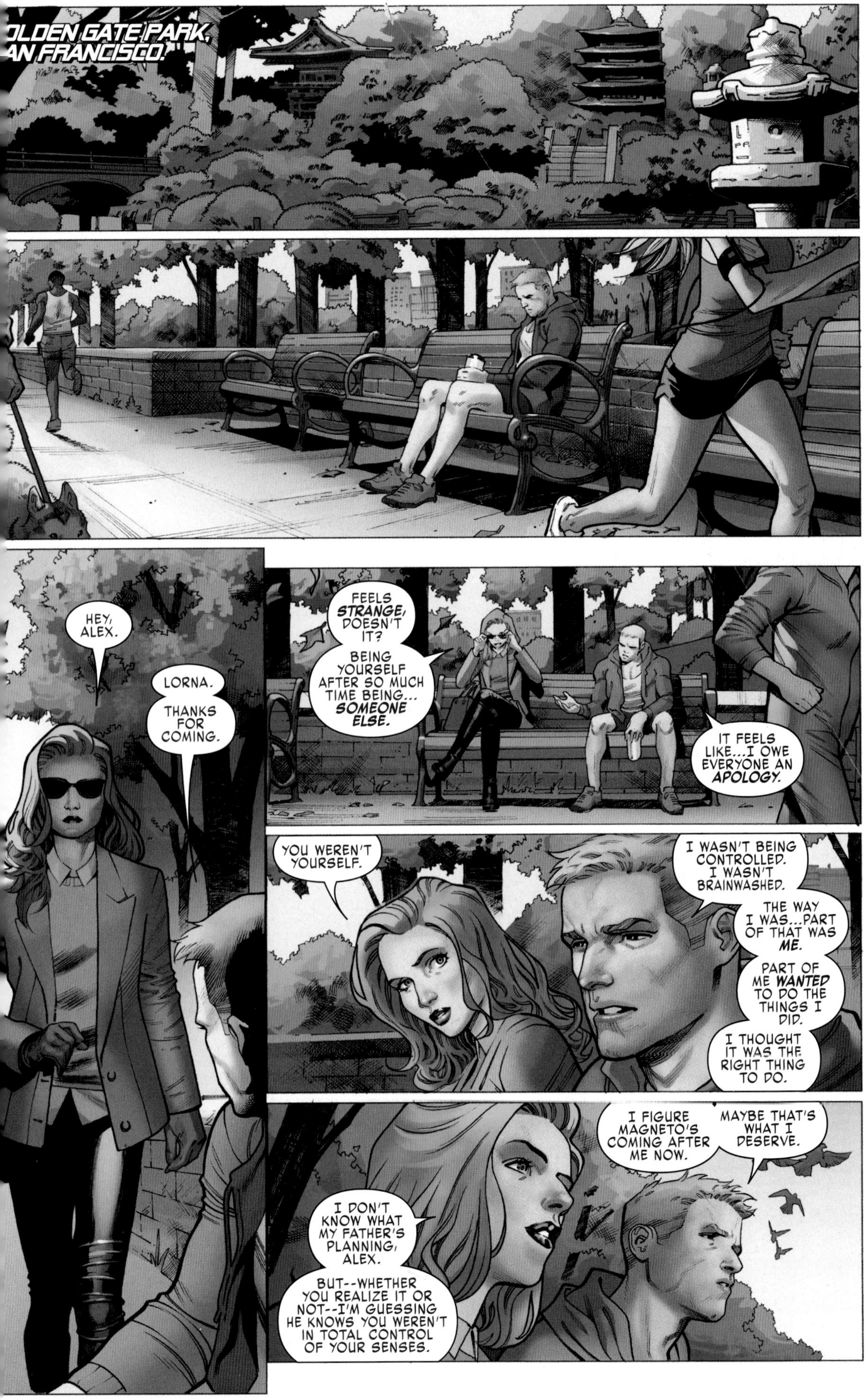
OLDEN GATE PARK, AN FRANCISCO.
HEY, ALEX.
LORNA.
THANKS FOR COMING.
FEELS STRANGE, DOESN'T IT?
BEING YOURSELF AFTER SO MUCH TIME BEING... SOMEONE ELSE.
IT FEELS LIKE...I OWE EVERYONE AN APOLOGY.
YOU WEREN'T YOURSELF.
I WASN'T BEING CONTROLLED. I WASN'T BRAINWASHED.
THE WAY I WAS...PART OF THAT WAS ME.
PART OF ME WANTED TO DO THE THINGS I DID.
I THOUGHT IT WAS THE RIGHT THING TO DO.
I FIGURE MAGNETO'S COMING AFTER ME NOW.
MAYBE THAT'S WHAT I DESERVE.
I DON'T KNOW WHAT MY FATHER'S PLANNING, ALEX.
BUT--WHETHER YOU REALIZE IT OR NOT--I'M GUESSING HE KNOWS YOU WEREN'T IN TOTAL CONTROL OF YOUR SENSES.

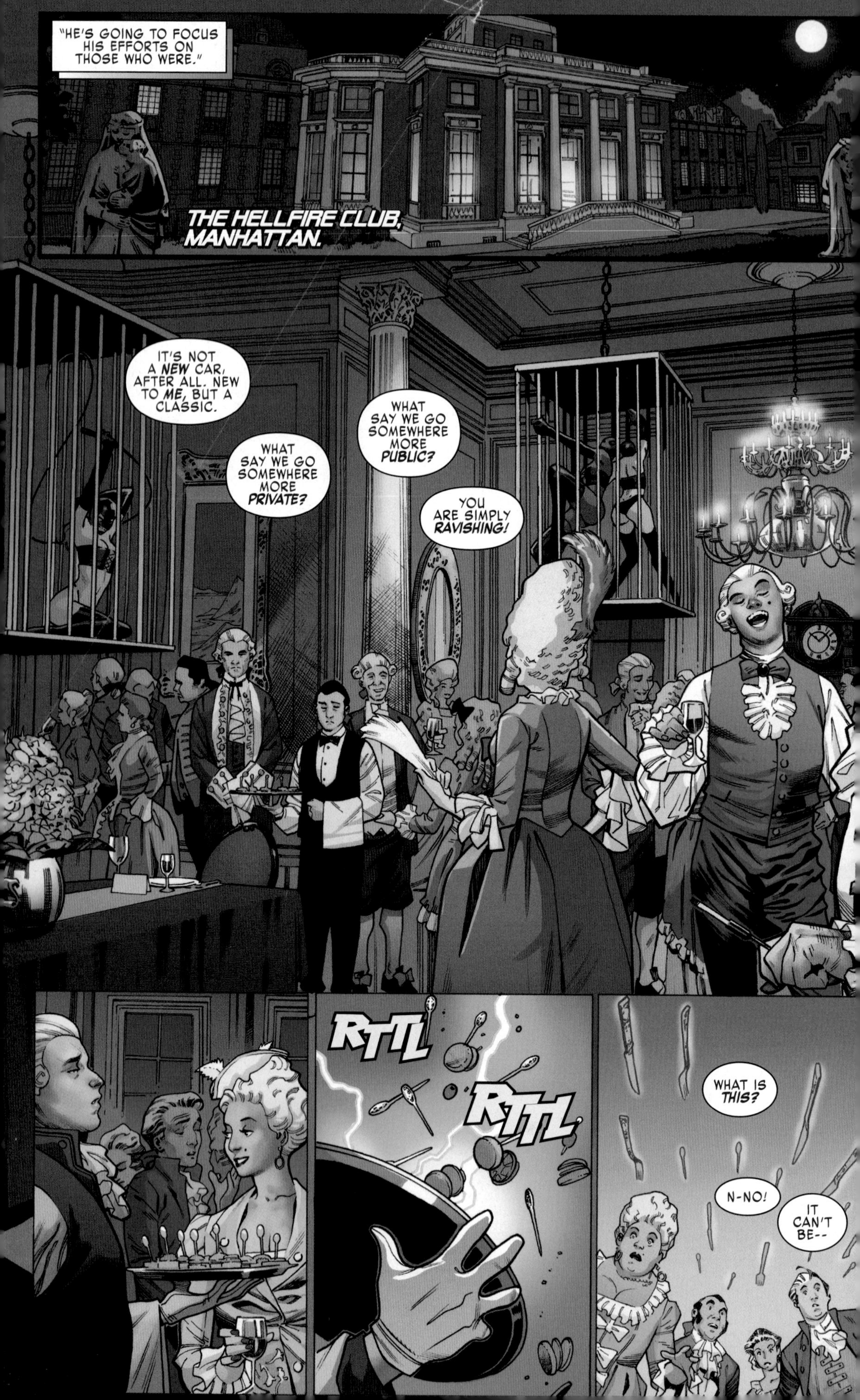
"HE'S GOING TO FOCUS HIS EFFORTS ON THOSE WHO WERE."
THE HELLFIRE CLUB, MANHATTAN.
IT'S NOT A NEW CAR, AFTER ALL. NEW TO ME, BUT A CLASSIC.
WHAT SAY WE GO SOMEWHERE MORE PRIVATE?
WHAT SAY WE GO SOMEWHERE MORE PUBLIC?
YOU ARE SIMPLY RAVISHING!
RTTL
RTTL
WHAT IS THIS?
N-NO!
IT CAN'T BE--

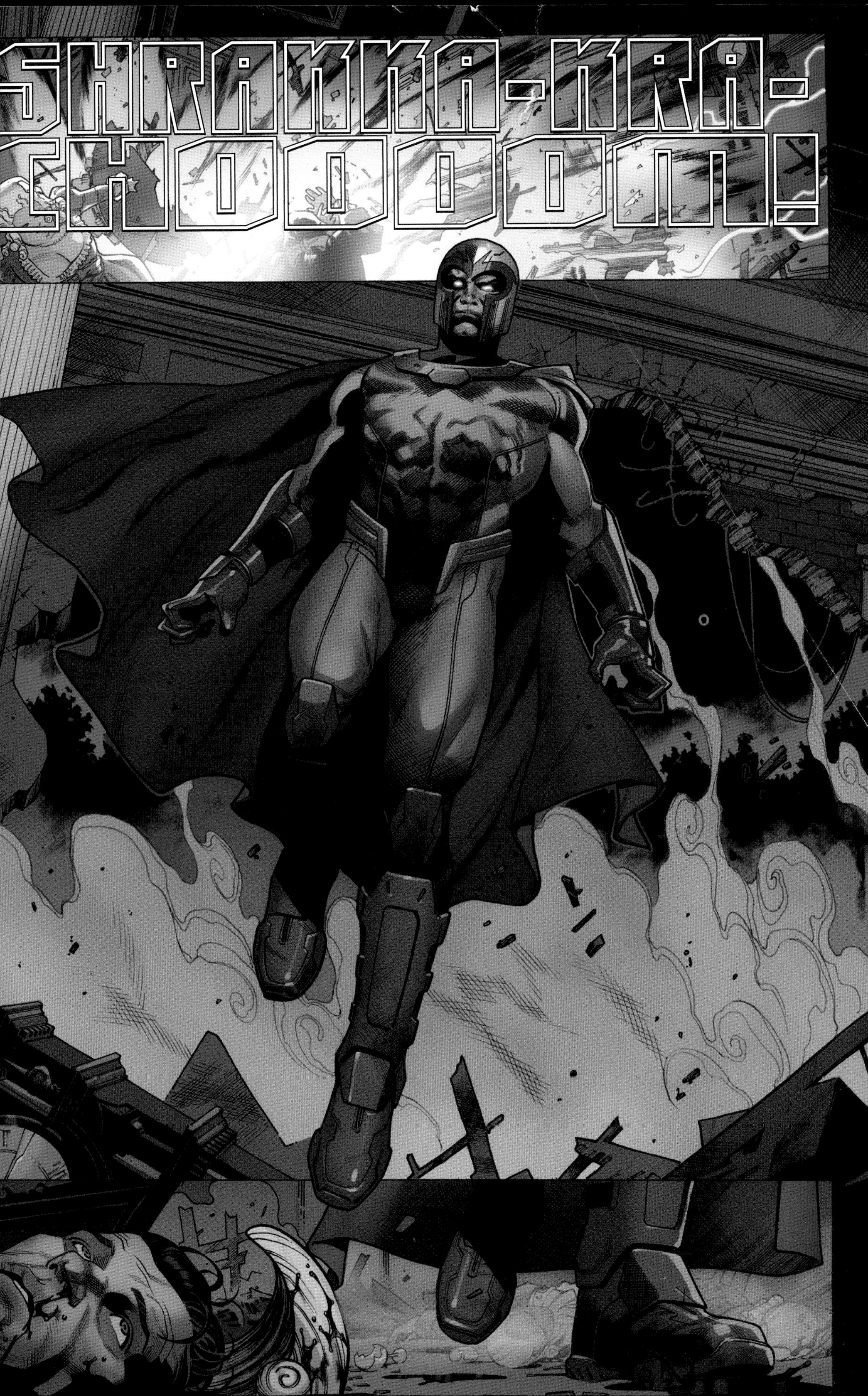
SHRAKKA-KRA-CHOOOOOM!

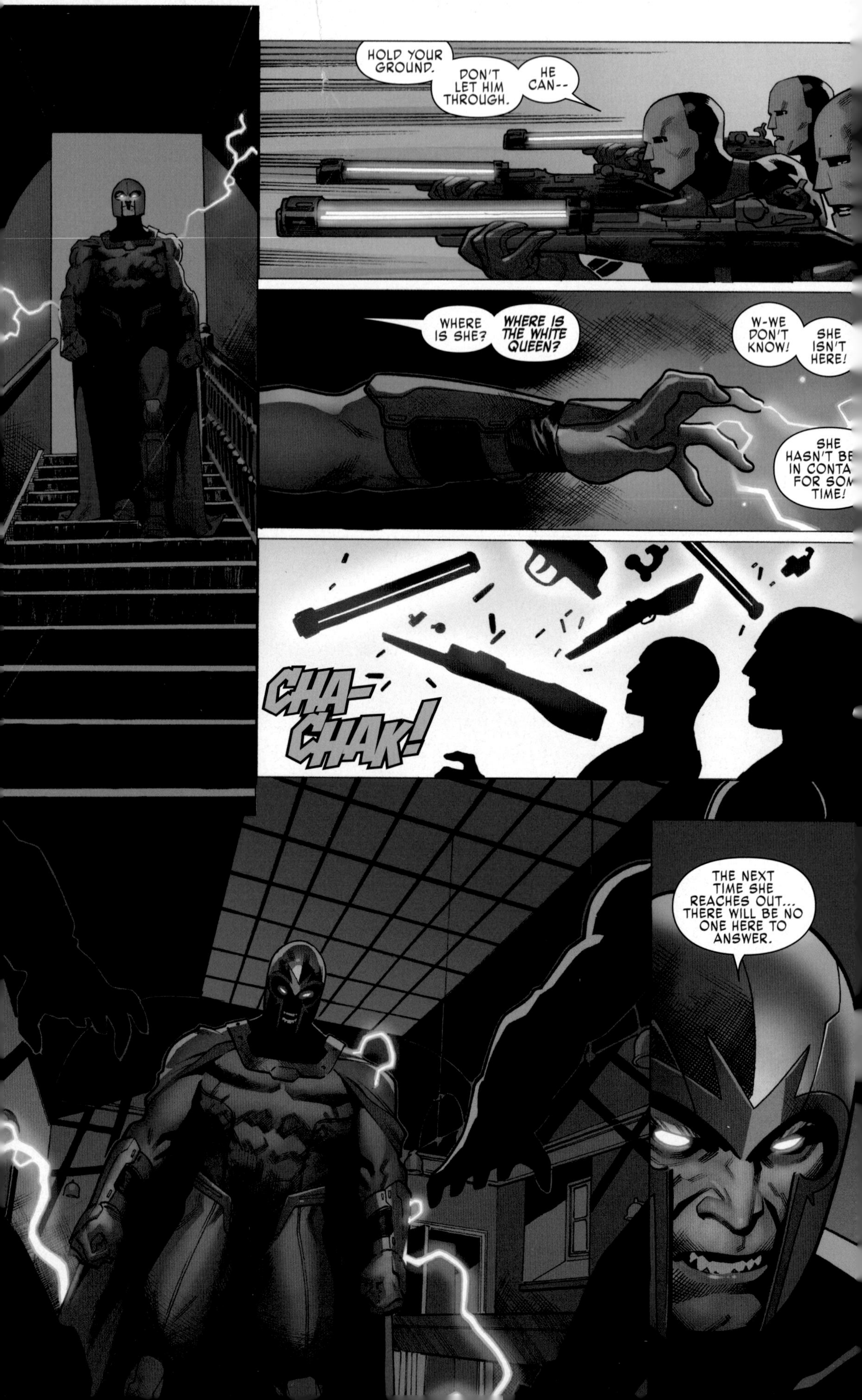
HOLD YOUR GROUND.
DON'T LET HIM THROUGH.
HE CAN--
WHERE IS SHE?
WHERE IS THE WHITE QUEEN?
W-WE DON'T KNOW!
SHE ISN'T HERE!
CHA-CHAK!
THE NEXT TIME SHE REACHES OUT... THERE WILL BE NO ONE HERE TO ANSWER.

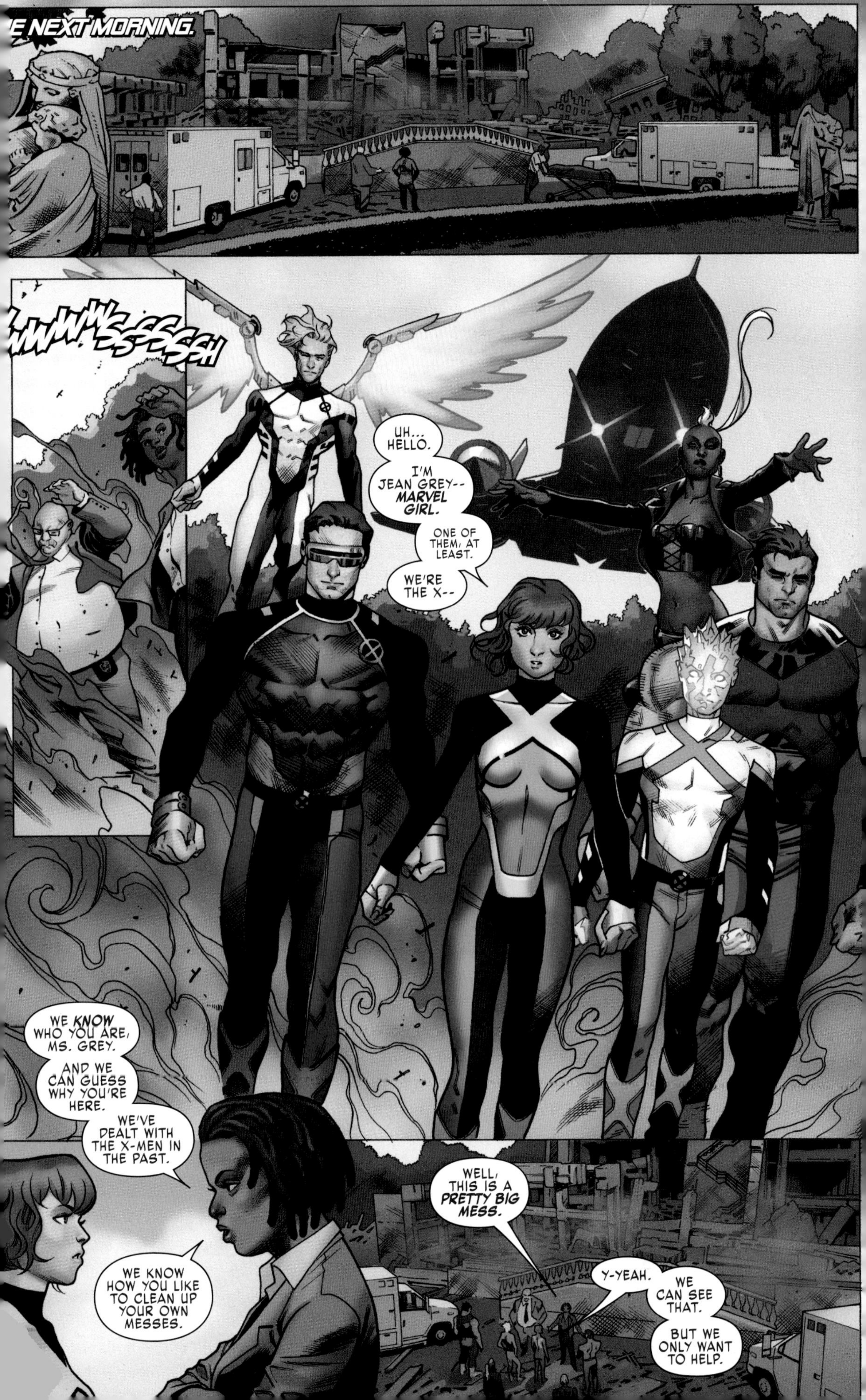

E NEXT MORNING.
WWWWSSSSSH
UH... HELLO.
I'M JEAN GREY-- MARVEL GIRL.
ONE OF THEM, AT LEAST.
WE'RE THE X--
WE KNOW WHO YOU ARE, MS. GREY.
AND WE CAN GUESS WHY YOU'RE HERE.
WE'VE DEALT WITH THE X-MEN IN THE PAST.
WE KNOW HOW YOU LIKE TO CLEAN UP YOUR OWN MESSES.
WELL, THIS IS A PRETTY BIG MESS.
Y-YEAH.
WE CAN SEE THAT.
BUT WE ONLY WANT TO HELP.

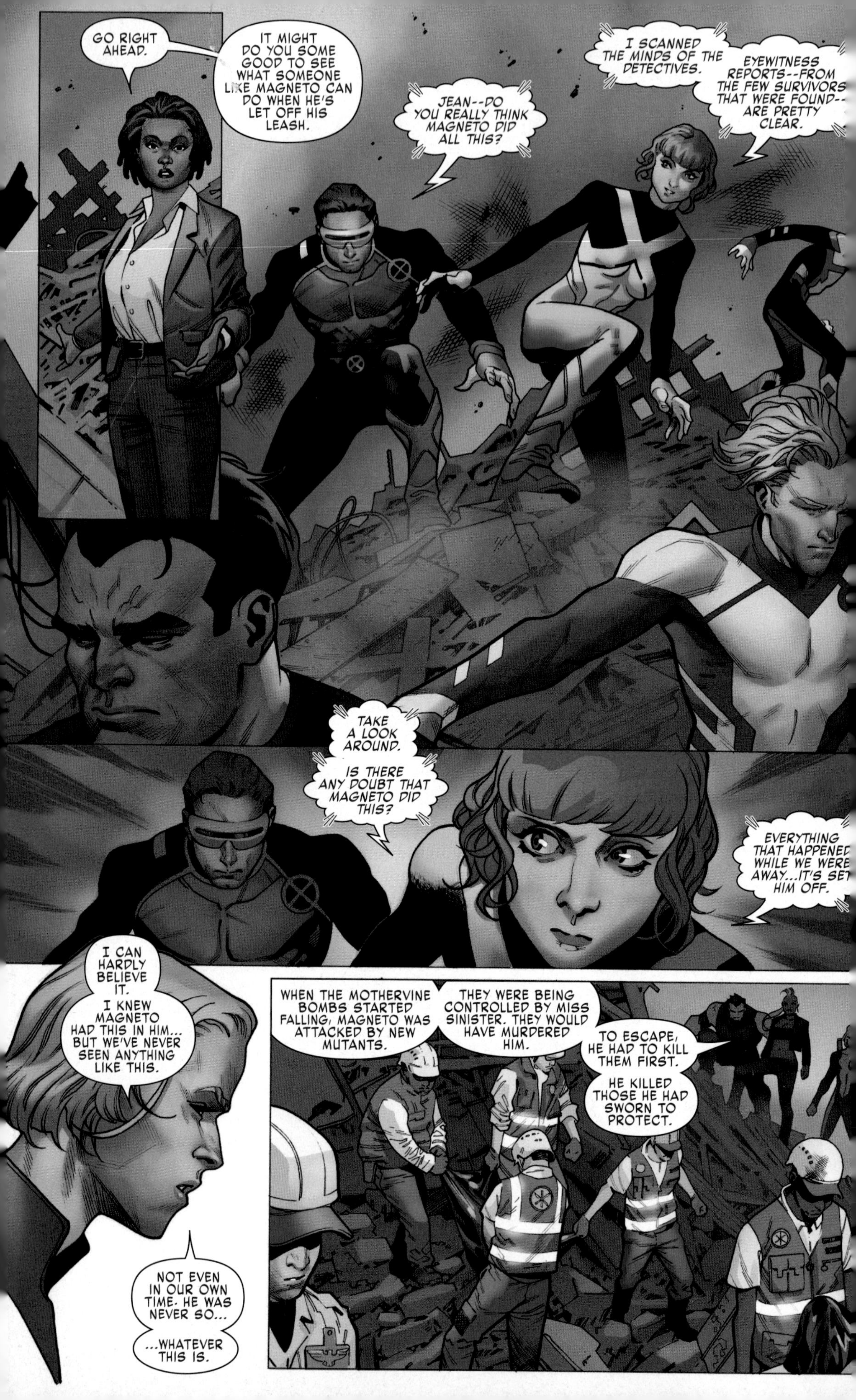
GO RIGHT AHEAD.
IT MIGHT DO YOU SOME GOOD TO SEE WHAT SOMEONE LIKE MAGNETO CAN DO WHEN HE'S LET OFF HIS LEASH.
JEAN--DO YOU REALLY THINK MAGNETO DID ALL THIS?
I SCANNED THE MINDS OF THE DETECTIVES.
EYEWITNESS REPORTS--FROM THE FEW SURVIVORS THAT WERE FOUND--ARE PRETTY CLEAR.
TAKE A LOOK AROUND.
IS THERE ANY DOUBT THAT MAGNETO DID THIS?
EVERYTHING THAT HAPPENED WHILE WE WERE AWAY...IT'S SET HIM OFF.
I CAN HARDLY BELIEVE IT.
I KNEW MAGNETO HAD THIS IN HIM... BUT WE'VE NEVER SEEN ANYTHING LIKE THIS.
NOT EVEN IN OUR OWN TIME. HE WAS NEVER SO...
...WHATEVER THIS IS.
WHEN THE MOTHERVINE BOMBS STARTED FALLING, MAGNETO WAS ATTACKED BY NEW MUTANTS.
THEY WERE BEING CONTROLLED BY MISS SINISTER. THEY WOULD HAVE MURDERED HIM.
TO ESCAPE, HE HAD TO KILL THEM FIRST.
HE KILLED THOSE HE HAD SWORN TO PROTECT.

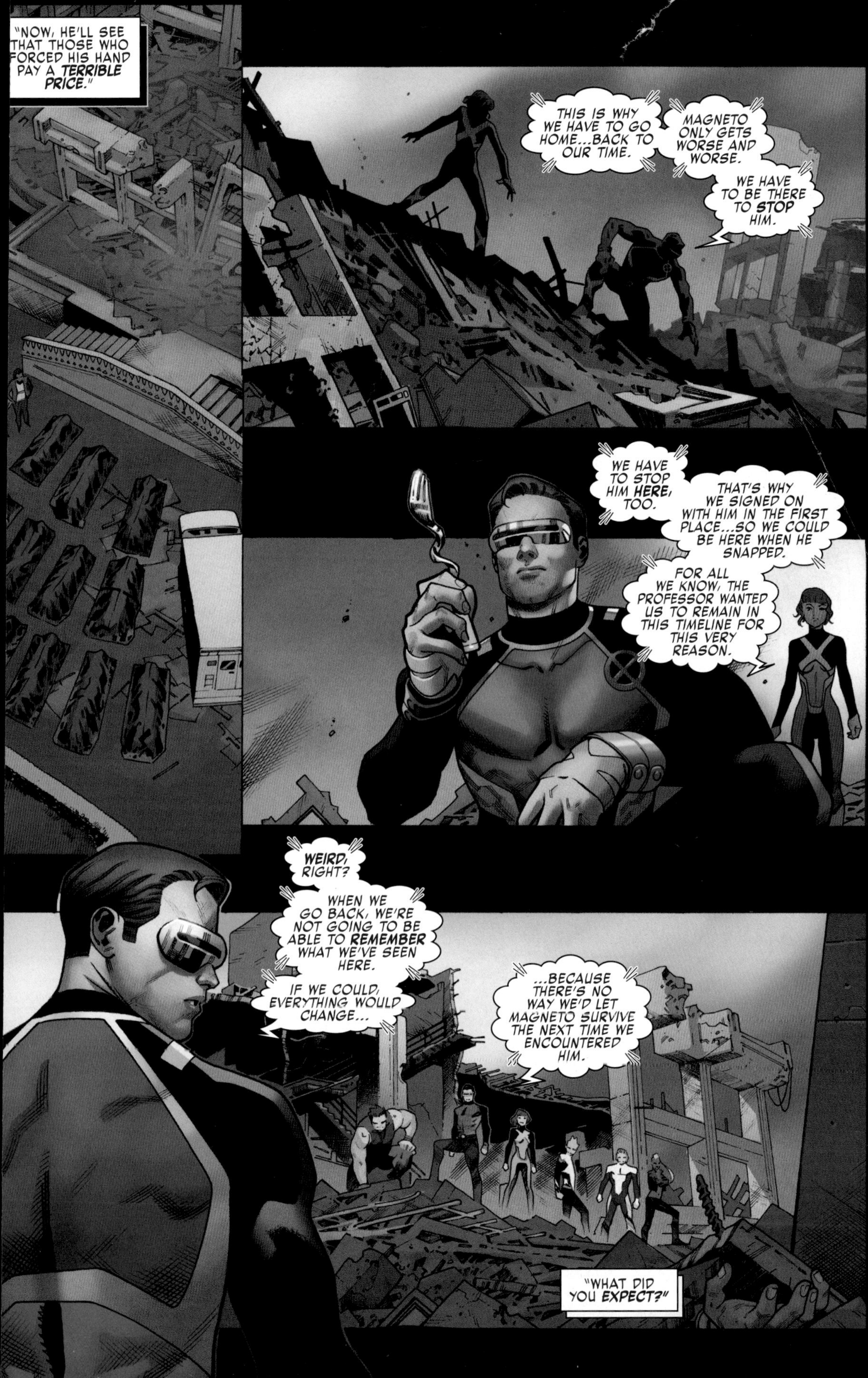
"NOW, HE'LL SEE THAT THOSE WHO FORCED HIS HAND PAY A **TERRIBLE PRICE**."
THIS IS WHY WE HAVE TO GO HOME...BACK TO OUR TIME.
MAGNETO ONLY GETS WORSE AND WORSE.
WE HAVE TO BE THERE TO **STOP** HIM.
WE HAVE TO STOP HIM **HERE**, TOO.
THAT'S WHY WE SIGNED ON WITH HIM IN THE FIRST PLACE...SO WE COULD BE HERE WHEN HE SNAPPED.
FOR ALL WE KNOW, THE PROFESSOR WANTED US TO REMAIN IN THIS TIMELINE FOR THIS VERY REASON.
**WEIRD**, RIGHT?
WHEN WE GO BACK, WE'RE NOT GOING TO BE ABLE TO **REMEMBER** WHAT WE'VE SEEN HERE.
IF WE COULD, EVERYTHING WOULD CHANGE...
...BECAUSE THERE'S NO WAY WE'D LET MAGNETO SURVIVE THE NEXT TIME WE ENCOUNTERED HIM.
"WHAT DID YOU **EXPECT**?"

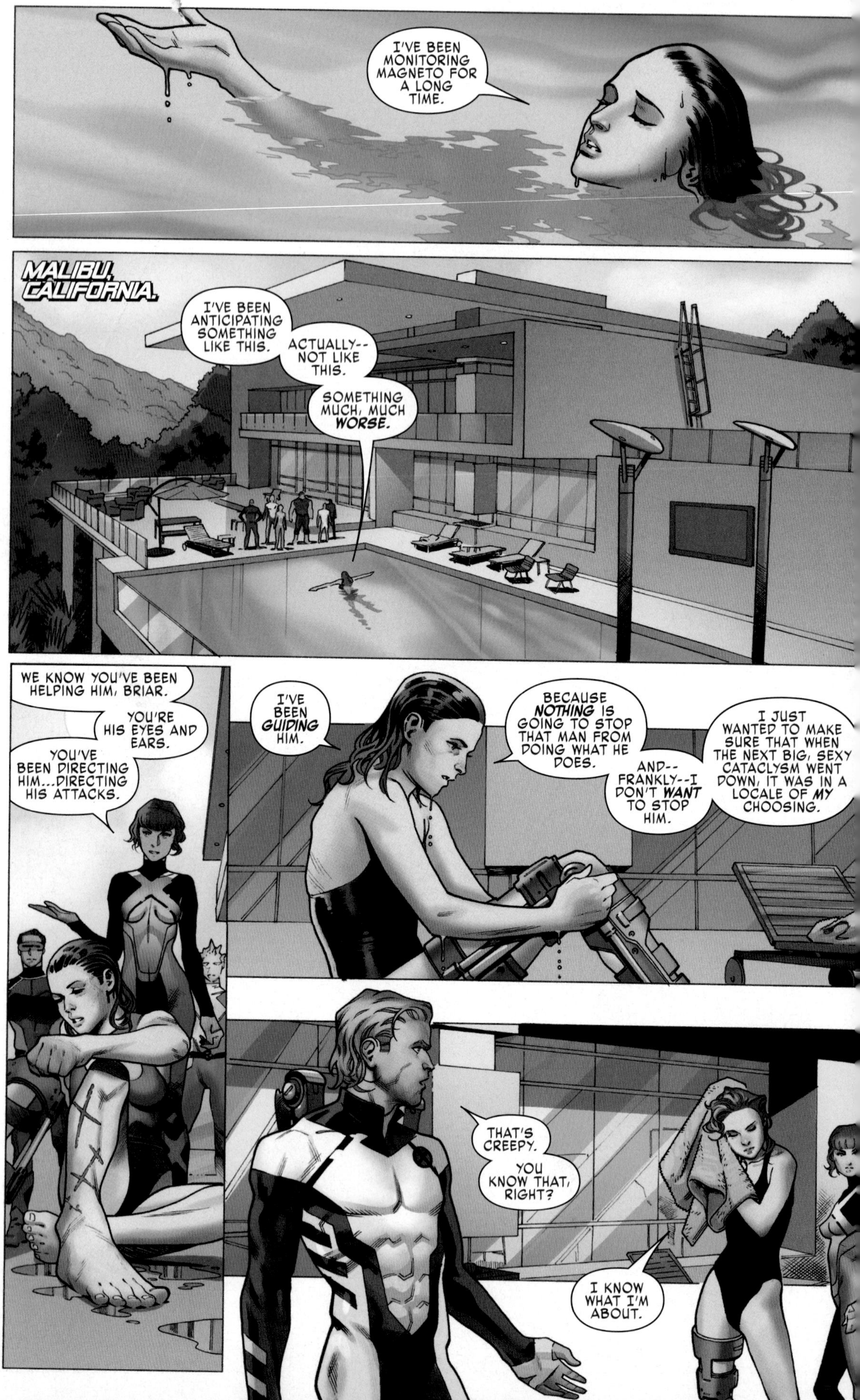
I'VE BEEN MONITORING MAGNETO FOR A LONG TIME.
MALIBU, CALIFORNIA.
I'VE BEEN ANTICIPATING SOMETHING LIKE THIS.
ACTUALLY-- NOT LIKE THIS.
SOMETHING MUCH, MUCH WORSE.
WE KNOW YOU'VE BEEN HELPING HIM, BRIAR.
YOU'RE HIS EYES AND EARS.
YOU'VE BEEN DIRECTING HIM...DIRECTING HIS ATTACKS.
I'VE BEEN GUIDING HIM.
BECAUSE NOTHING IS GOING TO STOP THAT MAN FROM DOING WHAT HE DOES.
AND-- FRANKLY--I DON'T WANT TO STOP HIM.
I JUST WANTED TO MAKE SURE THAT WHEN THE NEXT BIG, SEXY CATACLYSM WENT DOWN, IT WAS IN A LOCALE OF MY CHOOSING.
THAT'S CREEPY.
YOU KNOW THAT, RIGHT?
I KNOW WHAT I'M ABOUT.

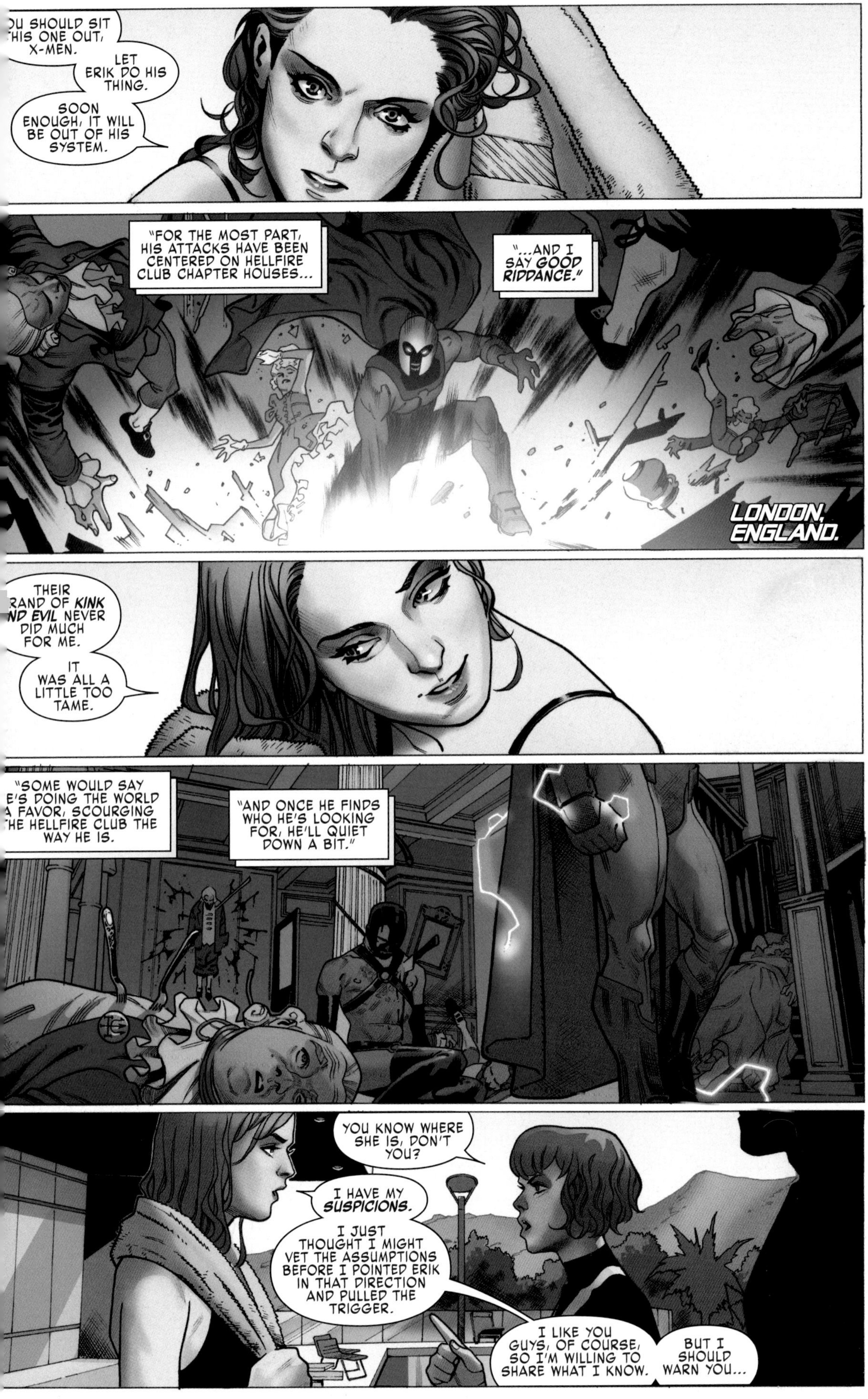
OU SHOULD SIT THIS ONE OUT, X-MEN.
LET ERIK DO HIS THING.
SOON ENOUGH, IT WILL BE OUT OF HIS SYSTEM.
"FOR THE MOST PART, HIS ATTACKS HAVE BEEN CENTERED ON HELLFIRE CLUB CHAPTER HOUSES...
"...AND I SAY GOOD RIDDANCE."
LONDON, ENGLAND.
THEIR RAND OF KINK ND EVIL NEVER DID MUCH FOR ME.
IT WAS ALL A LITTLE TOO TAME.
"SOME WOULD SAY E'S DOING THE WORLD A FAVOR, SCOURGING THE HELLFIRE CLUB THE WAY HE IS.
"AND ONCE HE FINDS WHO HE'S LOOKING FOR, HE'LL QUIET DOWN A BIT."
YOU KNOW WHERE SHE IS, DON'T YOU?
I HAVE MY SUSPICIONS.
I JUST THOUGHT I MIGHT VET THE ASSUMPTIONS BEFORE I POINTED ERIK IN THAT DIRECTION AND PULLED THE TRIGGER.
I LIKE YOU GUYS, OF COURSE, SO I'M WILLING TO SHARE WHAT I KNOW.
BUT I SHOULD WARN YOU...

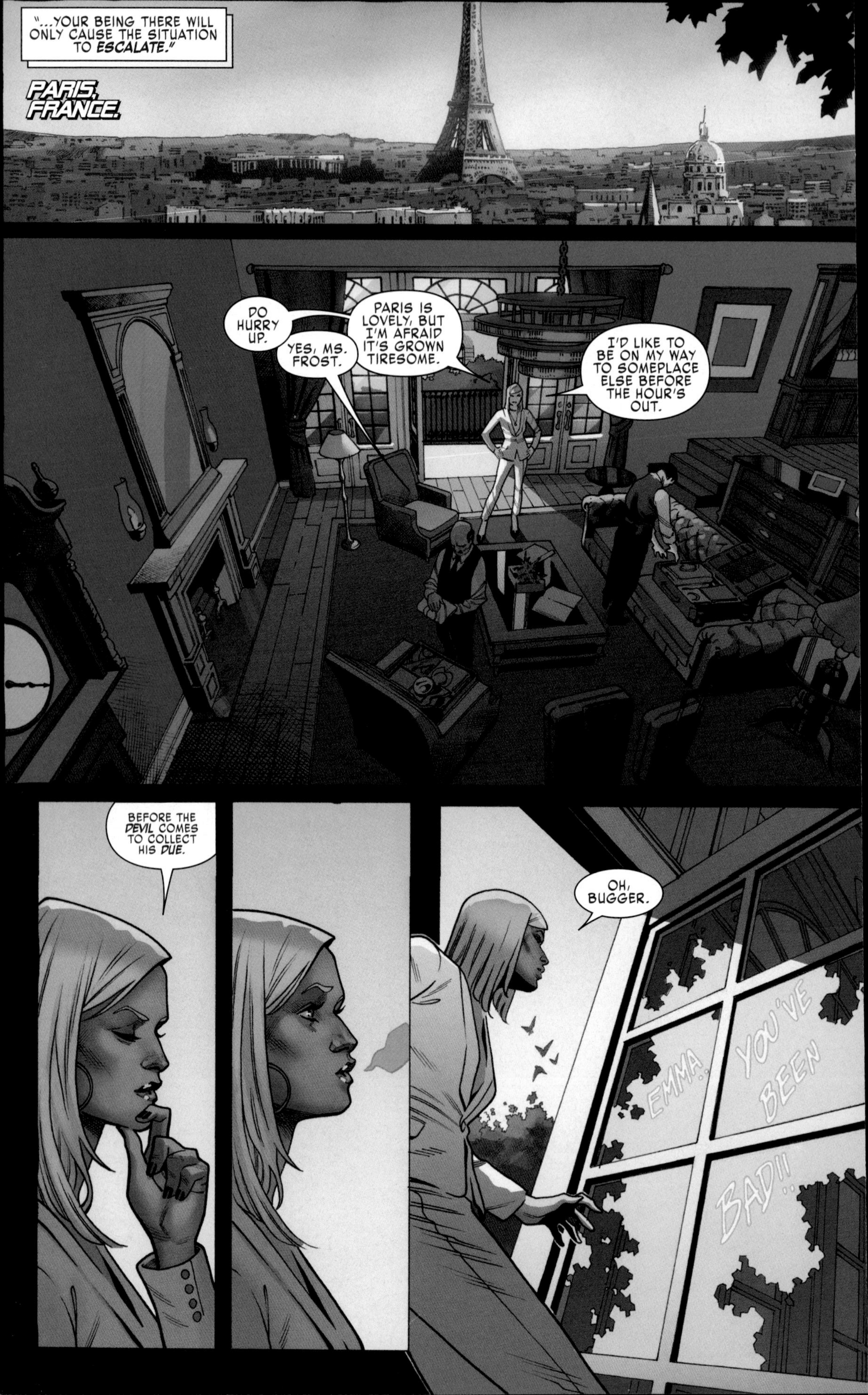
"...YOUR BEING THERE WILL ONLY CAUSE THE SITUATION TO ESCALATE."
PARIS, FRANCE.
DO HURRY UP.
YES, MS. FROST.
PARIS IS LOVELY, BUT I'M AFRAID IT'S GROWN TIRESOME.
I'D LIKE TO BE ON MY WAY TO SOMEPLACE ELSE BEFORE THE HOUR'S OUT.
BEFORE THE DEVIL COMES TO COLLECT HIS DUE.
OH, BUGGER.
EMMA... YOU'VE BEEN BAD!!

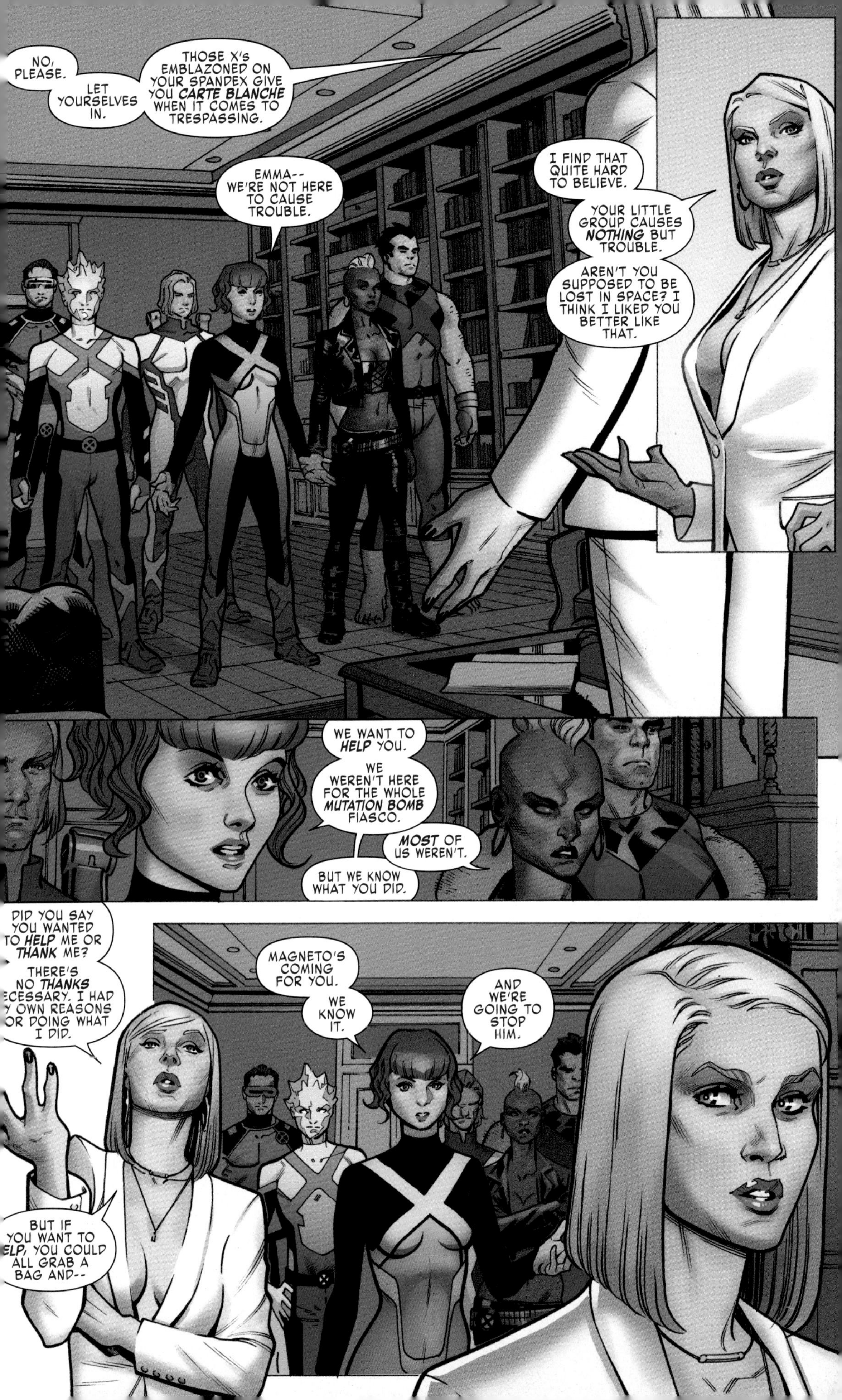
NO, PLEASE.
LET YOURSELVES IN.
THOSE X's EMBLAZONED ON YOUR SPANDEX GIVE YOU CARTE BLANCHE WHEN IT COMES TO TRESPASSING.
EMMA-- WE'RE NOT HERE TO CAUSE TROUBLE.
I FIND THAT QUITE HARD TO BELIEVE.
YOUR LITTLE GROUP CAUSES NOTHING BUT TROUBLE.
AREN'T YOU SUPPOSED TO BE LOST IN SPACE? I THINK I LIKED YOU BETTER LIKE THAT.
WE WANT TO HELP YOU.
WE WEREN'T HERE FOR THE WHOLE MUTATION BOMB FIASCO.
MOST OF US WEREN'T.
BUT WE KNOW WHAT YOU DID.
DID YOU SAY YOU WANTED TO HELP ME OR THANK ME?
THERE'S NO THANKS ECESSARY. I HAD Y OWN REASONS OR DOING WHAT I DID.
MAGNETO'S COMING FOR YOU.
WE KNOW IT.
AND WE'RE GOING TO STOP HIM.
BUT IF YOU WANT TO ELP, YOU COULD ALL GRAB A BAG AND--

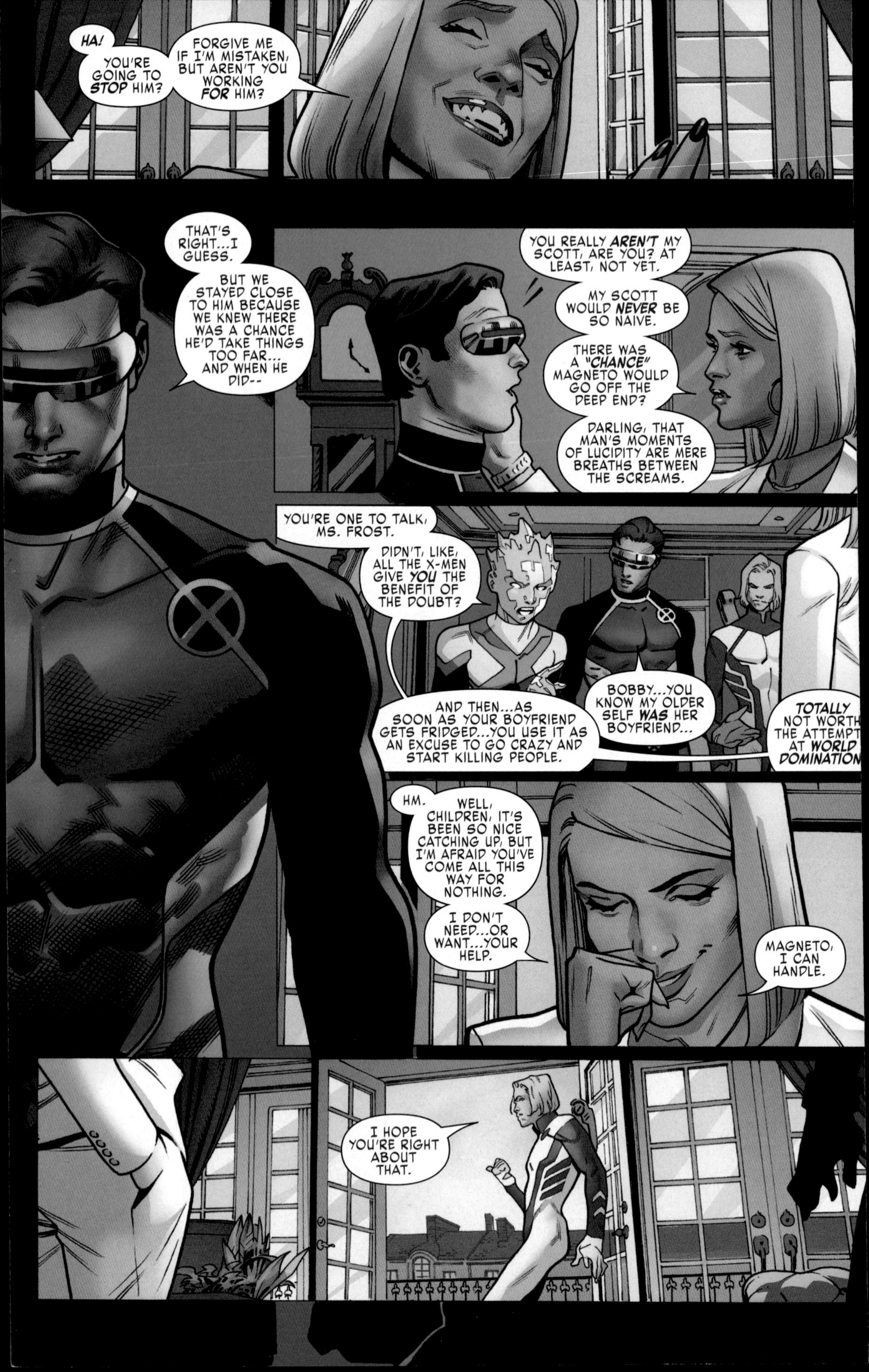

HA!
YOU'RE GOING TO STOP HIM?
FORGIVE ME IF I'M MISTAKEN, BUT AREN'T YOU WORKING FOR HIM?
THAT'S RIGHT...I GUESS.
BUT WE STAYED CLOSE TO HIM BECAUSE WE KNEW THERE WAS A CHANCE HE'D TAKE THINGS TOO FAR... AND WHEN HE DID--
YOU REALLY AREN'T MY SCOTT, ARE YOU? AT LEAST, NOT YET.
MY SCOTT WOULD NEVER BE SO NAIVE.
THERE WAS A "CHANCE" MAGNETO WOULD GO OFF THE DEEP END?
DARLING, THAT MAN'S MOMENTS OF LUCIDITY ARE MERE BREATHS BETWEEN THE SCREAMS.
YOU'RE ONE TO TALK, MS. FROST.
DIDN'T, LIKE, ALL THE X-MEN GIVE YOU THE BENEFIT OF THE DOUBT?
AND THEN...AS SOON AS YOUR BOYFRIEND GETS FRIDGED...YOU USE IT AS AN EXCUSE TO GO CRAZY AND START KILLING PEOPLE.
BOBBY...YOU KNOW MY OLDER SELF WAS HER BOYFRIEND...
TOTALLY NOT WORTH THE ATTEMPT AT WORLD DOMINATION
HM.
WELL, CHILDREN, IT'S BEEN SO NICE CATCHING UP, BUT I'M AFRAID YOU'VE COME ALL THIS WAY FOR NOTHING.
I DON'T NEED...OR WANT...YOUR HELP.
MAGNETO, I CAN HANDLE.
I HOPE YOU'RE RIGHT ABOUT THAT.

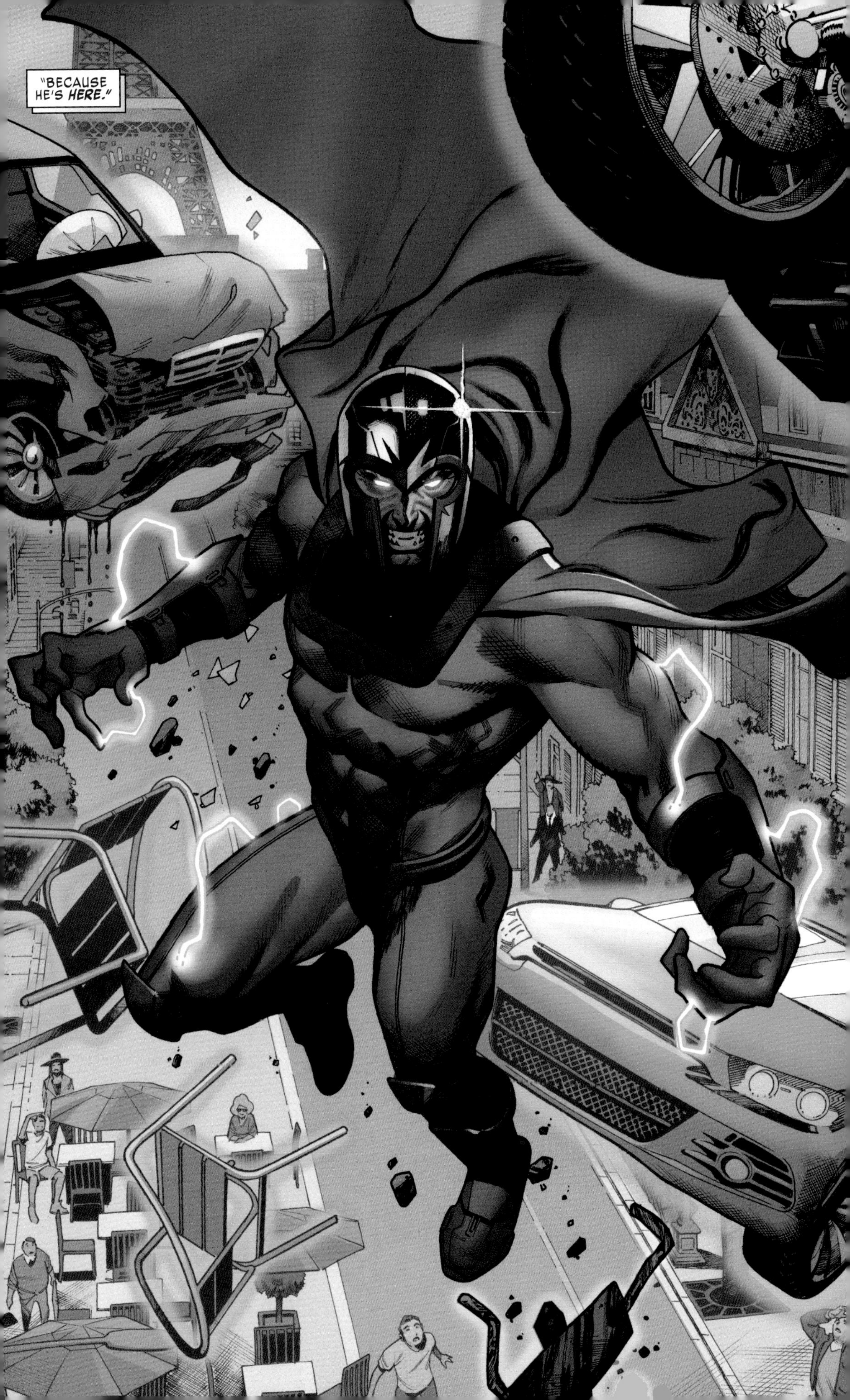
"BECAUSE HE'S HERE."

32

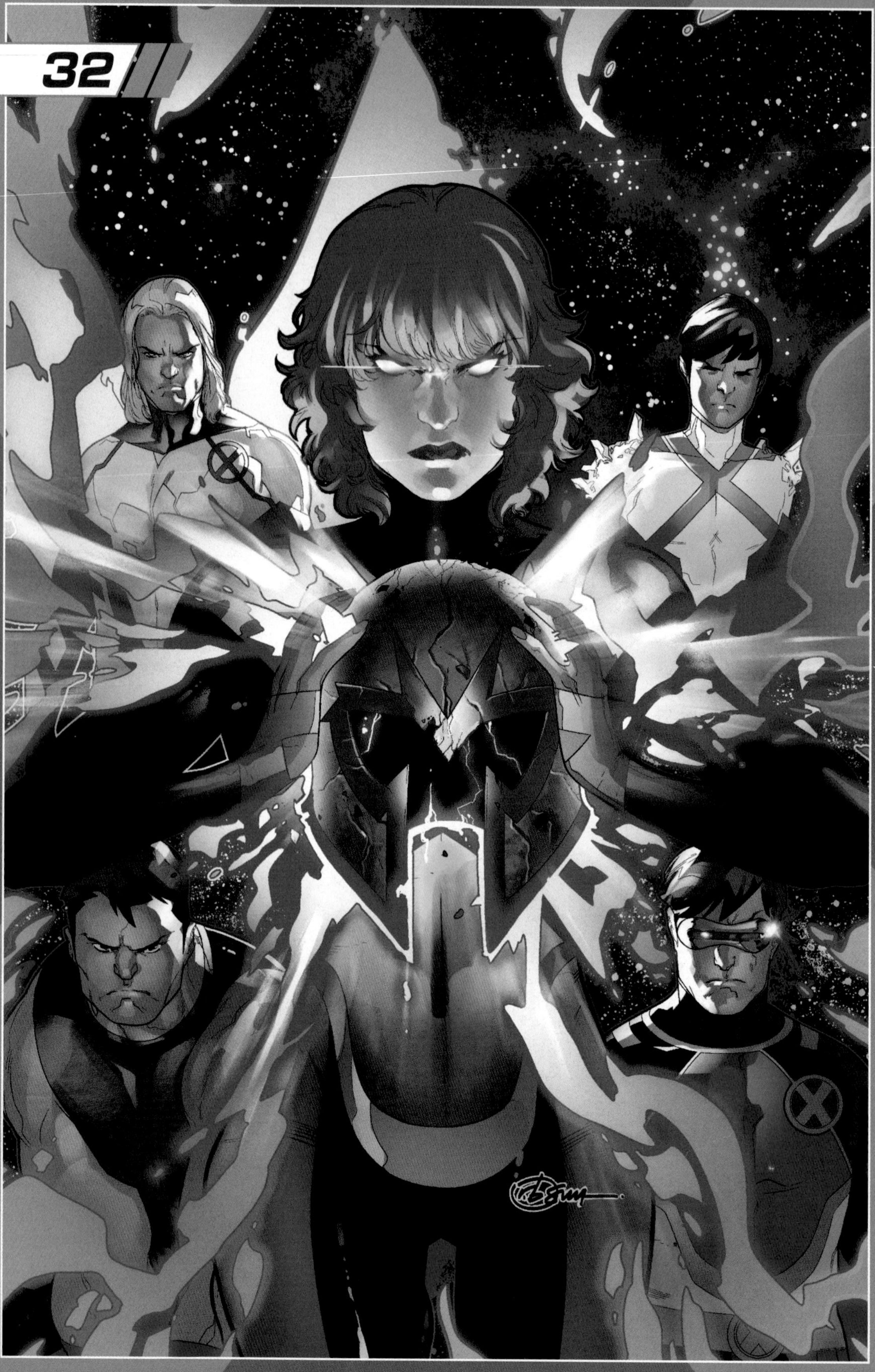

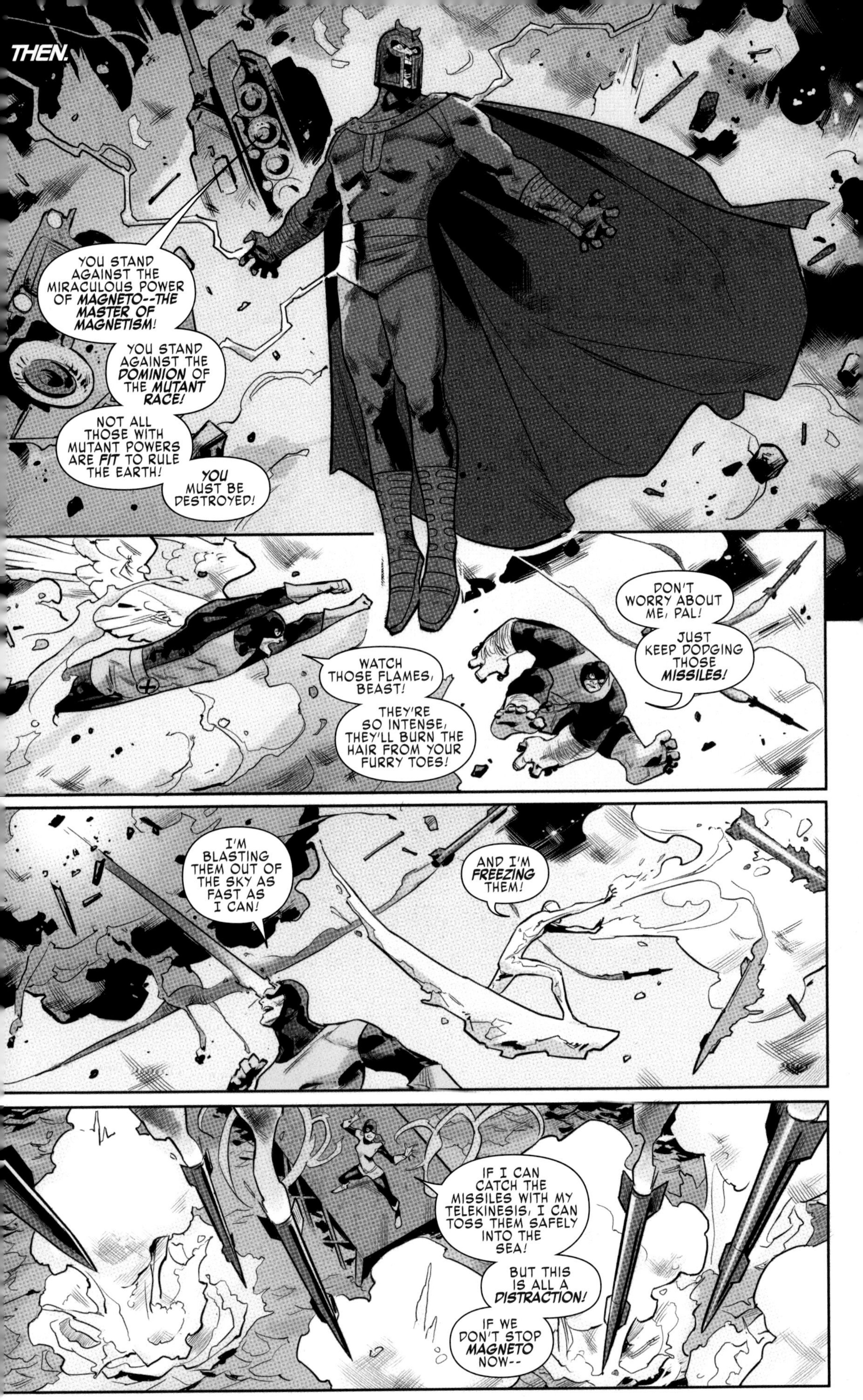
THEN.
YOU STAND AGAINST THE MIRACULOUS POWER OF MAGNETO--THE MASTER OF MAGNETISM!
YOU STAND AGAINST THE DOMINION OF THE MUTANT RACE!
NOT ALL THOSE WITH MUTANT POWERS ARE FIT TO RULE THE EARTH!
YOU MUST BE DESTROYED!
WATCH THOSE FLAMES, BEAST!
THEY'RE SO INTENSE, THEY'LL BURN THE HAIR FROM YOUR FURRY TOES!
DON'T WORRY ABOUT ME, PAL!
JUST KEEP DODGING THOSE MISSILES!
I'M BLASTING THEM OUT OF THE SKY AS FAST AS I CAN!
AND I'M FREEZING THEM!
IF I CAN CATCH THE MISSILES WITH MY TELEKINESIS, I CAN TOSS THEM SAFELY INTO THE SEA!
BUT THIS IS ALL A DISTRACTION!
IF WE DON'T STOP MAGNETO NOW--

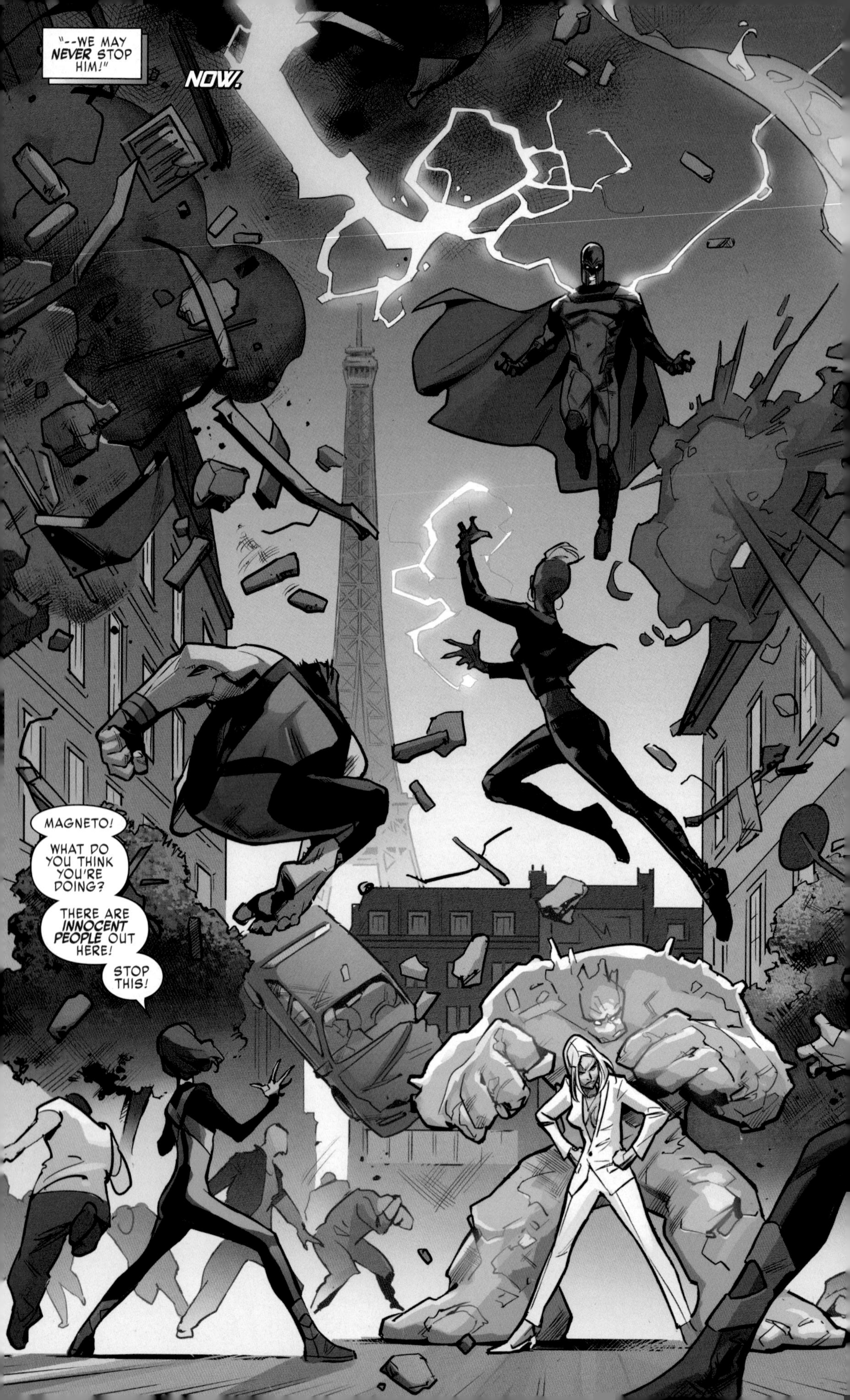
"--WE MAY NEVER STOP HIM!"
NOW.
MAGNETO!
WHAT DO YOU THINK YOU'RE DOING?
THERE ARE INNOCENT PEOPLE OUT HERE!
STOP THIS!

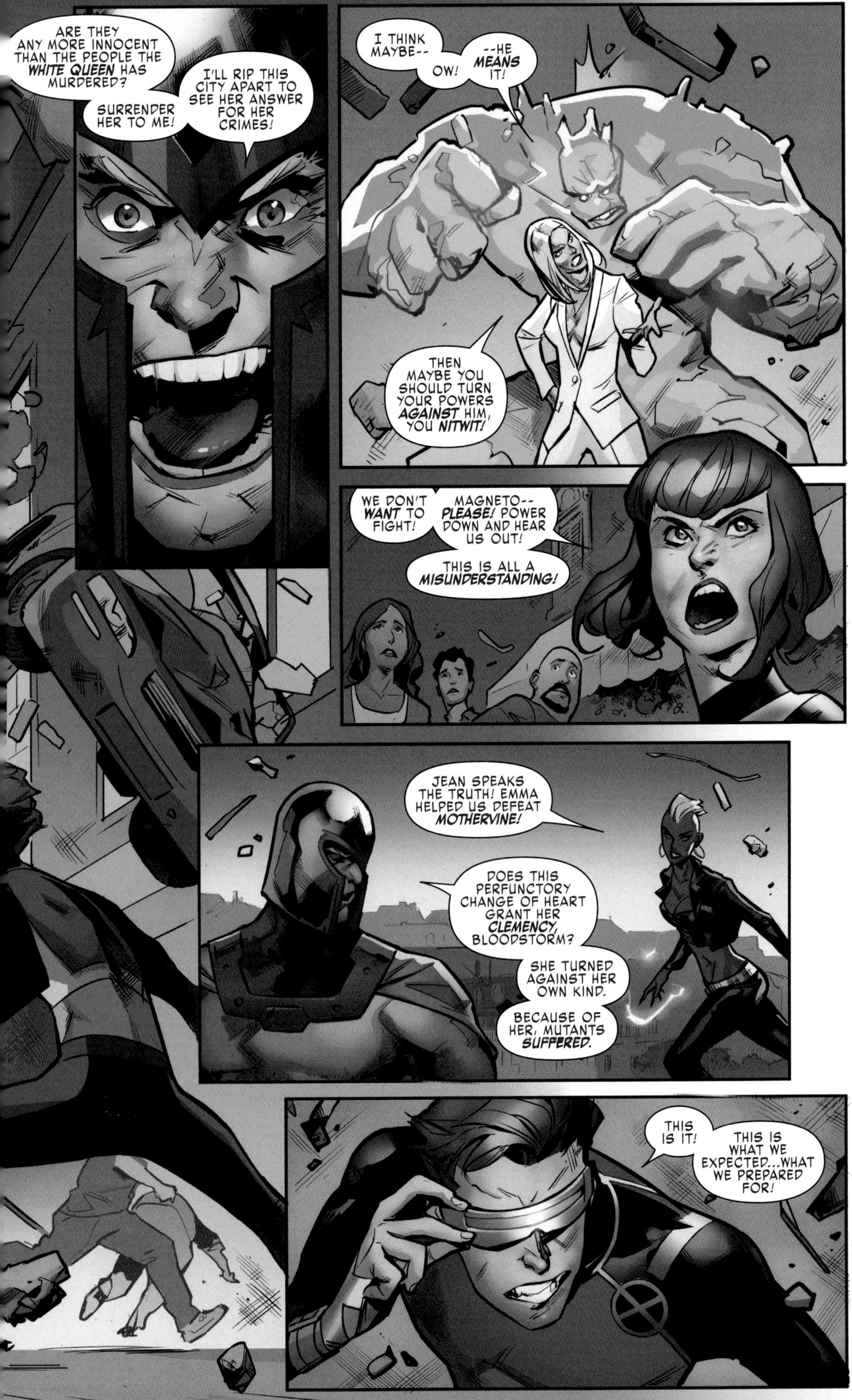
ARE THEY ANY MORE INNOCENT THAN THE PEOPLE THE WHITE QUEEN HAS MURDERED?
SURRENDER HER TO ME!
I'LL RIP THIS CITY APART TO SEE HER ANSWER FOR HER CRIMES!
I THINK MAYBE--
OW!
--HE MEANS IT!
THEN MAYBE YOU SHOULD TURN YOUR POWERS AGAINST HIM, YOU NITWIT!
WE DON'T WANT TO FIGHT!
MAGNETO-- PLEASE! POWER DOWN AND HEAR US OUT!
THIS IS ALL A MISUNDERSTANDING!
JEAN SPEAKS THE TRUTH! EMMA HELPED US DEFEAT MOTHERVINE!
DOES THIS PERFUNCTORY CHANGE OF HEART GRANT HER CLEMENCY, BLOODSTORM?
SHE TURNED AGAINST HER OWN KIND.
BECAUSE OF HER, MUTANTS SUFFERED.
THIS IS IT!
THIS IS WHAT WE EXPECTED...WHAT WE PREPARED FOR!

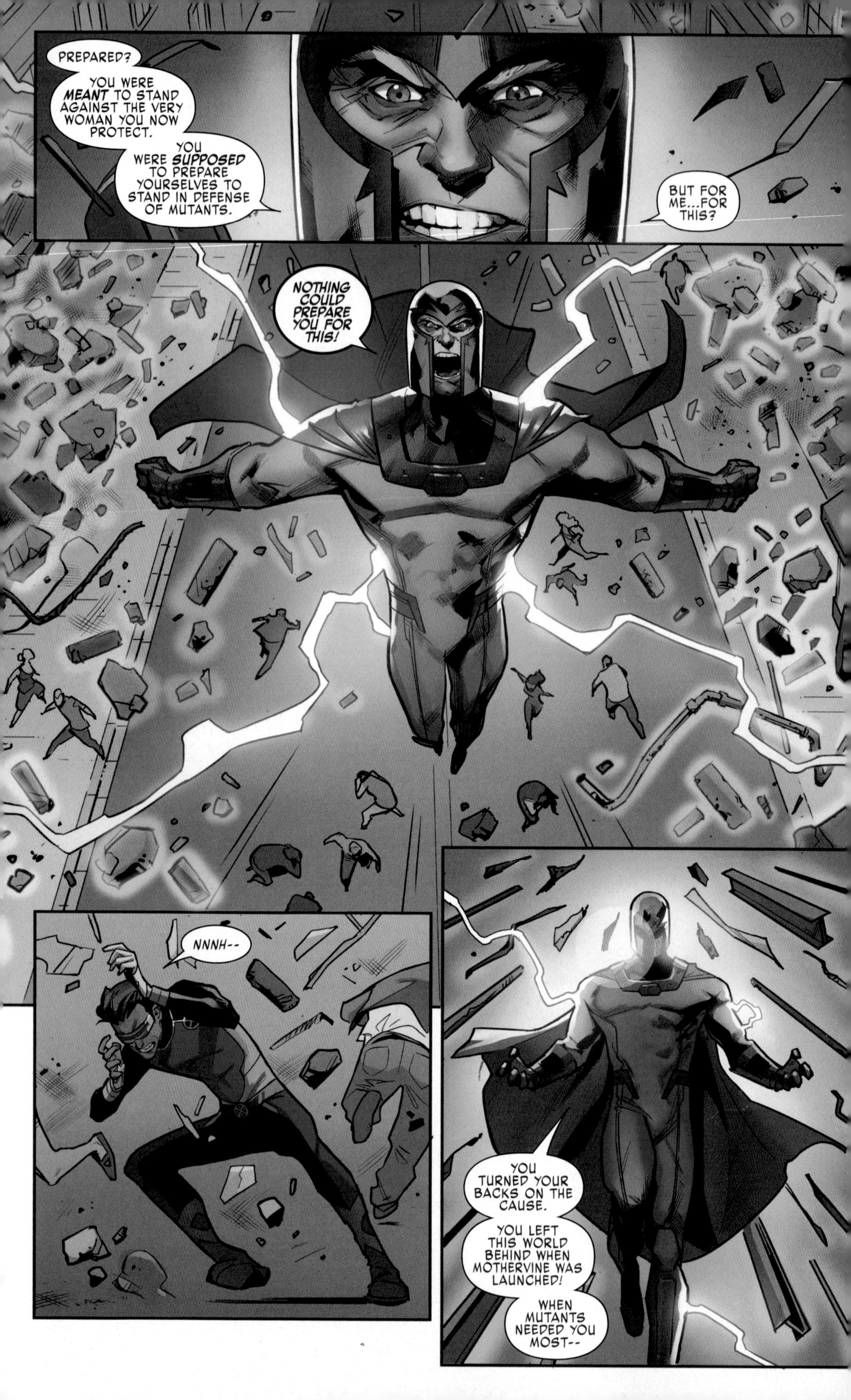
PREPARED?
YOU WERE MEANT TO STAND AGAINST THE VERY WOMAN YOU NOW PROTECT.
YOU WERE SUPPOSED TO PREPARE YOURSELVES TO STAND IN DEFENSE OF MUTANTS.
BUT FOR ME...FOR THIS?
NOTHING COULD PREPARE YOU FOR THIS!
NNNH--
YOU TURNED YOUR BACKS ON THE CAUSE.
YOU LEFT THIS WORLD BEHIND WHEN MOTHERVINE WAS LAUNCHED!
WHEN MUTANTS NEEDED YOU MOST--

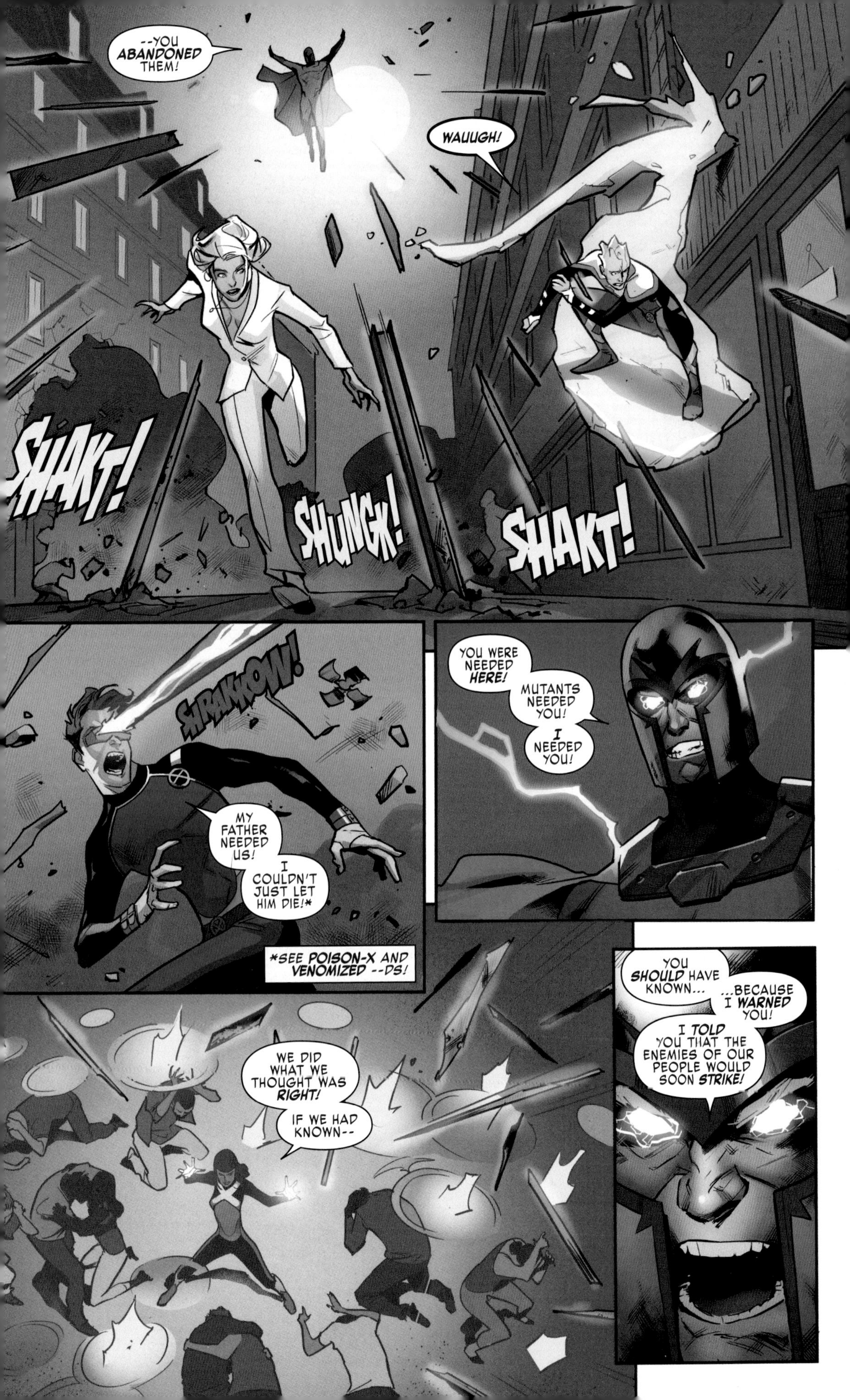

--YOU ABANDONED THEM!
WAUUGH!
SHAKT!
SHUNGK!
SHAKT!
SHRAKOOM!
MY FATHER NEEDED US!
I COULDN'T JUST LET HIM DIE!*
*SEE POISON-X AND VENOMIZED --DS!
YOU WERE NEEDED HERE!
MUTANTS NEEDED YOU!
I NEEDED YOU!
WE DID WHAT WE THOUGHT WAS RIGHT!
IF WE HAD KNOWN--
YOU SHOULD HAVE KNOWN...
...BECAUSE I WARNED YOU!
I TOLD YOU THAT THE ENEMIES OF OUR PEOPLE WOULD SOON STRIKE!

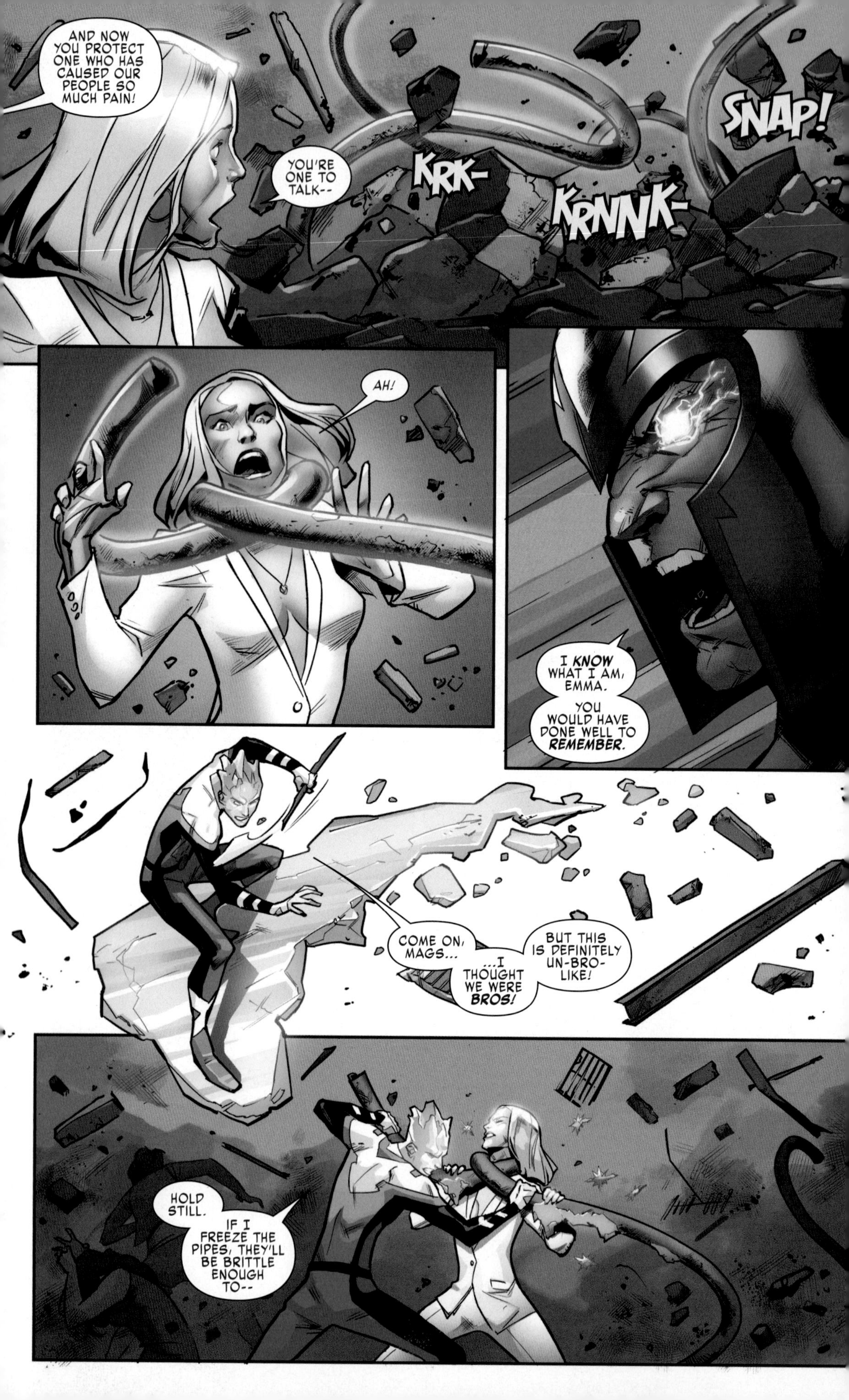
AND NOW YOU PROTECT ONE WHO HAS CAUSED OUR PEOPLE SO MUCH PAIN!
YOU'RE ONE TO TALK--
KRK-
KRNNK-
SNAP!
AH!
I KNOW WHAT I AM, EMMA.
YOU WOULD HAVE DONE WELL TO REMEMBER.
COME ON, MAGS...
...I THOUGHT WE WERE BROS!
BUT THIS IS DEFINITELY UN-BRO-LIKE!
HOLD STILL.
IF I FREEZE THE PIPES, THEY'LL BE BRITTLE ENOUGH TO--

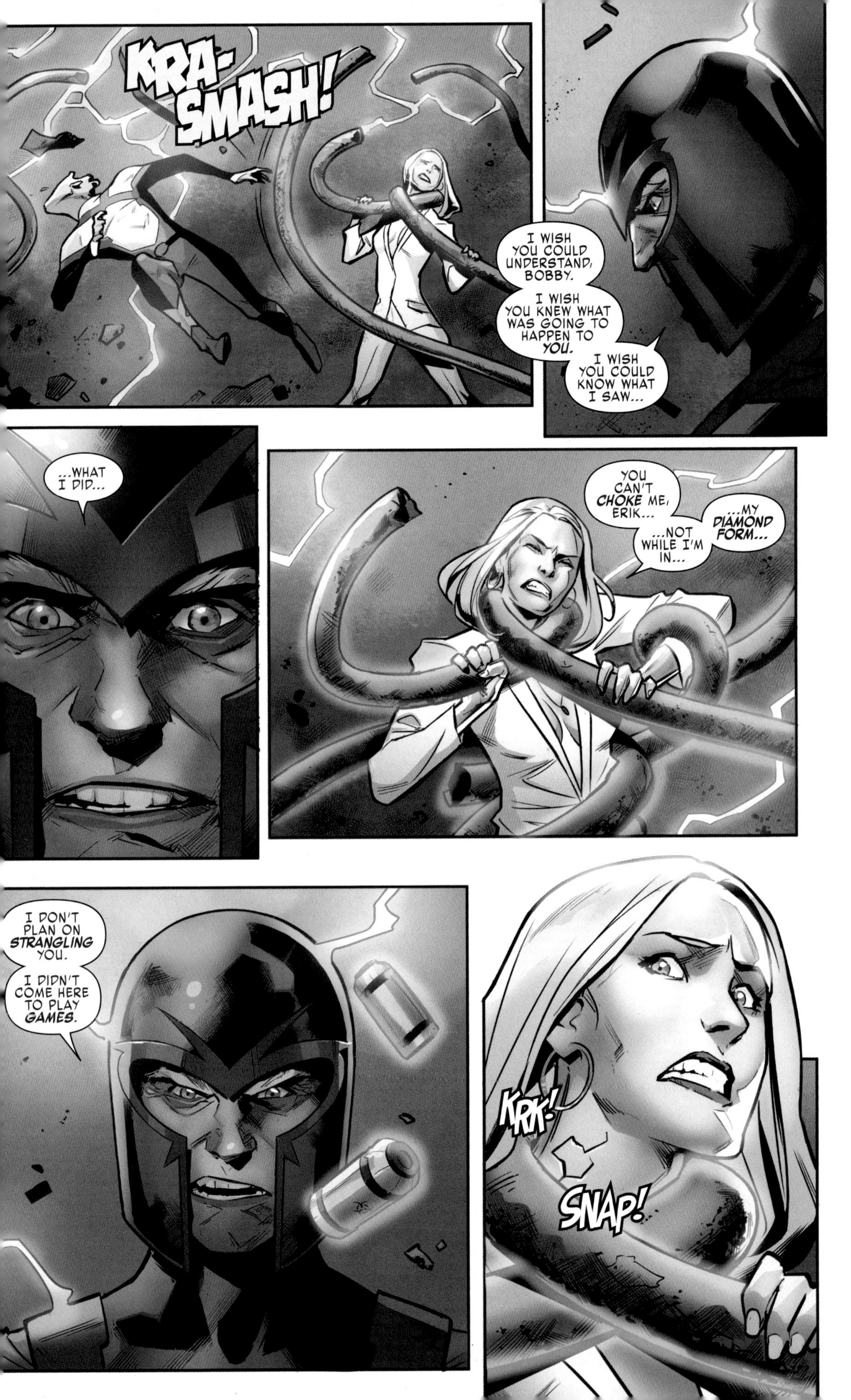
KRA-SMASH!
I WISH YOU COULD UNDERSTAND, BOBBY.
I WISH YOU KNEW WHAT WAS GOING TO HAPPEN TO YOU.
I WISH YOU COULD KNOW WHAT I SAW...
...WHAT I DID...
YOU CAN'T CHOKE ME, ERIK...
...NOT WHILE I'M IN...
...MY DIAMOND FORM...
I DON'T PLAN ON STRANGLING YOU.
I DIDN'T COME HERE TO PLAY GAMES.
KRK!
SNAP!

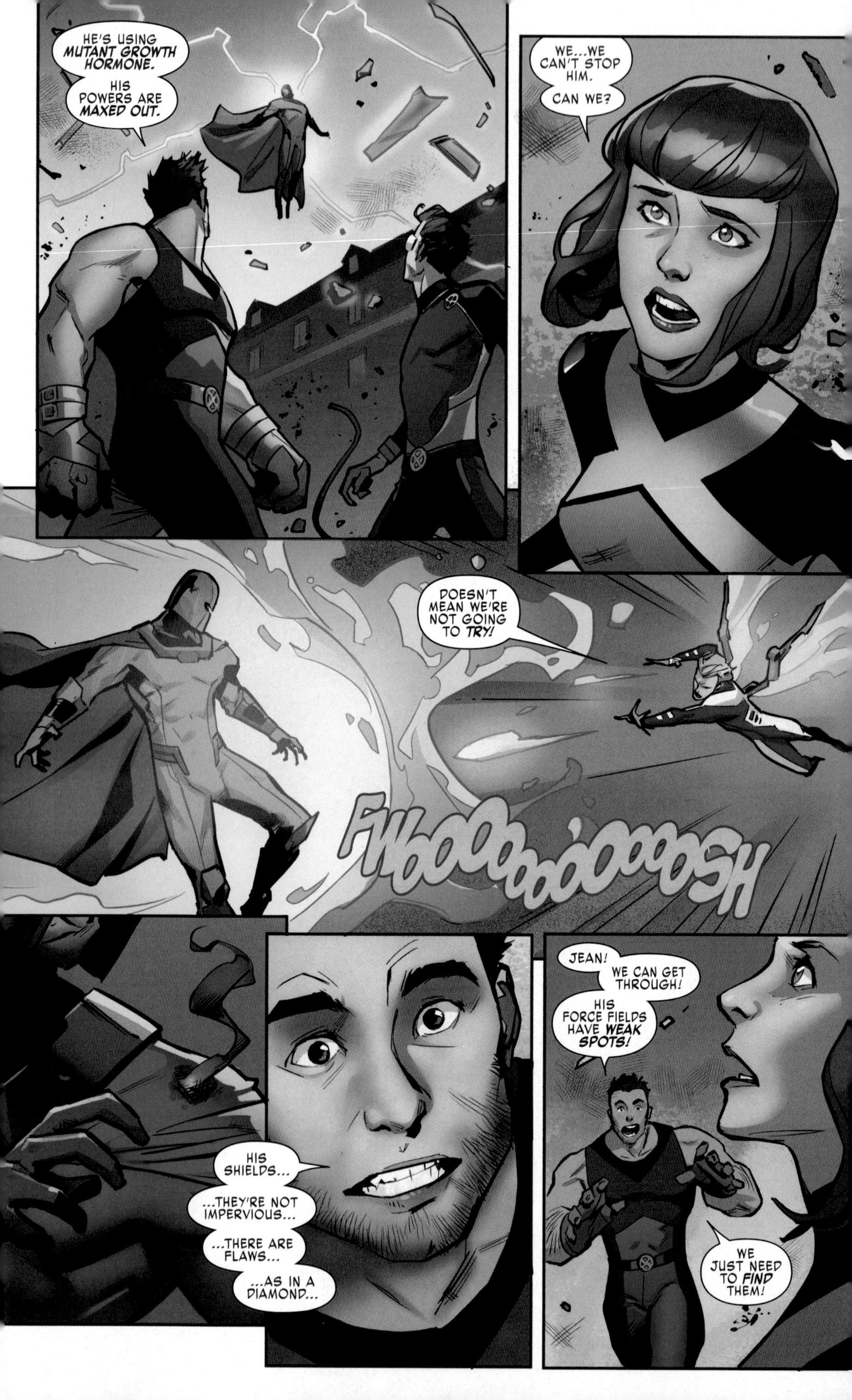
HE'S USING MUTANT GROWTH HORMONE.
HIS POWERS ARE MAXED OUT.
WE...WE CAN'T STOP HIM.
CAN WE?
DOESN'T MEAN WE'RE NOT GOING TO TRY!
FWOOOOOOOOOOSH
HIS SHIELDS...
...THEY'RE NOT IMPERVIOUS...
...THERE ARE FLAWS...
...AS IN A DIAMOND...
JEAN!
WE CAN GET THROUGH!
HIS FORCE FIELDS HAVE WEAK SPOTS!
WE JUST NEED TO FIND THEM!

ON IT.
DON'T DO THIS, MARVEL GIRL.
IT WILL NOT WORK THE WAY YOU THINK.
ST-STORY OF MY LIFE.
YOU CANNOT SAVE HER...
...NOT FROM ME...
...NOT FROM WHAT SHE HAS DONE.
SCOTT!
I'VE FOUND IT!
TAKE THE SHOT! I'LL GUIDE YOU!

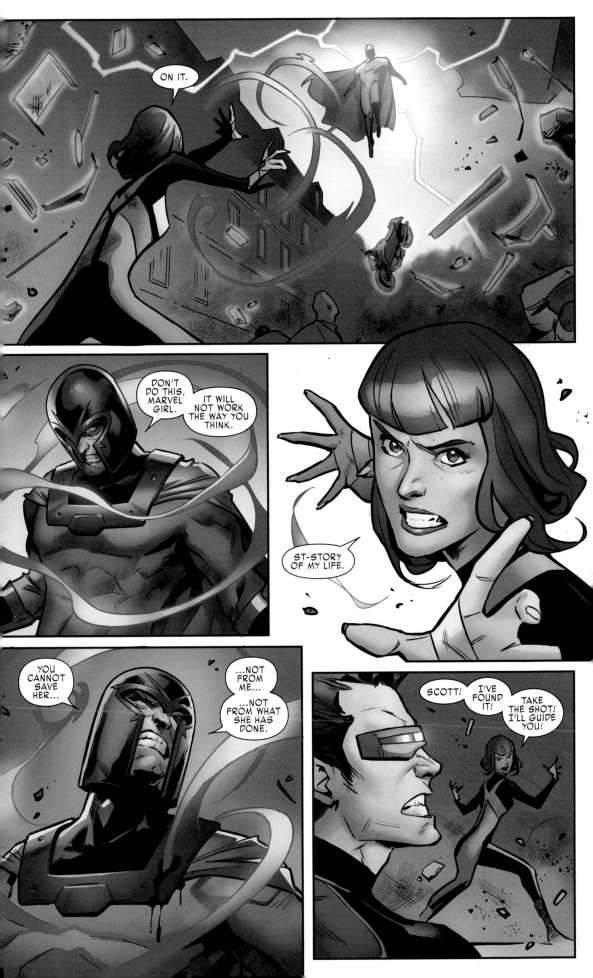

SKRA-KA-KOW!

I'M SORRY ABOUT THIS. I REALLY AM.

HIS SHIELDS ARE DOWN.

TAKE HIM

SHRAZZLK-KRAK!

VOOOOSH!

IT DID NOT HAVE TO BE THIS WAY.

YEAH. IT KINDA DID.

WHAP!

JUST STAY DOWN, MAN.

KRUNCH!

THAT'S IT. WE'VE GOT HIM.

NOW WHAT DO WE DO WITH HIM?

WE'LL FIGURE IT OUT, ICEMAN.

FOR THE MOMENT, HE IS CONTAINED.

N-NO. HE'S NOT--

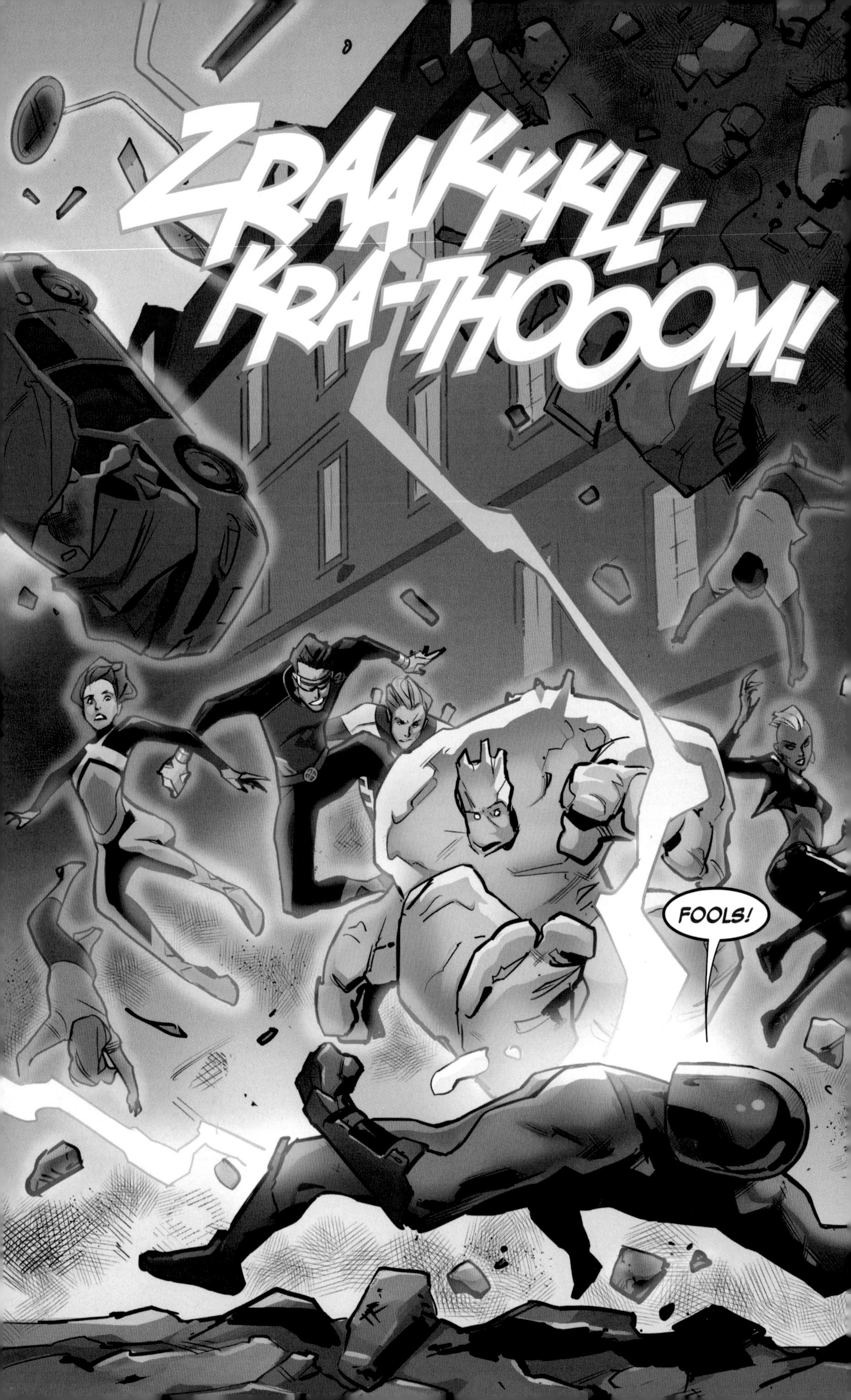
ZRAAKKLL-
KRA-THOOOOM!
FOOLS!

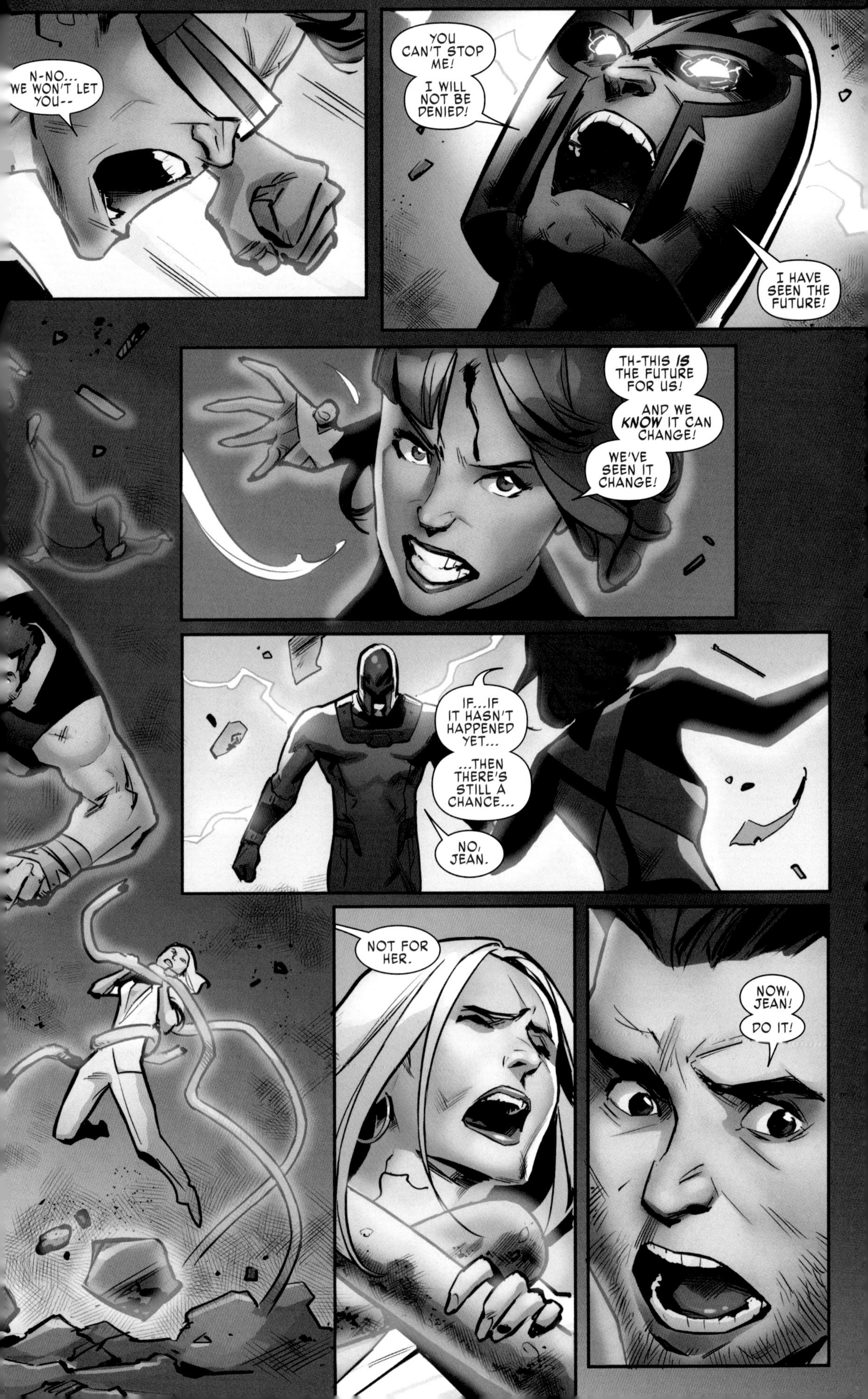
N-NO... WE WON'T LET YOU--
YOU CAN'T STOP ME!
I WILL NOT BE DENIED!
I HAVE SEEN THE FUTURE!
TH-THIS IS THE FUTURE FOR US!
AND WE KNOW IT CAN CHANGE!
WE'VE SEEN IT CHANGE!
IF...IF IT HASN'T HAPPENED YET...
...THEN THERE'S STILL A CHANCE...
NO, JEAN.
NOT FOR HER.
NOW, JEAN!
DO IT!

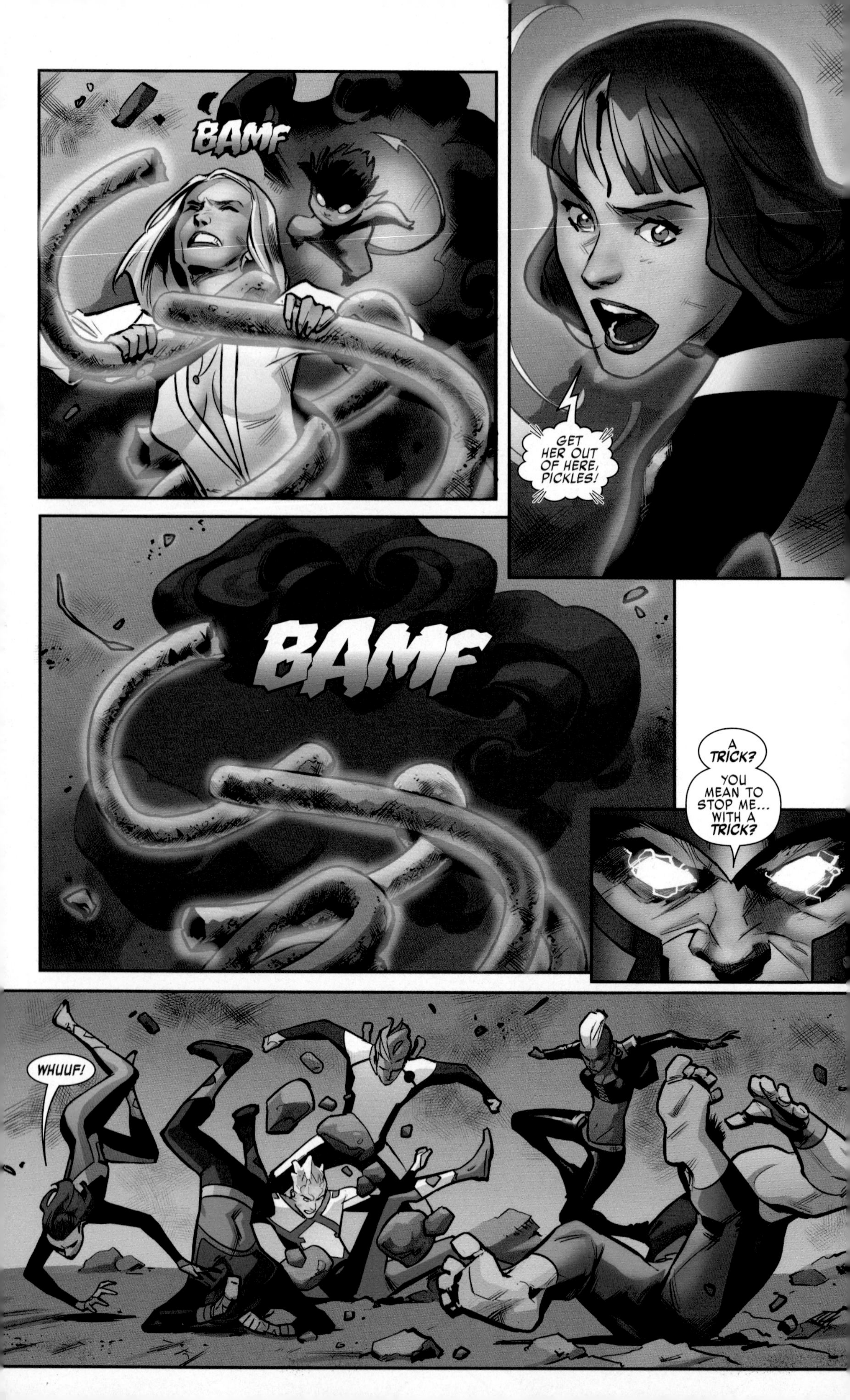
BAMF
GET HER OUT OF HERE, PICKLES!
BAMF
A TRICK?
YOU MEAN TO STOP ME... WITH A TRICK?
WHUUF!

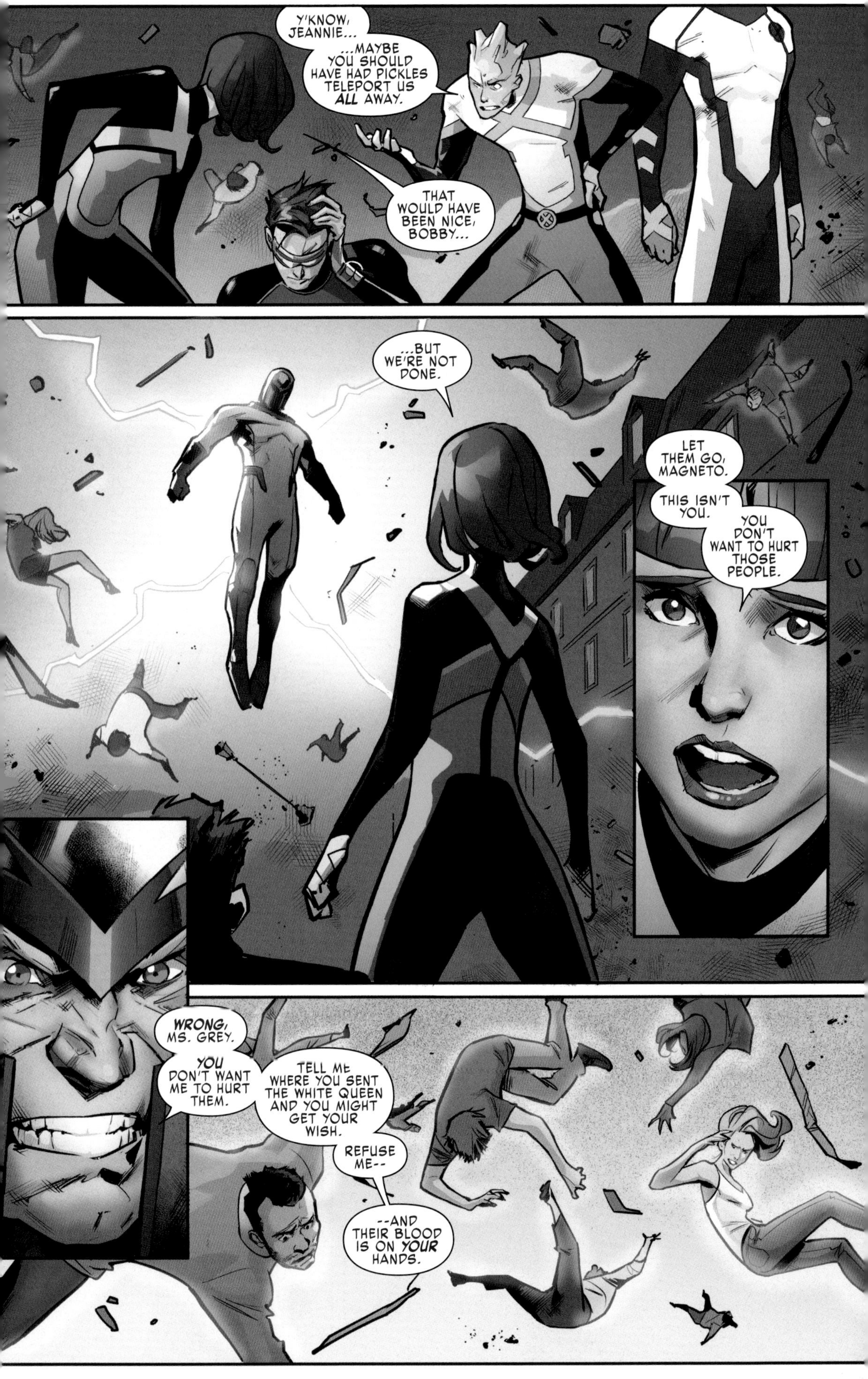
Y'KNOW, JEANNIE...
...MAYBE YOU SHOULD HAVE HAD PICKLES TELEPORT US ALL AWAY.
THAT WOULD HAVE BEEN NICE, BOBBY...
...BUT WE'RE NOT DONE.
LET THEM GO, MAGNETO.
THIS ISN'T YOU.
YOU DON'T WANT TO HURT THOSE PEOPLE.
WRONG, MS. GREY.
YOU DON'T WANT ME TO HURT THEM.
TELL ME WHERE YOU SENT THE WHITE QUEEN AND YOU MIGHT GET YOUR WISH.
REFUSE ME--
--AND THEIR BLOOD IS ON YOUR HANDS.

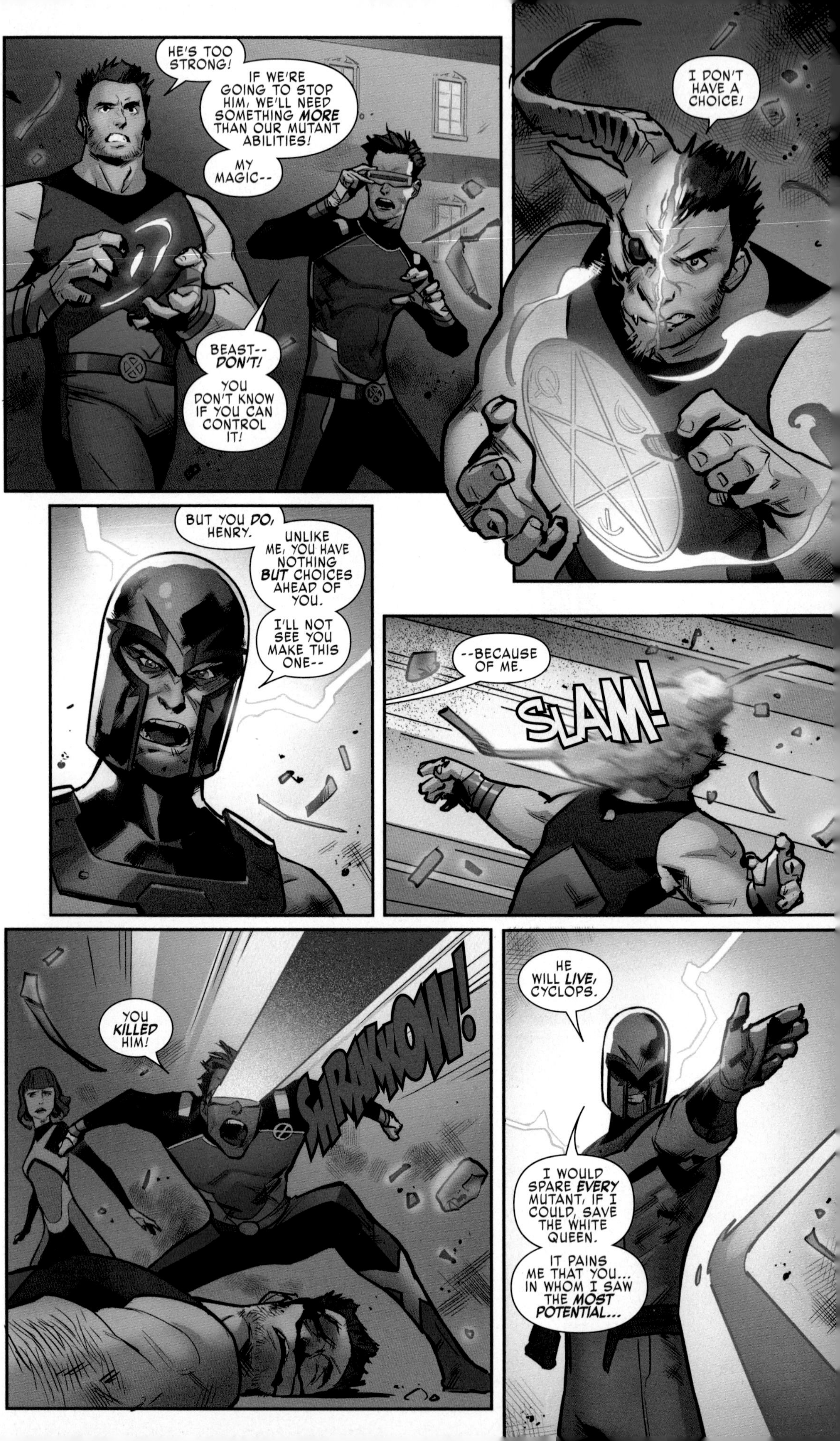
HE'S TOO STRONG!
IF WE'RE GOING TO STOP HIM, WE'LL NEED SOMETHING MORE THAN OUR MUTANT ABILITIES!
MY MAGIC--
BEAST-- DON'T!
YOU DON'T KNOW IF YOU CAN CONTROL IT!
I DON'T HAVE A CHOICE!
BUT YOU DO, HENRY.
UNLIKE ME, YOU HAVE NOTHING BUT CHOICES AHEAD OF YOU.
I'LL NOT SEE YOU MAKE THIS ONE--
--BECAUSE OF ME.
SLAM!
YOU KILLED HIM!
SHRAKKOW!
HE WILL LIVE, CYCLOPS.
I WOULD SPARE EVERY MUTANT, IF I COULD, SAVE THE WHITE QUEEN.
IT PAINS ME THAT YOU... IN WHOM I SAW THE MOST POTENTIAL...

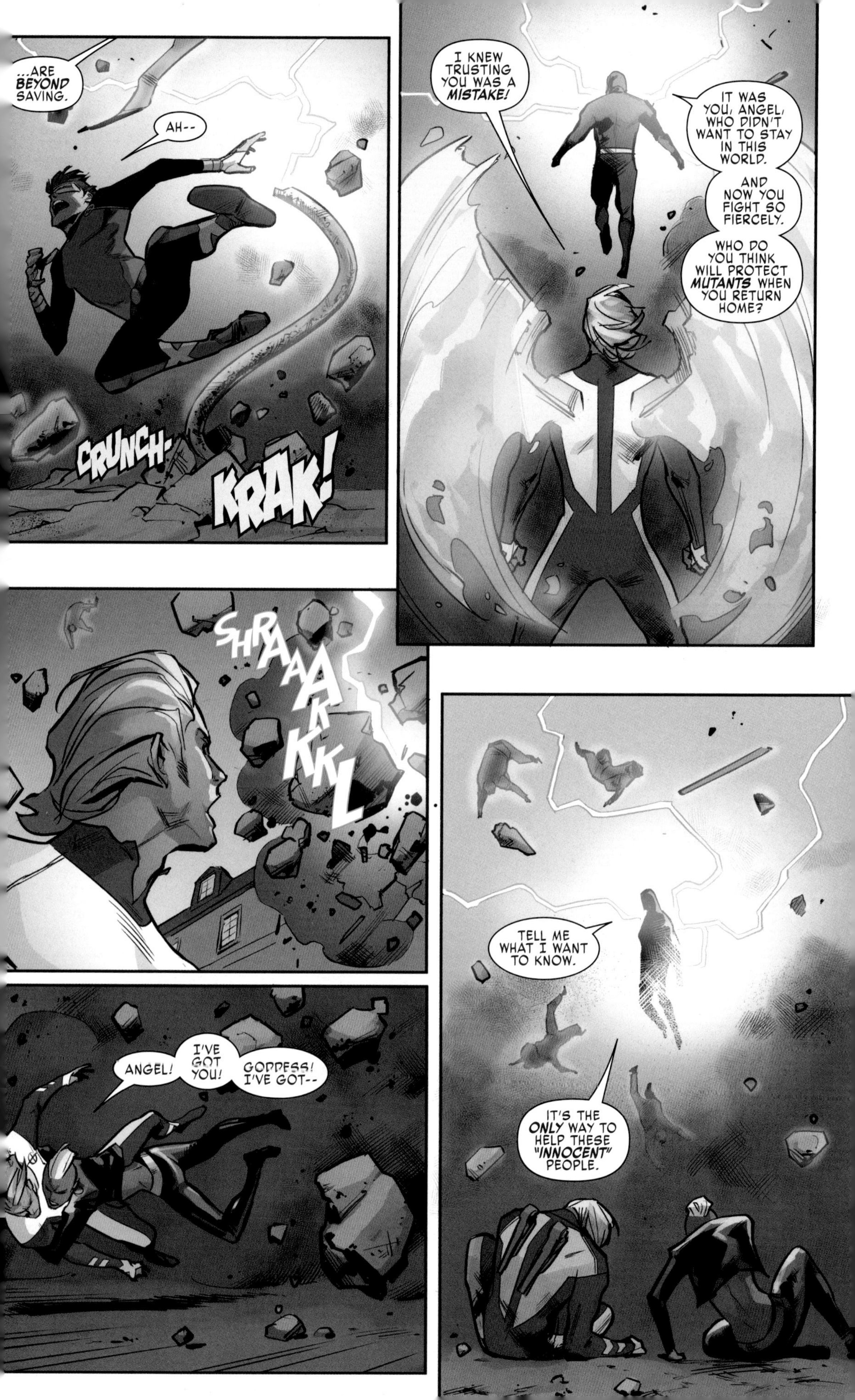
...ARE BEYOND SAVING.
AH--
CRUNCH-
KRAK!
I KNEW TRUSTING YOU WAS A MISTAKE!
IT WAS YOU, ANGEL, WHO DIDN'T WANT TO STAY IN THIS WORLD.
AND NOW YOU FIGHT SO FIERCELY.
WHO DO YOU THINK WILL PROTECT MUTANTS WHEN YOU RETURN HOME?
SHRAAAAKKL
ANGEL!
I'VE GOT YOU!
GODDESS! I'VE GOT--
TELL ME WHAT I WANT TO KNOW.
IT'S THE ONLY WAY TO HELP THESE "INNOCENT" PEOPLE.

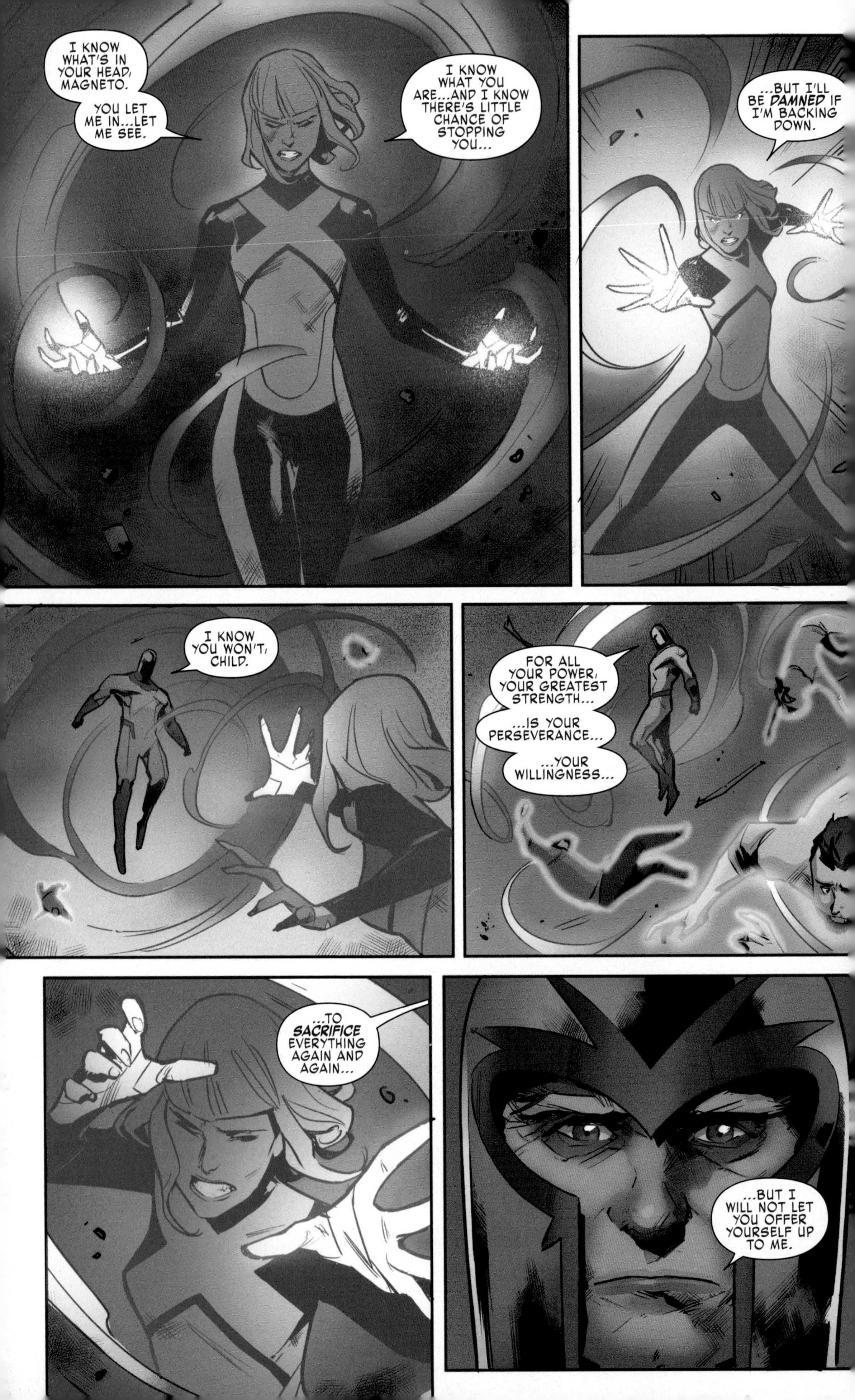
I KNOW WHAT'S IN YOUR HEAD, MAGNETO.
YOU LET ME IN...LET ME SEE.
I KNOW WHAT YOU ARE...AND I KNOW THERE'S LITTLE CHANCE OF STOPPING YOU...
...BUT I'LL BE DAMNED IF I'M BACKING DOWN.
I KNOW YOU WON'T, CHILD.
FOR ALL YOUR POWER, YOUR GREATEST STRENGTH...
...IS YOUR PERSEVERANCE...
...YOUR WILLINGNESS...
...TO SACRIFICE EVERYTHING AGAIN AND AGAIN...
...BUT I WILL NOT LET YOU OFFER YOURSELF UP TO ME.

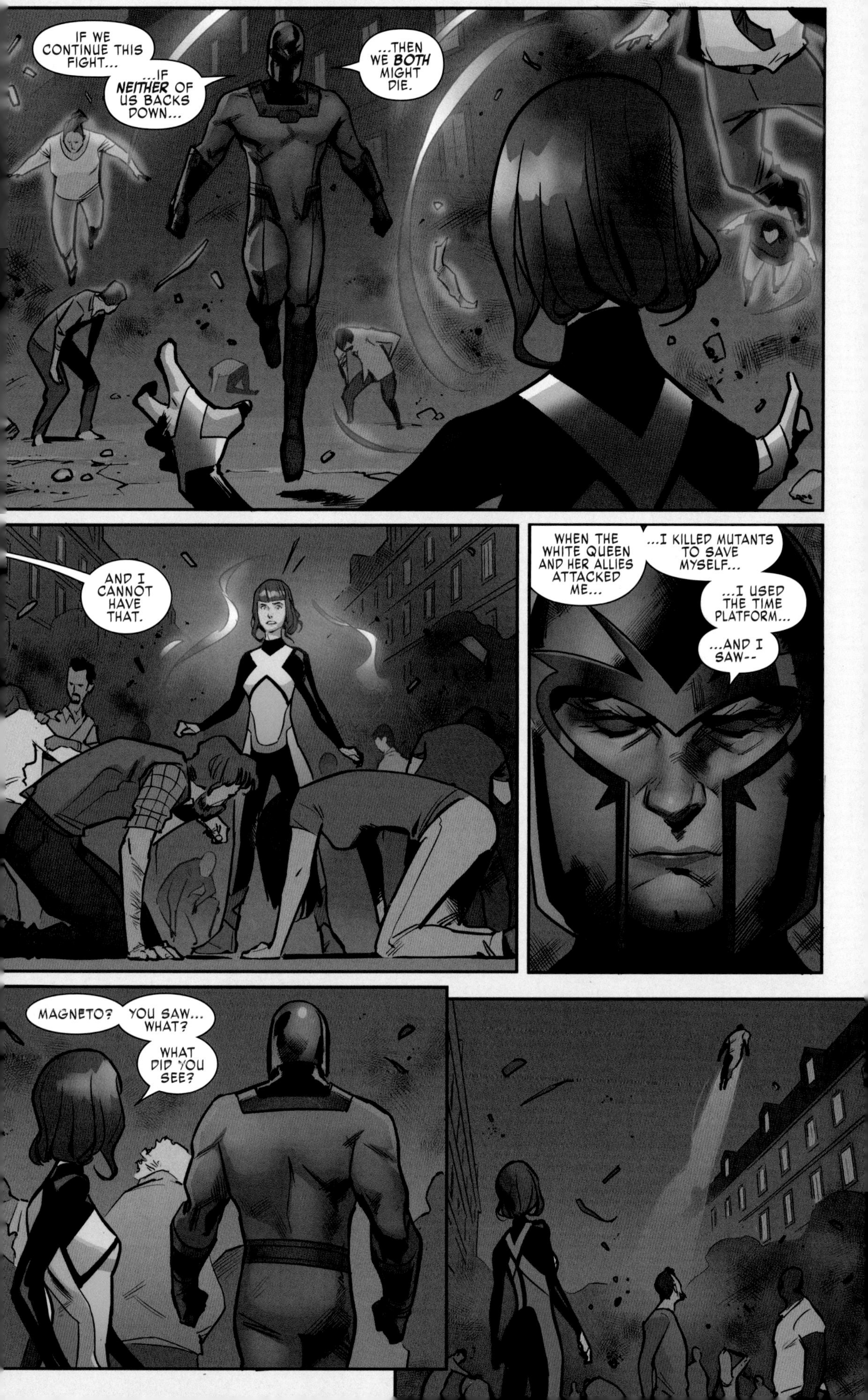
IF WE CONTINUE THIS FIGHT...
...IF NEITHER OF US BACKS DOWN...
...THEN WE BOTH MIGHT DIE.
AND I CANNOT HAVE THAT.
WHEN THE WHITE QUEEN AND HER ALLIES ATTACKED ME...
...I KILLED MUTANTS TO SAVE MYSELF...
...I USED THE TIME PLATFORM...
...AND I SAW--
MAGNETO?
YOU SAW... WHAT?
WHAT DID YOU SEE?

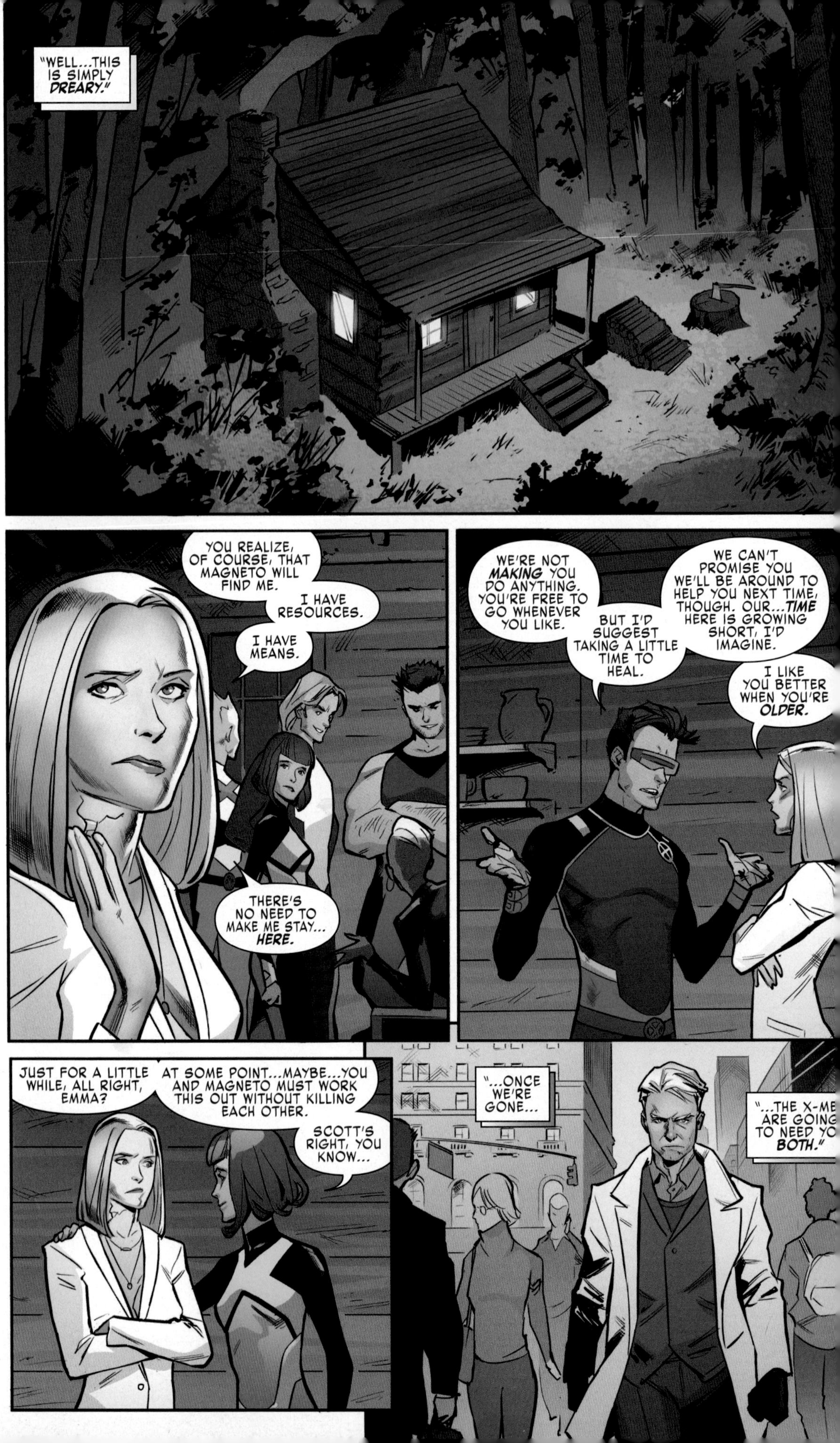
"WELL...THIS IS SIMPLY DREARY."
YOU REALIZE, OF COURSE, THAT MAGNETO WILL FIND ME.
I HAVE RESOURCES.
I HAVE MEANS.
THERE'S NO NEED TO MAKE ME STAY... HERE.
WE'RE NOT MAKING YOU DO ANYTHING. YOU'RE FREE TO GO WHENEVER YOU LIKE.
BUT I'D SUGGEST TAKING A LITTLE TIME TO HEAL.
WE CAN'T PROMISE YOU WE'LL BE AROUND TO HELP YOU NEXT TIME, THOUGH. OUR...TIME HERE IS GROWING SHORT, I'D IMAGINE.
I LIKE YOU BETTER WHEN YOU'RE OLDER.
JUST FOR A LITTLE WHILE, ALL RIGHT, EMMA?
AT SOME POINT...MAYBE...YOU AND MAGNETO MUST WORK THIS OUT WITHOUT KILLING EACH OTHER.
SCOTT'S RIGHT, YOU KNOW...
"...ONCE WE'RE GONE...
"...THE X-ME ARE GOING TO NEED YO BOTH."

33

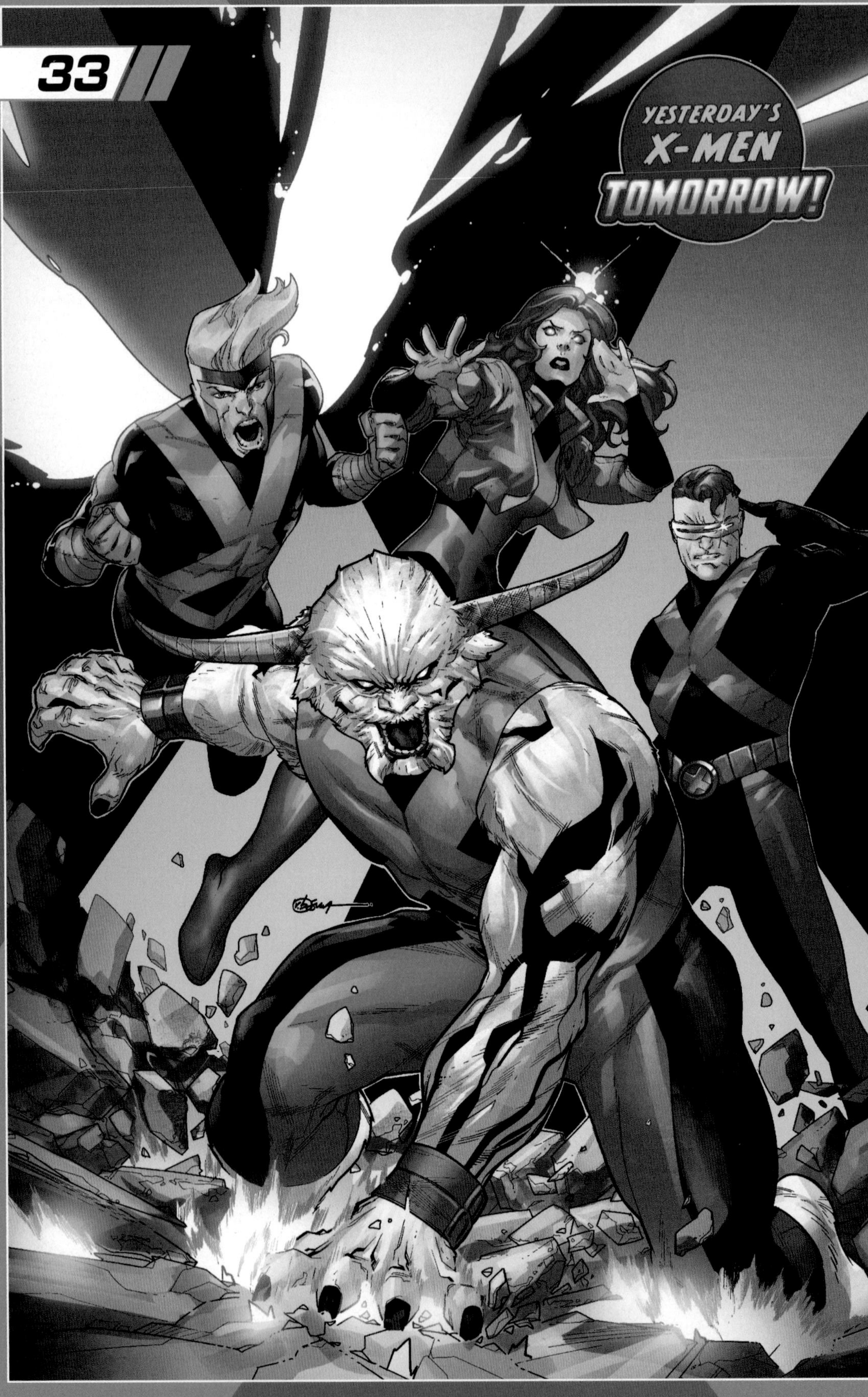
YESTERDAY'S
X-MEN
TOMORROW!

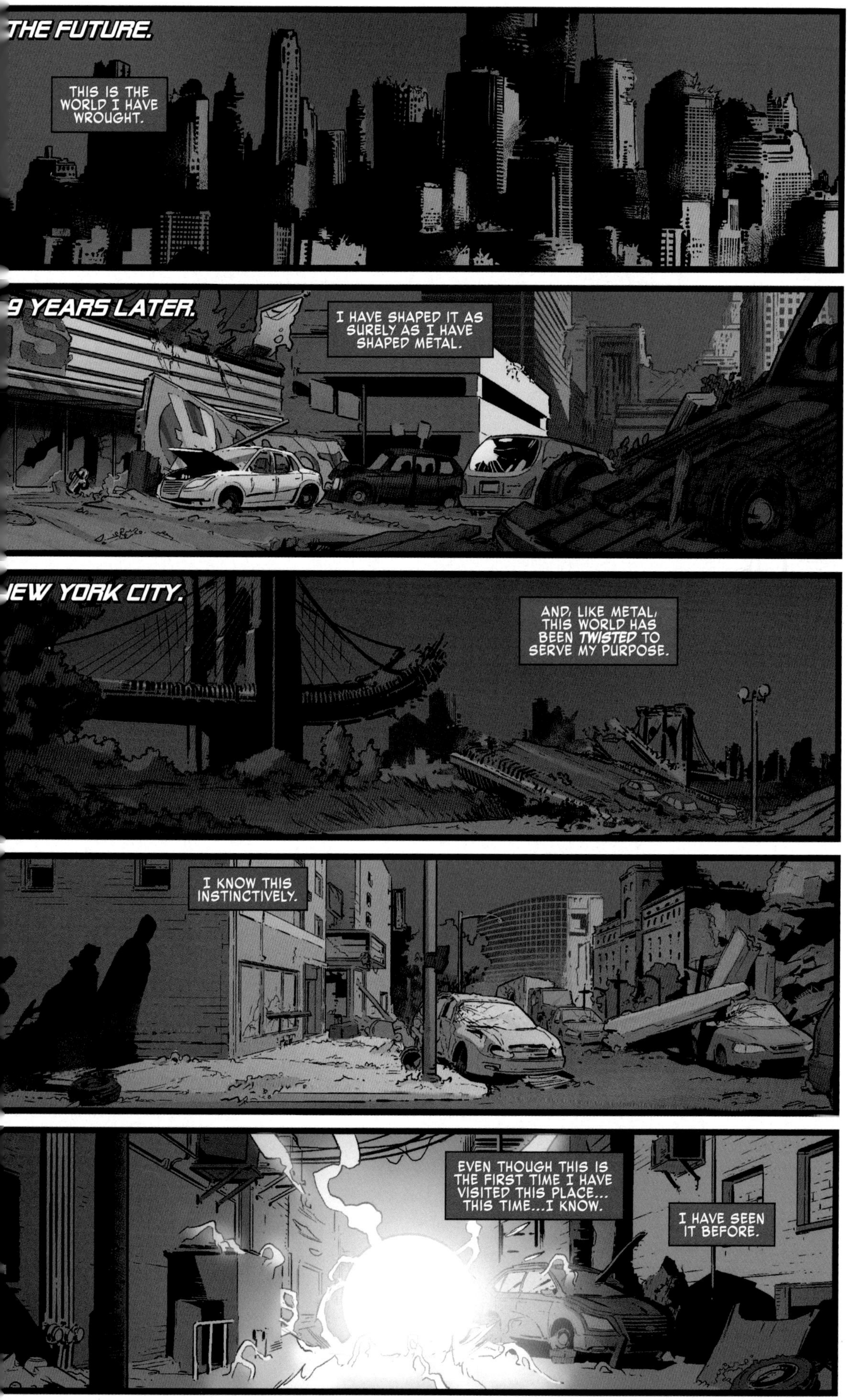
THE FUTURE.
THIS IS THE WORLD I HAVE WROUGHT.
9 YEARS LATER.
I HAVE SHAPED IT AS SURELY AS I HAVE SHAPED METAL.
EW YORK CITY.
AND, LIKE METAL, THIS WORLD HAS BEEN *TWISTED* TO SERVE MY PURPOSE.
I KNOW THIS INSTINCTIVELY.
EVEN THOUGH THIS IS THE FIRST TIME I HAVE VISITED THIS PLACE... THIS TIME...I KNOW.
I HAVE SEEN IT BEFORE.

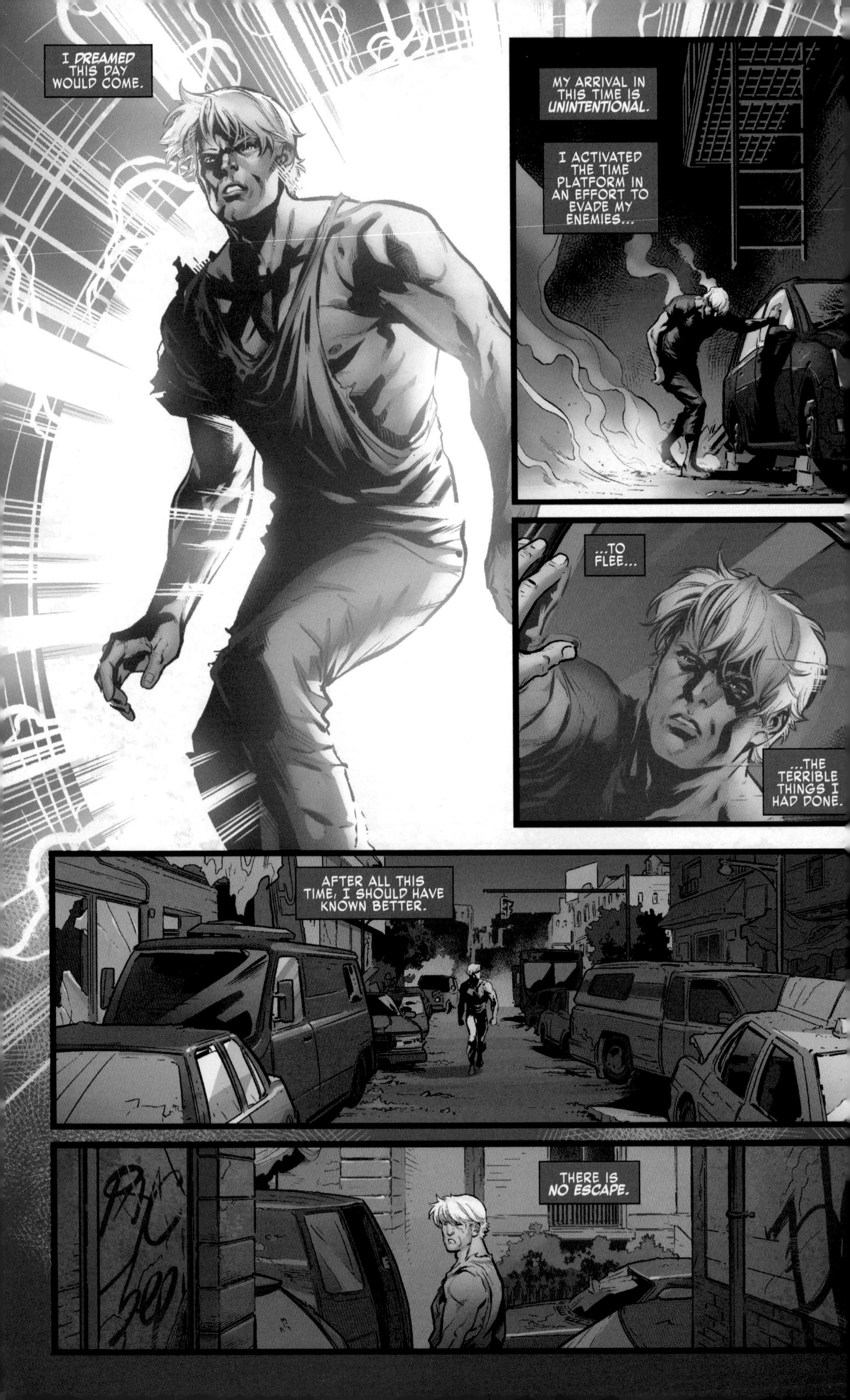

I DREAMED THIS DAY WOULD COME.
MY ARRIVAL IN THIS TIME IS UNINTENTIONAL.
I ACTIVATED THE TIME PLATFORM IN AN EFFORT TO EVADE MY ENEMIES...
...TO FLEE...
...THE TERRIBLE THINGS I HAD DONE.
AFTER ALL THIS TIME, I SHOULD HAVE KNOWN BETTER.
THERE IS NO ESCAPE.

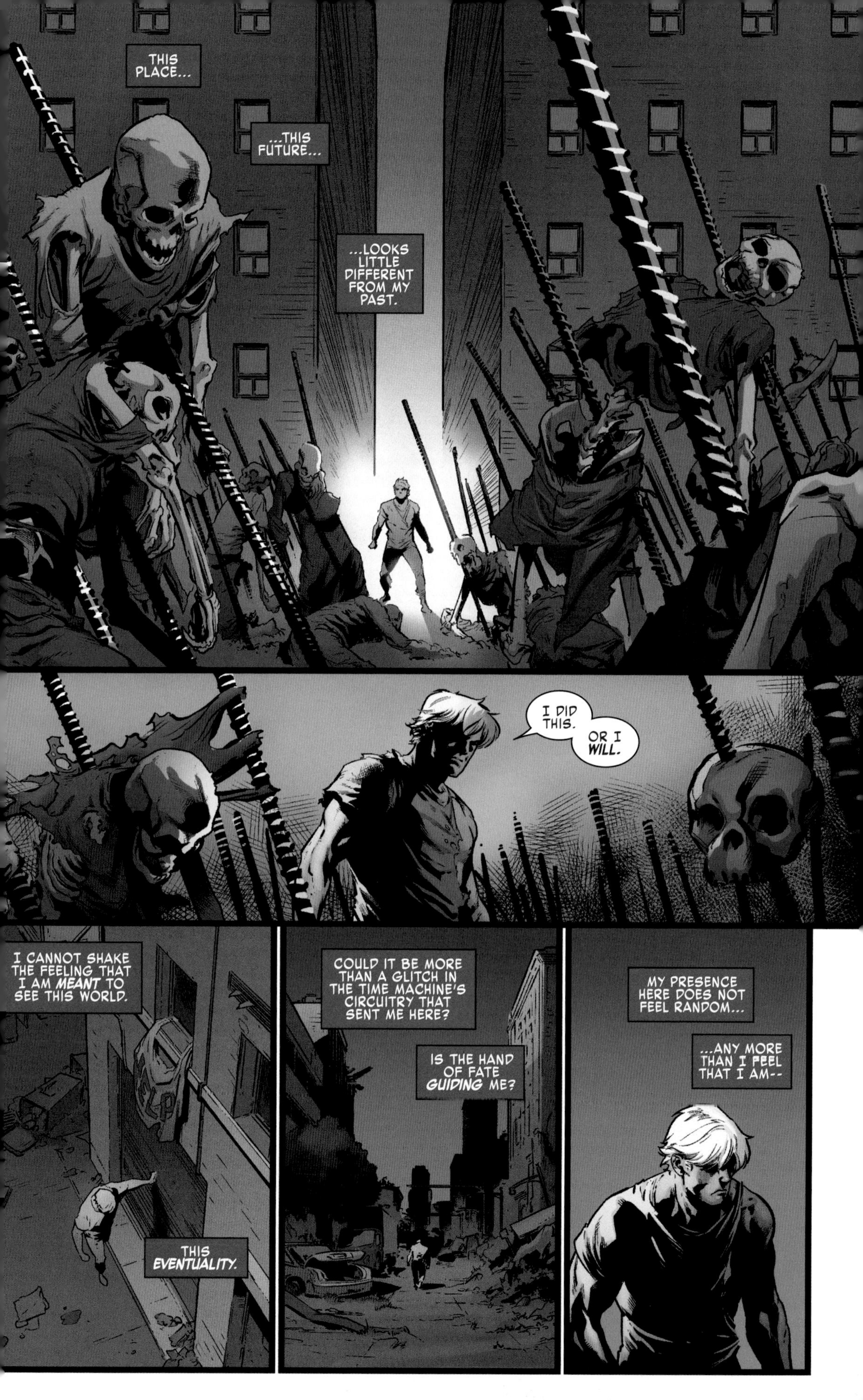
THIS PLACE...
...THIS FUTURE...
...LOOKS LITTLE DIFFERENT FROM MY PAST.
I DID THIS.
OR I *WILL.*
I CANNOT SHAKE THE FEELING THAT I AM *MEANT* TO SEE THIS WORLD.
THIS *EVENTUALITY.*
COULD IT BE MORE THAN A GLITCH IN THE TIME MACHINE'S CIRCUITRY THAT SENT ME HERE?
IS THE HAND OF FATE *GUIDING* ME?
MY PRESENCE HERE DOES NOT FEEL RANDOM...
...ANY MORE THAN I FEEL THAT I AM--

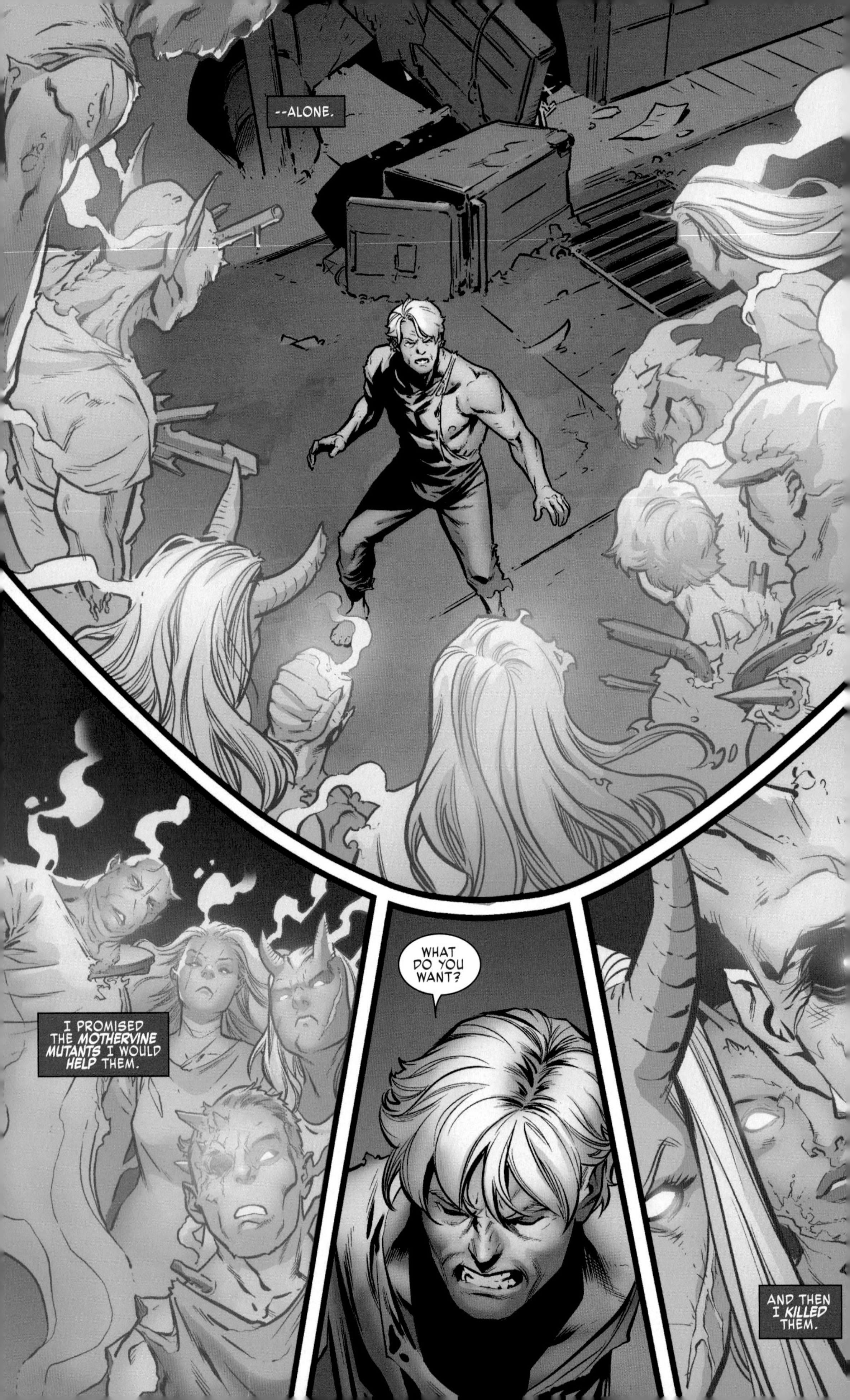
--ALONE.
I PROMISED THE MOTHERVINE MUTANTS I WOULD HELP THEM.
WHAT DO YOU WANT?
AND THEN I KILLED THEM.

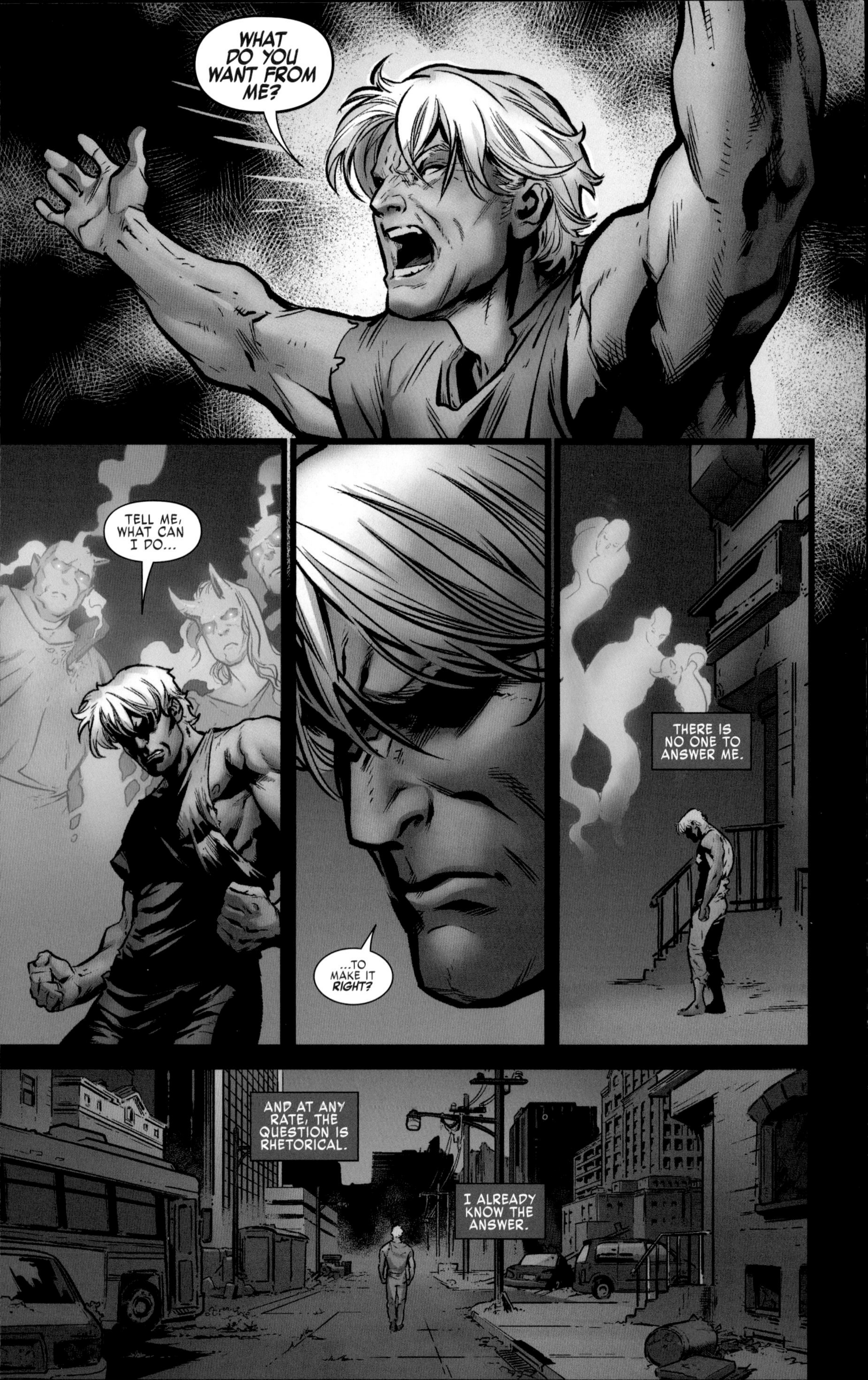
WHAT DO YOU WANT FROM ME?
TELL ME, WHAT CAN I DO...
...TO MAKE IT RIGHT?
THERE IS NO ONE TO ANSWER ME.
AND AT ANY RATE, THE QUESTION IS RHETORICAL.
I ALREADY KNOW THE ANSWER.

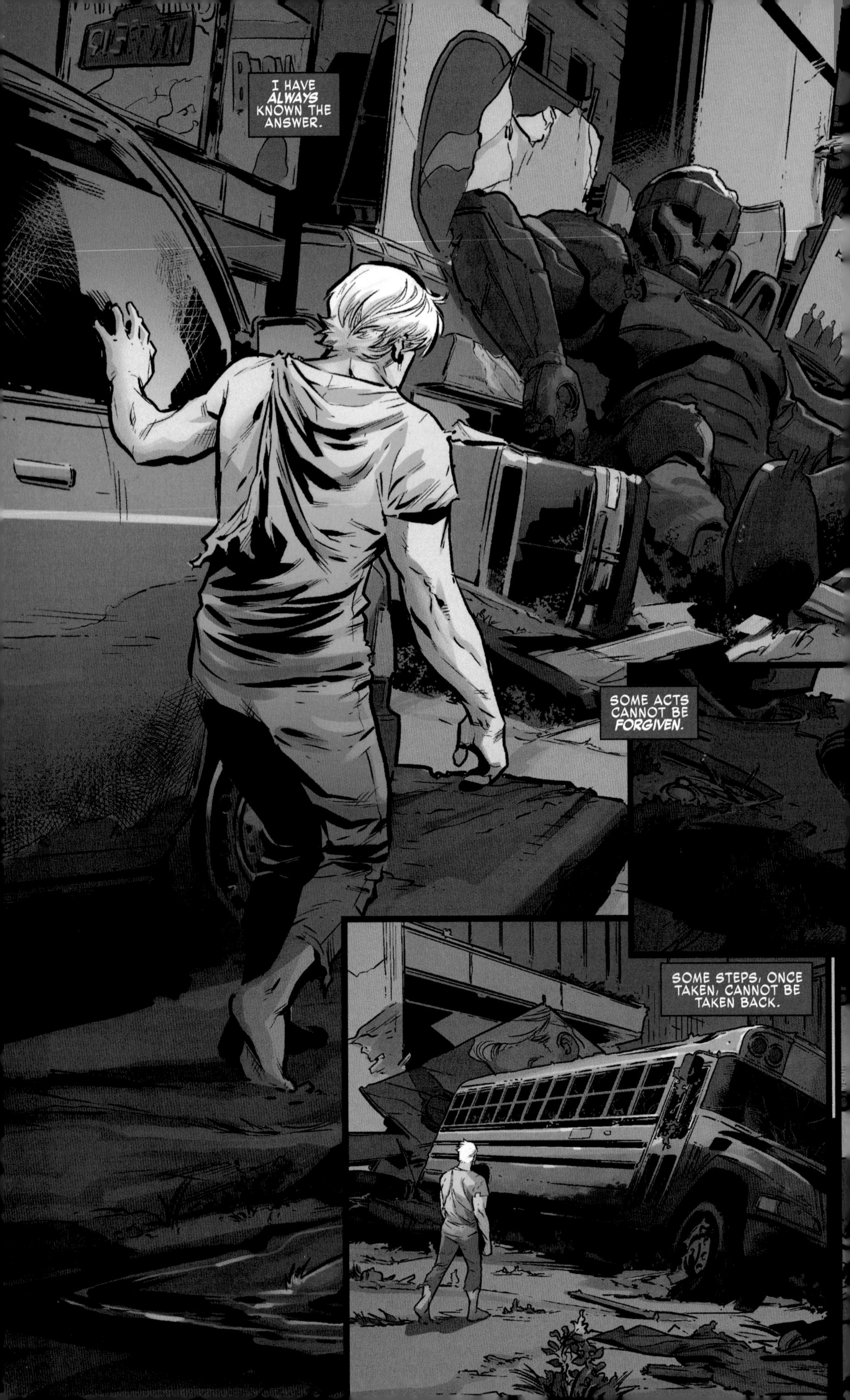
I HAVE ALWAYS KNOWN THE ANSWER.
SOME ACTS CANNOT BE FORGIVEN.
SOME STEPS, ONCE TAKEN, CANNOT BE TAKEN BACK.

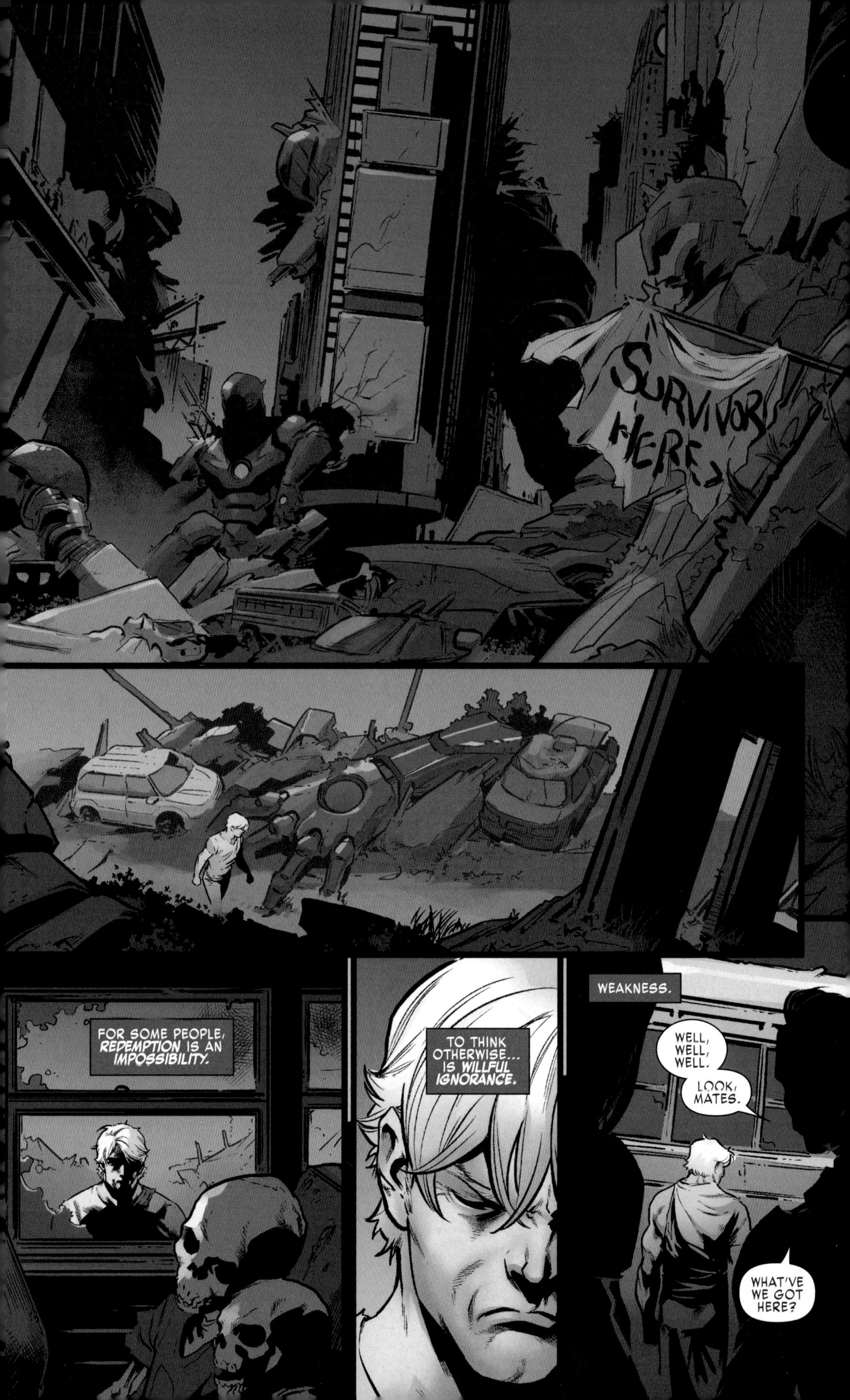
SURVIVOR HERE
FOR SOME PEOPLE, REDEMPTION IS AN IMPOSSIBILITY.
TO THINK OTHERWISE... IS WILLFUL IGNORANCE.
WEAKNESS.
WELL, WELL, WELL.
LOOK, MATES.
WHAT'VE WE GOT HERE?

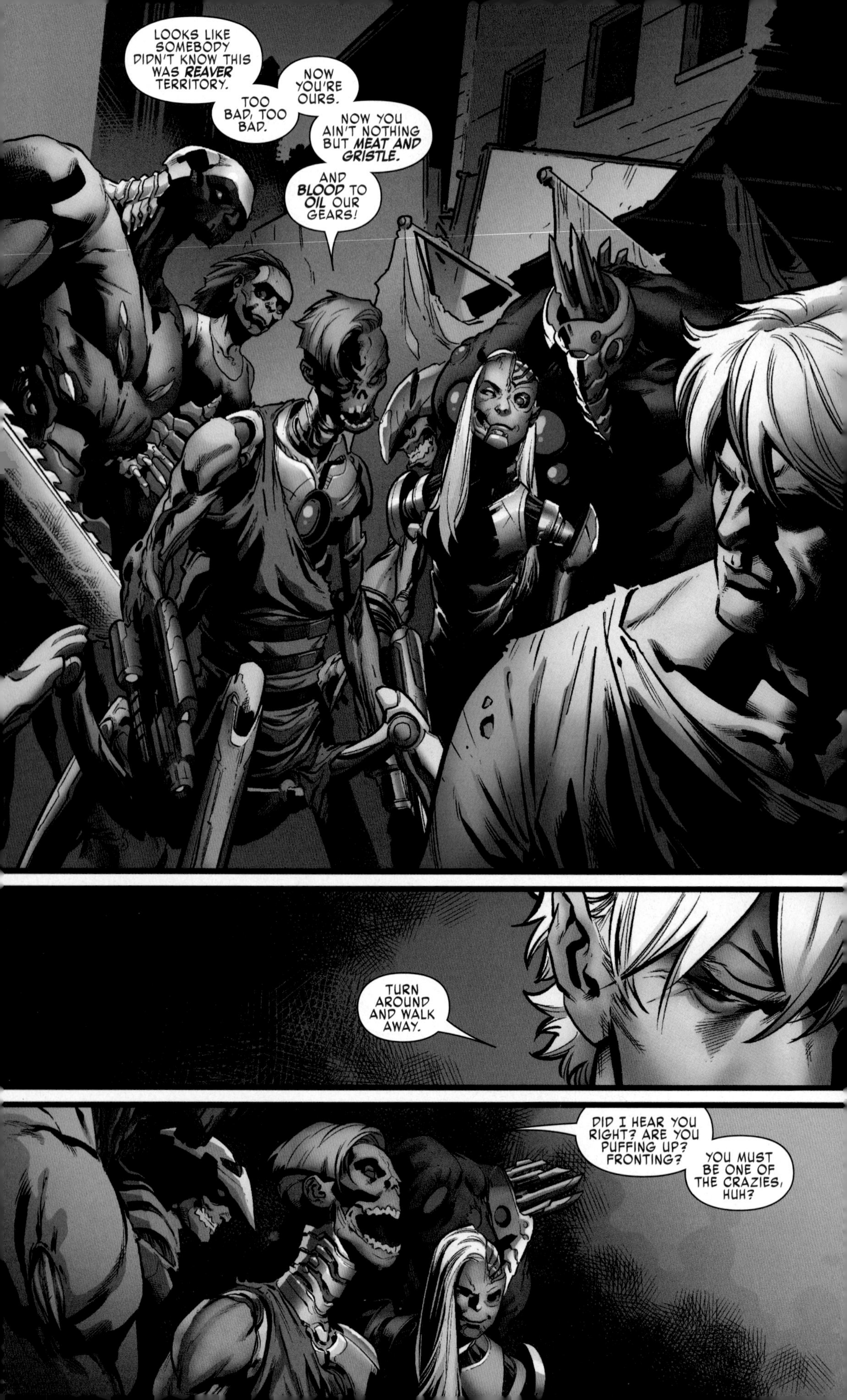
LOOKS LIKE SOMEBODY DIDN'T KNOW THIS WAS REAVER TERRITORY.
TOO BAD, TOO BAD.
NOW YOU'RE OURS.
NOW YOU AIN'T NOTHING BUT MEAT AND GRISTLE.
AND BLOOD TO OIL OUR GEARS!
TURN AROUND AND WALK AWAY.
DID I HEAR YOU RIGHT? ARE YOU PUFFING UP? FRONTING?
YOU MUST BE ONE OF THE CRAZIES, HUH?

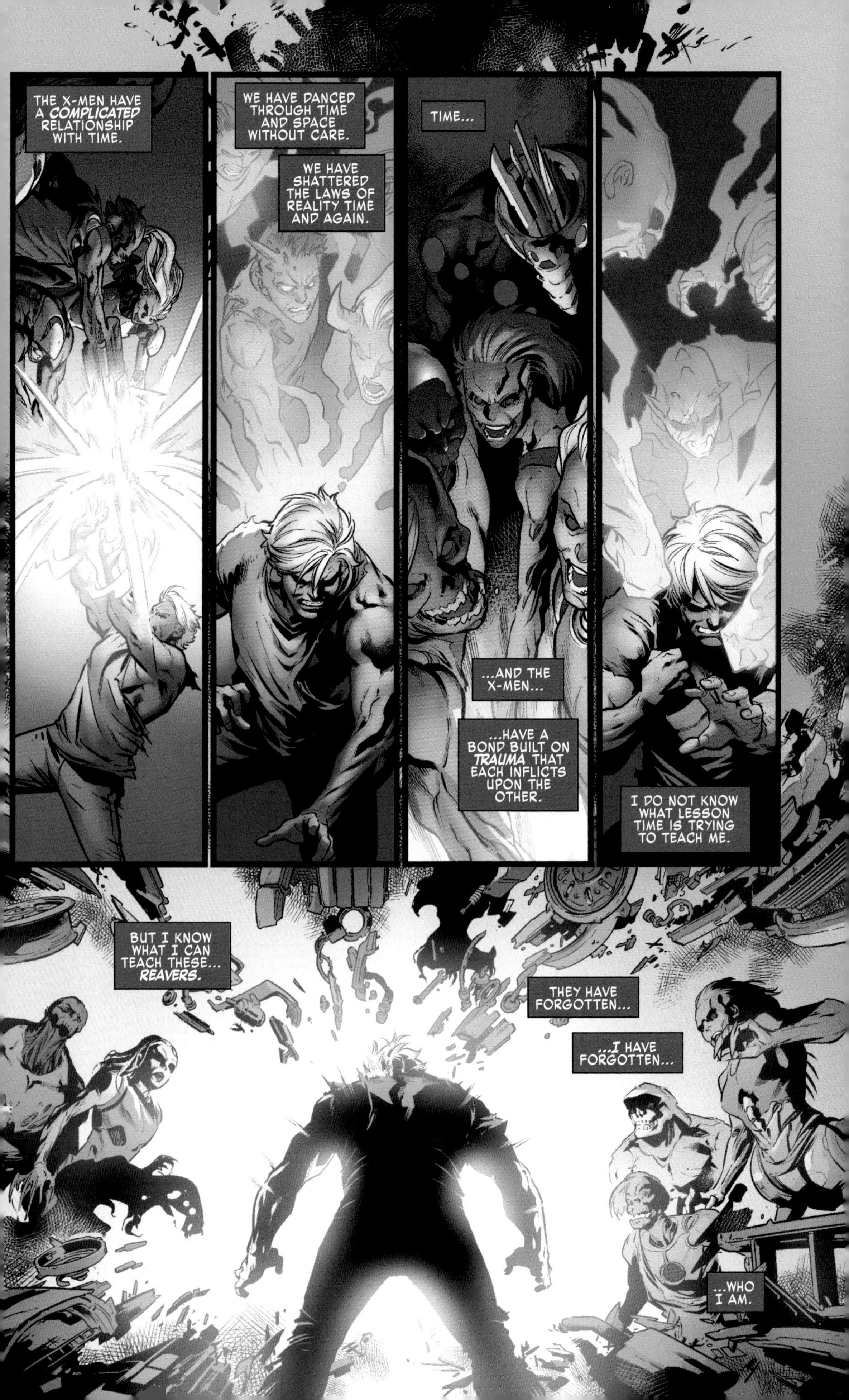
THE X-MEN HAVE A *COMPLICATED* RELATIONSHIP WITH TIME.
WE HAVE DANCED THROUGH TIME AND SPACE WITHOUT CARE.
WE HAVE SHATTERED THE LAWS OF REALITY TIME AND AGAIN.
TIME...
...AND THE X-MEN...
...HAVE A BOND BUILT ON *TRAUMA* THAT EACH INFLICTS UPON THE OTHER.
I DO NOT KNOW WHAT LESSON TIME IS TRYING TO TEACH ME.
BUT I KNOW WHAT I CAN TEACH THESE... *REAVERS.*
THEY HAVE FORGOTTEN...
...*I* HAVE FORGOTTEN...
...WHO I AM.

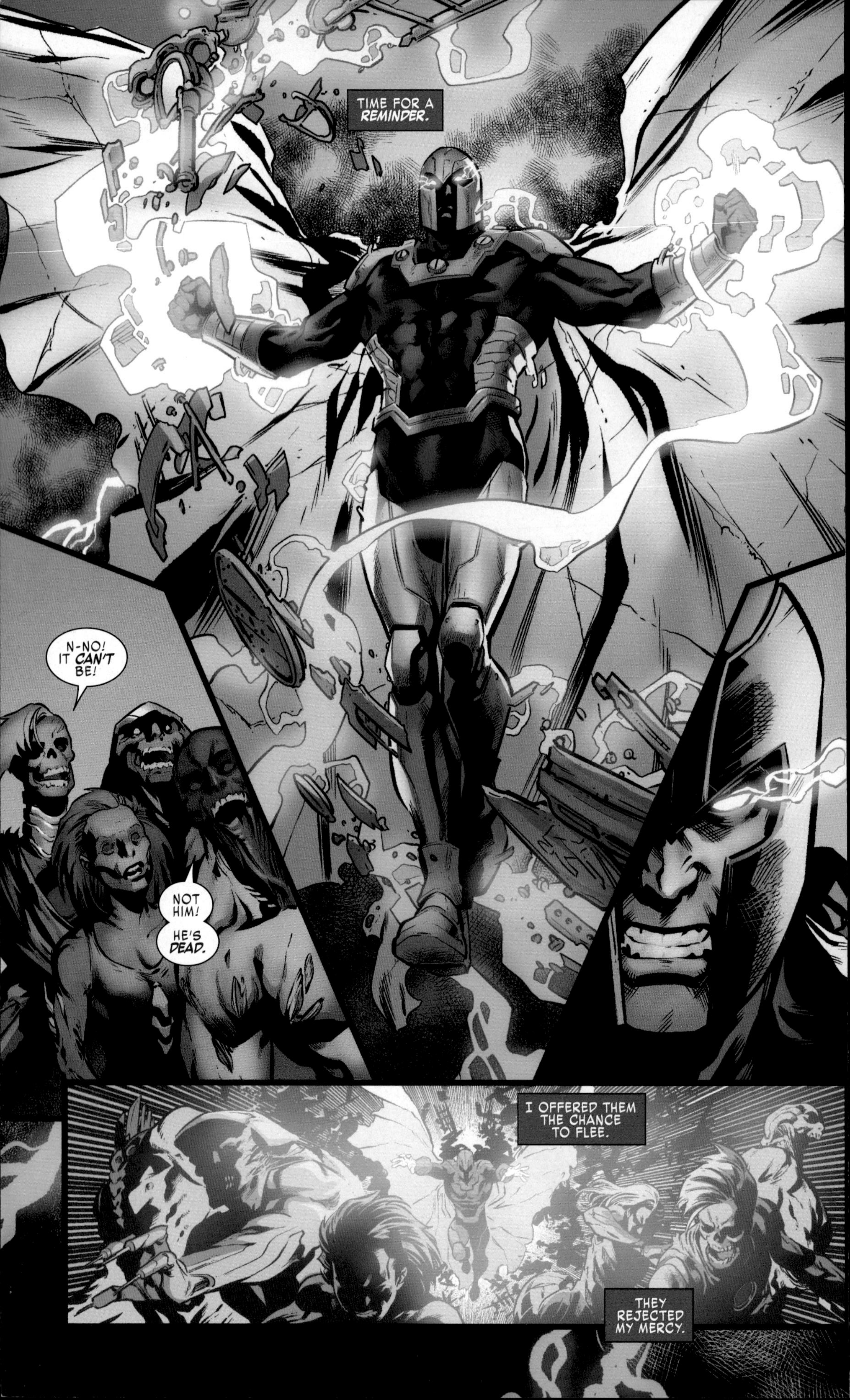
TIME FOR A REMINDER.
N-NO! IT CAN'T BE!
NOT HIM!
HE'S DEAD.
I OFFERED THEM THE CHANCE TO FLEE.
THEY REJECTED MY MERCY.

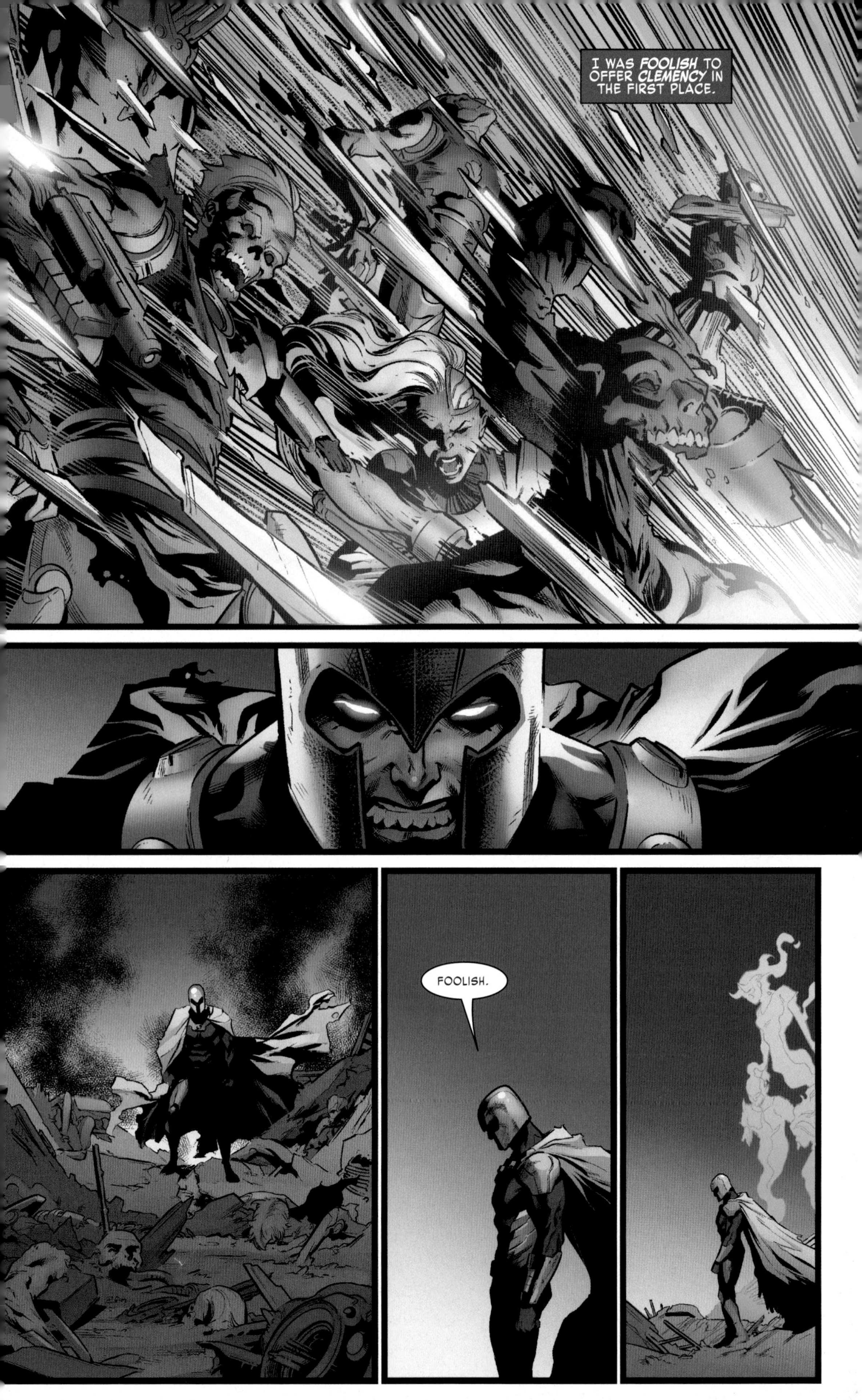
I WAS FOOLISH TO OFFER CLEMENCY IN THE FIRST PLACE.
FOOLISH.

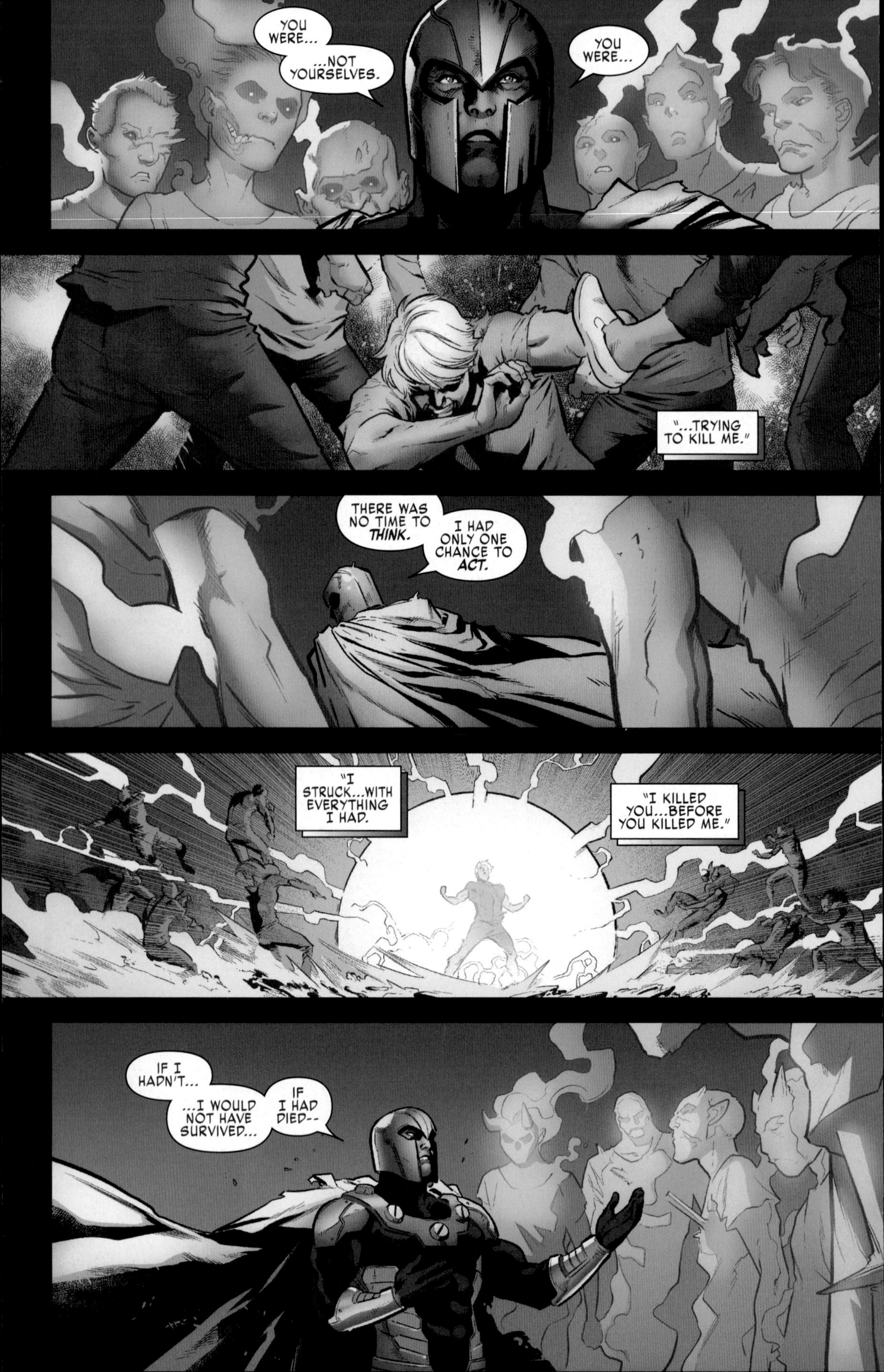
YOU WERE...
...NOT YOURSELVES.
YOU WERE...
"...TRYING TO KILL ME."
THERE WAS NO TIME TO *THINK.*
I HAD ONLY ONE CHANCE TO *ACT.*
"I STRUCK...WITH EVERYTHING I HAD.
"I KILLED YOU...BEFORE YOU KILLED ME."
IF I HADN'T...
...I WOULD NOT HAVE SURVIVED...
IF I HAD DIED--

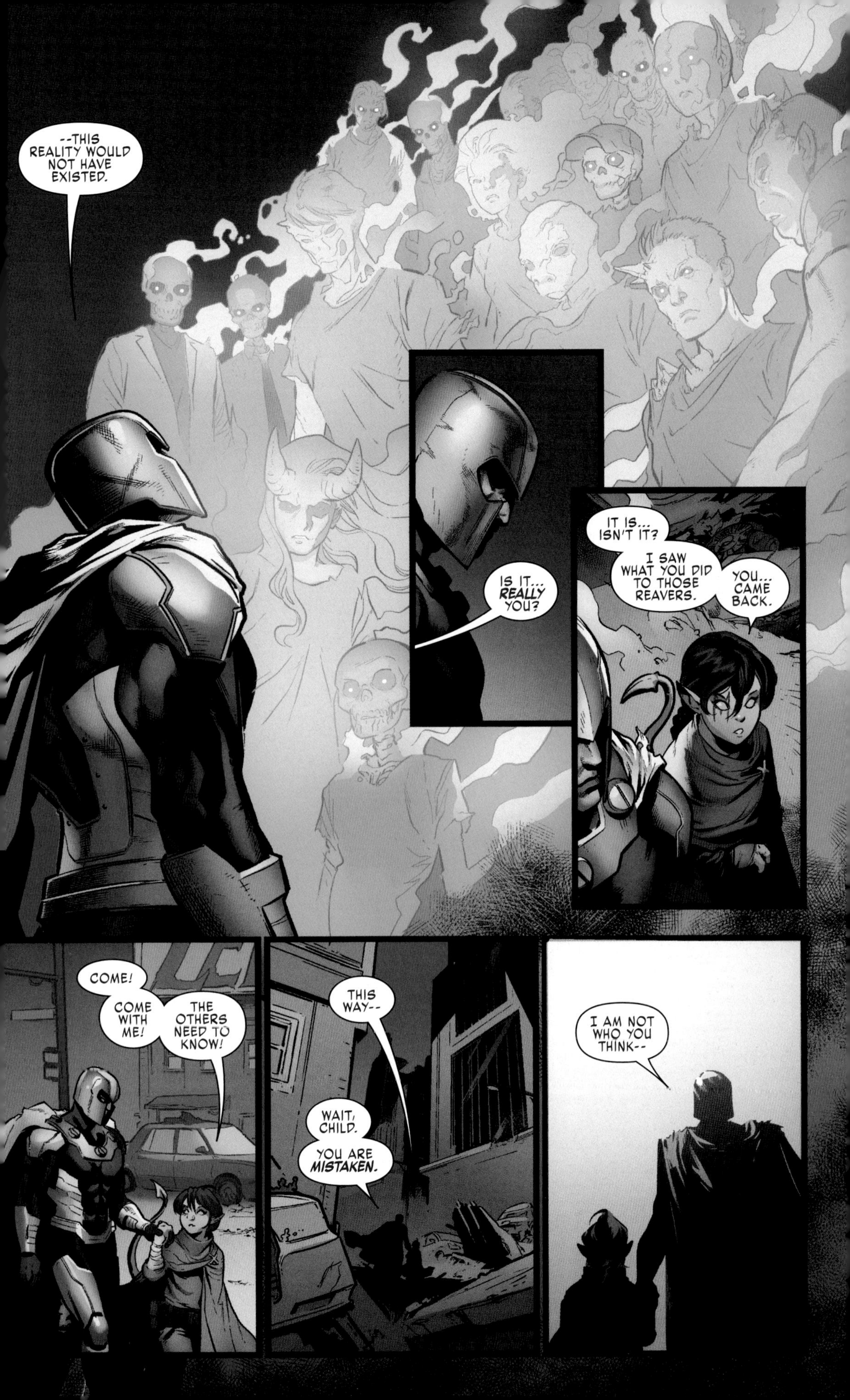
--THIS REALITY WOULD NOT HAVE EXISTED.
IS IT... REALLY YOU?
IT IS... ISN'T IT?
I SAW WHAT YOU DID TO THOSE REAVERS.
YOU... CAME BACK.
COME!
COME WITH ME!
THE OTHERS NEED TO KNOW!
THIS WAY--
WAIT, CHILD.
YOU ARE MISTAKEN.
I AM NOT WHO YOU THINK--

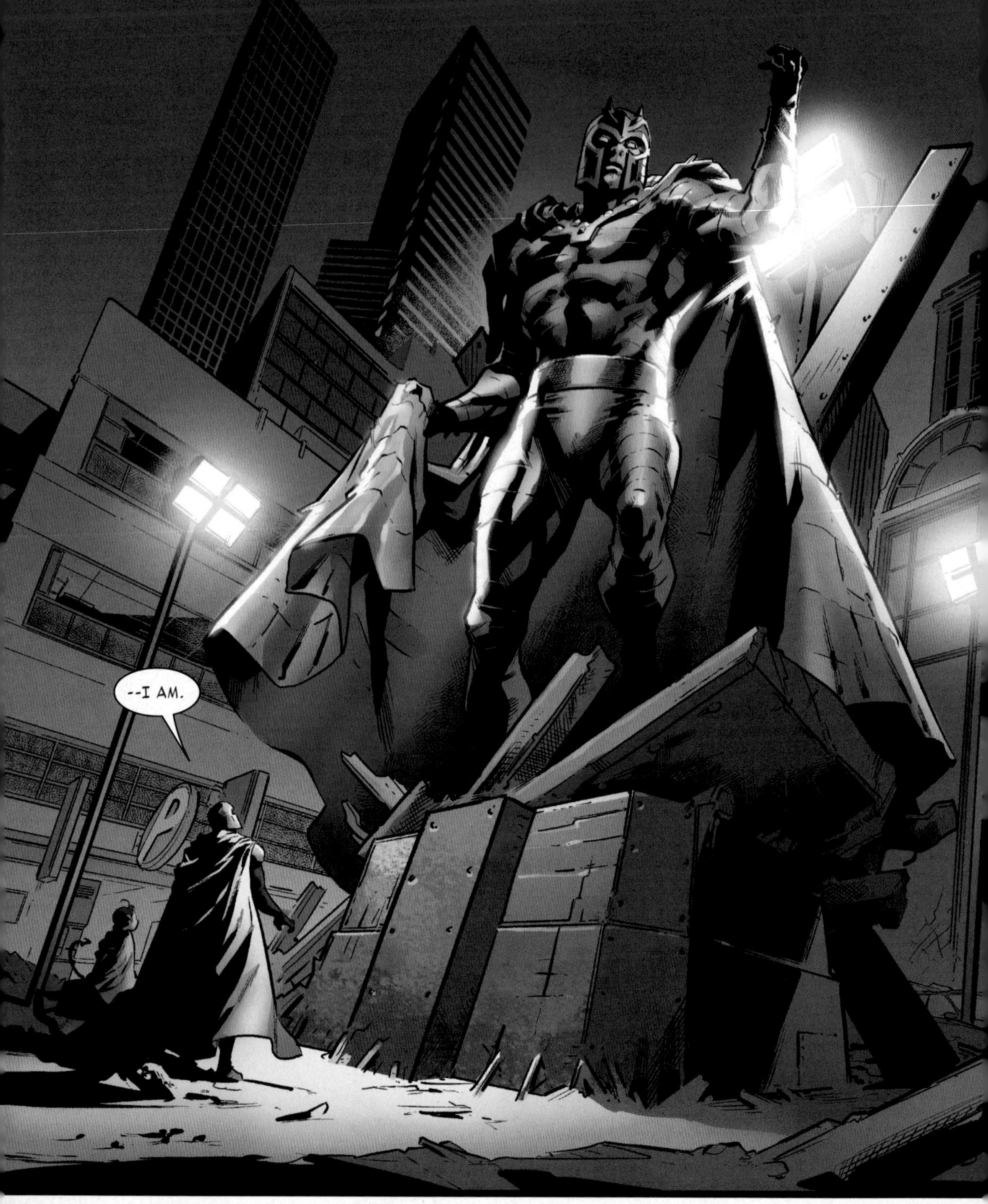
--I AM.

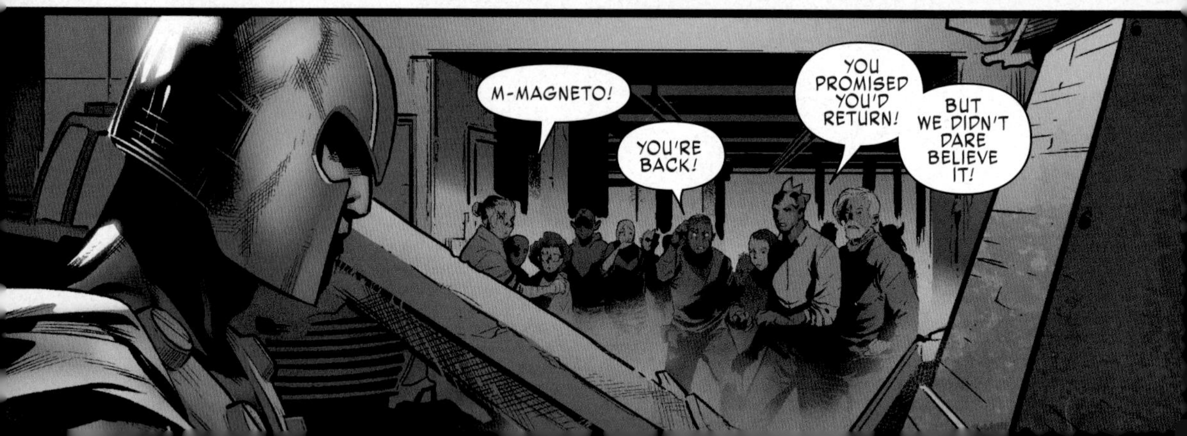
M-MAGNETO!
YOU'RE BACK!
YOU PROMISED YOU'D RETURN!
BUT WE DIDN'T DARE BELIEVE IT!

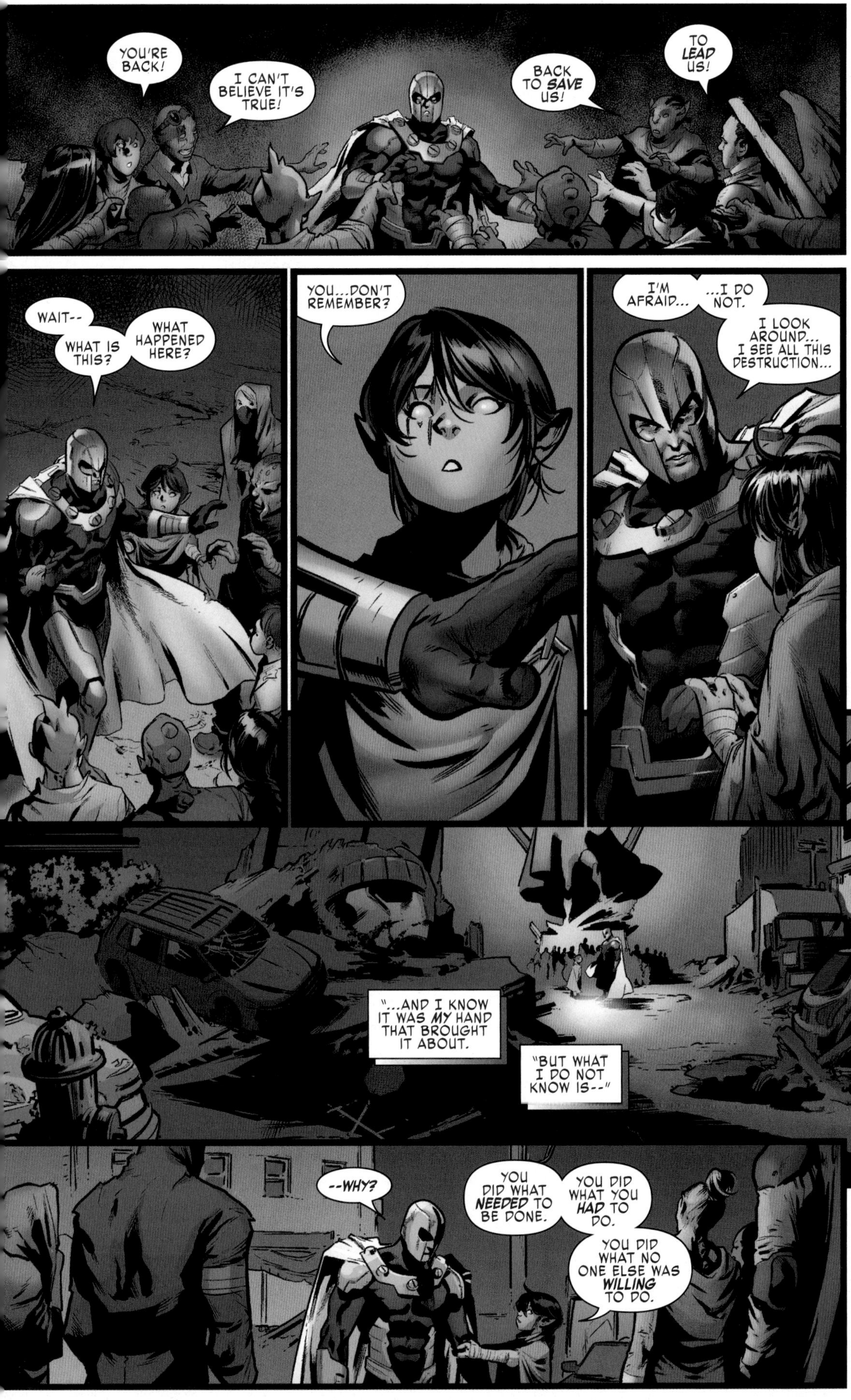
YOU'RE BACK!
I CAN'T BELIEVE IT'S TRUE!
BACK TO SAVE US!
TO LEAD US!
WAIT--
WHAT IS THIS?
WHAT HAPPENED HERE?
YOU...DON'T REMEMBER?
I'M AFRAID...
...I DO NOT.
I LOOK AROUND... I SEE ALL THIS DESTRUCTION...
"...AND I KNOW IT WAS MY HAND THAT BROUGHT IT ABOUT.
"BUT WHAT I DO NOT KNOW IS--"
--WHY?
YOU DID WHAT NEEDED TO BE DONE.
YOU DID WHAT YOU HAD TO DO.
YOU DID WHAT NO ONE ELSE WAS WILLING TO DO.

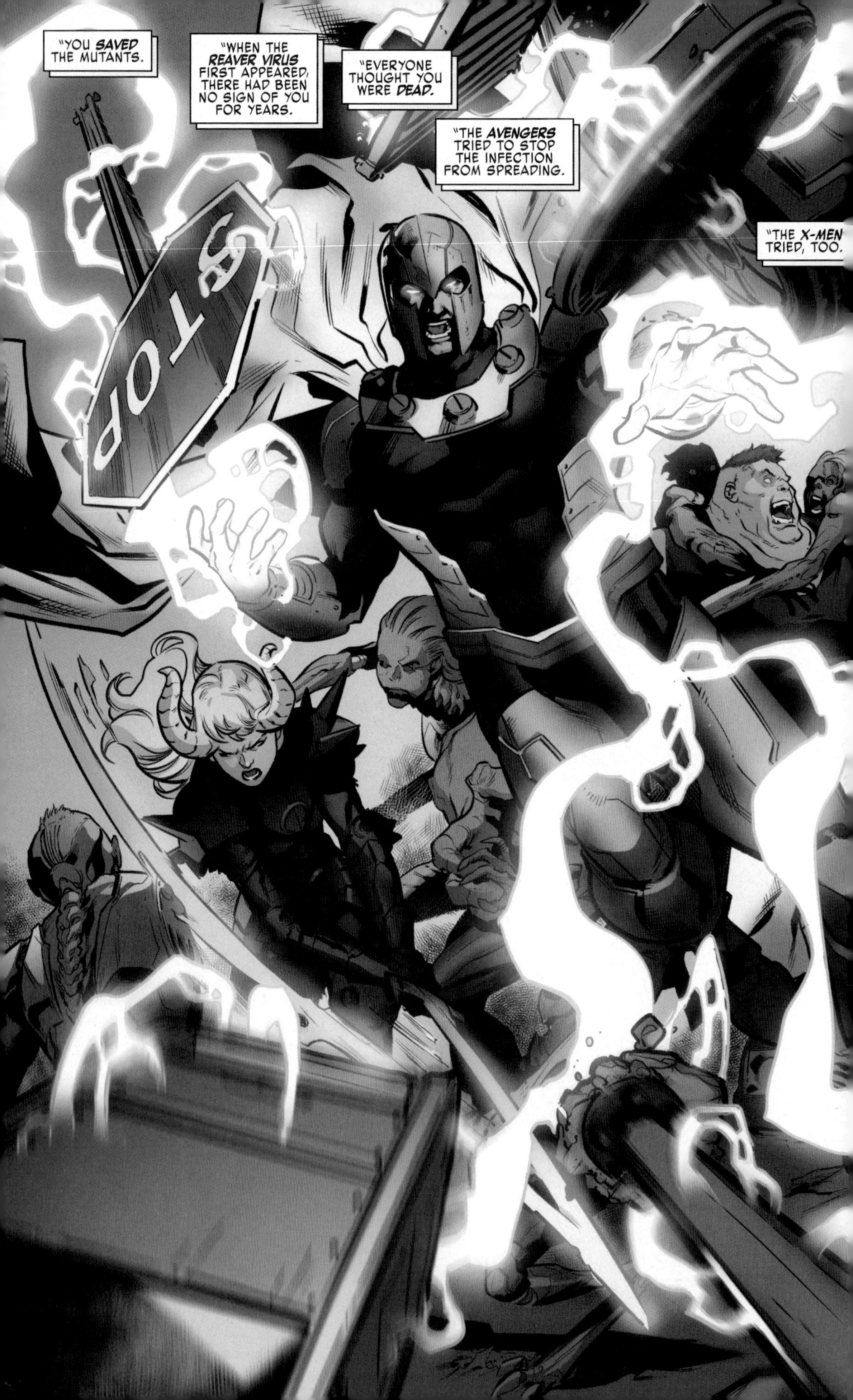
"YOU SAVED THE MUTANTS.
"WHEN THE REAVER VIRUS FIRST APPEARED, THERE HAD BEEN NO SIGN OF YOU FOR YEARS.
"EVERYONE THOUGHT YOU WERE DEAD.
"THE AVENGERS TRIED TO STOP THE INFECTION FROM SPREADING.
"THE X-MEN TRIED, TOO.
STOP

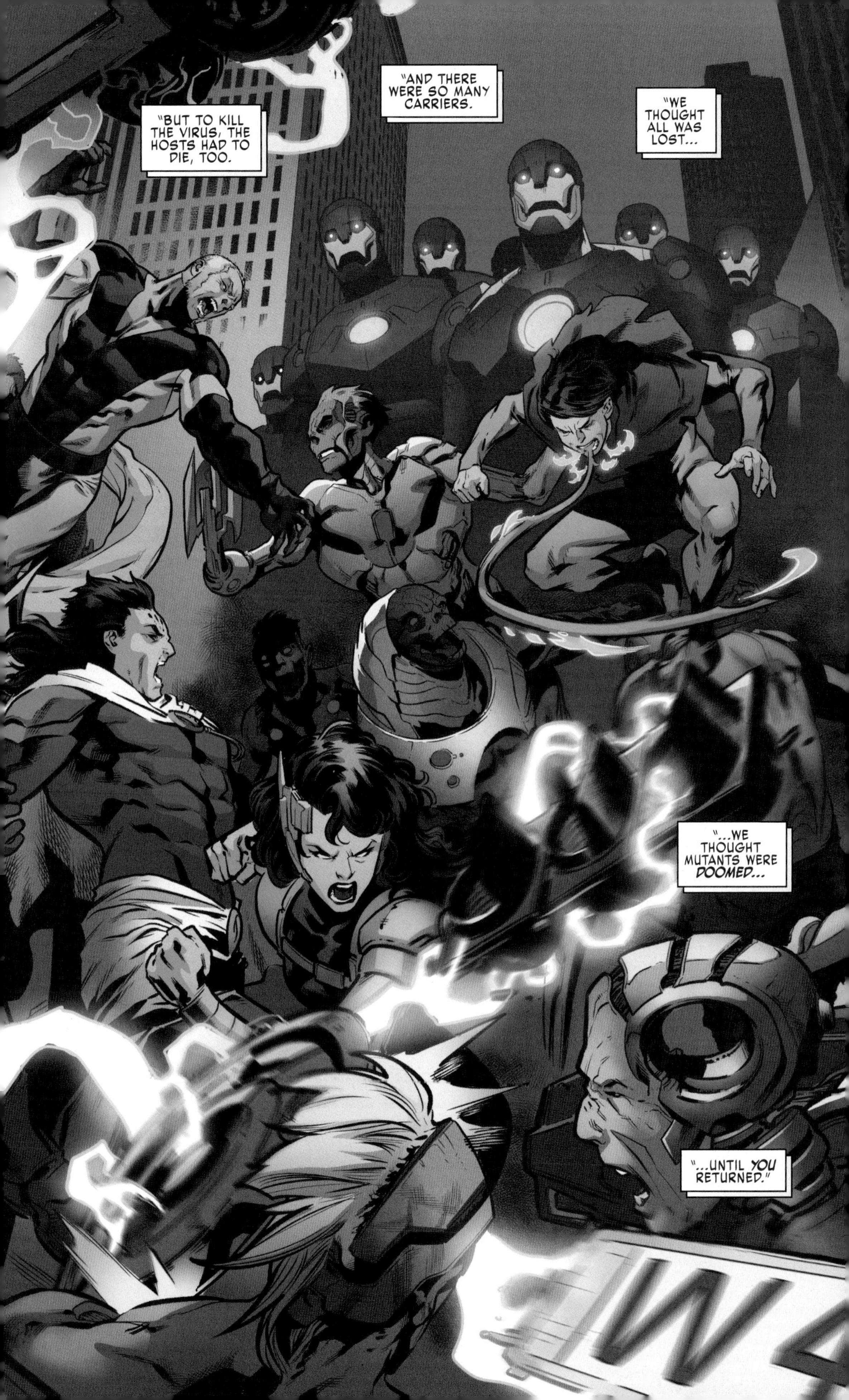
"BUT TO KILL THE VIRUS, THE HOSTS HAD TO DIE, TOO.
"AND THERE WERE SO MANY CARRIERS.
"WE THOUGHT ALL WAS LOST...
"...WE THOUGHT MUTANTS WERE DOOMED...
"...UNTIL YOU RETURNED."

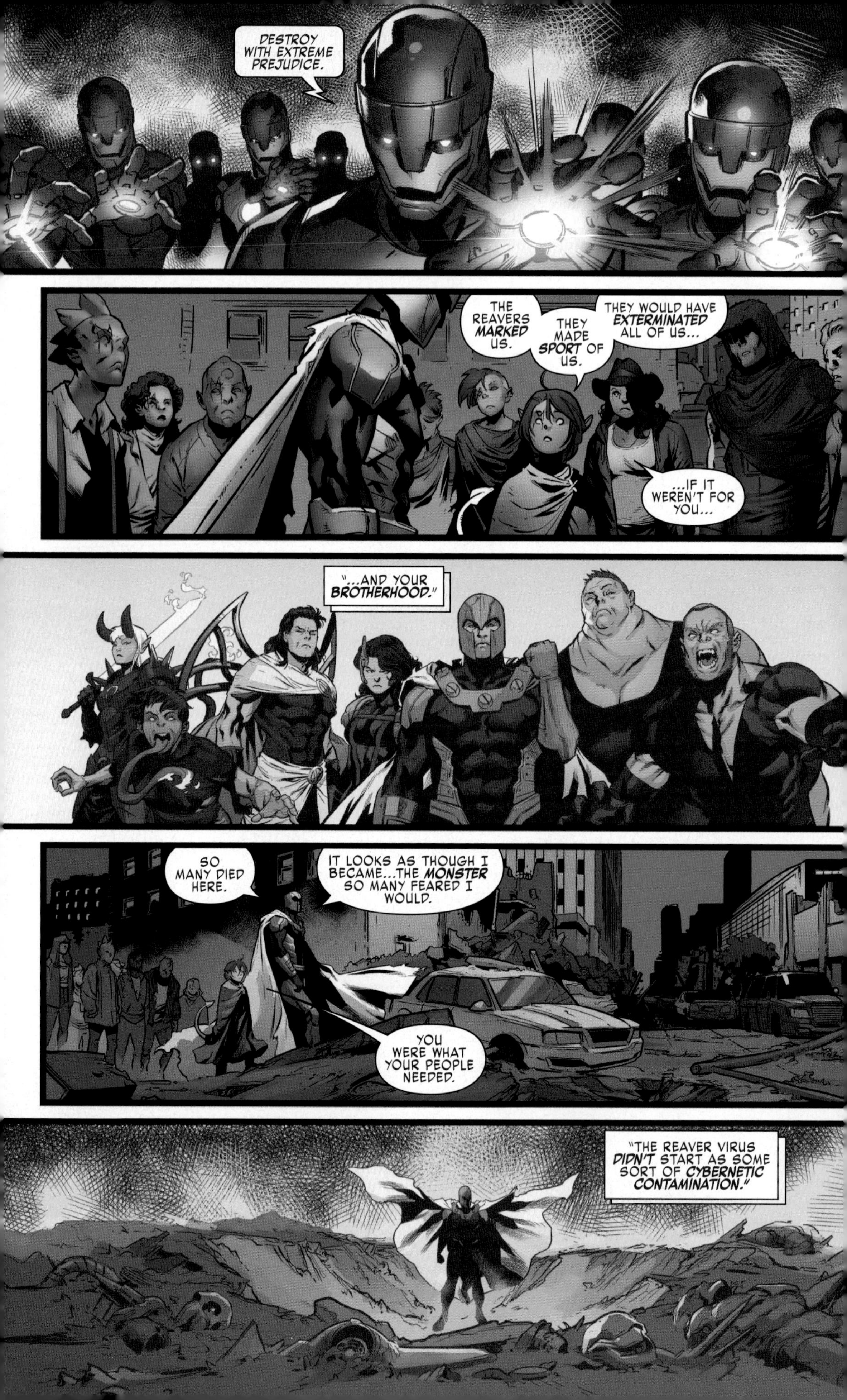

DESTROY WITH EXTREME PREJUDICE.
THE REAVERS MARKED US.
THEY MADE SPORT OF US.
THEY WOULD HAVE EXTERMINATED ALL OF US...
...IF IT WEREN'T FOR YOU...
"...AND YOUR BROTHERHOOD."
SO MANY DIED HERE.
IT LOOKS AS THOUGH I BECAME...THE MONSTER SO MANY FEARED I WOULD.
YOU WERE WHAT YOUR PEOPLE NEEDED.
"THE REAVER VIRUS DIDN'T START AS SOME SORT OF CYBERNETIC CONTAMINATION."

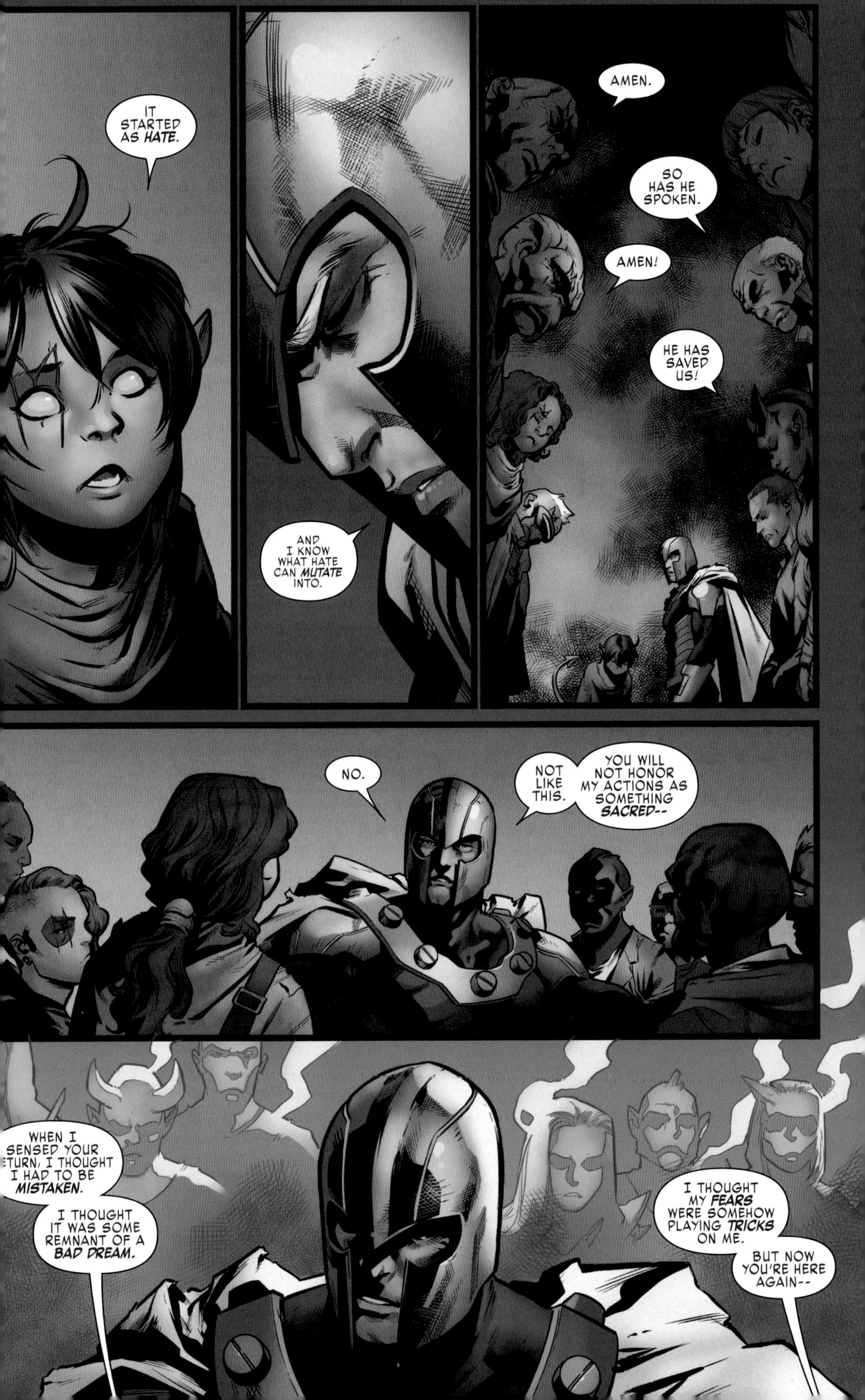
IT STARTED AS HATE.
AND I KNOW WHAT HATE CAN MUTATE INTO.
AMEN.
SO HAS HE SPOKEN.
AMEN!
HE HAS SAVED US!
NO.
NOT LIKE THIS.
YOU WILL NOT HONOR MY ACTIONS AS SOMETHING SACRED--
WHEN I SENSED YOUR ETURN, I THOUGHT I HAD TO BE MISTAKEN.
I THOUGHT IT WAS SOME REMNANT OF A BAD DREAM.
I THOUGHT MY FEARS WERE SOMEHOW PLAYING TRICKS ON ME.
BUT NOW YOU'RE HERE AGAIN--

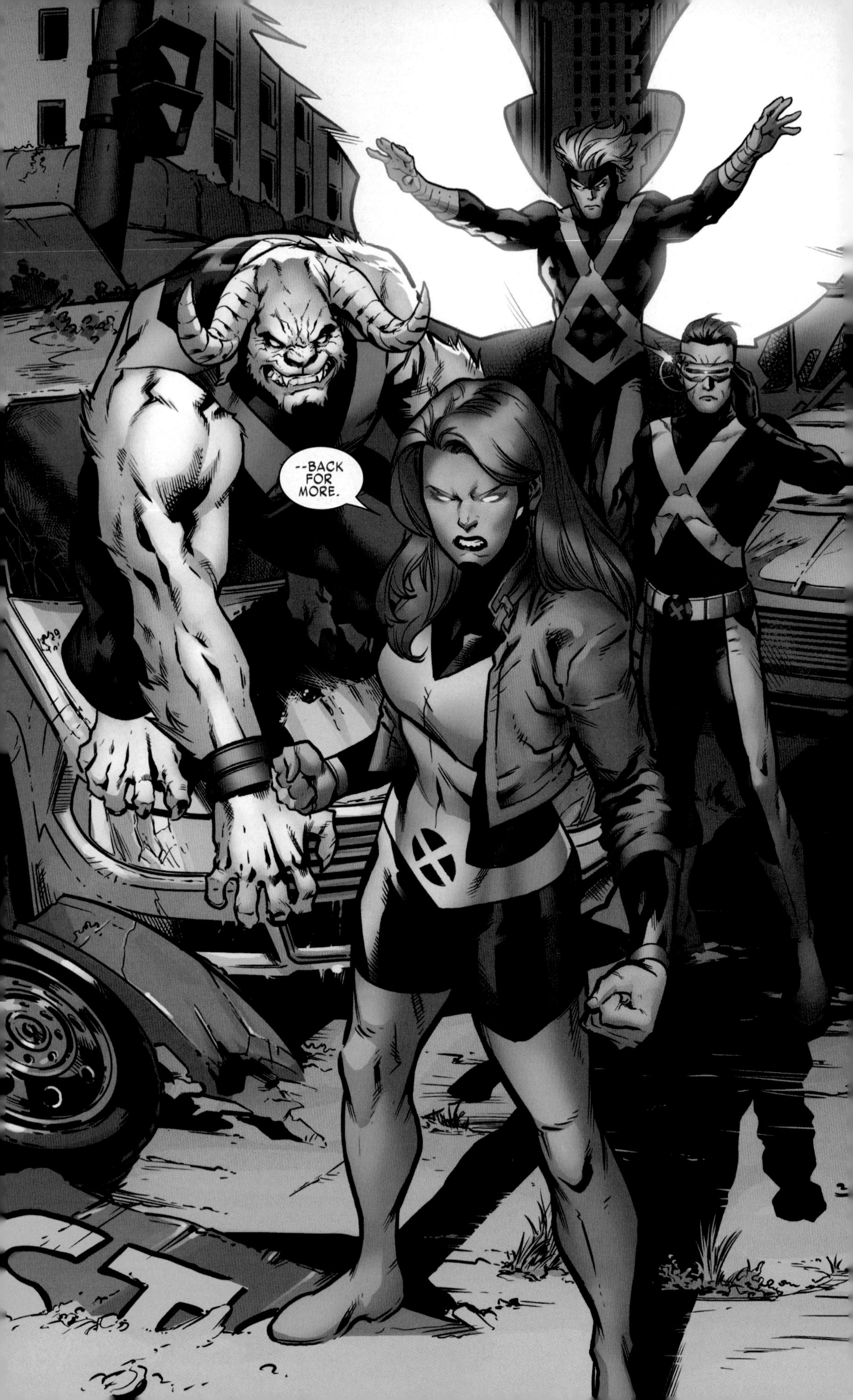
--BACK FOR MORE.

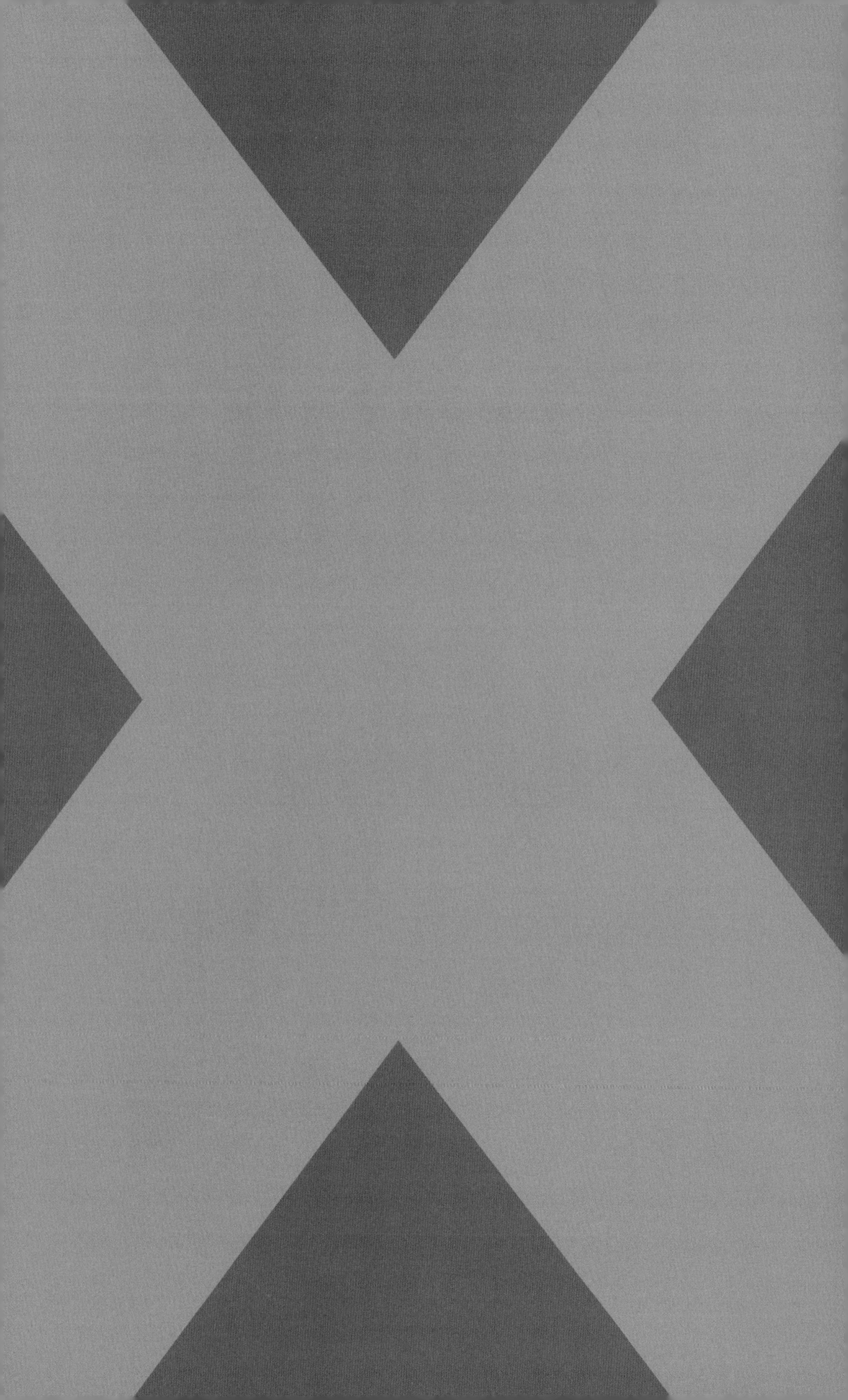

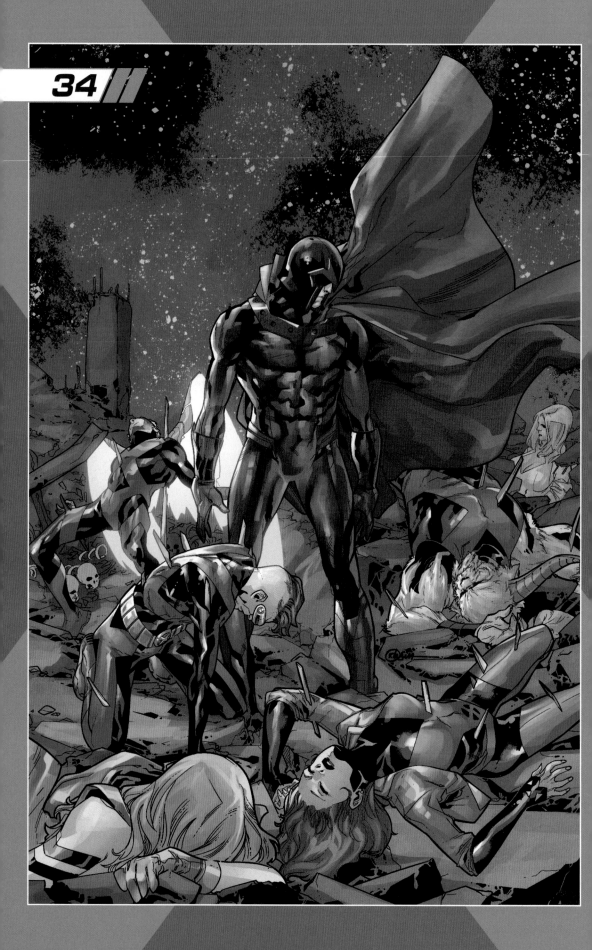

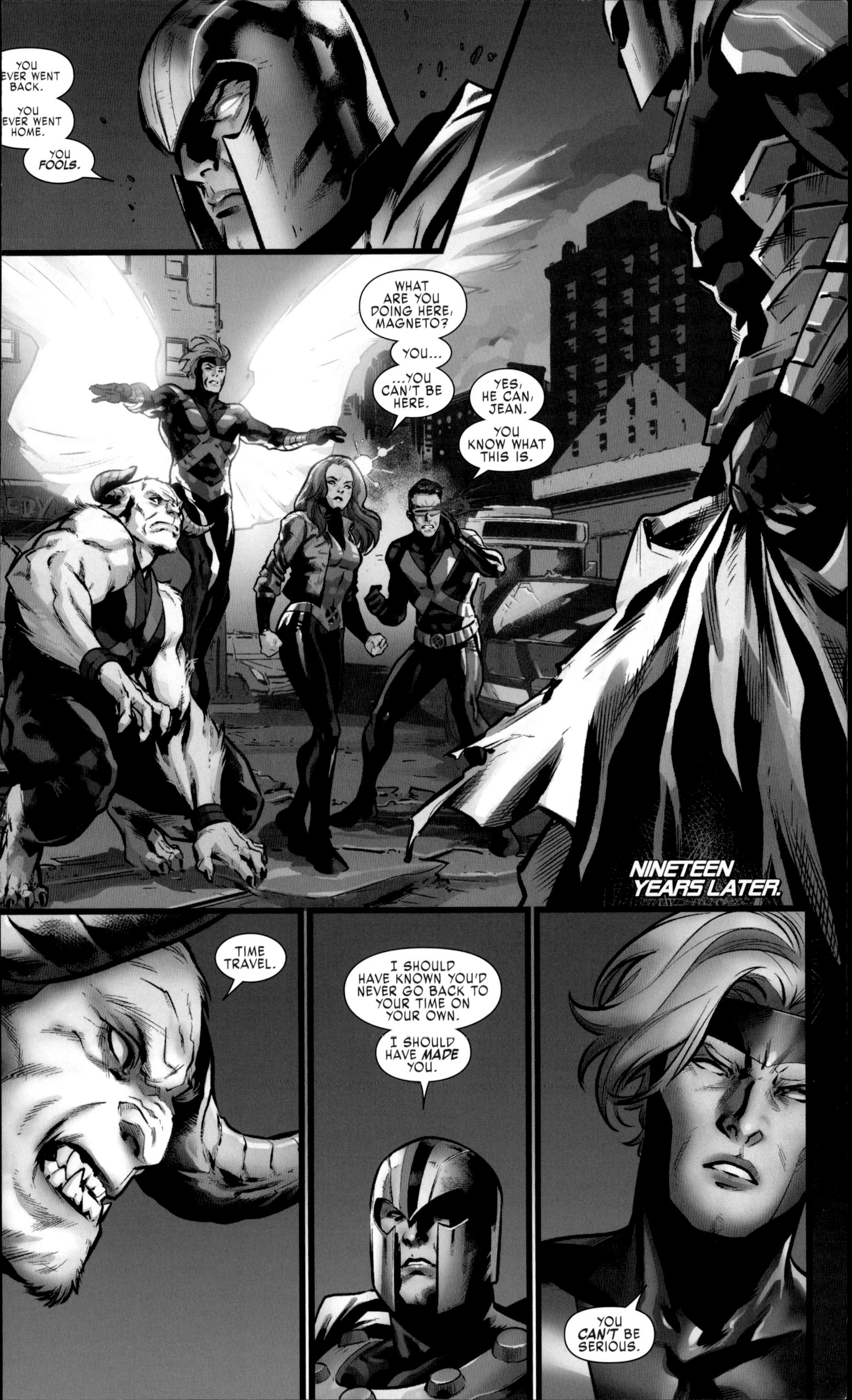
YOU
EVER WENT
BACK.
YOU
EVER WENT
HOME.
YOU
FOOLS.
WHAT ARE YOU DOING HERE, MAGNETO?
YOU...
...YOU CAN'T BE HERE.
YES, HE CAN, JEAN.
YOU KNOW WHAT THIS IS.
NINETEEN YEARS LATER.
TIME TRAVEL.
I SHOULD HAVE KNOWN YOU'D NEVER GO BACK TO YOUR TIME ON YOUR OWN.
I SHOULD HAVE MADE YOU.
YOU CAN'T BE SERIOUS.

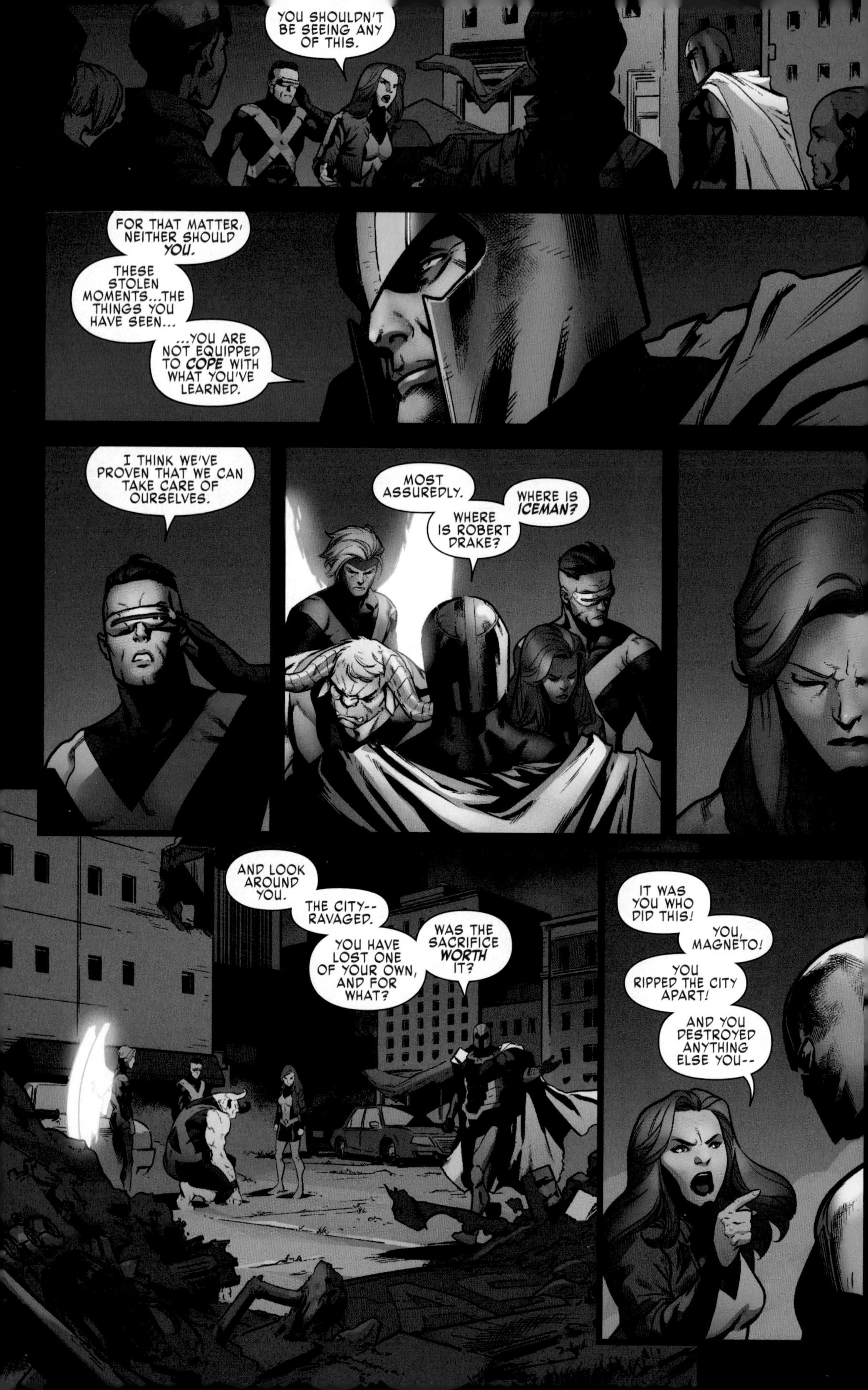
YOU SHOULDN'T BE SEEING ANY OF THIS.
FOR THAT MATTER, NEITHER SHOULD *YOU.*
THESE STOLEN MOMENTS...THE THINGS YOU HAVE SEEN...
...YOU ARE NOT EQUIPPED TO *COPE* WITH WHAT YOU'VE LEARNED.
I THINK WE'VE PROVEN THAT WE CAN TAKE CARE OF OURSELVES.
MOST ASSUREDLY.
WHERE IS ROBERT DRAKE?
WHERE IS *ICEMAN?*
AND LOOK AROUND YOU.
THE CITY-- RAVAGED.
YOU HAVE LOST ONE OF YOUR OWN, AND FOR WHAT?
WAS THE SACRIFICE *WORTH* IT?
IT WAS YOU WHO DID THIS!
YOU, MAGNETO!
YOU RIPPED THE CITY APART!
AND YOU DESTROYED ANYTHING ELSE YOU--

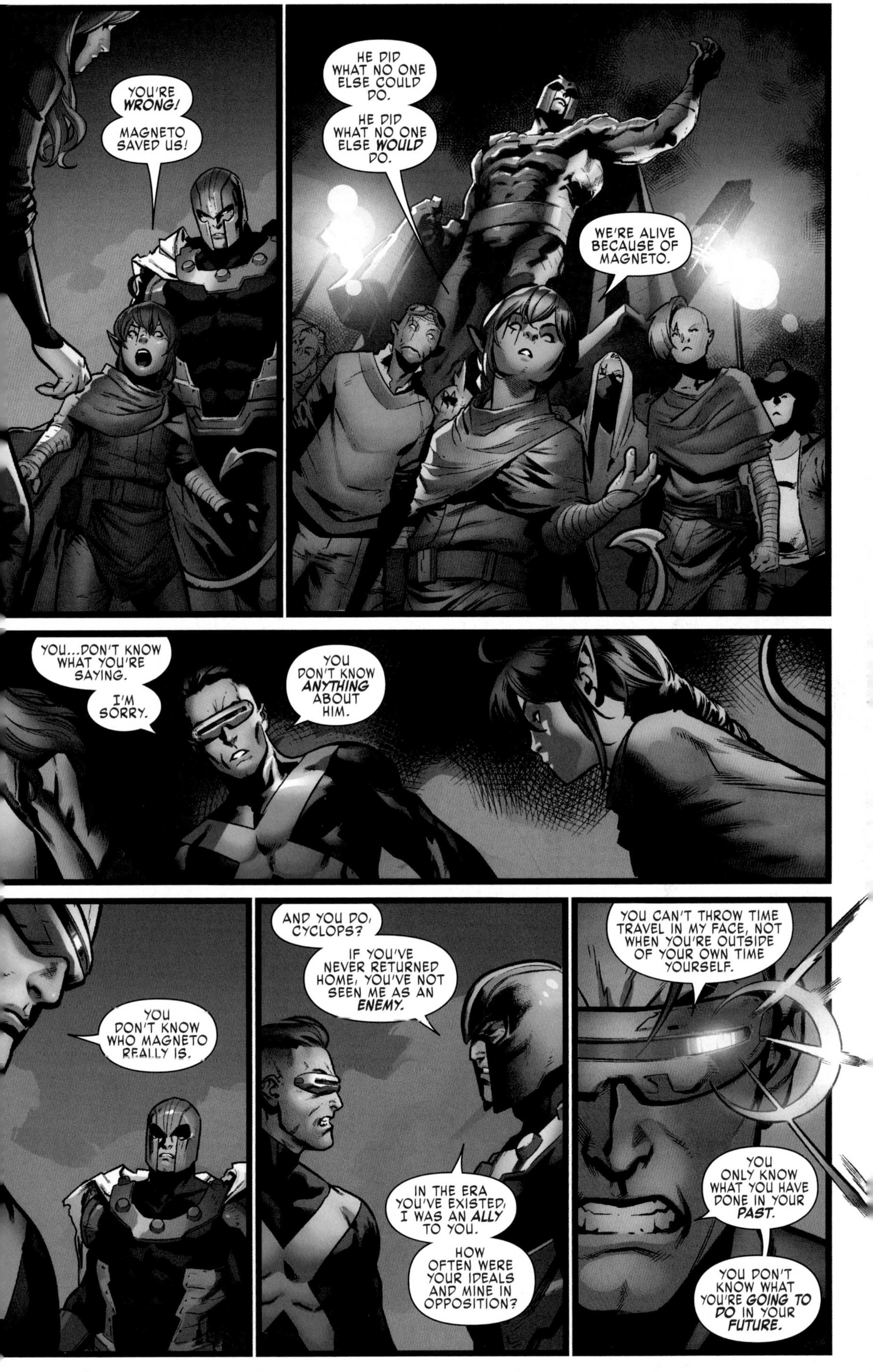
YOU'RE WRONG!
MAGNETO SAVED US!
HE DID WHAT NO ONE ELSE COULD DO.
HE DID WHAT NO ONE ELSE WOULD DO.
WE'RE ALIVE BECAUSE OF MAGNETO.
YOU...DON'T KNOW WHAT YOU'RE SAYING.
I'M SORRY.
YOU DON'T KNOW ANYTHING ABOUT HIM.
YOU DON'T KNOW WHO MAGNETO REALLY IS.
AND YOU DO, CYCLOPS?
IF YOU'VE NEVER RETURNED HOME, YOU'VE NOT SEEN ME AS AN ENEMY.
IN THE ERA YOU'VE EXISTED, I WAS AN ALLY TO YOU.
HOW OFTEN WERE YOUR IDEALS AND MINE IN OPPOSITION?
YOU CAN'T THROW TIME TRAVEL IN MY FACE, NOT WHEN YOU'RE OUTSIDE OF YOUR OWN TIME YOURSELF.
YOU ONLY KNOW WHAT YOU HAVE DONE IN YOUR PAST.
YOU DON'T KNOW WHAT YOU'RE GOING TO DO IN YOUR FUTURE.

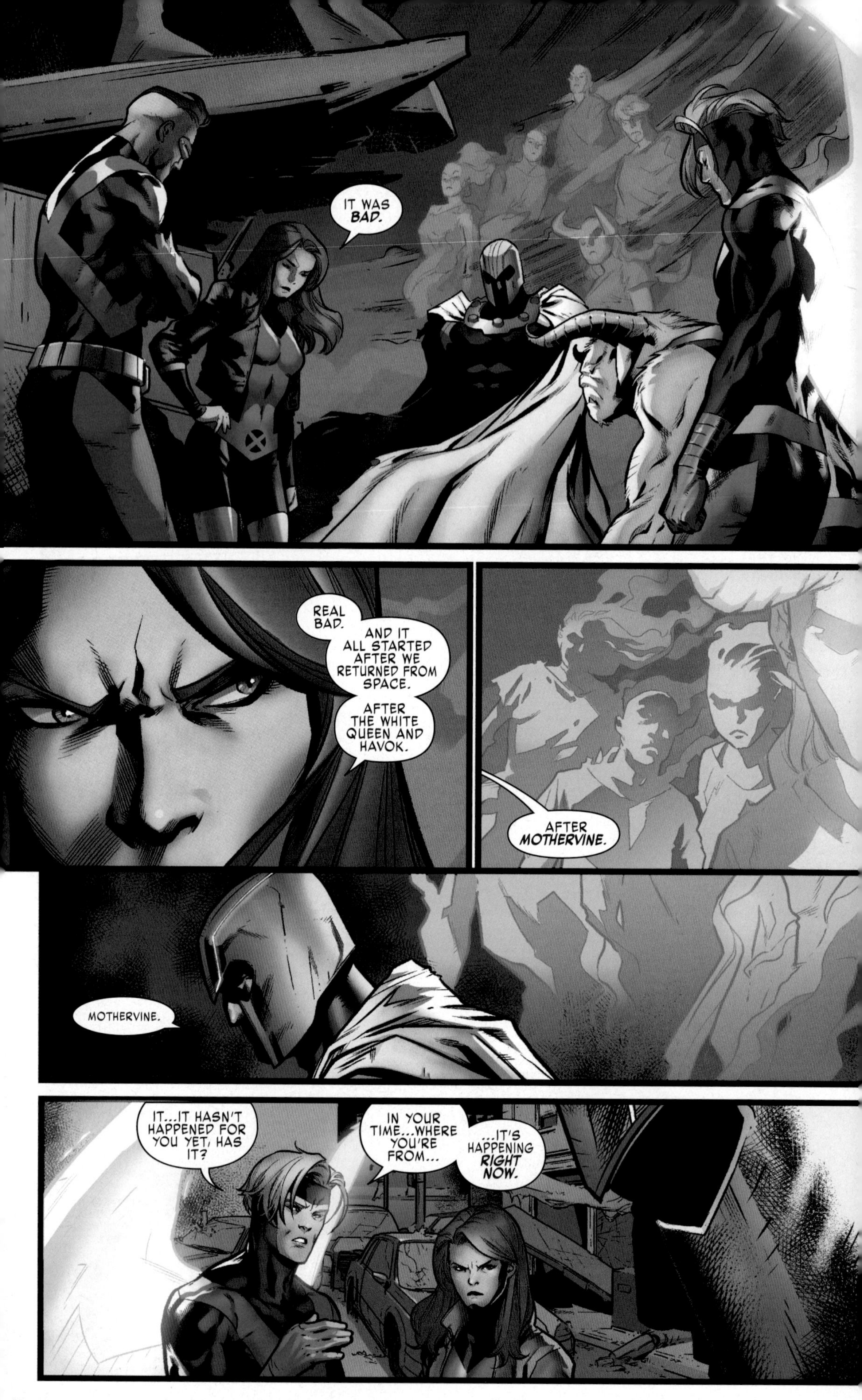
IT WAS BAD.
REAL BAD.
AND IT ALL STARTED AFTER WE RETURNED FROM SPACE.
AFTER THE WHITE QUEEN AND HAVOK.
AFTER MOTHERVINE.
MOTHERVINE.
IT...IT HASN'T HAPPENED FOR YOU YET, HAS IT?
IN YOUR TIME...WHERE YOU'RE FROM...
...IT'S HAPPENING RIGHT NOW.

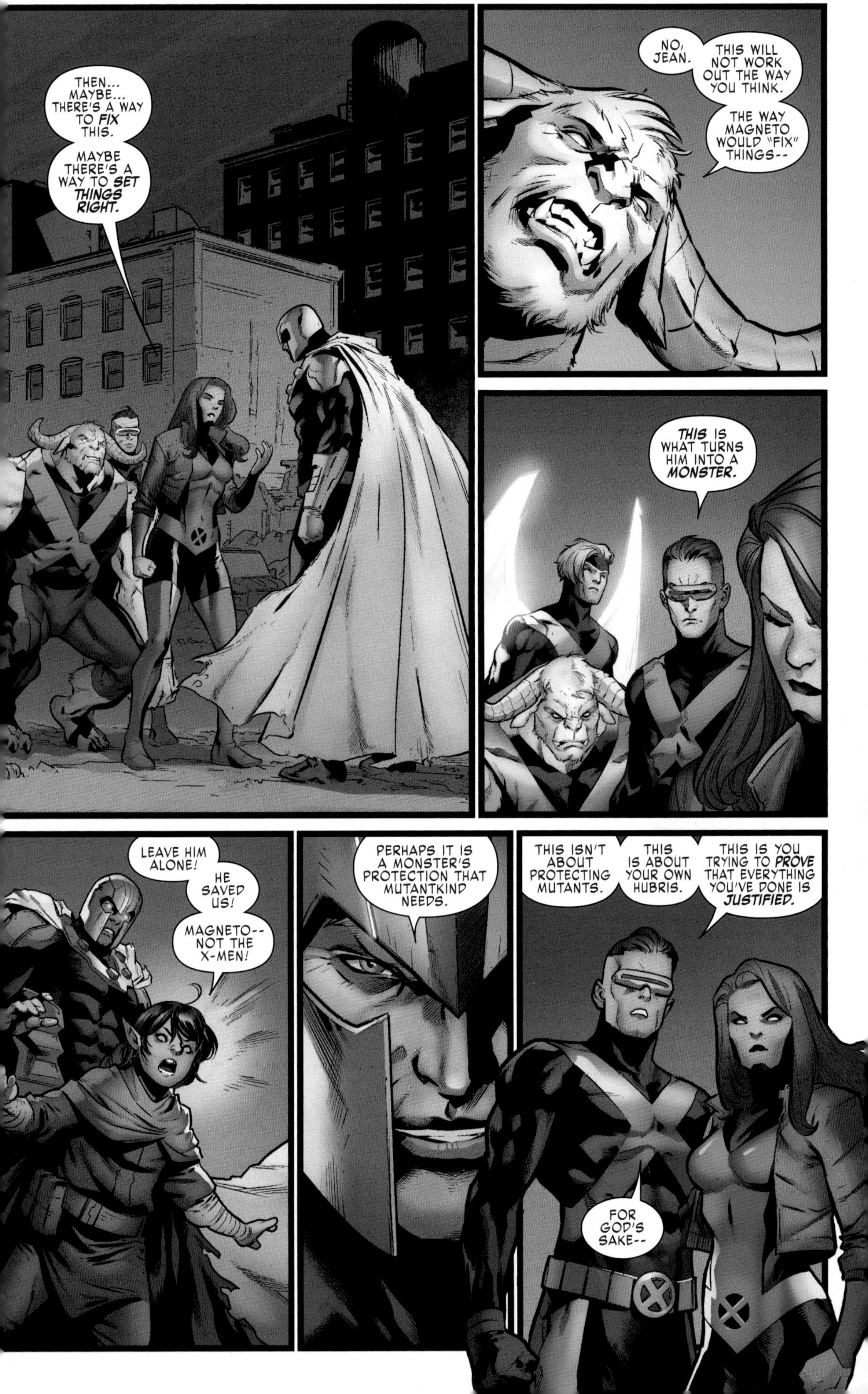
THEN... MAYBE... THERE'S A WAY TO FIX THIS.
MAYBE THERE'S A WAY TO SET THINGS RIGHT.
NO, JEAN.
THIS WILL NOT WORK OUT THE WAY YOU THINK.
THE WAY MAGNETO WOULD "FIX" THINGS--
THIS IS WHAT TURNS HIM INTO A MONSTER.
LEAVE HIM ALONE!
HE SAVED US!
MAGNETO--NOT THE X-MEN!
PERHAPS IT IS A MONSTER'S PROTECTION THAT MUTANTKIND NEEDS.
THIS ISN'T ABOUT PROTECTING MUTANTS.
THIS IS ABOUT YOUR OWN HUBRIS.
THIS IS YOU TRYING TO PROVE THAT EVERYTHING YOU'VE DONE IS JUSTIFIED.
FOR GOD'S SAKE--

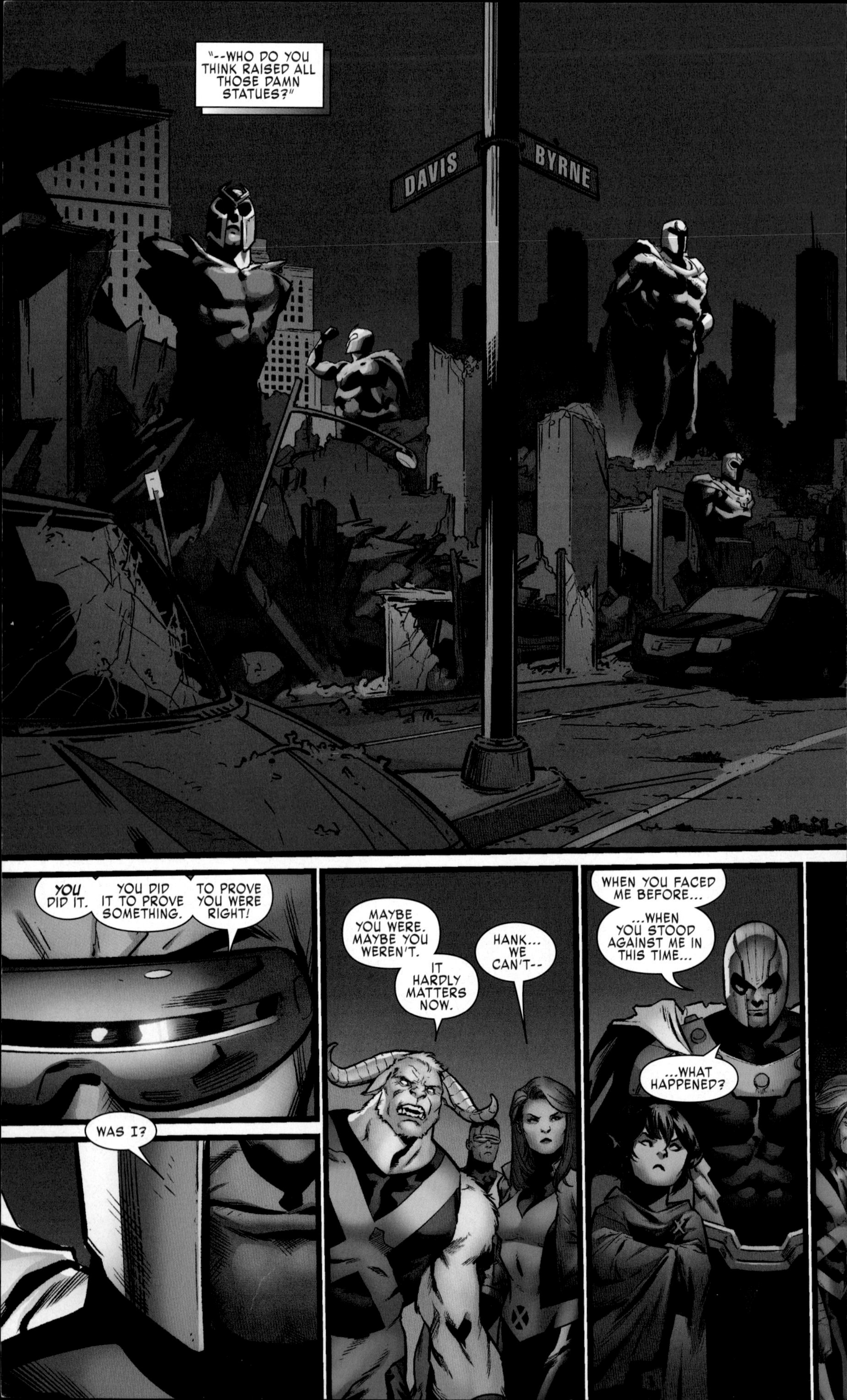
"--WHO DO YOU THINK RAISED ALL THOSE DAMN STATUES?"
DAVIS
BYRNE
YOU DID IT.
YOU DID IT TO PROVE SOMETHING.
TO PROVE YOU WERE RIGHT!
WAS I?
MAYBE YOU WERE. MAYBE YOU WEREN'T.
IT HARDLY MATTERS NOW.
HANK... WE CAN'T--
WHEN YOU FACED ME BEFORE...
...WHEN YOU STOOD AGAINST ME IN THIS TIME...
...WHAT HAPPENED?

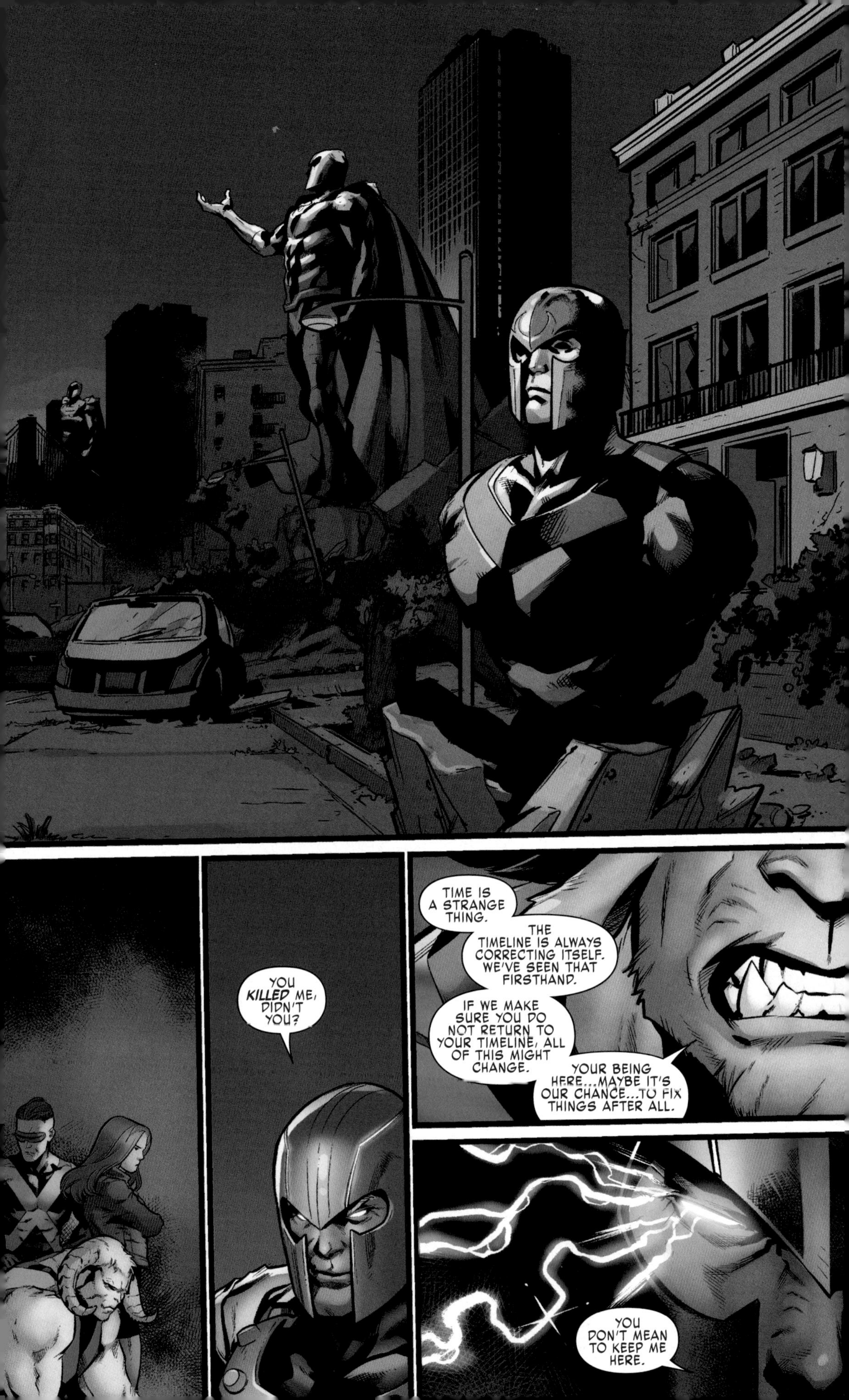
YOU KILLED ME, DIDN'T YOU?
TIME IS A STRANGE THING.
THE TIMELINE IS ALWAYS CORRECTING ITSELF. WE'VE SEEN THAT FIRSTHAND.
IF WE MAKE SURE YOU DO NOT RETURN TO YOUR TIMELINE, ALL OF THIS MIGHT CHANGE.
YOUR BEING HERE...MAYBE IT'S OUR CHANCE...TO FIX THINGS AFTER ALL.
YOU DON'T MEAN TO KEEP ME HERE.

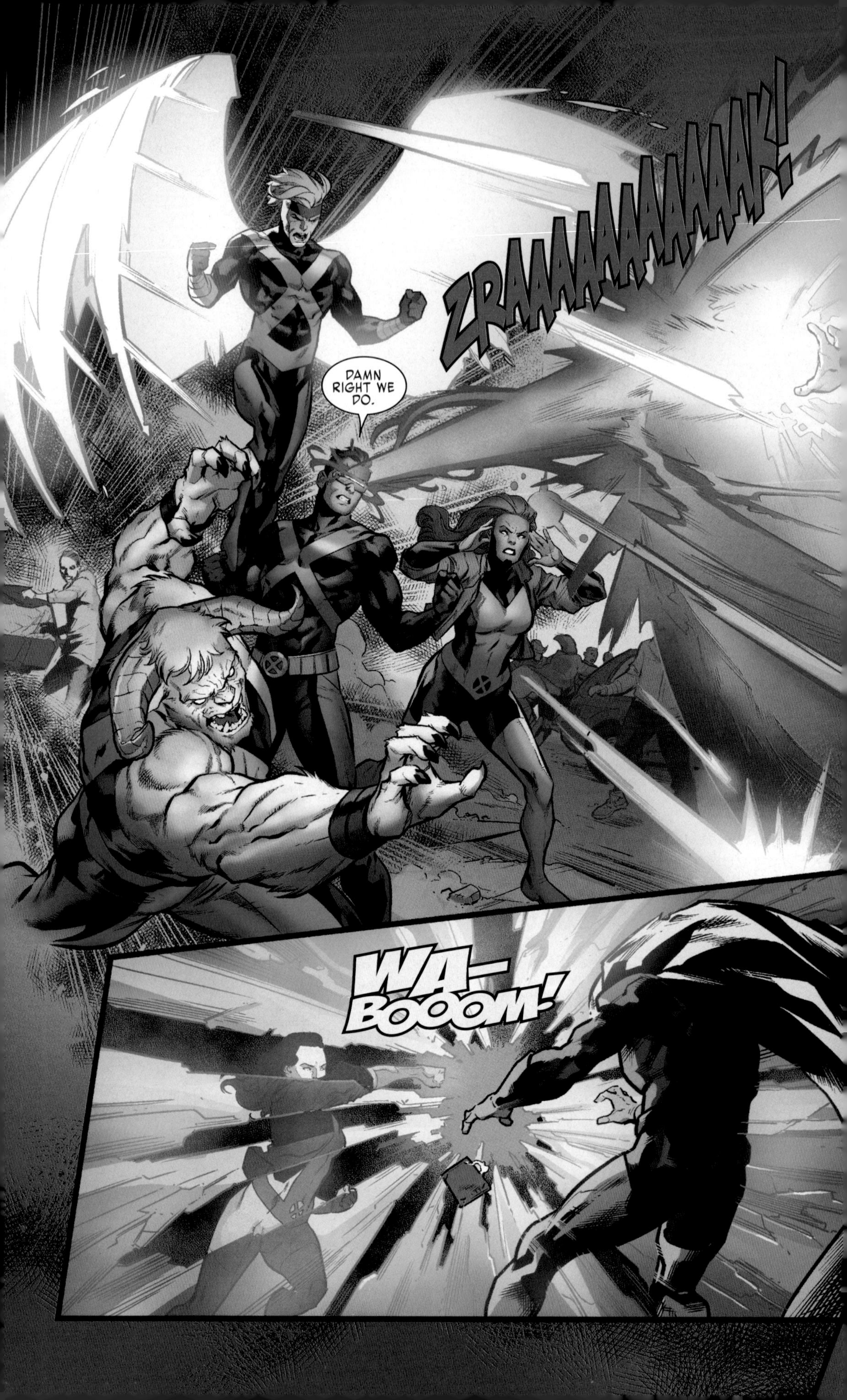
ZRAAAAAAAAAAK!
DAMN RIGHT WE DO.
WA-BOOOM!

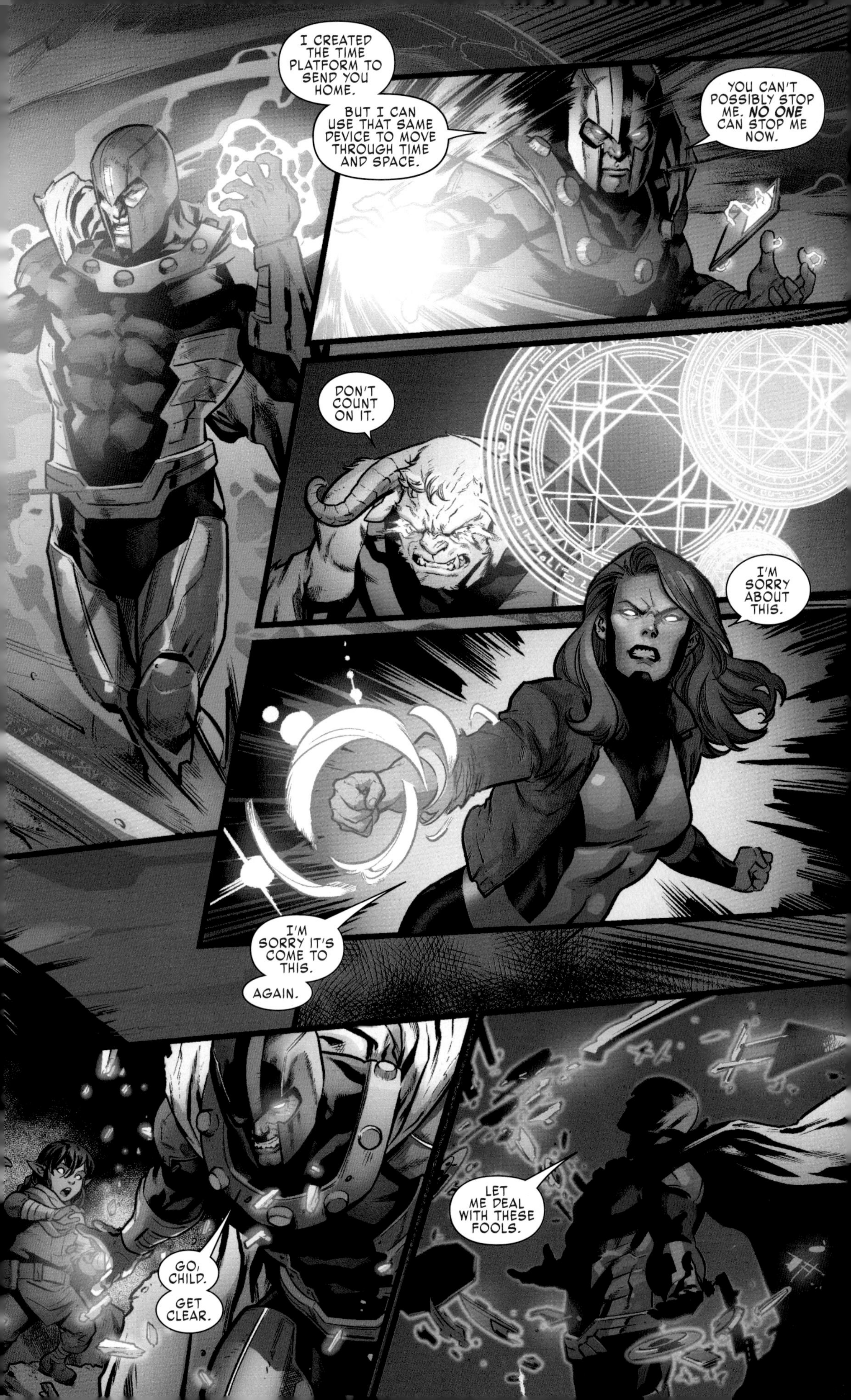
I CREATED THE TIME PLATFORM TO SEND YOU HOME.
BUT I CAN USE THAT SAME DEVICE TO MOVE THROUGH TIME AND SPACE.
YOU CAN'T POSSIBLY STOP ME. NO ONE CAN STOP ME NOW.
DON'T COUNT ON IT.
I'M SORRY ABOUT THIS.
I'M SORRY IT'S COME TO THIS.
AGAIN.
GO, CHILD.
GET CLEAR.
LET ME DEAL WITH THESE FOOLS.

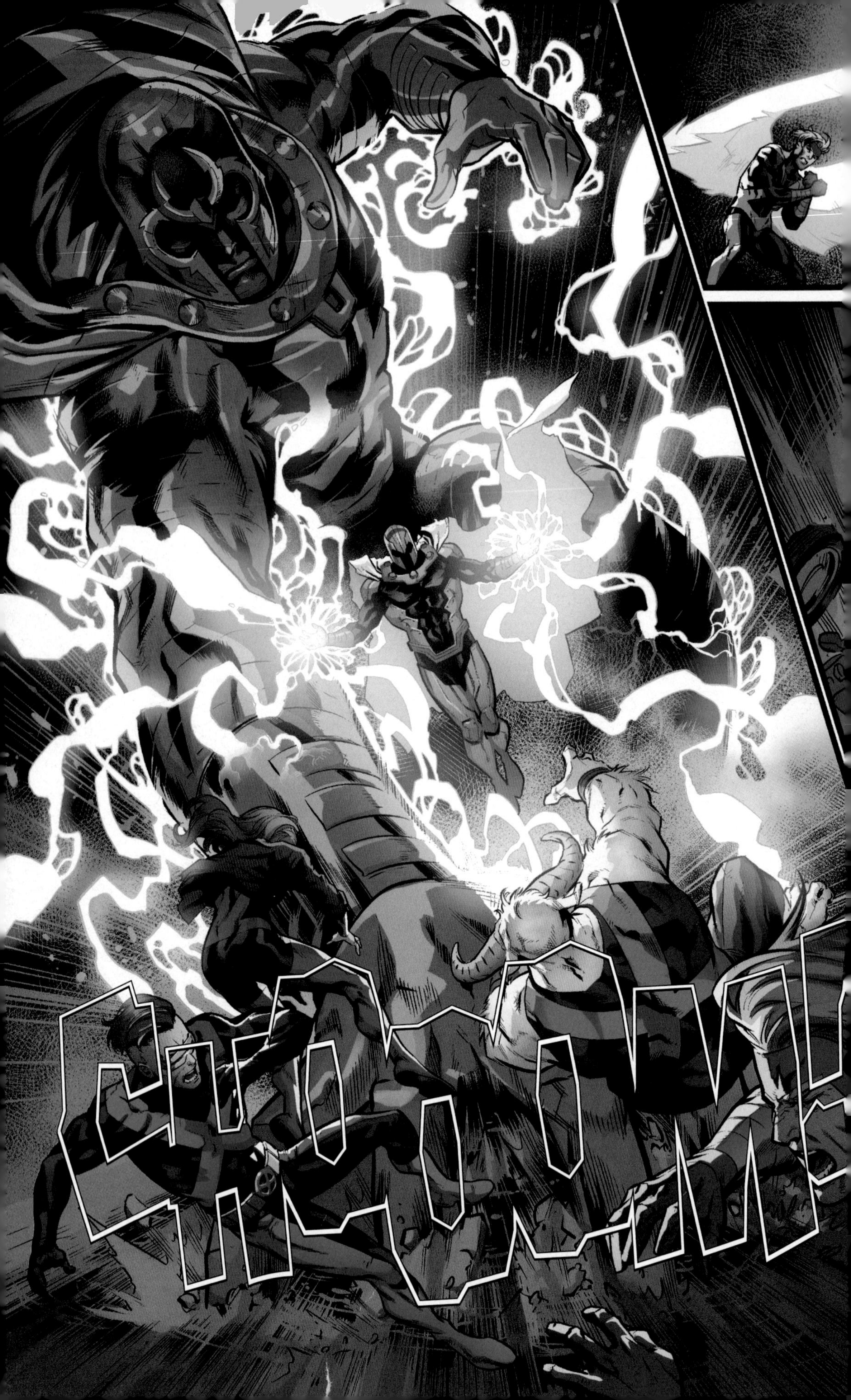
CHOOOM!

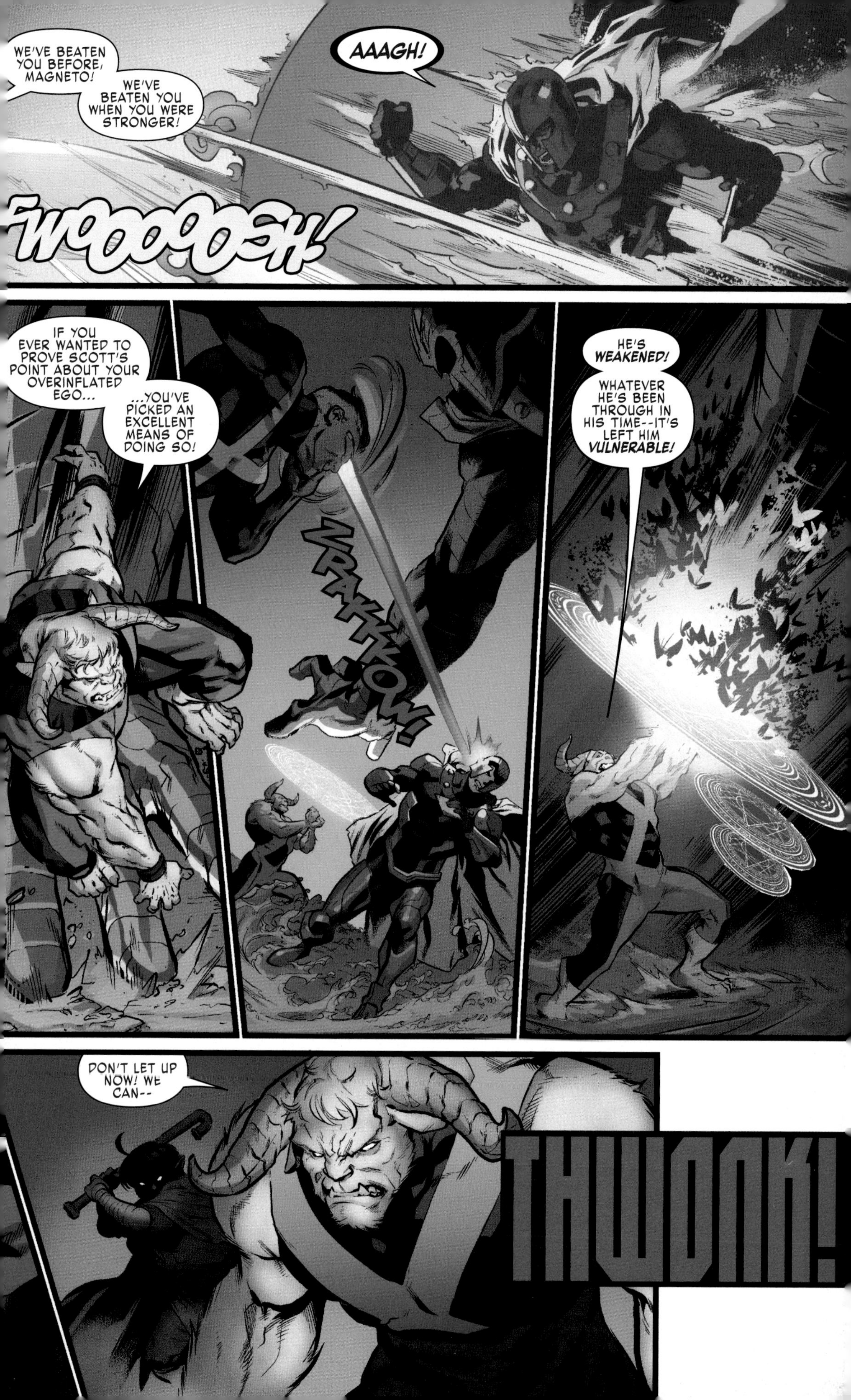
WE'VE BEATEN YOU BEFORE, MAGNETO!
WE'VE BEATEN YOU WHEN YOU WERE STRONGER!
AAAGH!
FWOOOOOSH!
IF YOU EVER WANTED TO PROVE SCOTT'S POINT ABOUT YOUR OVERINFLATED EGO...
...YOU'VE PICKED AN EXCELLENT MEANS OF DOING SO!
ZRAKKKOW!
HE'S WEAKENED!
WHATEVER HE'S BEEN THROUGH IN HIS TIME--IT'S LEFT HIM VULNERABLE!
DON'T LET UP NOW! WE CAN--
THWONK!

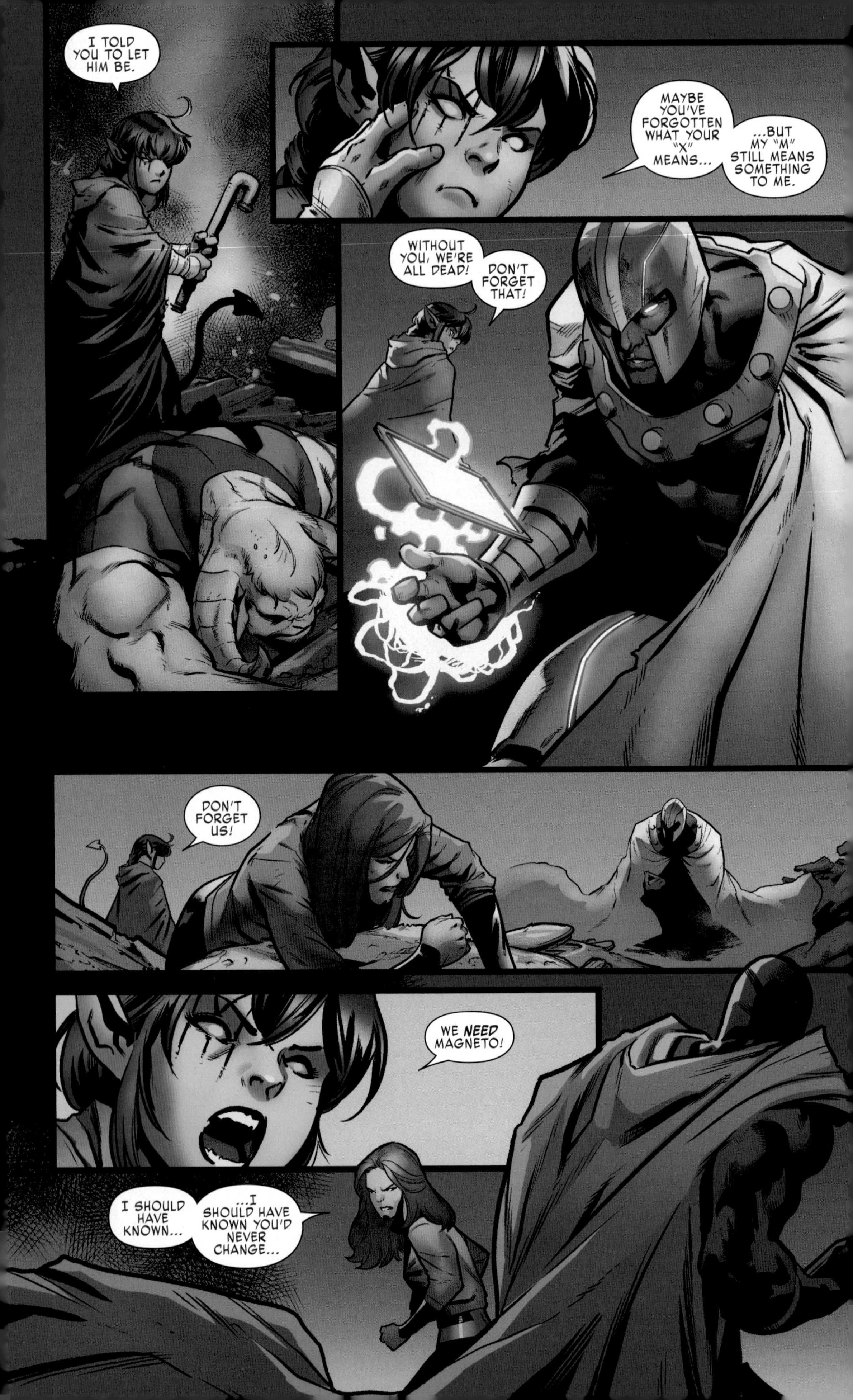
I TOLD YOU TO LET HIM BE.
MAYBE YOU'VE FORGOTTEN WHAT YOUR "X" MEANS...
...BUT MY "M" STILL MEANS SOMETHING TO ME.
WITHOUT YOU, WE'RE ALL DEAD!
DON'T FORGET THAT!
DON'T FORGET US!
WE NEED MAGNETO!
I SHOULD HAVE KNOWN...
...I SHOULD HAVE KNOWN YOU'D NEVER CHANGE...

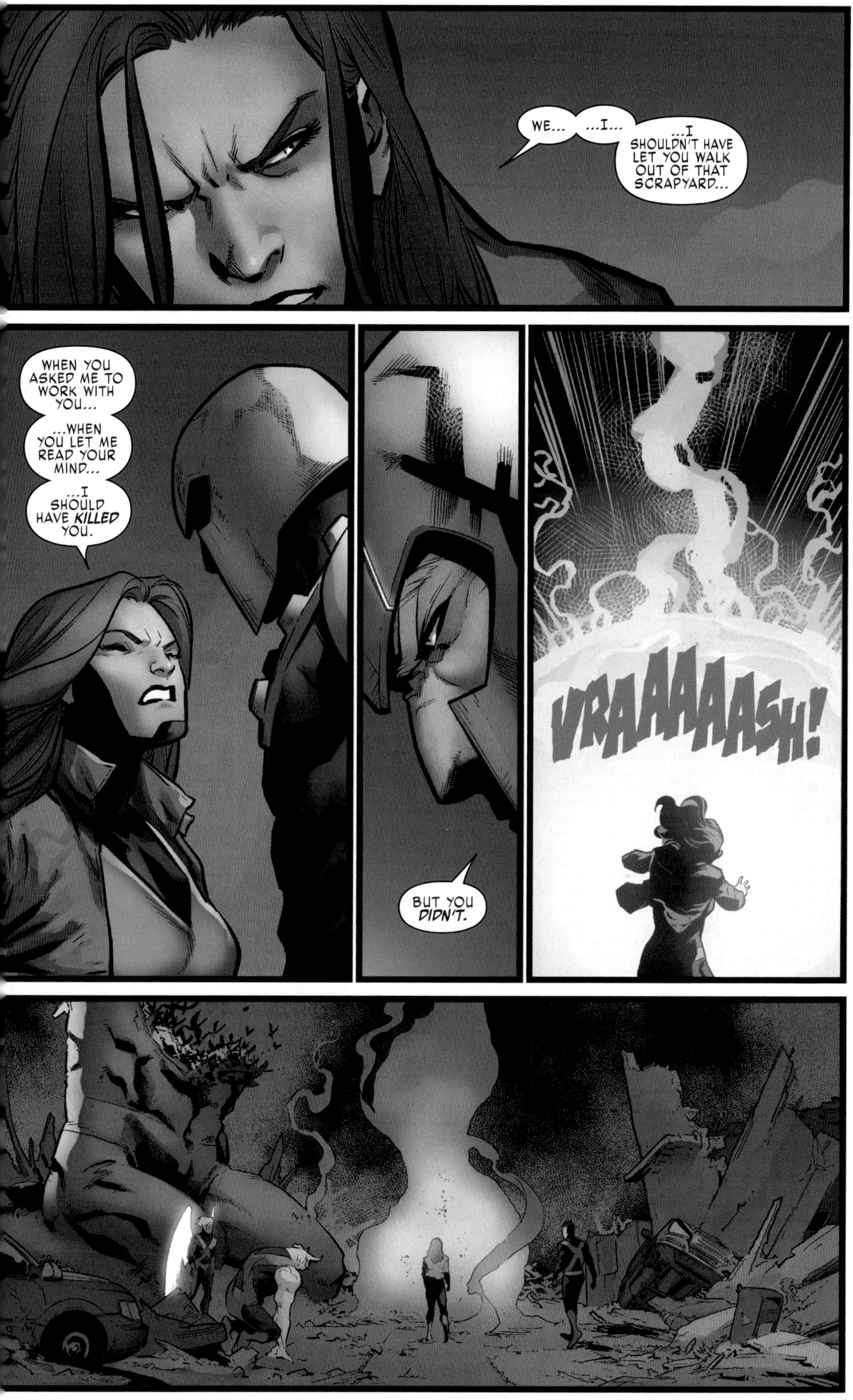
WE...
...I...
...I SHOULDN'T HAVE LET YOU WALK OUT OF THAT SCRAPYARD...
WHEN YOU ASKED ME TO WORK WITH YOU...
...WHEN YOU LET ME READ YOUR MIND...
...I SHOULD HAVE KILLED YOU.
BUT YOU DIDN'T.
VRAAAAASH!

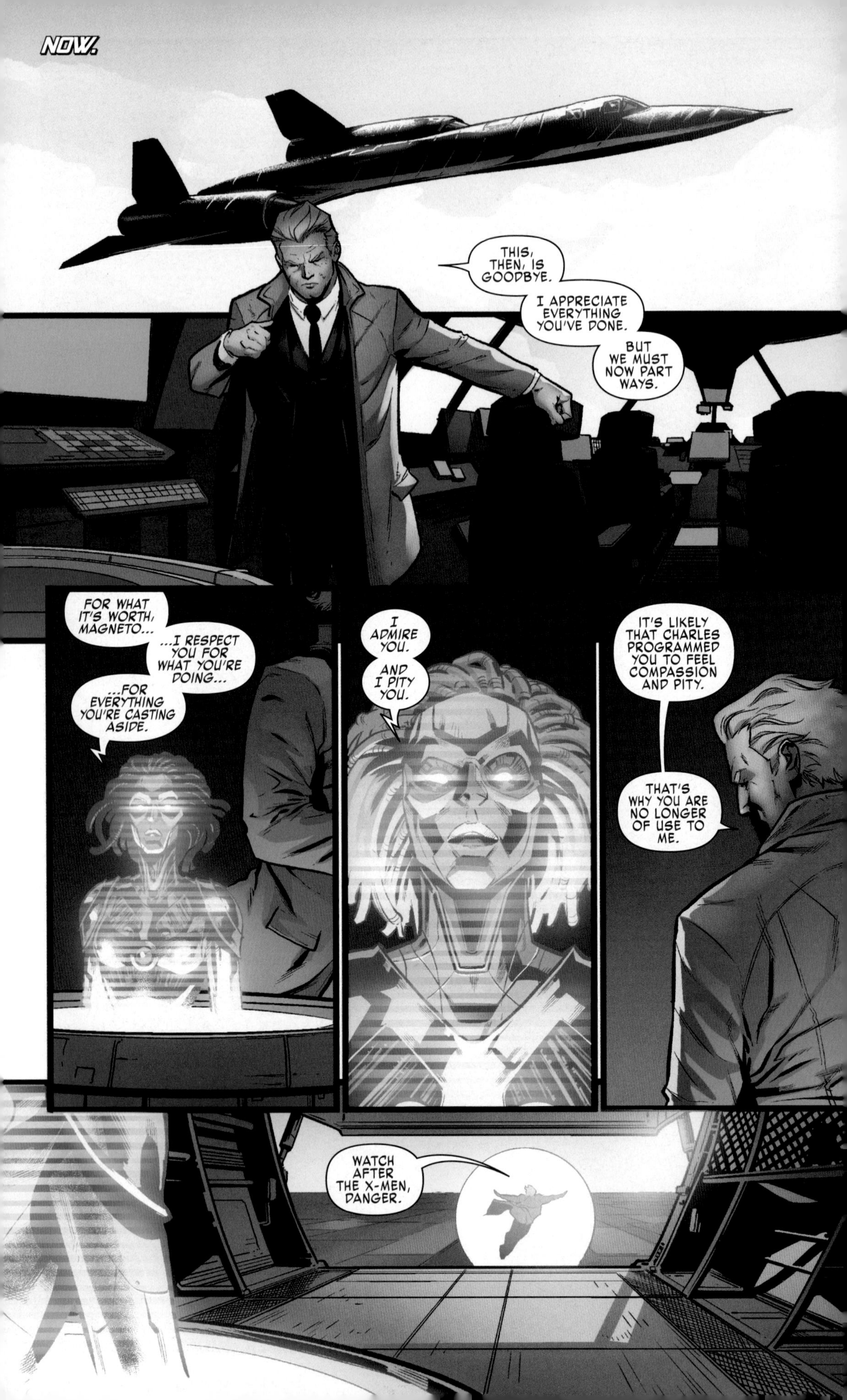
NOW.
THIS, THEN, IS GOODBYE.
I APPRECIATE EVERYTHING YOU'VE DONE.
BUT WE MUST NOW PART WAYS.
FOR WHAT IT'S WORTH, MAGNETO...
...I RESPECT YOU FOR WHAT YOU'RE DOING...
...FOR EVERYTHING YOU'RE CASTING ASIDE.
I ADMIRE YOU.
AND I PITY YOU.
IT'S LIKELY THAT CHARLES PROGRAMMED YOU TO FEEL COMPASSION AND PITY.
THAT'S WHY YOU ARE NO LONGER OF USE TO ME.
WATCH AFTER THE X-MEN, DANGER.

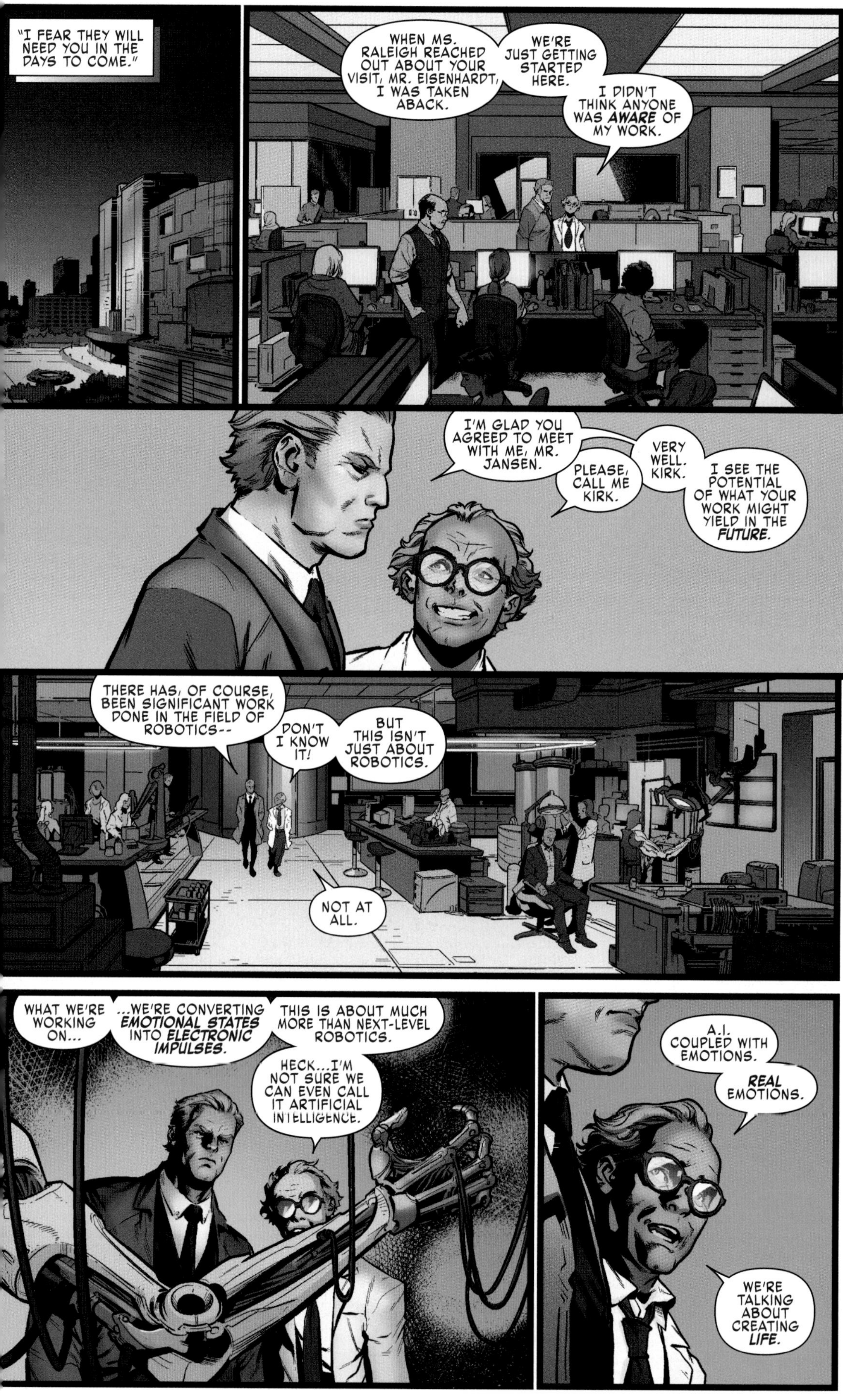
"I FEAR THEY WILL NEED YOU IN THE DAYS TO COME."
WHEN MS. RALEIGH REACHED OUT ABOUT YOUR VISIT, MR. EISENHARDT, I WAS TAKEN ABACK.
WE'RE JUST GETTING STARTED HERE.
I DIDN'T THINK ANYONE WAS AWARE OF MY WORK.
I'M GLAD YOU AGREED TO MEET WITH ME, MR. JANSEN.
PLEASE, CALL ME KIRK.
VERY WELL. KIRK.
I SEE THE POTENTIAL OF WHAT YOUR WORK MIGHT YIELD IN THE FUTURE.
THERE HAS, OF COURSE, BEEN SIGNIFICANT WORK DONE IN THE FIELD OF ROBOTICS--
DON'T I KNOW IT!
BUT THIS ISN'T JUST ABOUT ROBOTICS.
NOT AT ALL.
WHAT WE'RE WORKING ON...
...WE'RE CONVERTING EMOTIONAL STATES INTO ELECTRONIC IMPULSES.
THIS IS ABOUT MUCH MORE THAN NEXT-LEVEL ROBOTICS.
HECK...I'M NOT SURE WE CAN EVEN CALL IT ARTIFICIAL INTELLIGENCE.
A.I. COUPLED WITH EMOTIONS.
REAL EMOTIONS.
WE'RE TALKING ABOUT CREATING LIFE.

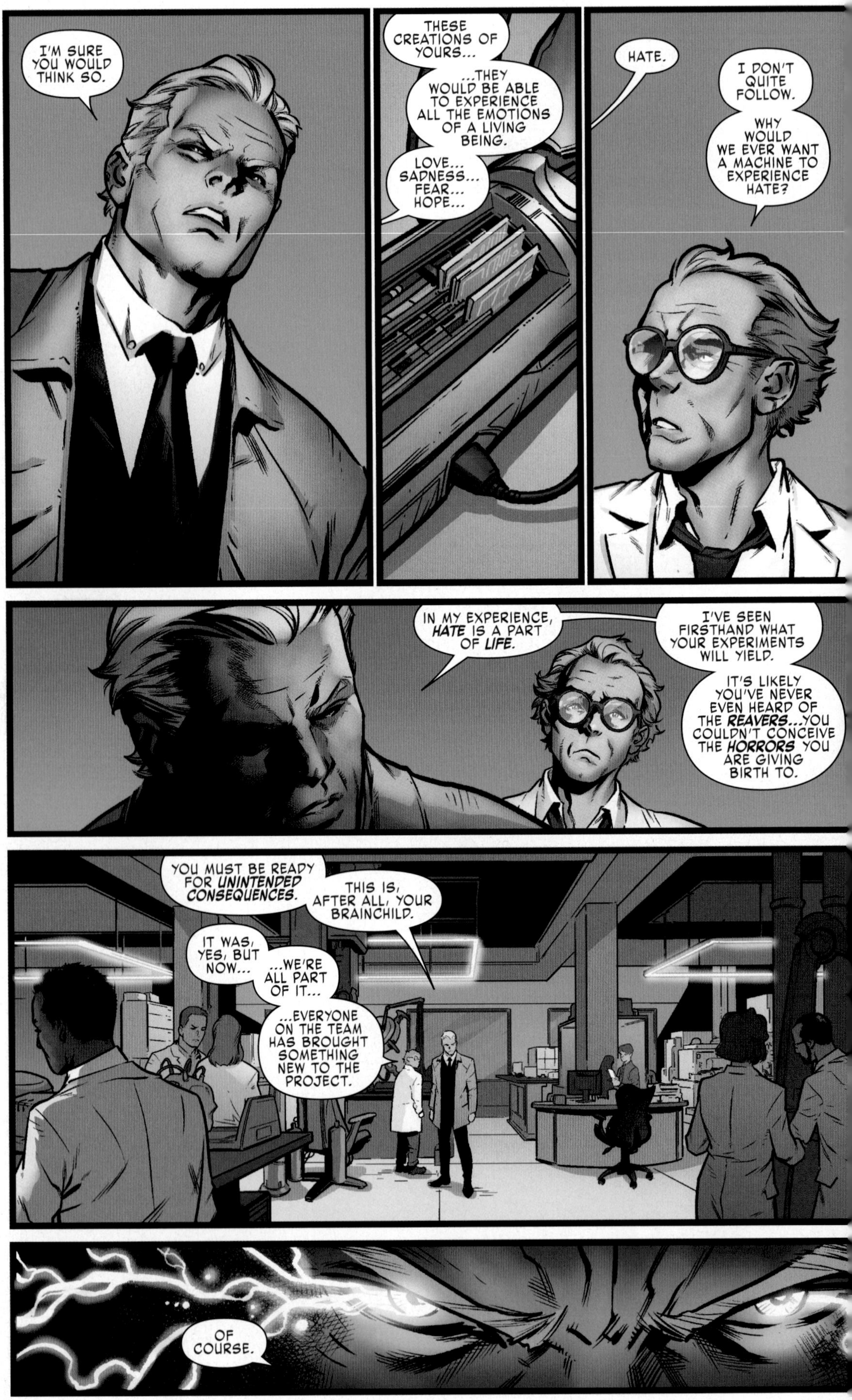

I'M SURE YOU WOULD THINK SO.
THESE CREATIONS OF YOURS...
...THEY WOULD BE ABLE TO EXPERIENCE ALL THE EMOTIONS OF A LIVING BEING.
LOVE... SADNESS... FEAR... HOPE...
HATE.
I DON'T QUITE FOLLOW.
WHY WOULD WE EVER WANT A MACHINE TO EXPERIENCE HATE?
IN MY EXPERIENCE, HATE IS A PART OF LIFE.
I'VE SEEN FIRSTHAND WHAT YOUR EXPERIMENTS WILL YIELD.
IT'S LIKELY YOU'VE NEVER EVEN HEARD OF THE REAVERS...YOU COULDN'T CONCEIVE THE HORRORS YOU ARE GIVING BIRTH TO.
YOU MUST BE READY FOR UNINTENDED CONSEQUENCES.
THIS IS, AFTER ALL, YOUR BRAINCHILD.
IT WAS, YES, BUT NOW...
...WE'RE ALL PART OF IT...
...EVERYONE ON THE TEAM HAS BROUGHT SOMETHING NEW TO THE PROJECT.
OF COURSE.

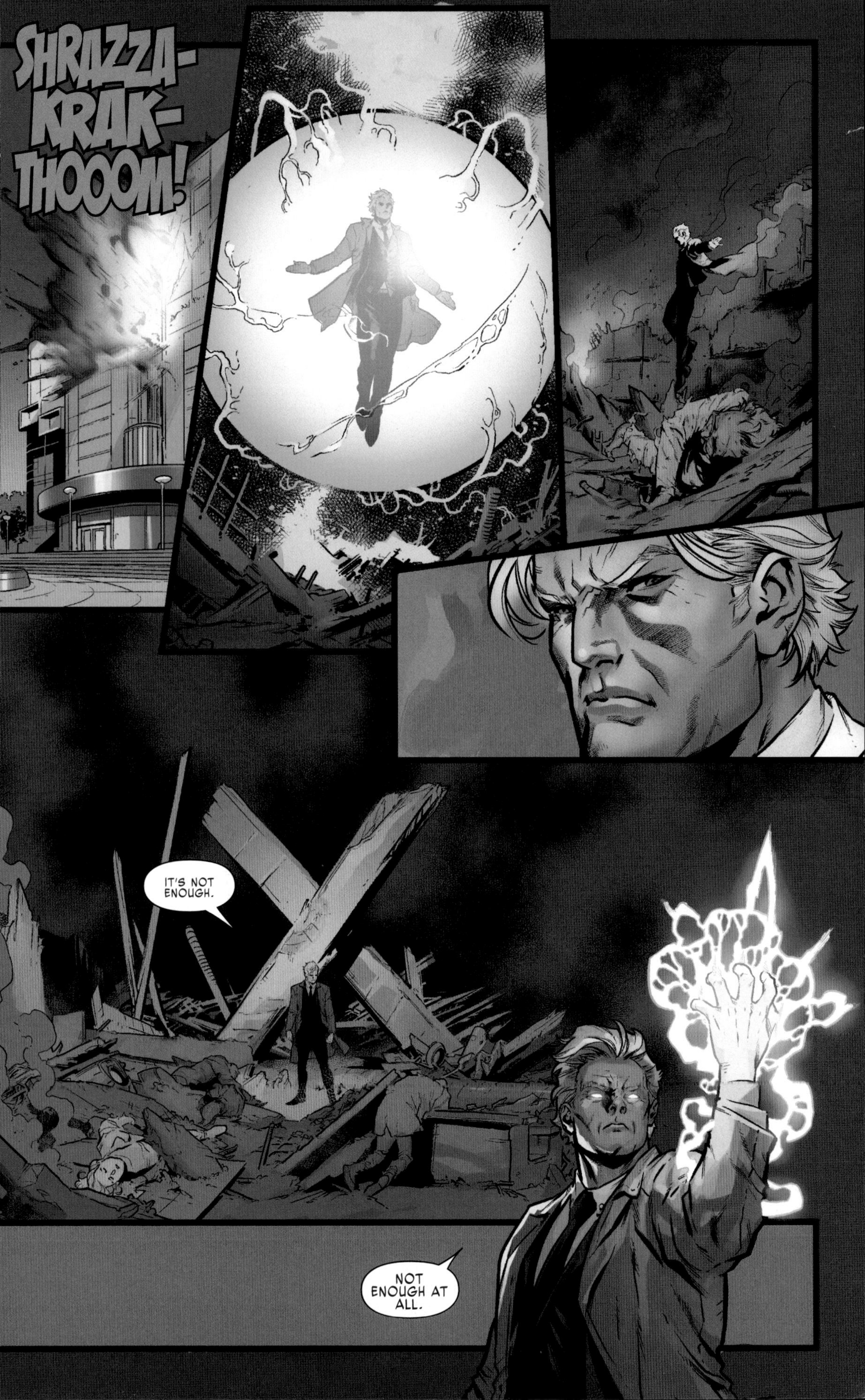
SHRAZZA-KRAK-THOOOM!
IT'S NOT ENOUGH.
NOT ENOUGH AT ALL.

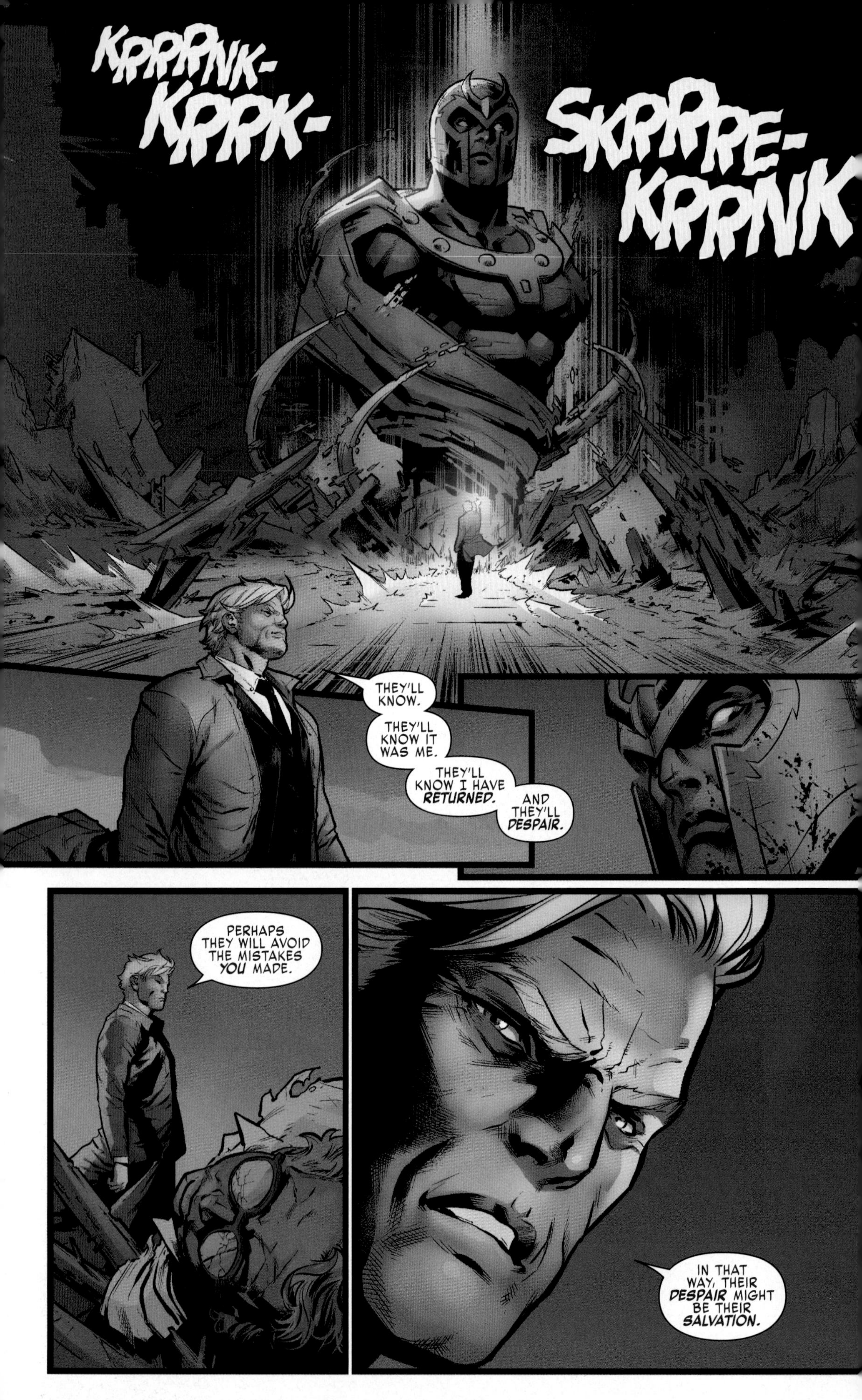
KRRRNK-
KRRRK-
SKRRRE-
KRRRNK
THEY'LL KNOW.
THEY'LL KNOW IT WAS ME.
THEY'LL KNOW I HAVE RETURNED.
AND THEY'LL DESPAIR.
PERHAPS THEY WILL AVOID THE MISTAKES YOU MADE.
IN THAT WAY, THEIR DESPAIR MIGHT BE THEIR SALVATION.

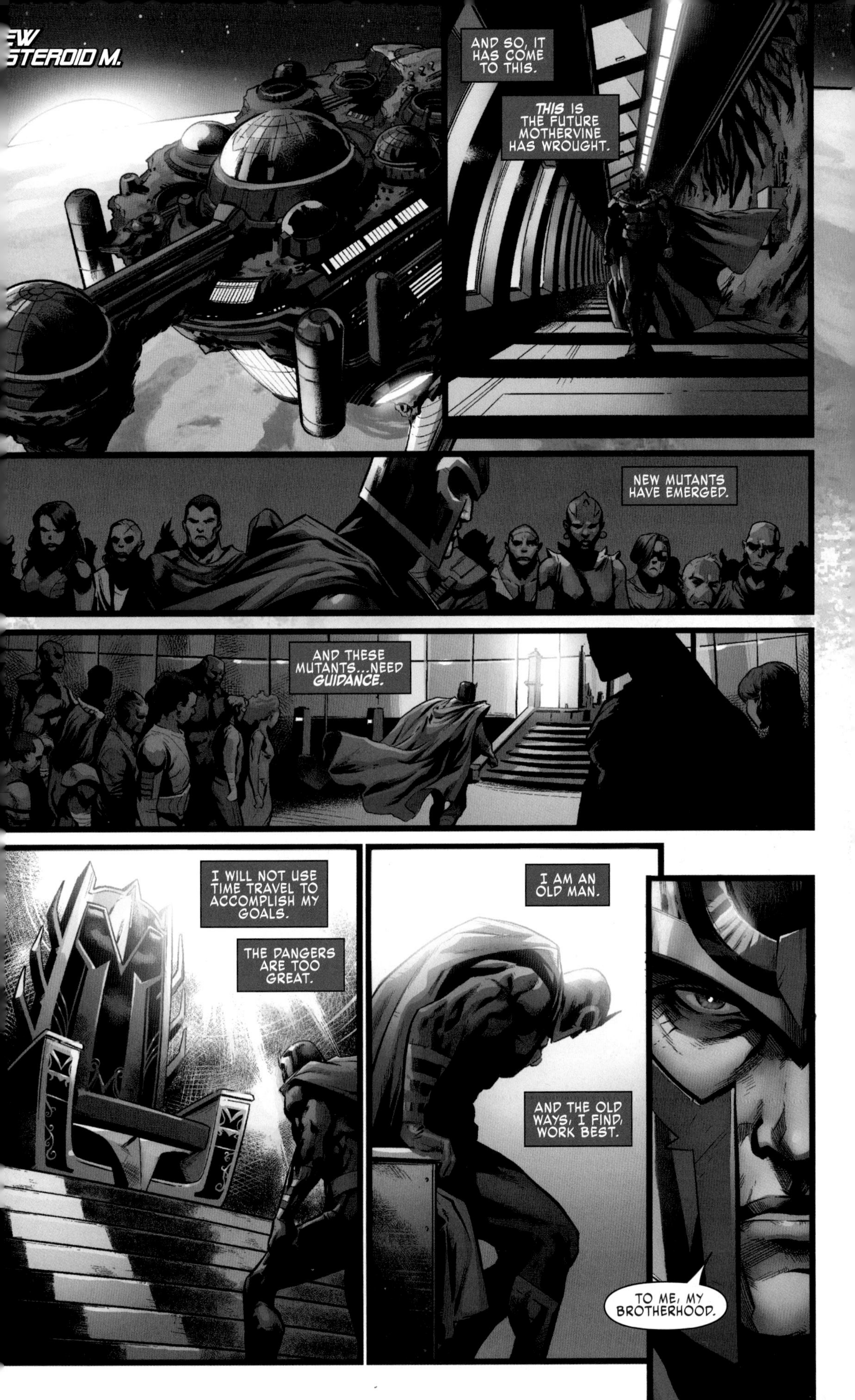
EW
STEROID M.
AND SO, IT HAS COME TO THIS.
THIS IS THE FUTURE MOTHERVINE HAS WROUGHT.
NEW MUTANTS HAVE EMERGED.
AND THESE MUTANTS...NEED GUIDANCE.
I WILL NOT USE TIME TRAVEL TO ACCOMPLISH MY GOALS.
THE DANGERS ARE TOO GREAT.
I AM AN OLD MAN.
AND THE OLD WAYS, I FIND, WORK BEST.
TO ME, MY BROTHERHOOD.

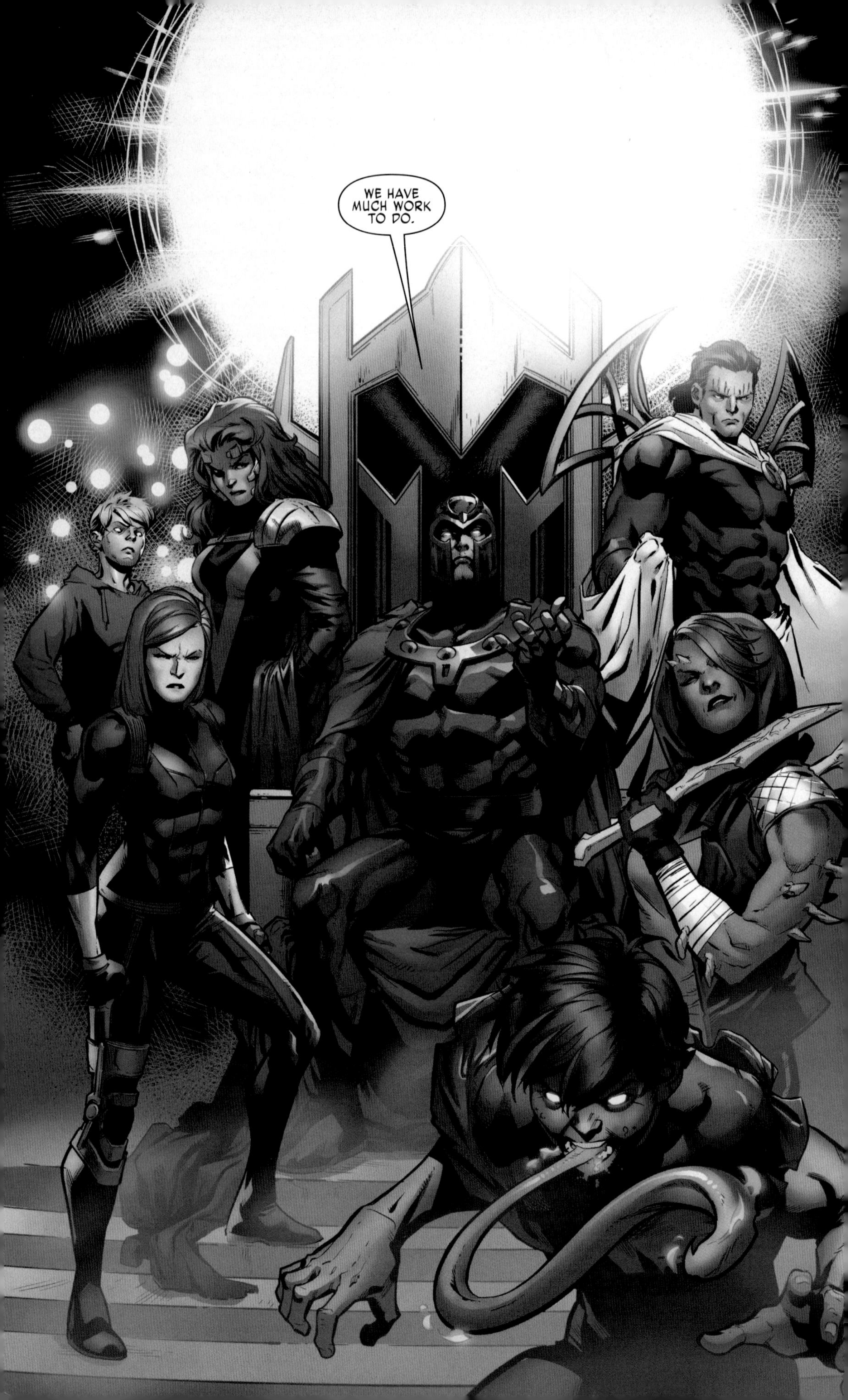
WE HAVE MUCH WORK TO DO.

35

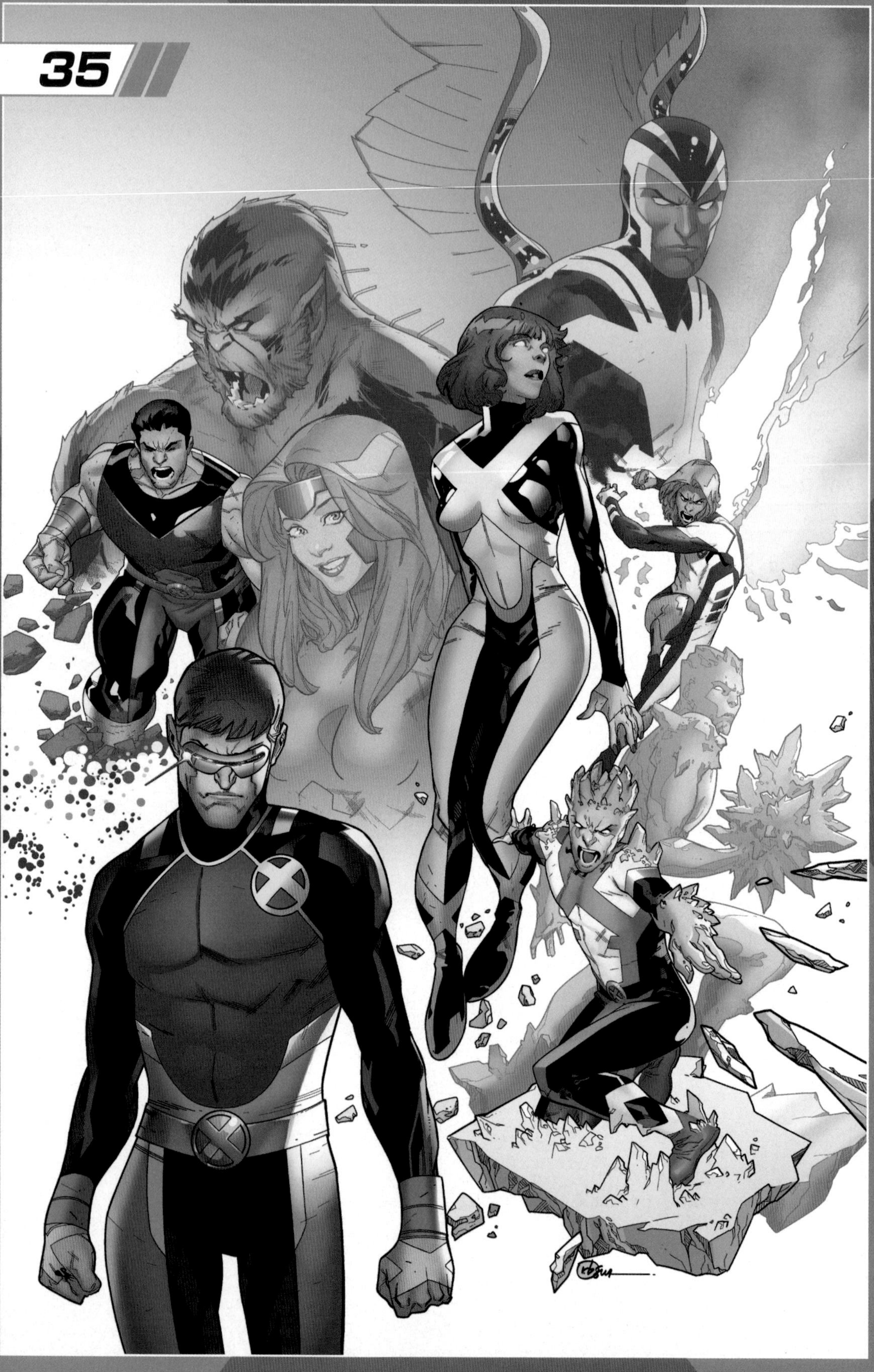

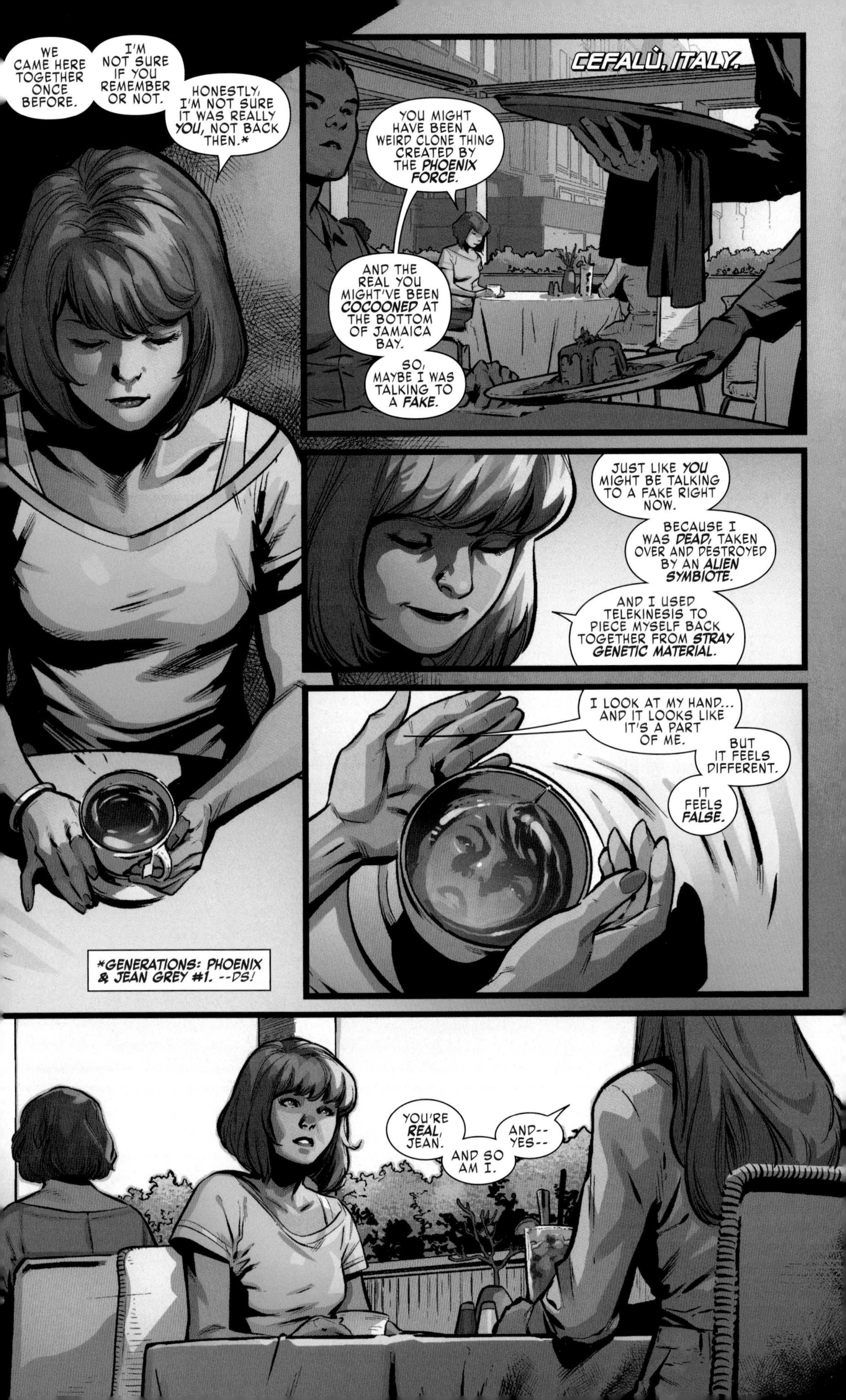
WE CAME HERE TOGETHER ONCE BEFORE.
I'M NOT SURE IF YOU REMEMBER OR NOT.
HONESTLY, I'M NOT SURE IT WAS REALLY YOU, NOT BACK THEN.*
CEFALÙ, ITALY.
YOU MIGHT HAVE BEEN A WEIRD CLONE THING CREATED BY THE PHOENIX FORCE.
AND THE REAL YOU MIGHT'VE BEEN COCOONED AT THE BOTTOM OF JAMAICA BAY.
SO, MAYBE I WAS TALKING TO A FAKE.
JUST LIKE YOU MIGHT BE TALKING TO A FAKE RIGHT NOW.
BECAUSE I WAS DEAD, TAKEN OVER AND DESTROYED BY AN ALIEN SYMBIOTE.
AND I USED TELEKINESIS TO PIECE MYSELF BACK TOGETHER FROM STRAY GENETIC MATERIAL.
I LOOK AT MY HAND... AND IT LOOKS LIKE IT'S A PART OF ME.
BUT IT FEELS DIFFERENT.
IT FEELS FALSE.
*GENERATIONS: PHOENIX & JEAN GREY #1. --DS!
YOU'RE REAL, JEAN.
AND SO AM I.
AND-- YES--

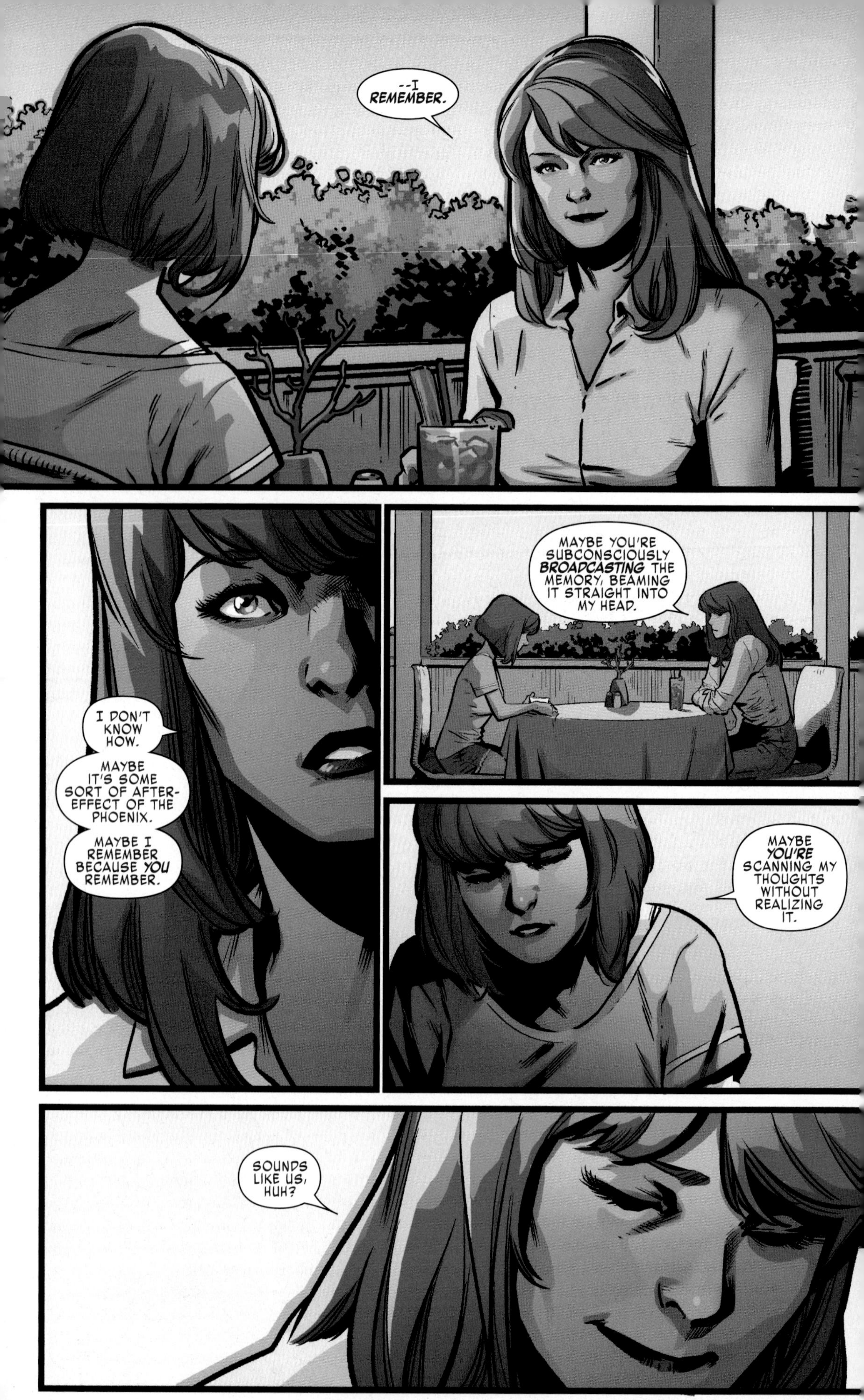
--I REMEMBER.
MAYBE YOU'RE SUBCONSCIOUSLY BROADCASTING THE MEMORY, BEAMING IT STRAIGHT INTO MY HEAD.
I DON'T KNOW HOW.
MAYBE IT'S SOME SORT OF AFTER-EFFECT OF THE PHOENIX.
MAYBE I REMEMBER BECAUSE YOU REMEMBER.
MAYBE YOU'RE SCANNING MY THOUGHTS WITHOUT REALIZING IT.
SOUNDS LIKE US, HUH?

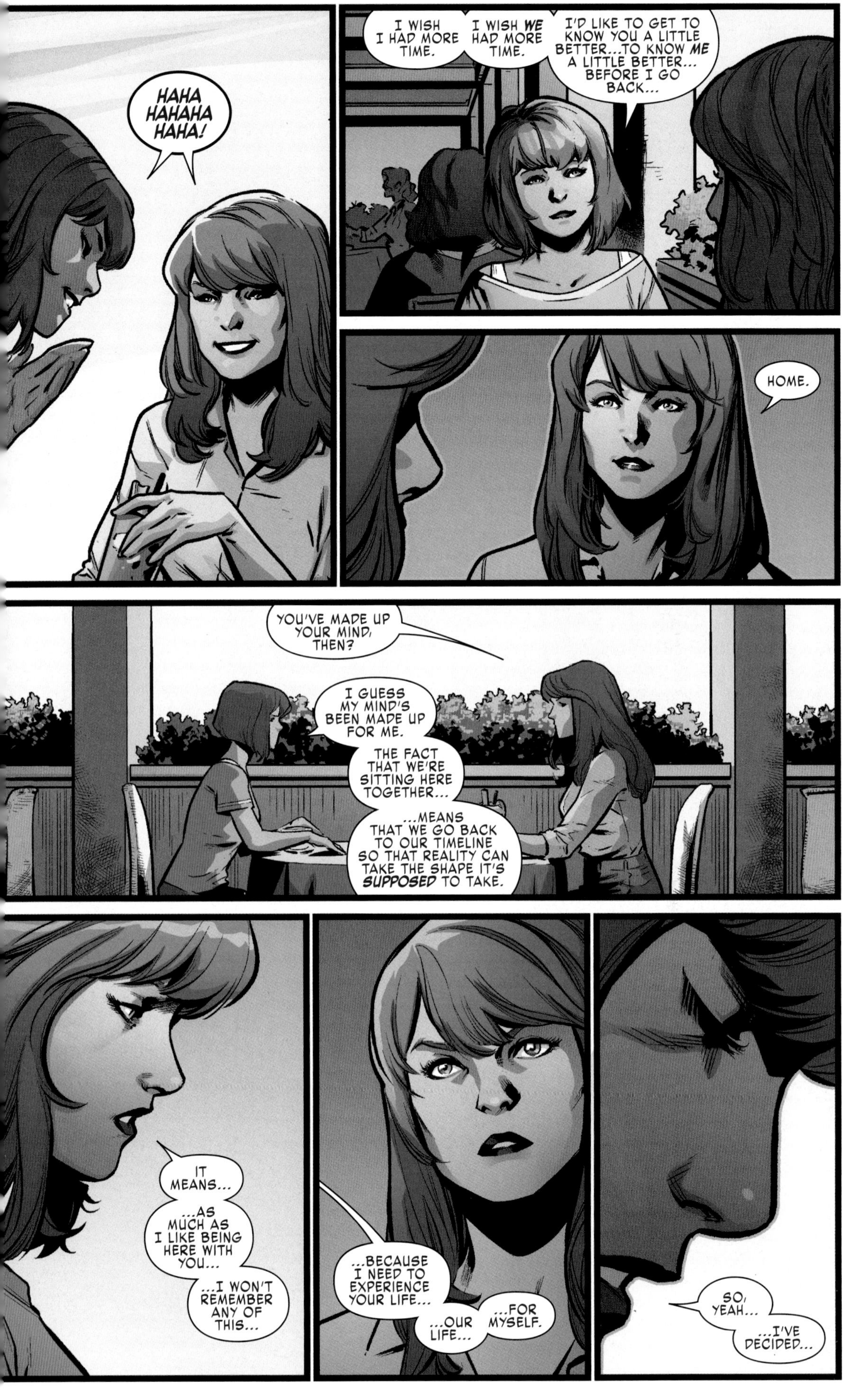
HAHA HAHAHA HAHA!
I WISH I HAD MORE TIME.
I WISH WE HAD MORE TIME.
I'D LIKE TO GET TO KNOW YOU A LITTLE BETTER...TO KNOW ME A LITTLE BETTER... BEFORE I GO BACK...
HOME.
YOU'VE MADE UP YOUR MIND, THEN?
I GUESS MY MIND'S BEEN MADE UP FOR ME.
THE FACT THAT WE'RE SITTING HERE TOGETHER...
...MEANS THAT WE GO BACK TO OUR TIMELINE SO THAT REALITY CAN TAKE THE SHAPE IT'S SUPPOSED TO TAKE.
IT MEANS...
...AS MUCH AS I LIKE BEING HERE WITH YOU...
...I WON'T REMEMBER ANY OF THIS...
...BECAUSE I NEED TO EXPERIENCE YOUR LIFE...
...OUR LIFE...
...FOR MYSELF.
SO, YEAH...
...I'VE DECIDED...

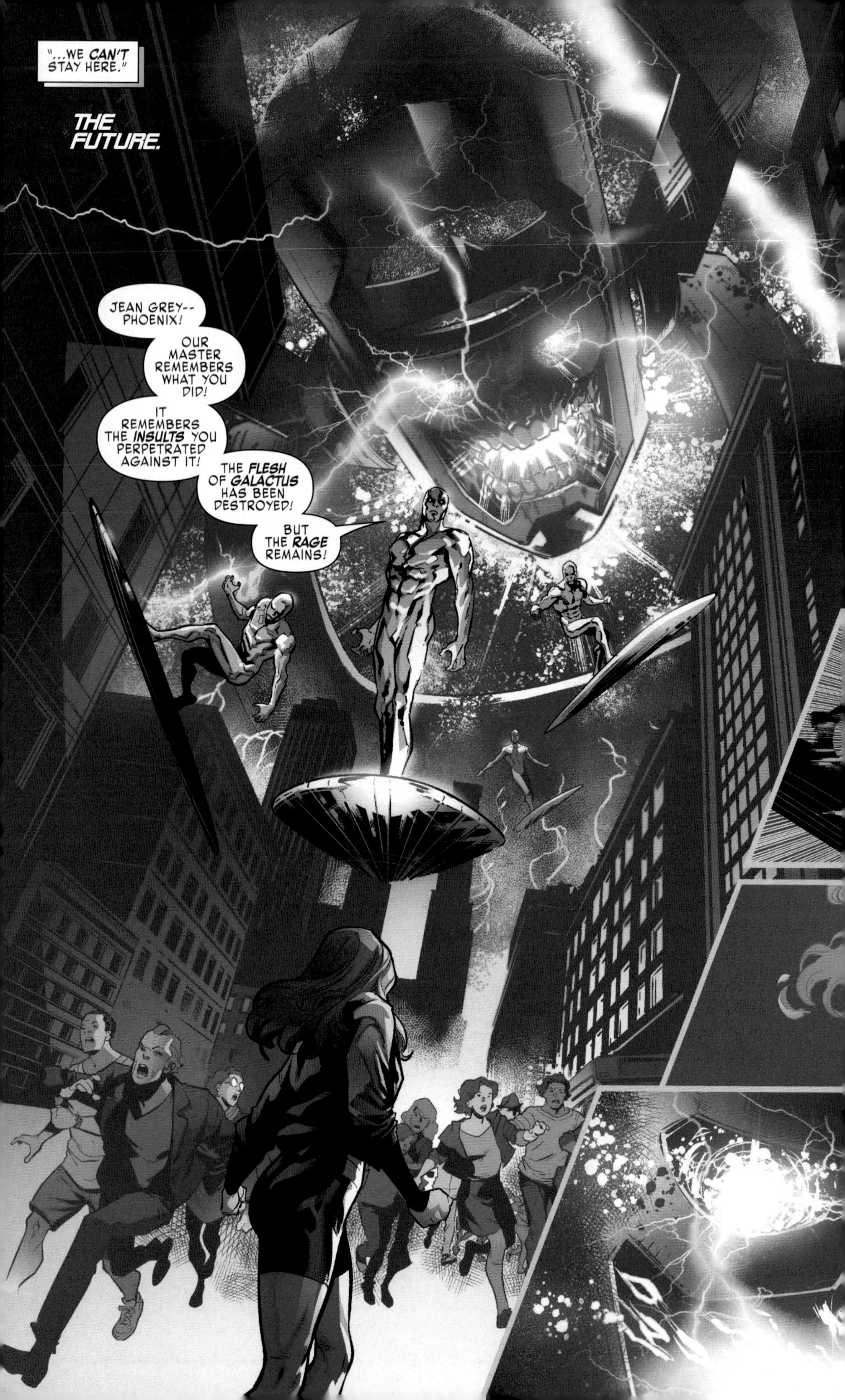
"...WE CAN'T STAY HERE."
THE FUTURE.
JEAN GREY--PHOENIX!
OUR MASTER REMEMBERS WHAT YOU DID!
IT REMEMBERS THE INSULTS YOU PERPETRATED AGAINST IT!
THE FLESH OF GALACTUS HAS BEEN DESTROYED!
BUT THE RAGE REMAINS!

AND NOW THE EARTH MUST DIE!
AND YOU FIRST OF ALL!
SHOOM!
SHRA-SHROOM!
THOOM!
YOU'RE NOT SERIOUS.
GALACTUS AS COME HERE...
..COME TO ESTROY THE PLANET...
...ALL BECAUSE I PUNCHED HIM ONCE?
I'VE GOT BAD NEWS FOR HIM.
HIS PRIDE'S ABOUT TO TAKE ANOTHER HIT.

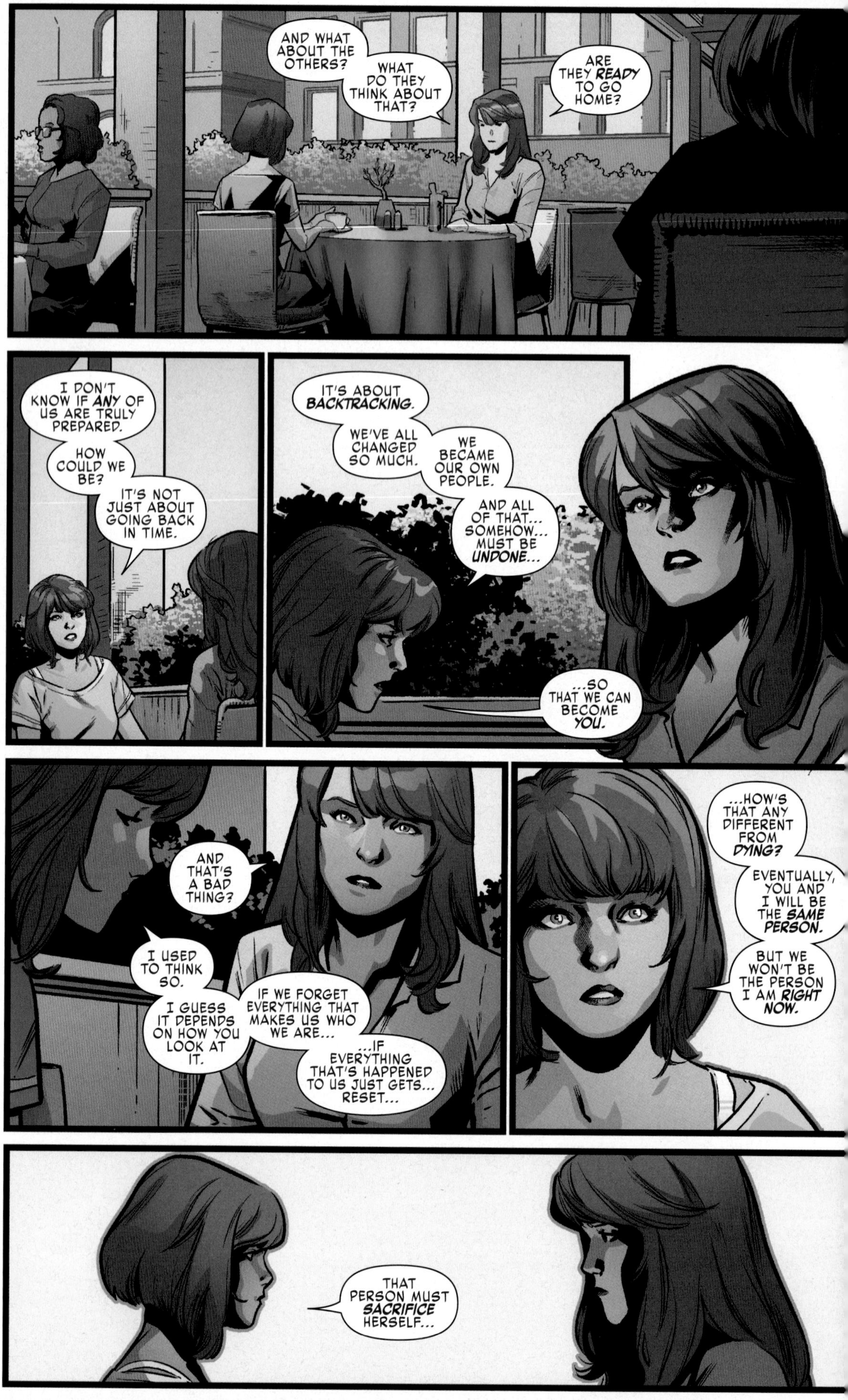
AND WHAT ABOUT THE OTHERS?
WHAT DO THEY THINK ABOUT THAT?
ARE THEY READY TO GO HOME?
I DON'T KNOW IF ANY OF US ARE TRULY PREPARED.
HOW COULD WE BE?
IT'S NOT JUST ABOUT GOING BACK IN TIME.
IT'S ABOUT BACKTRACKING.
WE'VE ALL CHANGED SO MUCH.
WE BECAME OUR OWN PEOPLE.
AND ALL OF THAT... SOMEHOW... MUST BE UNDONE...
...SO THAT WE CAN BECOME YOU.
AND THAT'S A BAD THING?
I USED TO THINK SO.
I GUESS IT DEPENDS ON HOW YOU LOOK AT IT.
IF WE FORGET EVERYTHING THAT MAKES US WHO WE ARE...
...IF EVERYTHING THAT'S HAPPENED TO US JUST GETS... RESET...
...HOW'S THAT ANY DIFFERENT FROM DYING?
EVENTUALLY, YOU AND I WILL BE THE SAME PERSON.
BUT WE WON'T BE THE PERSON I AM RIGHT NOW.
THAT PERSON MUST SACRIFICE HERSELF...

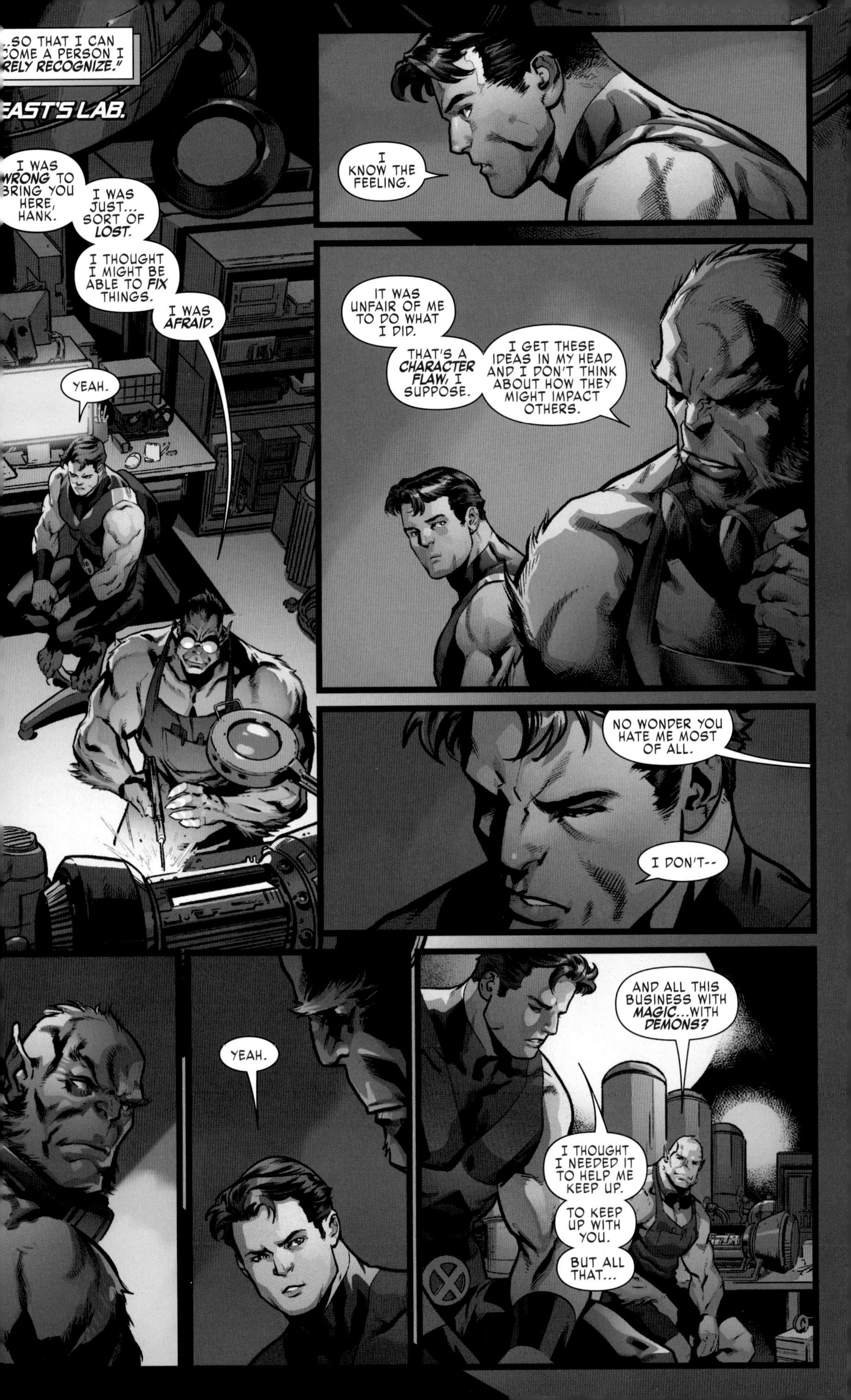
..SO THAT I CAN
COME A PERSON I
RELY RECOGNIZE."
EAST'S LAB.
I WAS WRONG TO BRING YOU HERE, HANK.
I WAS JUST... SORT OF LOST.
I THOUGHT I MIGHT BE ABLE TO FIX THINGS.
I WAS AFRAID.
YEAH.
I KNOW THE FEELING.
IT WAS UNFAIR OF ME TO DO WHAT I DID.
THAT'S A CHARACTER FLAW, I SUPPOSE.
I GET THESE IDEAS IN MY HEAD AND I DON'T THINK ABOUT HOW THEY MIGHT IMPACT OTHERS.
NO WONDER YOU HATE ME MOST OF ALL.
I DON'T--
YEAH.
AND ALL THIS BUSINESS WITH MAGIC...WITH DEMONS?
I THOUGHT I NEEDED IT TO HELP ME KEEP UP.
TO KEEP UP WITH YOU.
BUT ALL THAT...

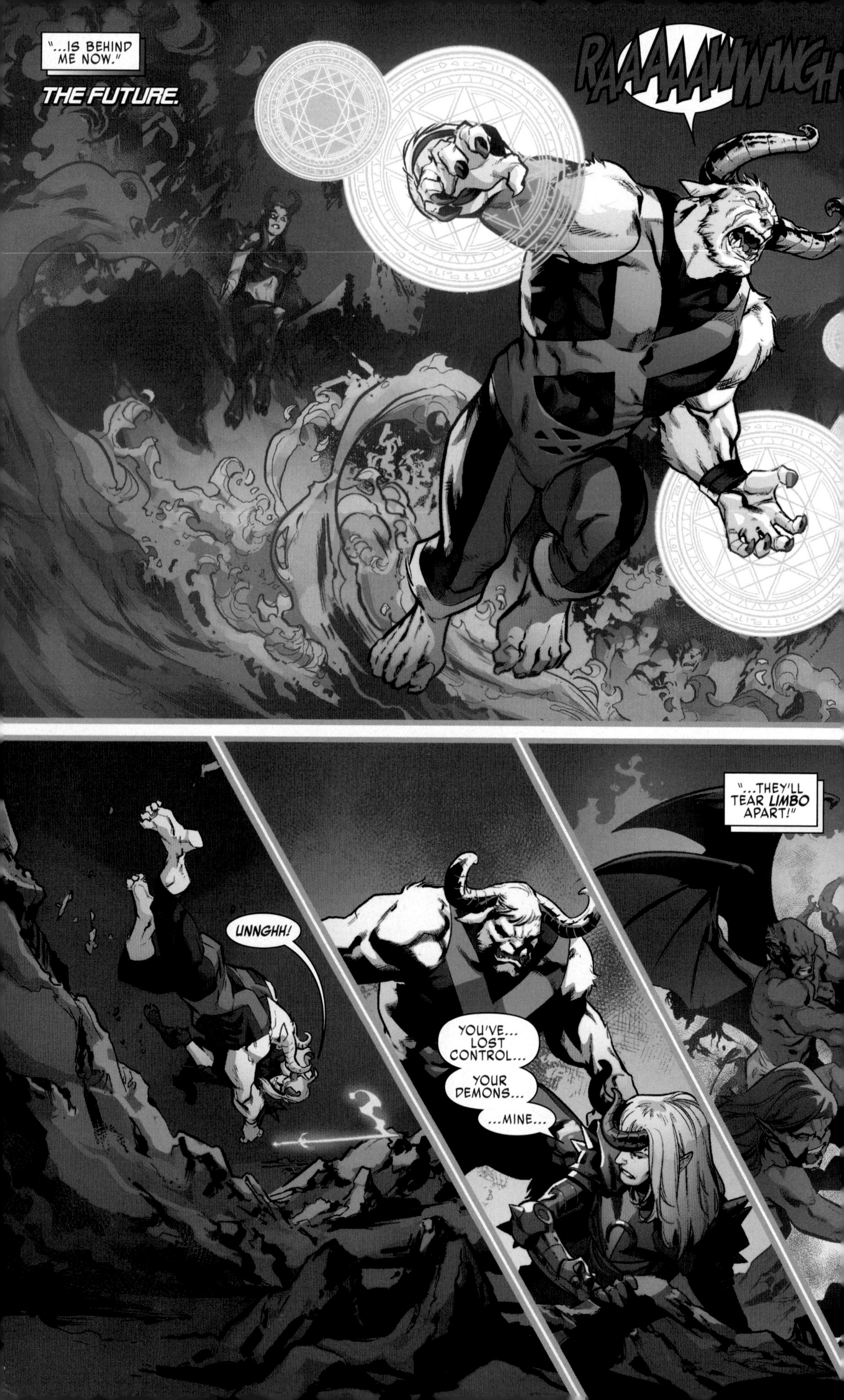
"...IS BEHIND ME NOW."
THE FUTURE.
RAAAAAWWWGH
UNNGHH!
YOU'VE... LOST CONTROL...
YOUR DEMONS...
...MINE...
"...THEY'LL TEAR LIMBO APART!"

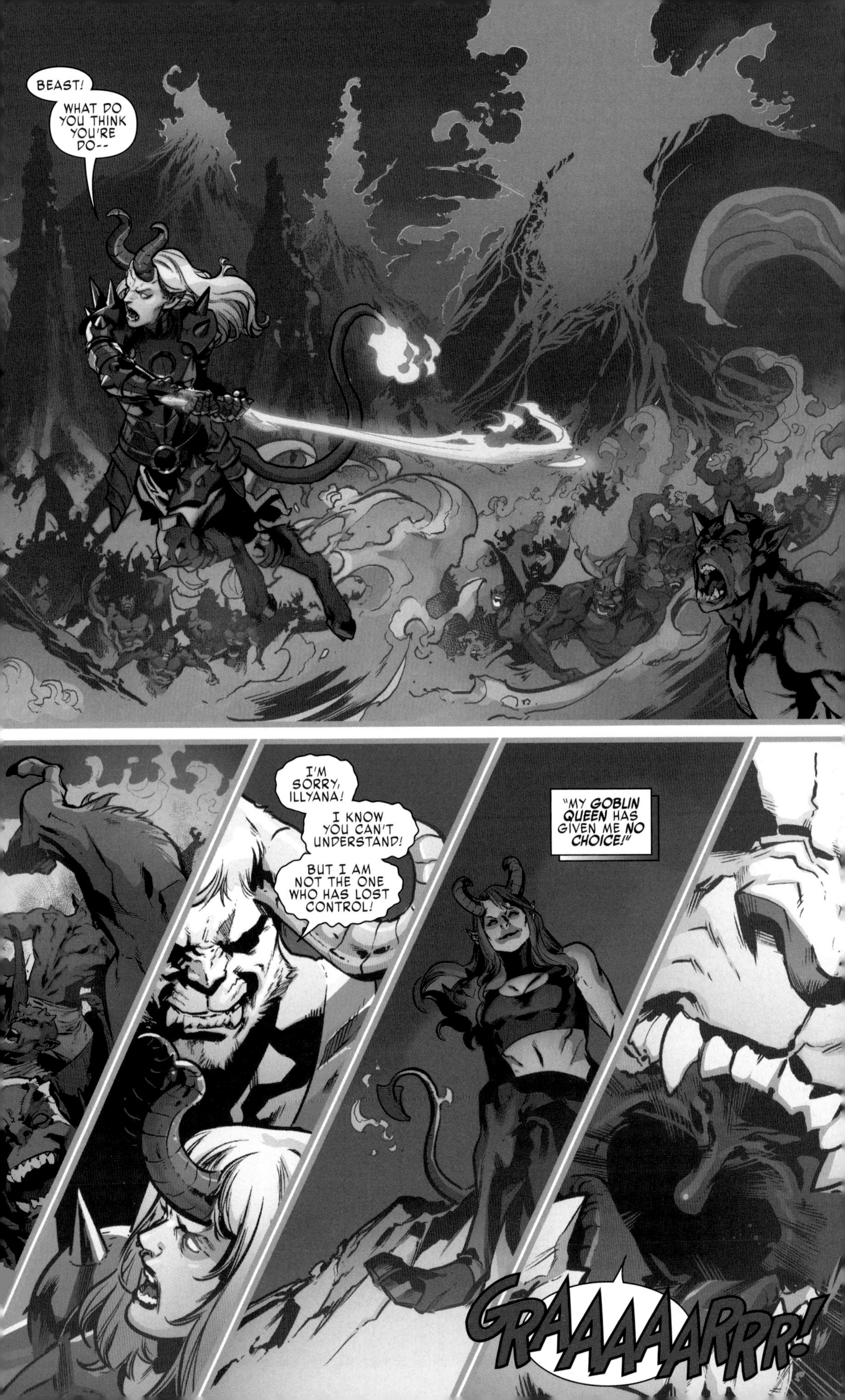
BEAST!
WHAT DO YOU THINK YOU'RE DO--
I'M SORRY, ILLYANA!
I KNOW YOU CAN'T UNDERSTAND!
BUT I AM NOT THE ONE WHO HAS LOST CONTROL!
"MY GOBLIN QUEEN HAS GIVEN ME NO CHOICE!"
GRAAAAARRR!

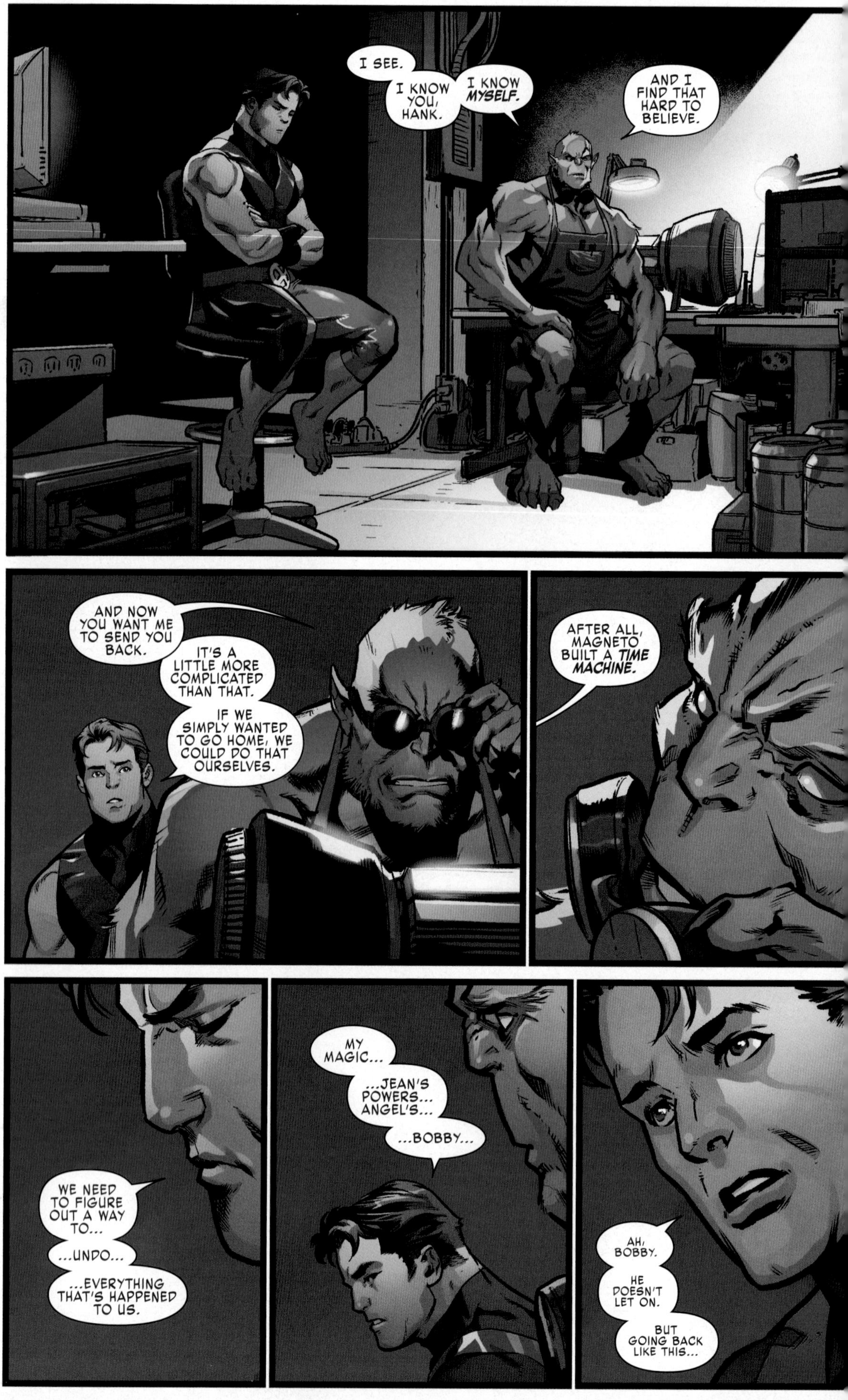

I SEE.
I KNOW YOU, HANK.
I KNOW *MYSELF.*
AND I FIND THAT HARD TO BELIEVE.
AND NOW YOU WANT ME TO SEND YOU BACK.
IT'S A LITTLE MORE COMPLICATED THAN THAT.
IF WE SIMPLY WANTED TO GO HOME, WE COULD DO THAT OURSELVES.
AFTER ALL, MAGNETO BUILT A *TIME MACHINE.*
WE NEED TO FIGURE OUT A WAY TO...
...UNDO...
...EVERYTHING THAT'S HAPPENED TO US.
MY MAGIC...
...JEAN'S POWERS... ANGEL'S...
...BOBBY...
AH, BOBBY.
HE DOESN'T LET ON.
BUT GOING BACK LIKE THIS...

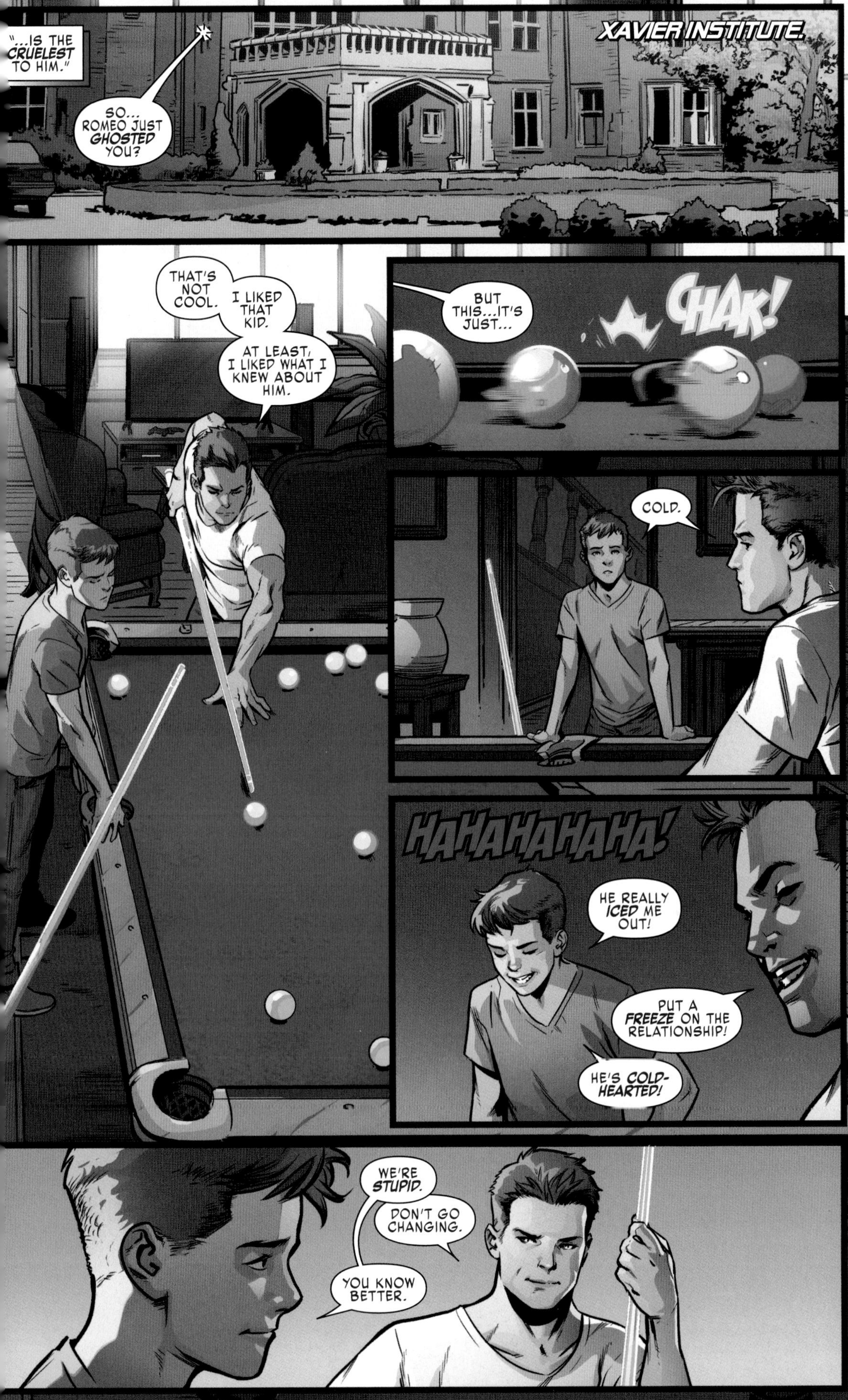
"...IS THE CRUELEST TO HIM."
XAVIER INSTITUTE.
SO... ROMEO JUST GHOSTED YOU?
THAT'S NOT COOL.
I LIKED THAT KID.
AT LEAST, I LIKED WHAT I KNEW ABOUT HIM.
BUT THIS...IT'S JUST...
CHAK!
COLD.
HAHAHAHAHAHA!
HE REALLY ICED ME OUT!
PUT A FREEZE ON THE RELATIONSHIP!
HE'S COLD-HEARTED!
WE'RE STUPID.
DON'T GO CHANGING.
YOU KNOW BETTER.

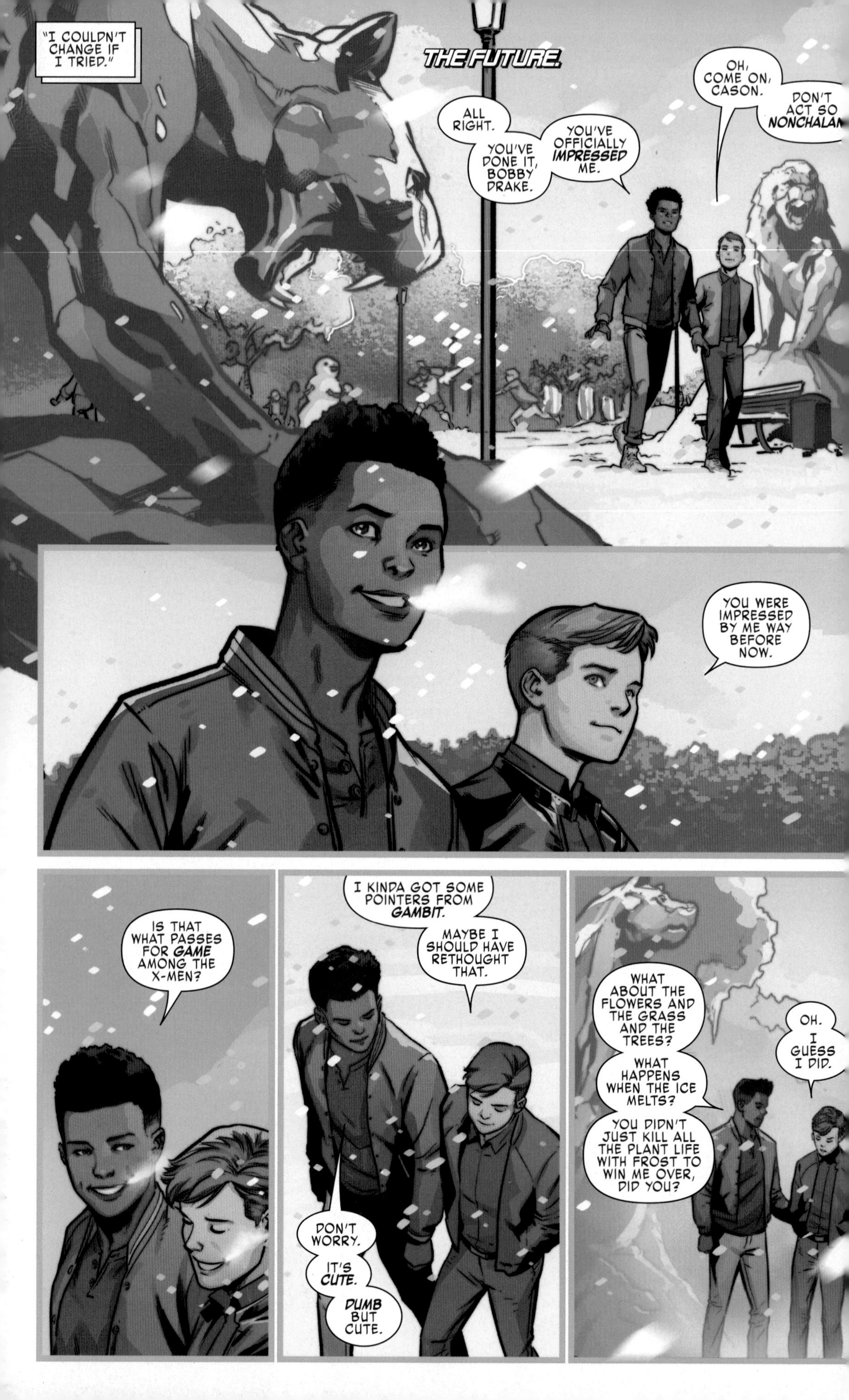
"I COULDN'T CHANGE IF I TRIED."
THE FUTURE.
ALL RIGHT.
YOU'VE DONE IT, BOBBY DRAKE.
YOU'VE OFFICIALLY IMPRESSED ME.
OH, COME ON, CASON.
DON'T ACT SO NONCHALAN
YOU WERE IMPRESSED BY ME WAY BEFORE NOW.
IS THAT WHAT PASSES FOR GAME AMONG THE X-MEN?
I KINDA GOT SOME POINTERS FROM GAMBIT.
MAYBE I SHOULD HAVE RETHOUGHT THAT.
DON'T WORRY.
IT'S CUTE.
DUMB BUT CUTE.
WHAT ABOUT THE FLOWERS AND THE GRASS AND THE TREES?
WHAT HAPPENS WHEN THE ICE MELTS?
YOU DIDN'T JUST KILL ALL THE PLANT LIFE WITH FROST TO WIN ME OVER, DID YOU?
OH.
I GUESS I DID.

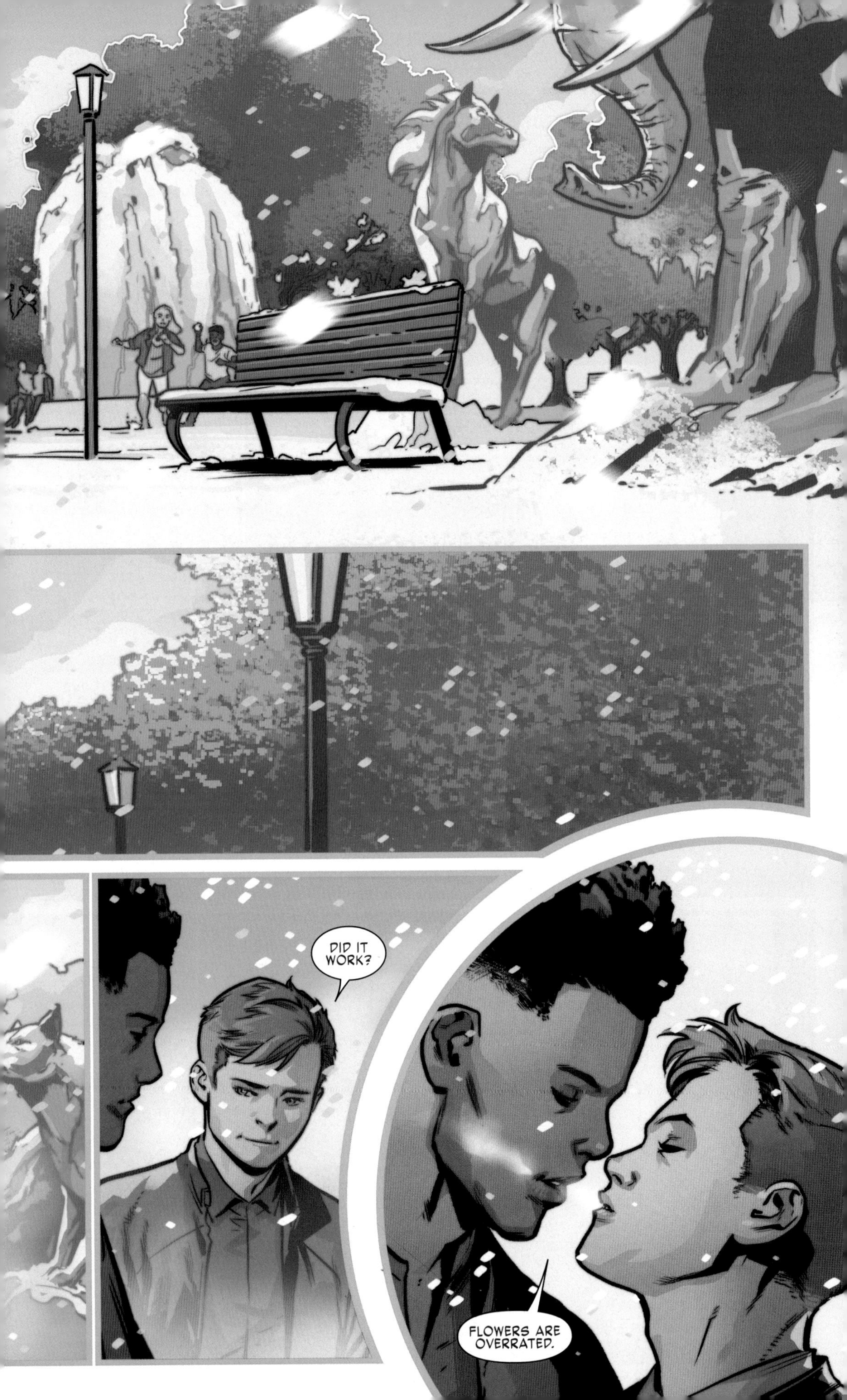
DID IT WORK?
FLOWERS ARE OVERRATED.

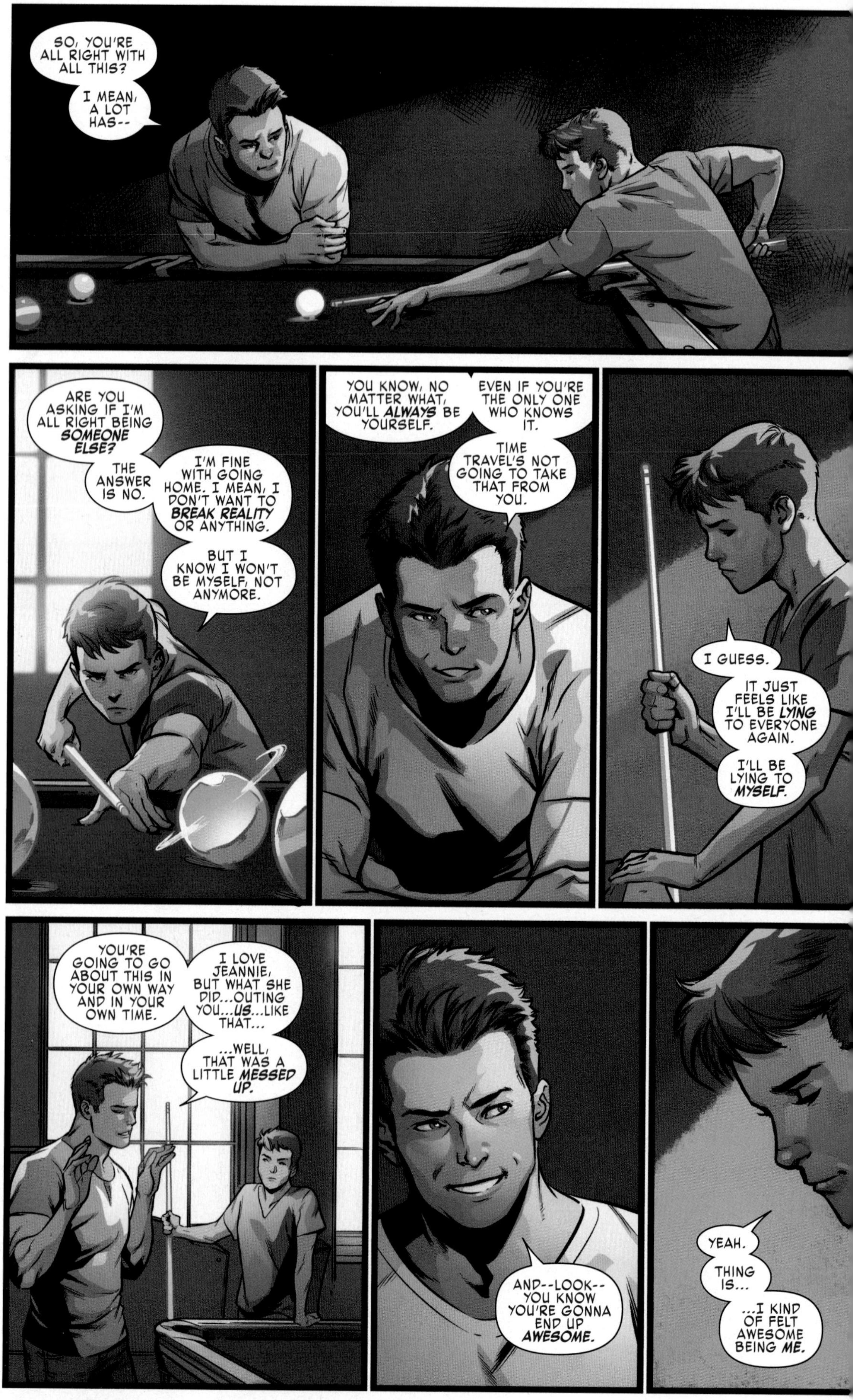
SO, YOU'RE ALL RIGHT WITH ALL THIS?
I MEAN, A LOT HAS--
ARE YOU ASKING IF I'M ALL RIGHT BEING SOMEONE ELSE?
THE ANSWER IS NO.
I'M FINE WITH GOING HOME. I MEAN, I DON'T WANT TO BREAK REALITY OR ANYTHING.
BUT I KNOW I WON'T BE MYSELF, NOT ANYMORE.
YOU KNOW, NO MATTER WHAT, YOU'LL ALWAYS BE YOURSELF.
EVEN IF YOU'RE THE ONLY ONE WHO KNOWS IT.
TIME TRAVEL'S NOT GOING TO TAKE THAT FROM YOU.
I GUESS.
IT JUST FEELS LIKE I'LL BE LYING TO EVERYONE AGAIN.
I'LL BE LYING TO MYSELF.
YOU'RE GOING TO GO ABOUT THIS IN YOUR OWN WAY AND IN YOUR OWN TIME.
I LOVE JEANNIE, BUT WHAT SHE DID...OUTING YOU...US...LIKE THAT...
...WELL, THAT WAS A LITTLE MESSED UP.
AND--LOOK--YOU KNOW YOU'RE GONNA END UP AWESOME.
YEAH.
THING IS...
...I KIND OF FELT AWESOME BEING ME.

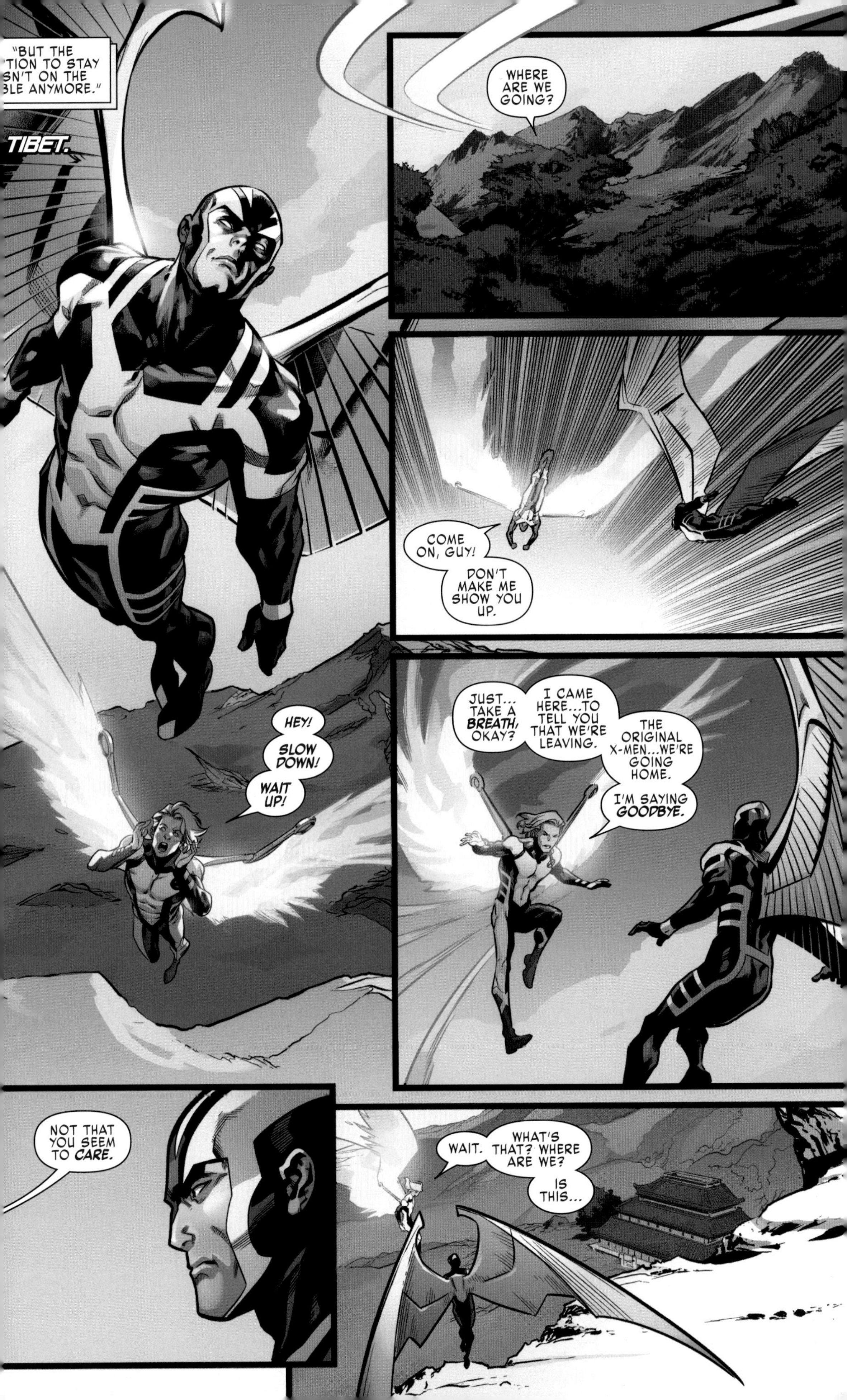
"BUT THE
TION TO STAY
SN'T ON THE
BLE ANYMORE."
TIBET.
WHERE ARE WE GOING?
COME ON, GUY!
DON'T MAKE ME SHOW YOU UP.
HEY!
SLOW DOWN!
WAIT UP!
JUST... TAKE A BREATH, OKAY?
I CAME HERE...TO TELL YOU THAT WE'RE LEAVING.
THE ORIGINAL X-MEN...WE'RE GOING HOME.
I'M SAYING GOODBYE.
NOT THAT YOU SEEM TO CARE.
WAIT.
WHAT'S THAT? WHERE ARE WE?
IS THIS...

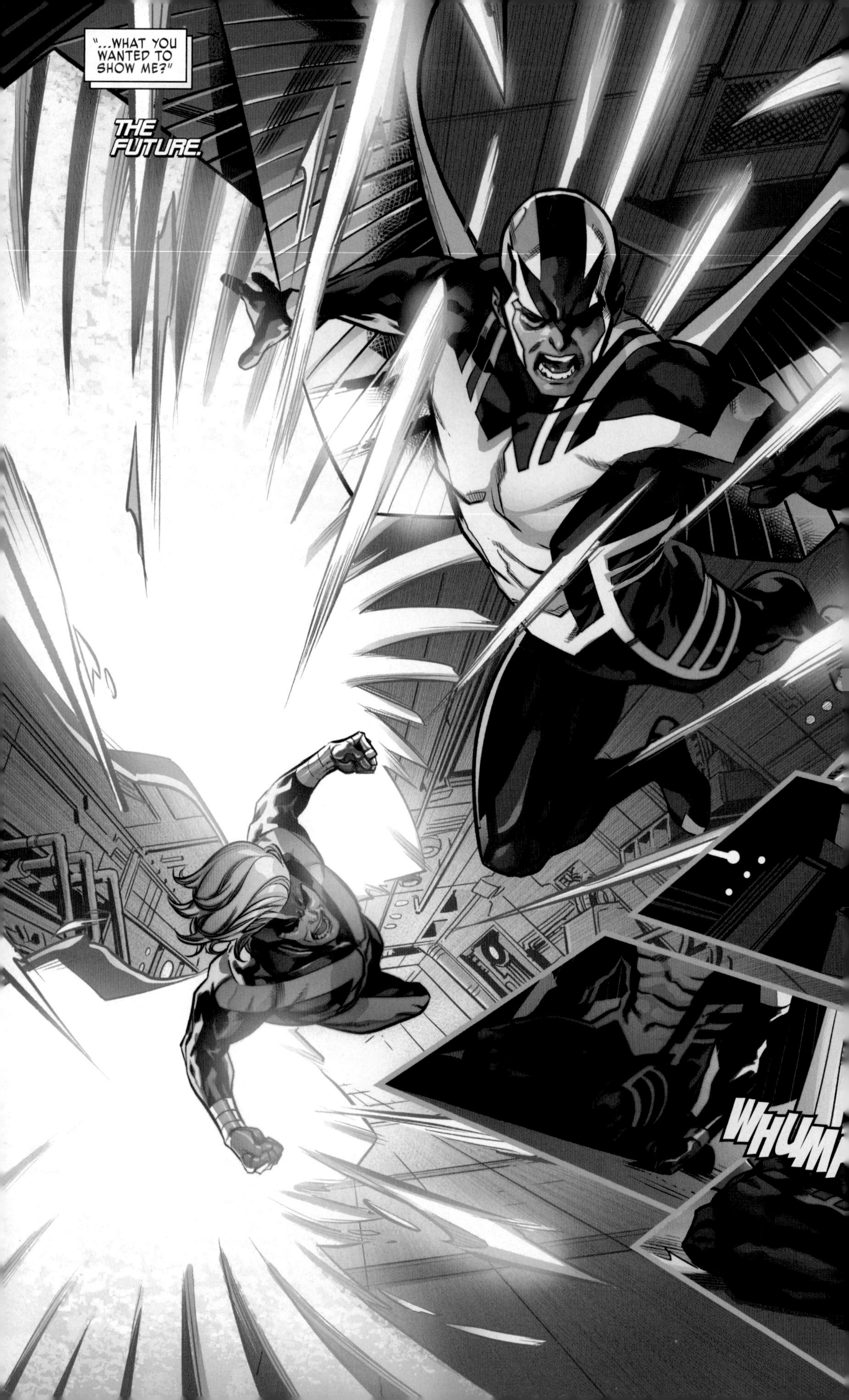
"...WHAT YOU WANTED TO SHOW ME?"
THE FUTURE.
WHUM

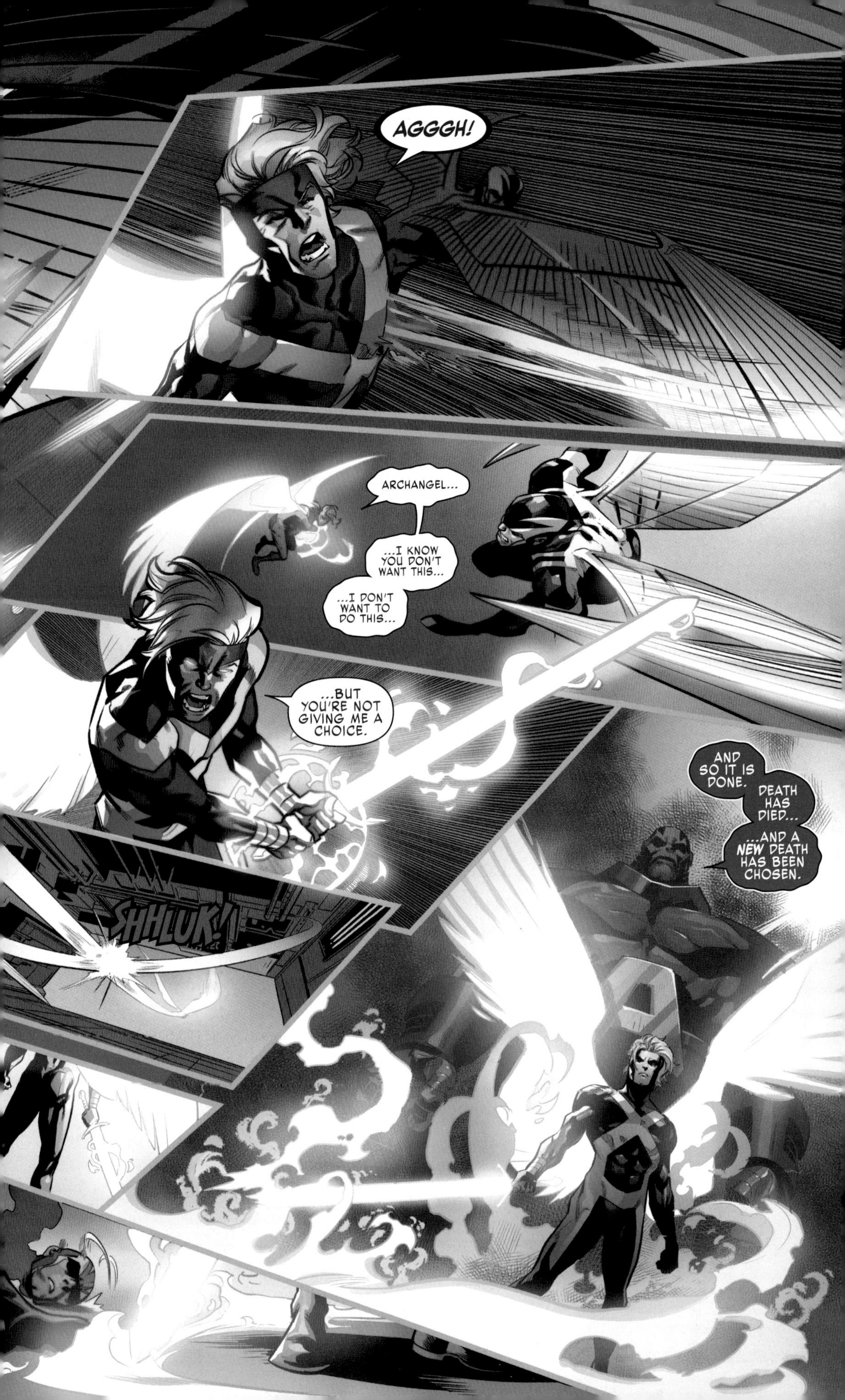

AGGGH!
ARCHANGEL...
...I KNOW YOU DON'T WANT THIS...
...I DON'T WANT TO DO THIS...
...BUT YOU'RE NOT GIVING ME A CHOICE.
SHHLUK!
AND SO IT IS DONE.
DEATH HAS DIED...
...AND A *NEW* DEATH HAS BEEN CHOSEN.

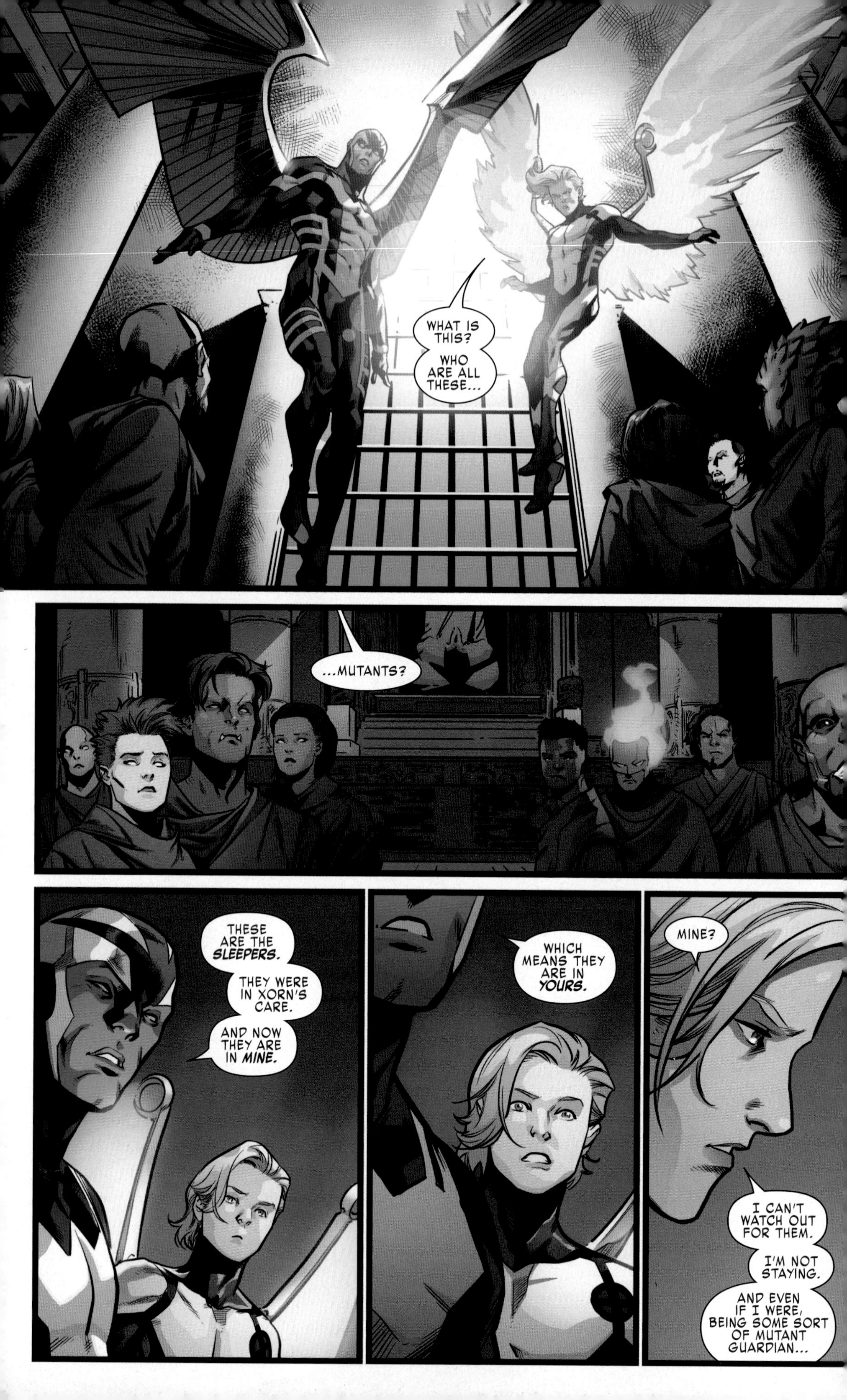
WHAT IS THIS?
WHO ARE ALL THESE...
...MUTANTS?
THESE ARE THE SLEEPERS.
THEY WERE IN XORN'S CARE.
AND NOW THEY ARE IN MINE.
WHICH MEANS THEY ARE IN YOURS.
MINE?
I CAN'T WATCH OUT FOR THEM.
I'M NOT STAYING.
AND EVEN IF I WERE, BEING SOME SORT OF MUTANT GUARDIAN...

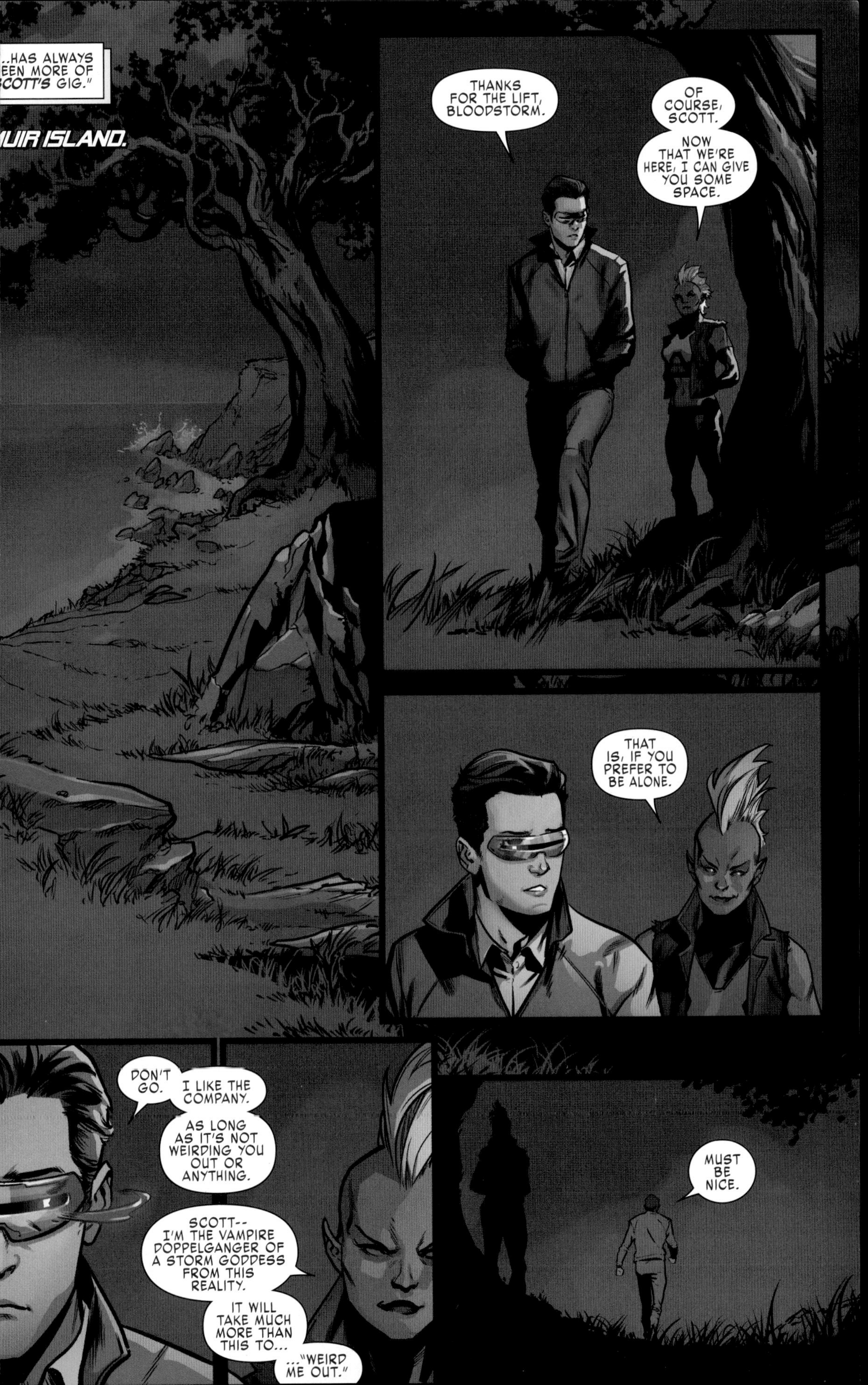
...HAS ALWAYS BEEN MORE OF SCOTT'S GIG."
MUIR ISLAND.
THANKS FOR THE LIFT, BLOODSTORM.
OF COURSE, SCOTT.
NOW THAT WE'RE HERE, I CAN GIVE YOU SOME SPACE.
THAT IS, IF YOU PREFER TO BE ALONE.
DON'T GO.
I LIKE THE COMPANY.
AS LONG AS IT'S NOT WEIRDING YOU OUT OR ANYTHING.
SCOTT-- I'M THE VAMPIRE DOPPELGANGER OF A STORM GODDESS FROM THIS REALITY.
IT WILL TAKE MUCH MORE THAN THIS TO...
..."WEIRD ME OUT."
MUST BE NICE.

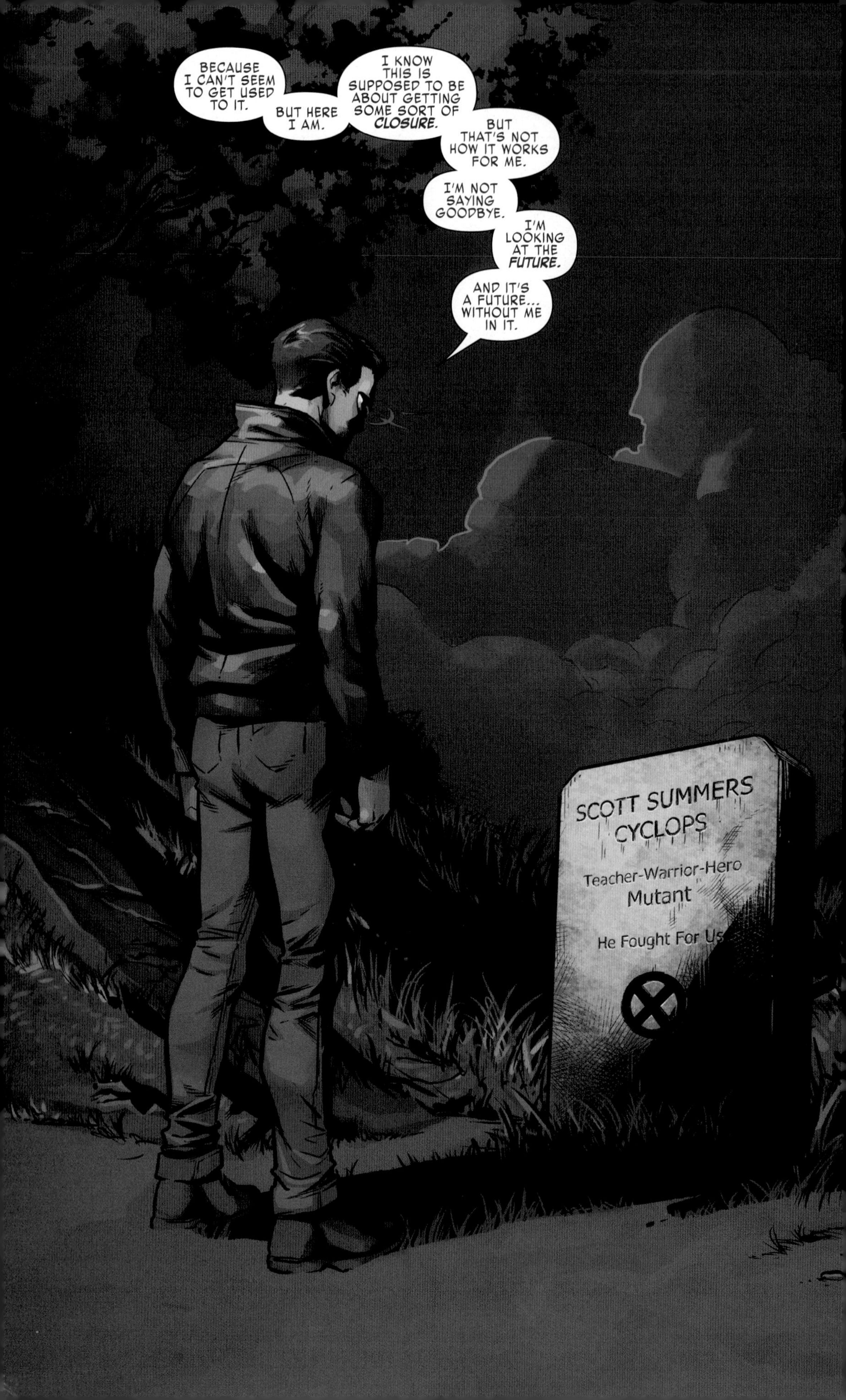
BECAUSE I CAN'T SEEM TO GET USED TO IT.
BUT HERE I AM.
I KNOW THIS IS SUPPOSED TO BE ABOUT GETTING SOME SORT OF *CLOSURE*.
BUT THAT'S NOT HOW IT WORKS FOR ME.
I'M NOT SAYING GOODBYE.
I'M LOOKING AT THE *FUTURE*.
AND IT'S A FUTURE... WITHOUT ME IN IT.
SCOTT SUMMERS
CYCLOPS
Teacher-Warrior-Hero
Mutant
He Fought For Us

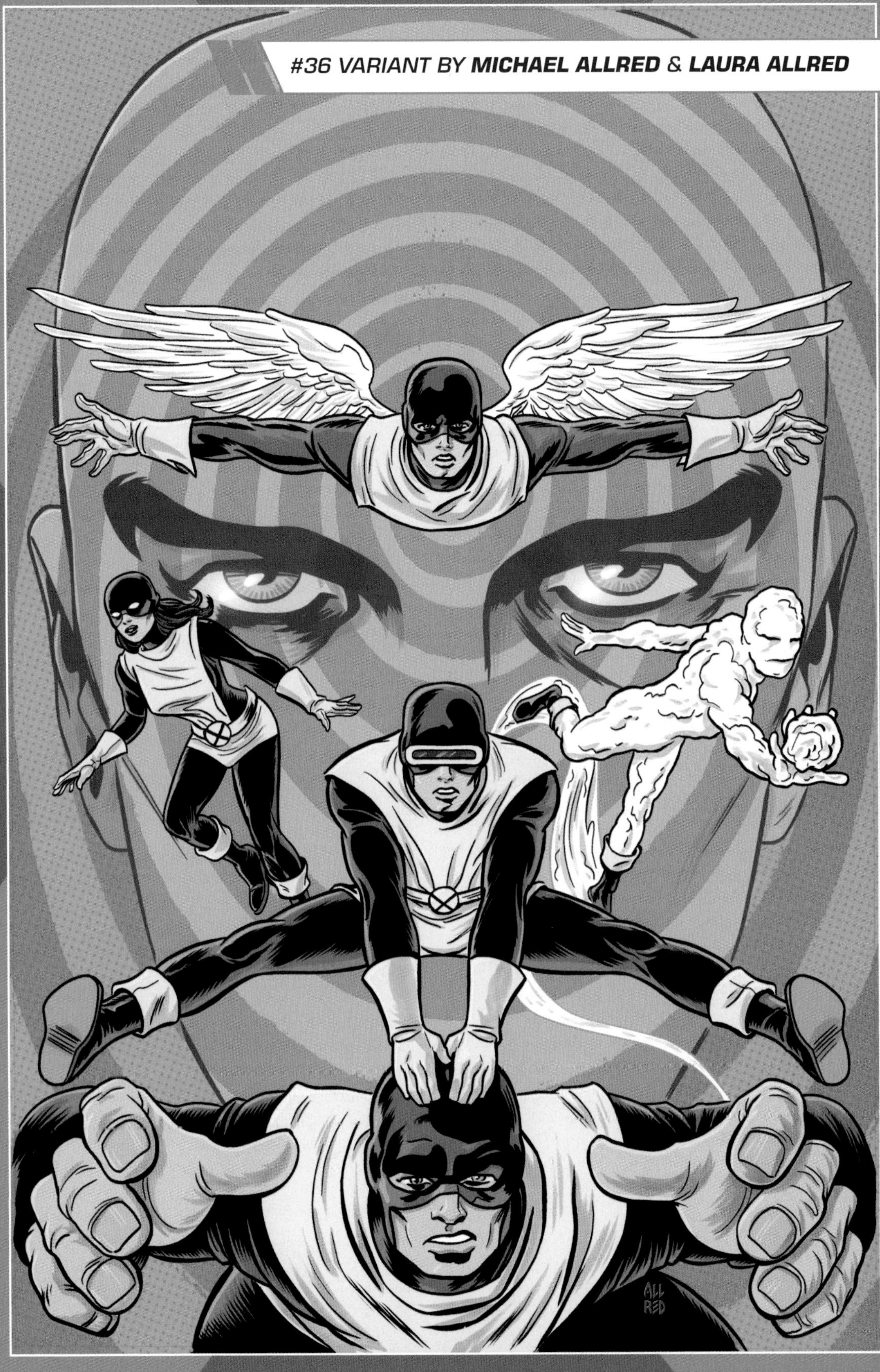

#36 VARIANT BY **MICHAEL ALLRED** & **LAURA ALLRED**

36

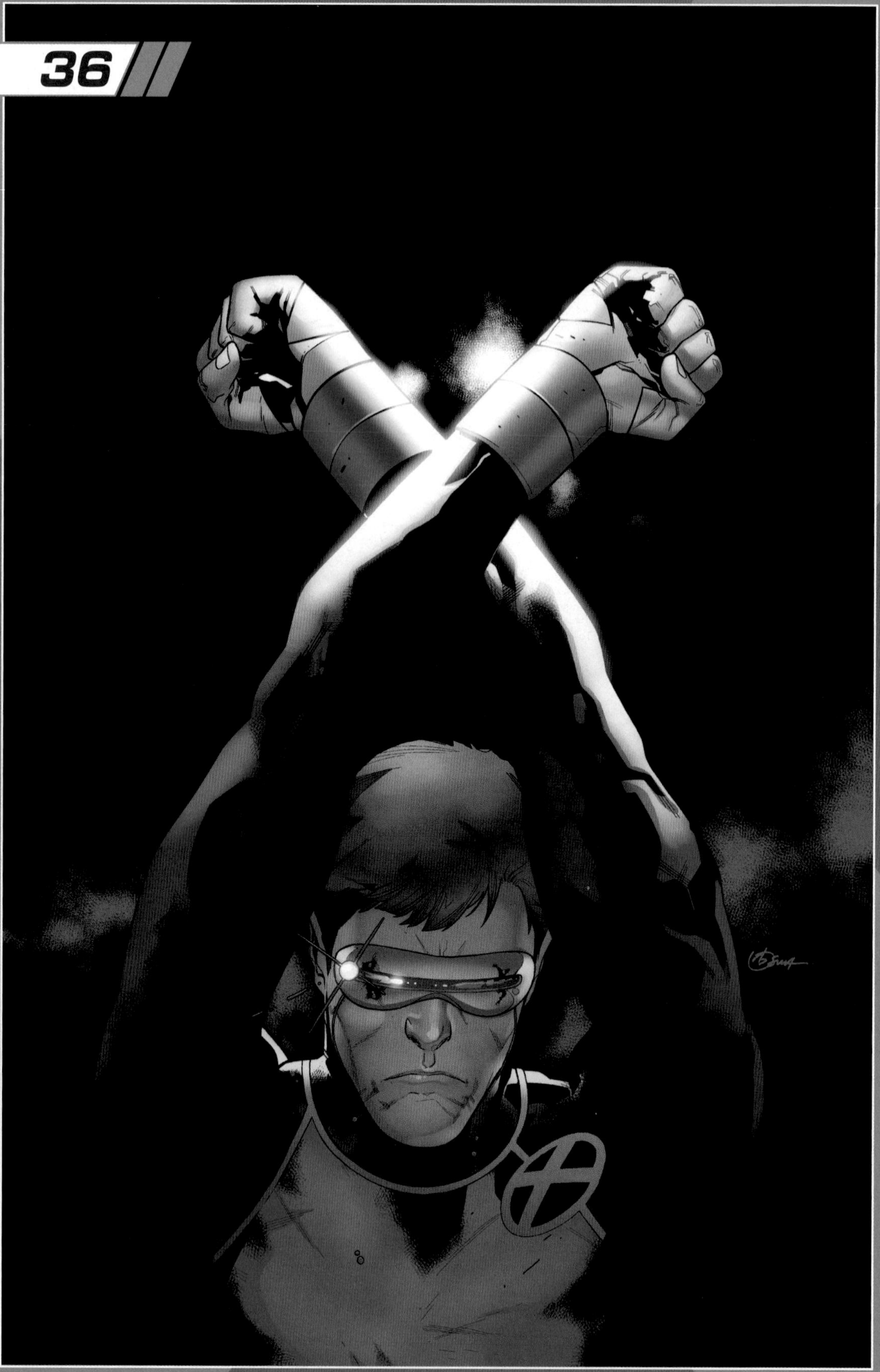

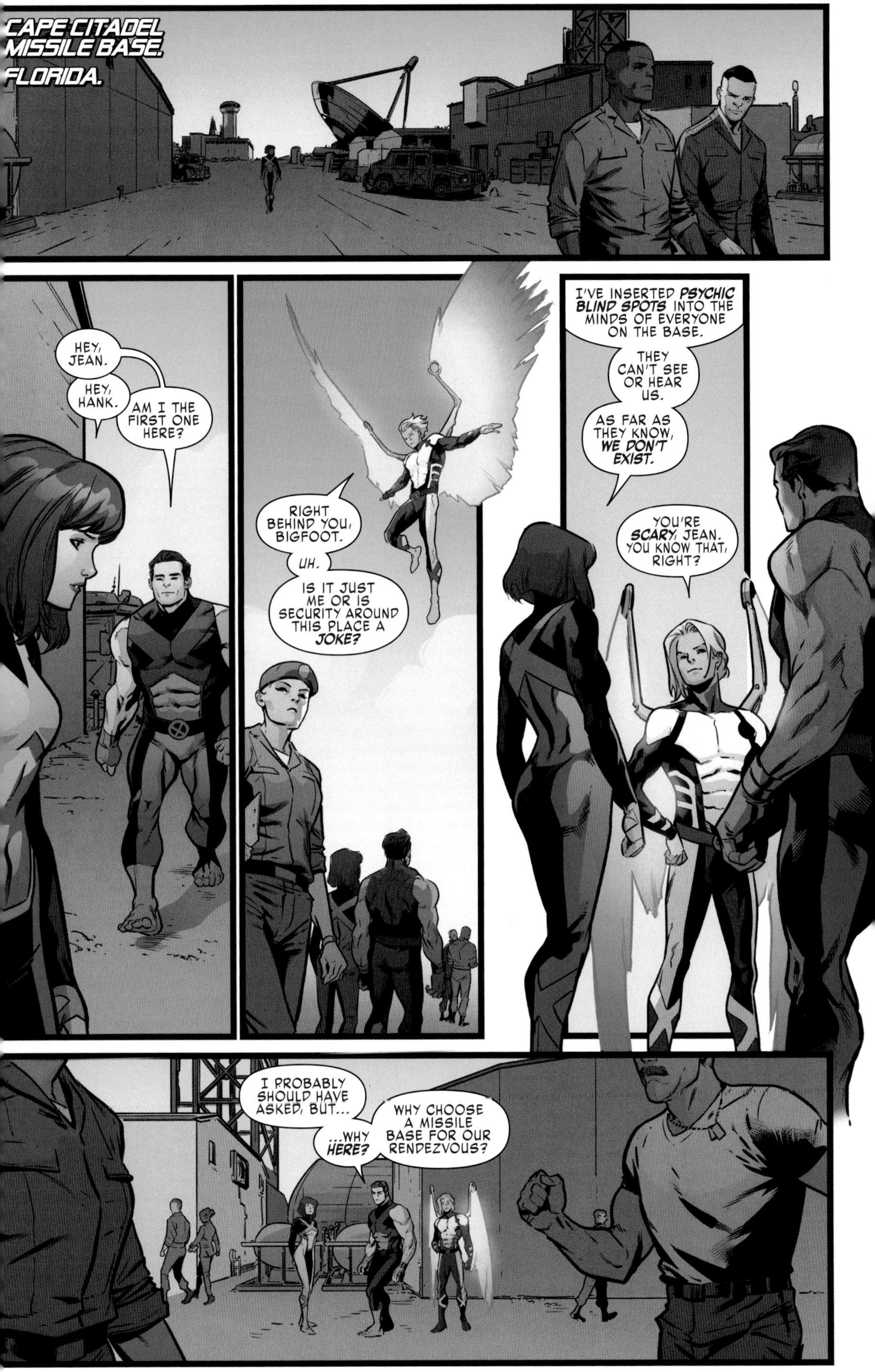
CAPE CITADEL MISSILE BASE.
FLORIDA.
HEY, JEAN.
HEY, HANK.
AM I THE FIRST ONE HERE?
RIGHT BEHIND YOU, BIGFOOT.
UH.
IS IT JUST ME OR IS SECURITY AROUND THIS PLACE A JOKE?
I'VE INSERTED PSYCHIC BLIND SPOTS INTO THE MINDS OF EVERYONE ON THE BASE.
THEY CAN'T SEE OR HEAR US.
AS FAR AS THEY KNOW, WE DON'T EXIST.
YOU'RE SCARY, JEAN. YOU KNOW THAT, RIGHT?
I PROBABLY SHOULD HAVE ASKED, BUT...
...WHY HERE?
WHY CHOOSE A MISSILE BASE FOR OUR RENDEZVOUS?

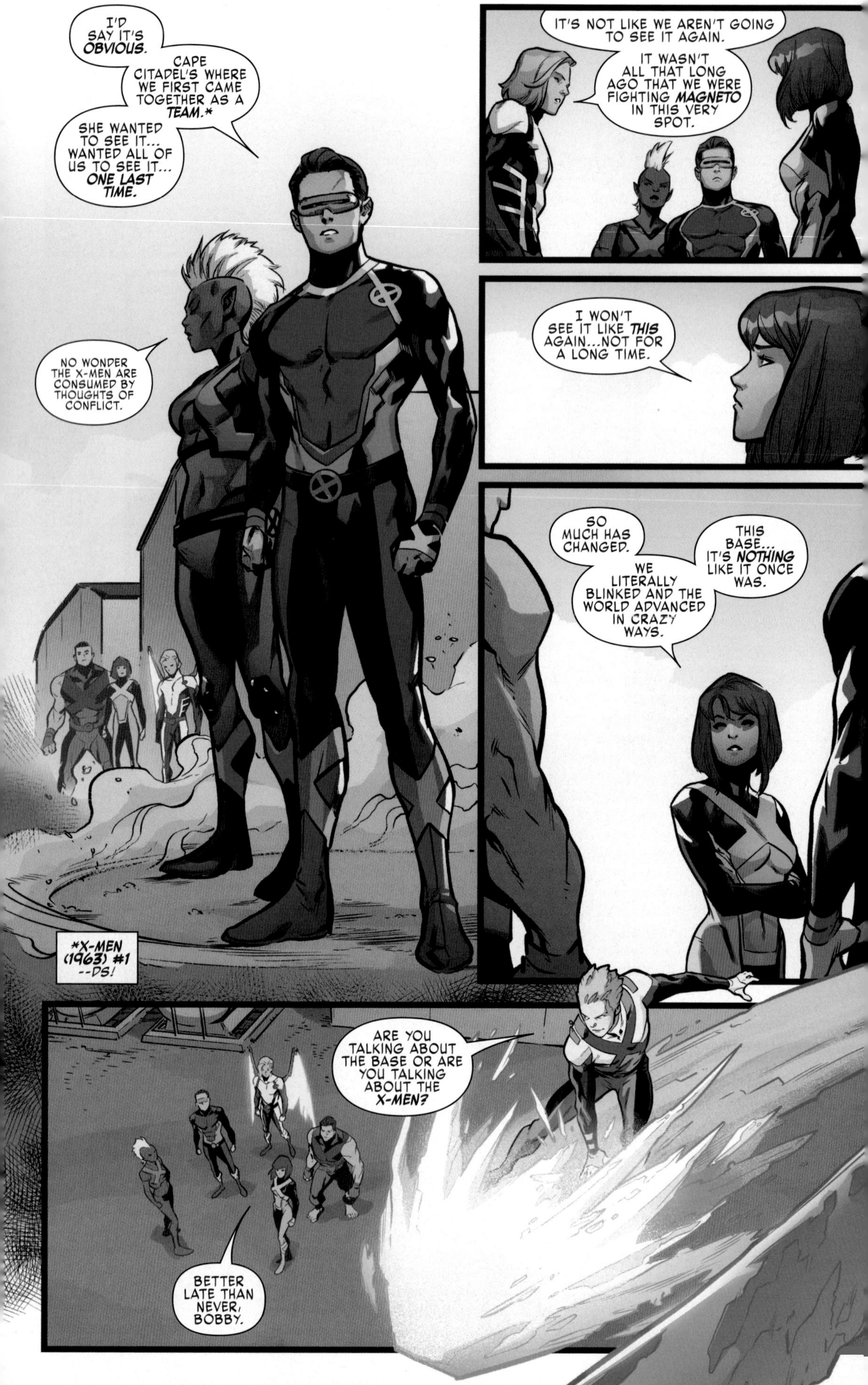
I'D SAY IT'S OBVIOUS.
CAPE CITADEL'S WHERE WE FIRST CAME TOGETHER AS A TEAM.*
SHE WANTED TO SEE IT... WANTED ALL OF US TO SEE IT... ONE LAST TIME.
NO WONDER THE X-MEN ARE CONSUMED BY THOUGHTS OF CONFLICT.
*X-MEN (1963) #1 --DS!
IT'S NOT LIKE WE AREN'T GOING TO SEE IT AGAIN.
IT WASN'T ALL THAT LONG AGO THAT WE WERE FIGHTING MAGNETO IN THIS VERY SPOT.
I WON'T SEE IT LIKE THIS AGAIN...NOT FOR A LONG TIME.
THIS BASE... IT'S NOTHING LIKE IT ONCE WAS.
SO MUCH HAS CHANGED.
WE LITERALLY BLINKED AND THE WORLD ADVANCED IN CRAZY WAYS.
ARE YOU TALKING ABOUT THE BASE OR ARE YOU TALKING ABOUT THE X-MEN?
BETTER LATE THAN NEVER, BOBBY.

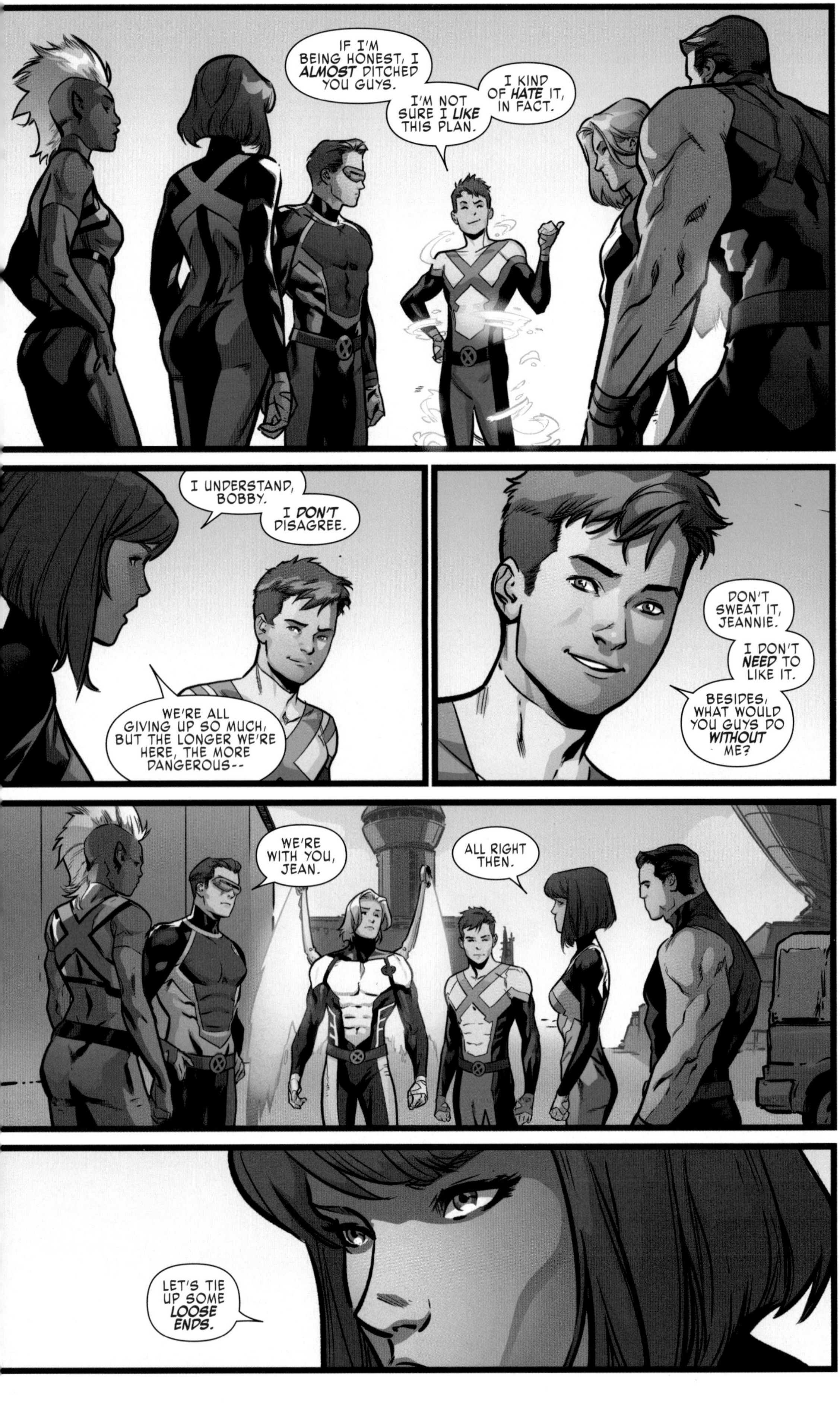
IF I'M BEING HONEST, I ALMOST DITCHED YOU GUYS.
I'M NOT SURE I LIKE THIS PLAN.
I KIND OF HATE IT, IN FACT.
I UNDERSTAND, BOBBY.
I DON'T DISAGREE.
WE'RE ALL GIVING UP SO MUCH, BUT THE LONGER WE'RE HERE, THE MORE DANGEROUS--
DON'T SWEAT IT, JEANNIE.
I DON'T NEED TO LIKE IT.
BESIDES, WHAT WOULD YOU GUYS DO WITHOUT ME?
WE'RE WITH YOU, JEAN.
ALL RIGHT THEN.
LET'S TIE UP SOME LOOSE ENDS.

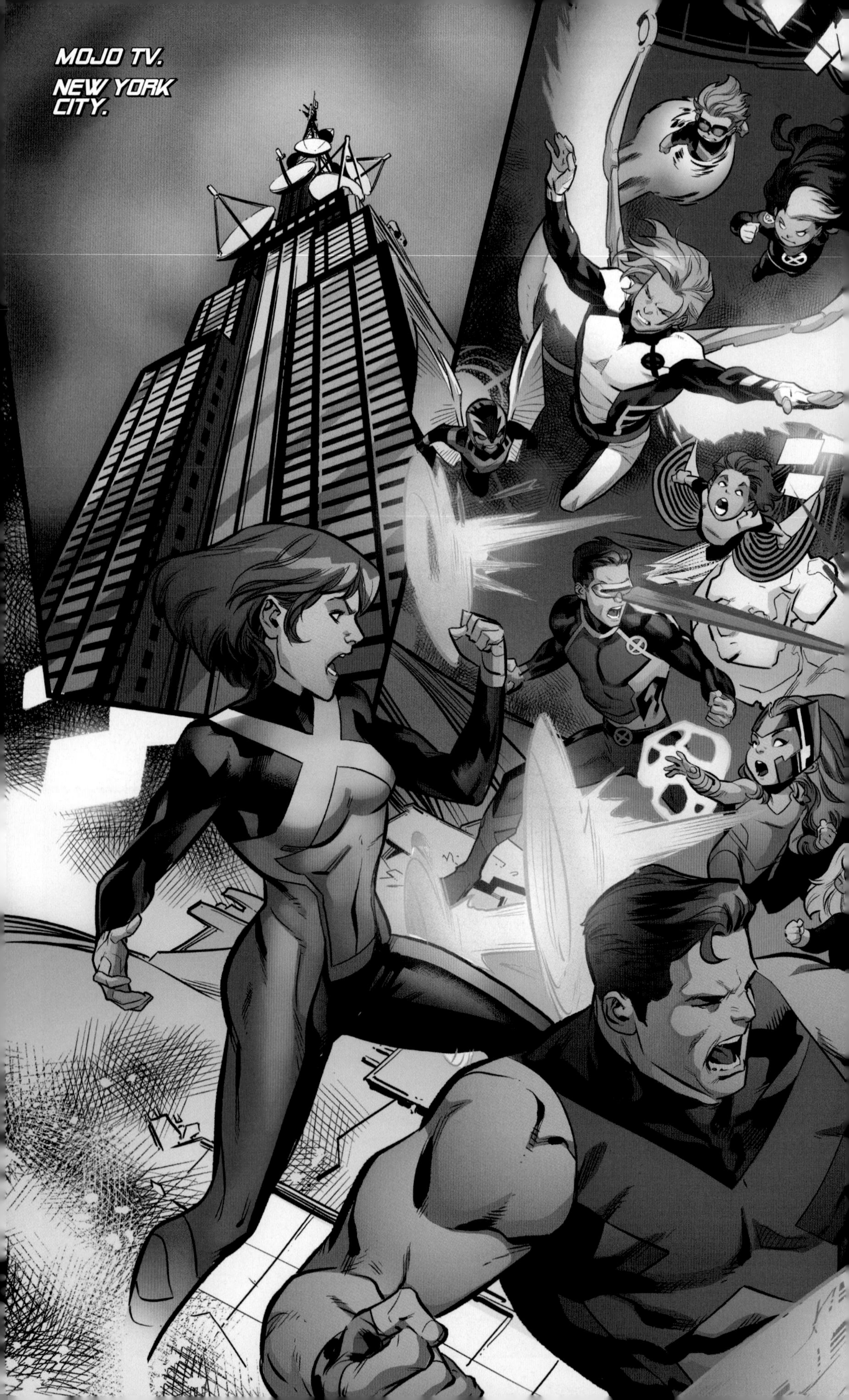
MOJO TV.
NEW YORK CITY.

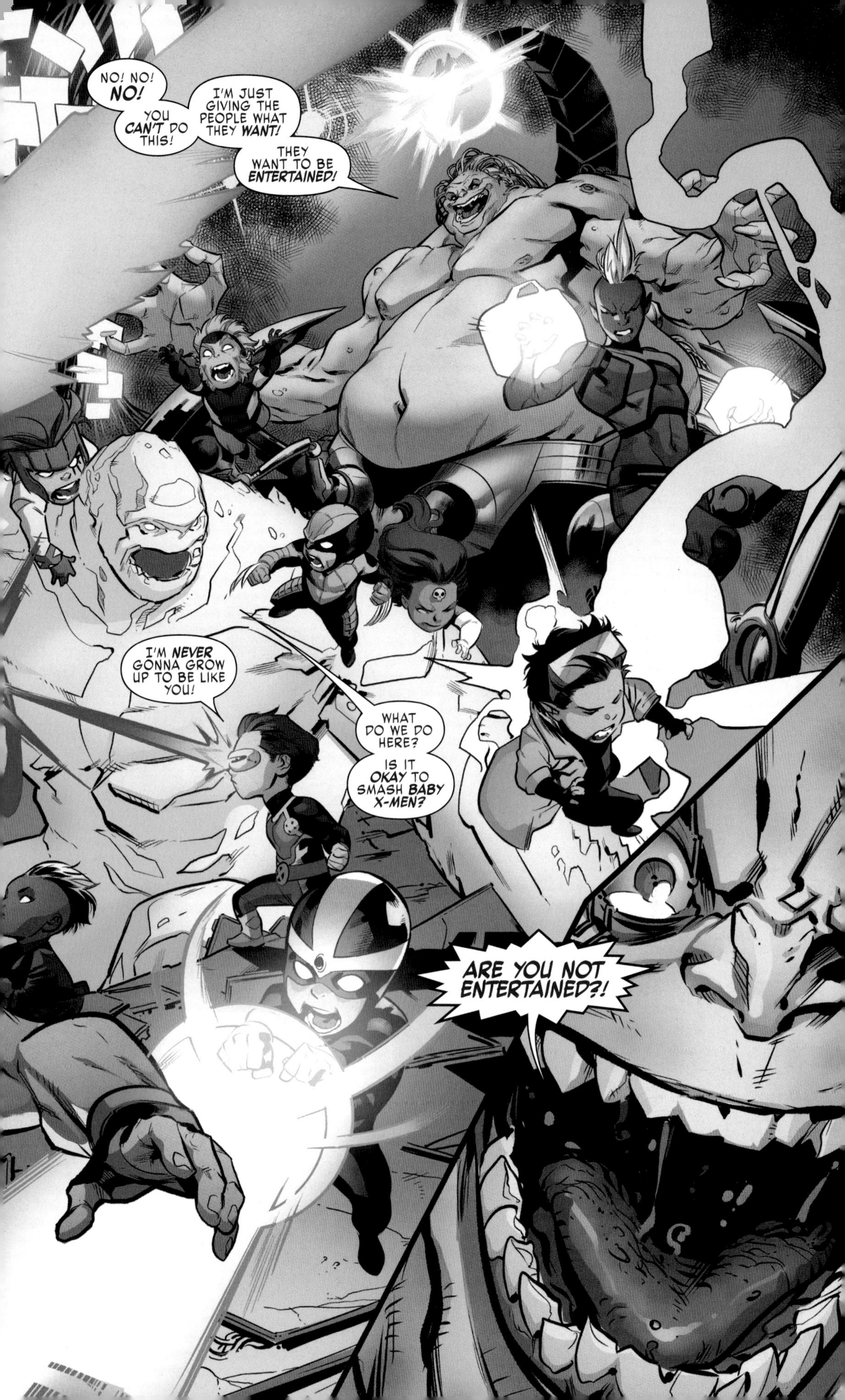
NO! NO! NO!
YOU CAN'T DO THIS!
I'M JUST GIVING THE PEOPLE WHAT THEY WANT!
THEY WANT TO BE ENTERTAINED!
I'M NEVER GONNA GROW UP TO BE LIKE YOU!
WHAT DO WE DO HERE?
IS IT OKAY TO SMASH BABY X-MEN?
ARE YOU NOT ENTERTAINED?!

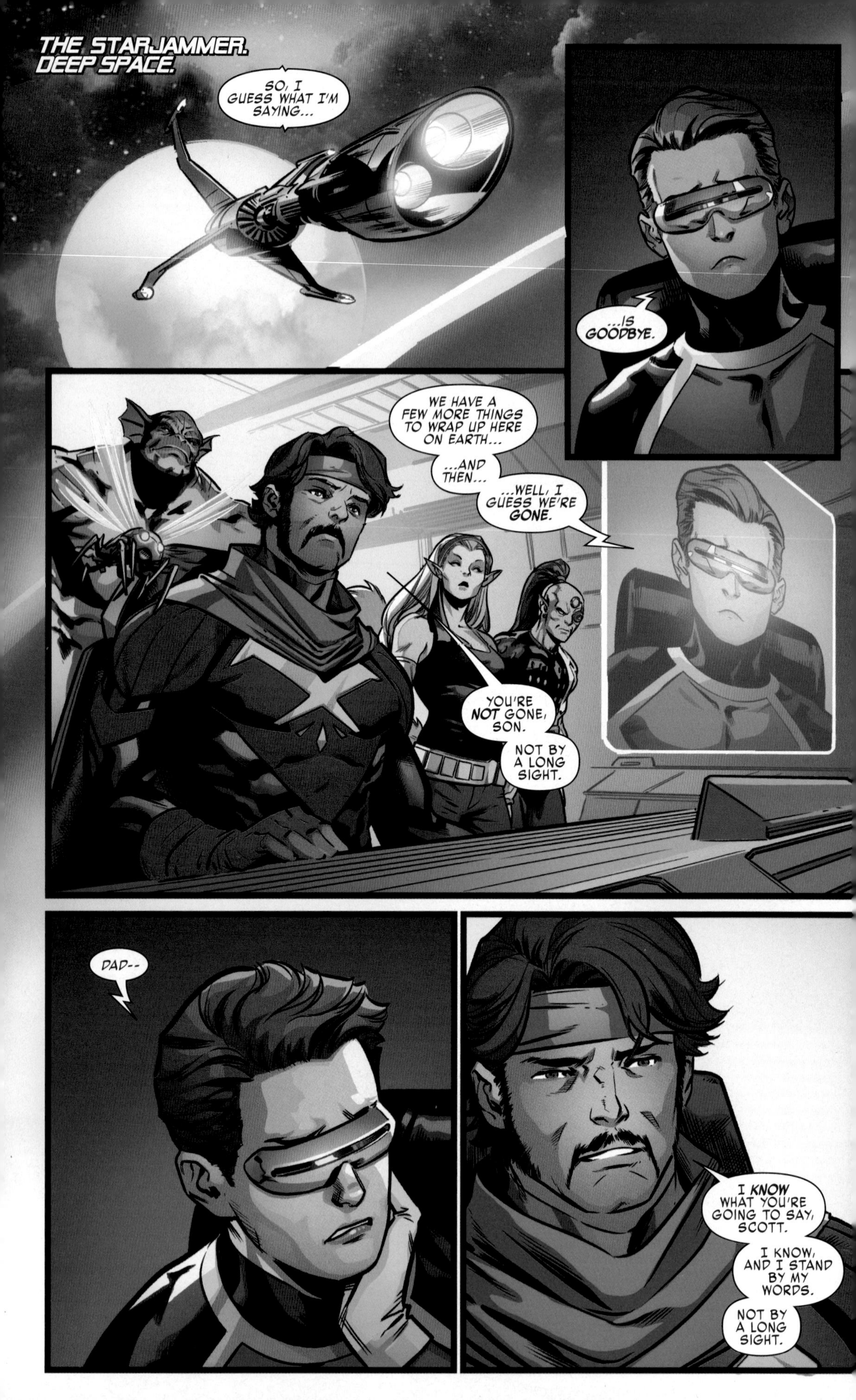
THE STARJAMMER. DEEP SPACE.
SO, I GUESS WHAT I'M SAYING...
...IS GOODBYE.
WE HAVE A FEW MORE THINGS TO WRAP UP HERE ON EARTH...
...AND THEN...
...WELL, I GUESS WE'RE GONE.
YOU'RE NOT GONE, SON.
NOT BY A LONG SIGHT.
DAD--
I KNOW WHAT YOU'RE GOING TO SAY, SCOTT.
I KNOW, AND I STAND BY MY WORDS.
NOT BY A LONG SIGHT.

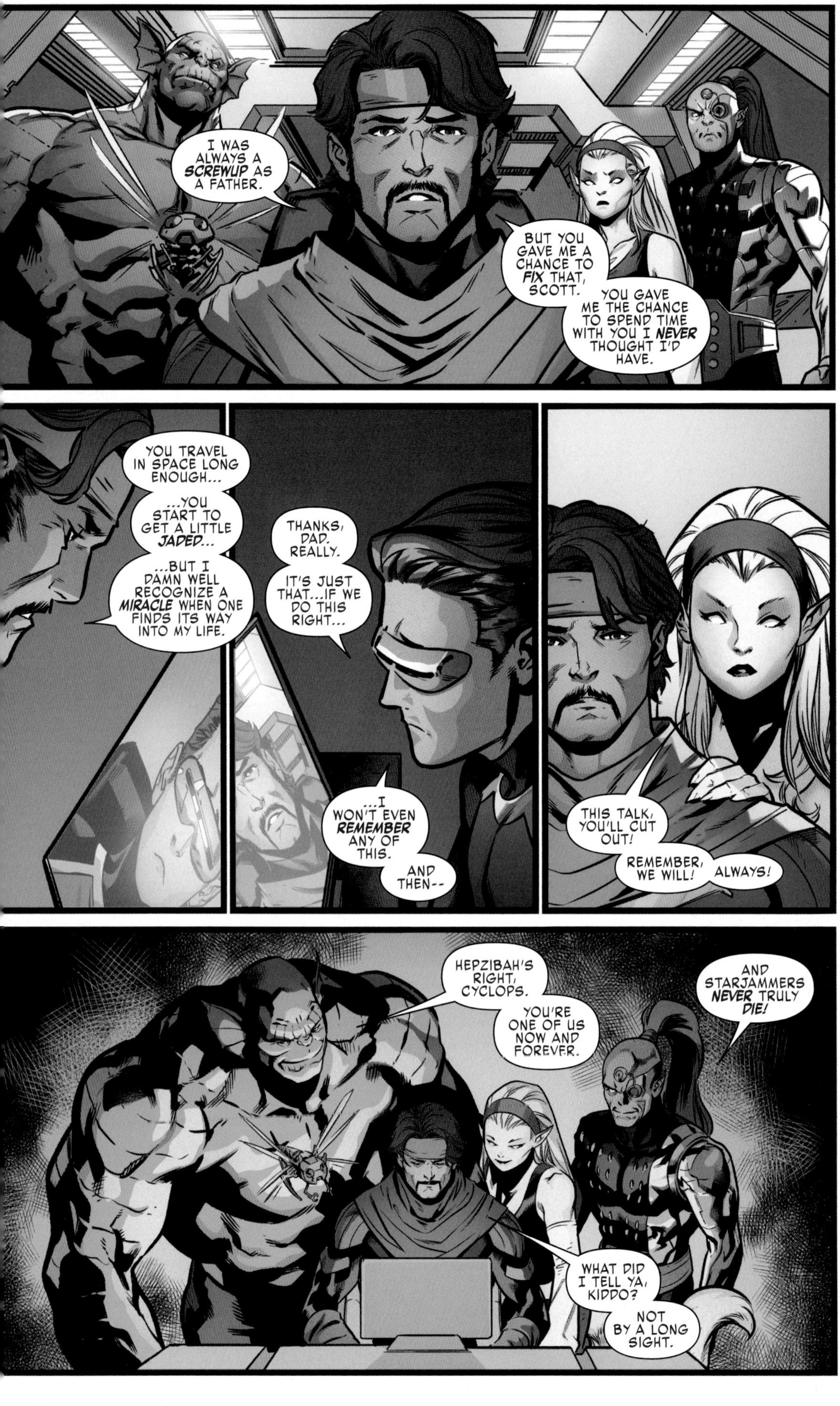

I WAS ALWAYS A SCREWUP AS A FATHER.
BUT YOU GAVE ME A CHANCE TO FIX THAT, SCOTT.
YOU GAVE ME THE CHANCE TO SPEND TIME WITH YOU I NEVER THOUGHT I'D HAVE.
YOU TRAVEL IN SPACE LONG ENOUGH...
...YOU START TO GET A LITTLE JADED...
...BUT I DAMN WELL RECOGNIZE A MIRACLE WHEN ONE FINDS ITS WAY INTO MY LIFE.
THANKS, DAD. REALLY.
IT'S JUST THAT...IF WE DO THIS RIGHT...
...I WON'T EVEN REMEMBER ANY OF THIS.
AND THEN--
THIS TALK, YOU'LL CUT OUT!
REMEMBER, WE WILL!
ALWAYS!
HEPZIBAH'S RIGHT, CYCLOPS.
YOU'RE ONE OF US NOW AND FOREVER.
AND STARJAMMERS NEVER TRULY DIE!
WHAT DID I TELL YA, KIDDO?
NOT BY A LONG SIGHT.

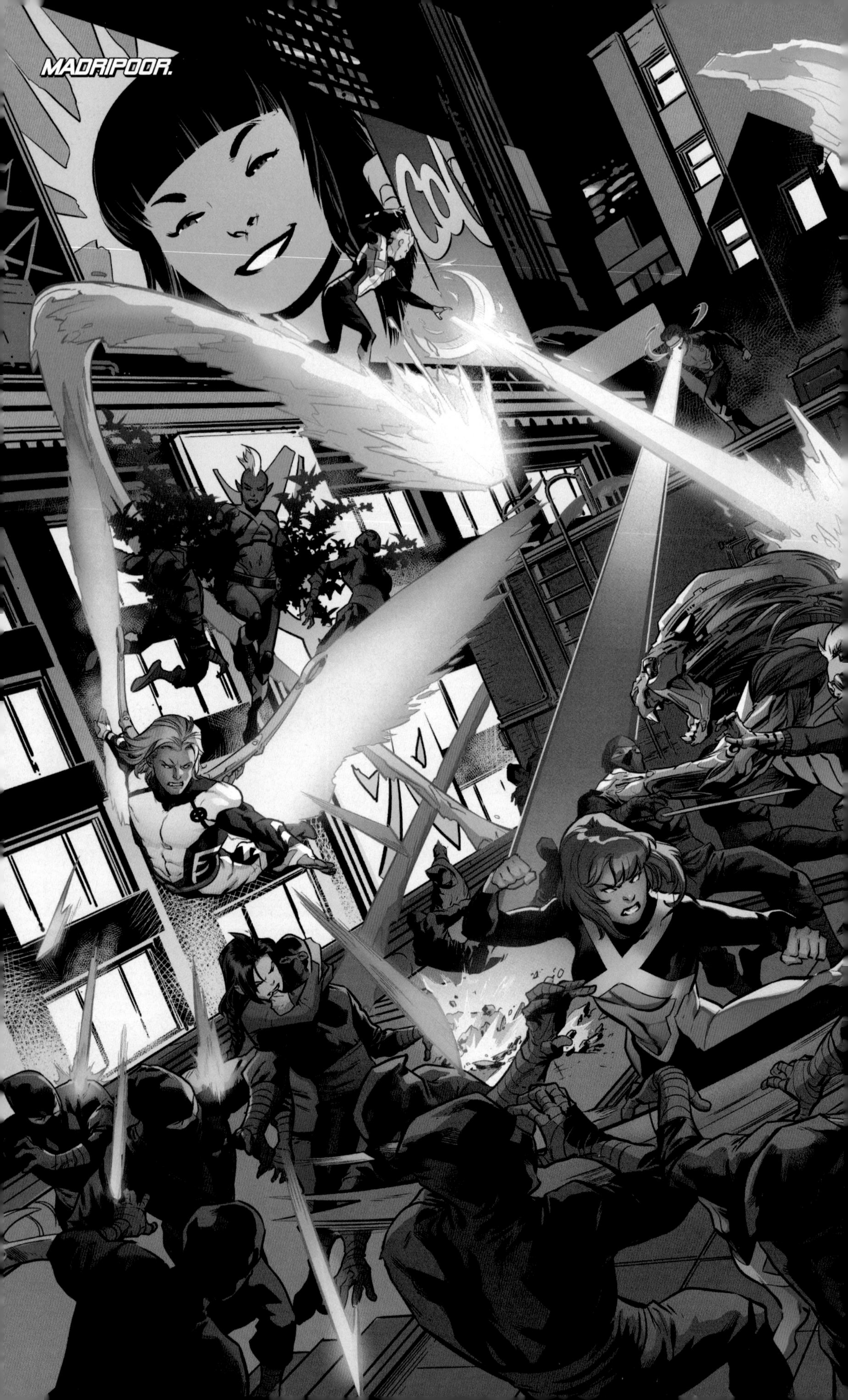
MADRIPOOR.

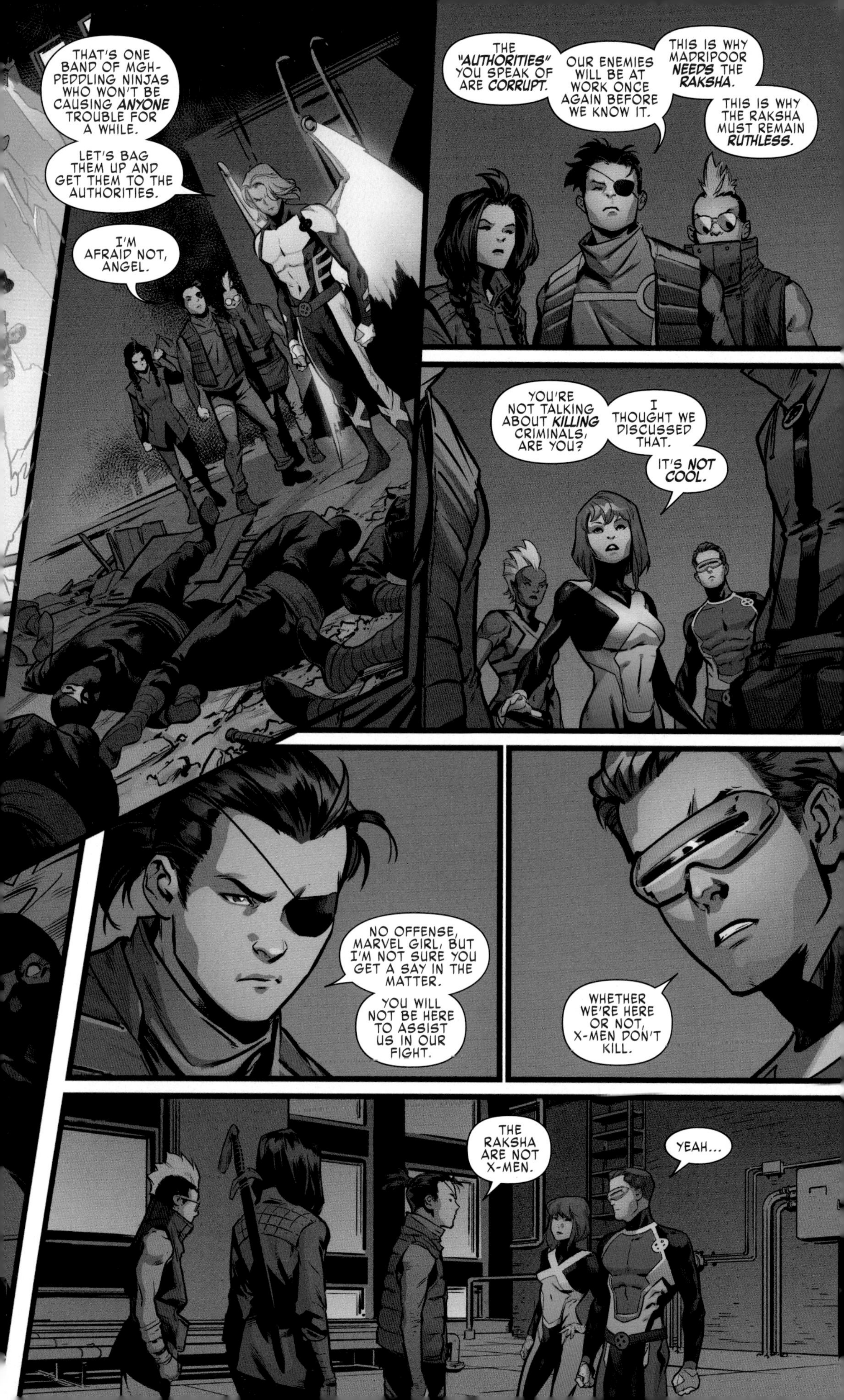
THAT'S ONE BAND OF MGH-PEDDLING NINJAS WHO WON'T BE CAUSING ANYONE TROUBLE FOR A WHILE.
LET'S BAG THEM UP AND GET THEM TO THE AUTHORITIES.
I'M AFRAID NOT, ANGEL.
THE "AUTHORITIES" YOU SPEAK OF ARE CORRUPT.
OUR ENEMIES WILL BE AT WORK ONCE AGAIN BEFORE WE KNOW IT.
THIS IS WHY MADRIPOOR NEEDS THE RAKSHA.
THIS IS WHY THE RAKSHA MUST REMAIN RUTHLESS.
YOU'RE NOT TALKING ABOUT KILLING CRIMINALS, ARE YOU?
I THOUGHT WE DISCUSSED THAT.
IT'S NOT COOL.
NO OFFENSE, MARVEL GIRL, BUT I'M NOT SURE YOU GET A SAY IN THE MATTER.
YOU WILL NOT BE HERE TO ASSIST US IN OUR FIGHT.
WHETHER WE'RE HERE OR NOT, X-MEN DON'T KILL.
THE RAKSHA ARE NOT X-MEN.
YEAH...

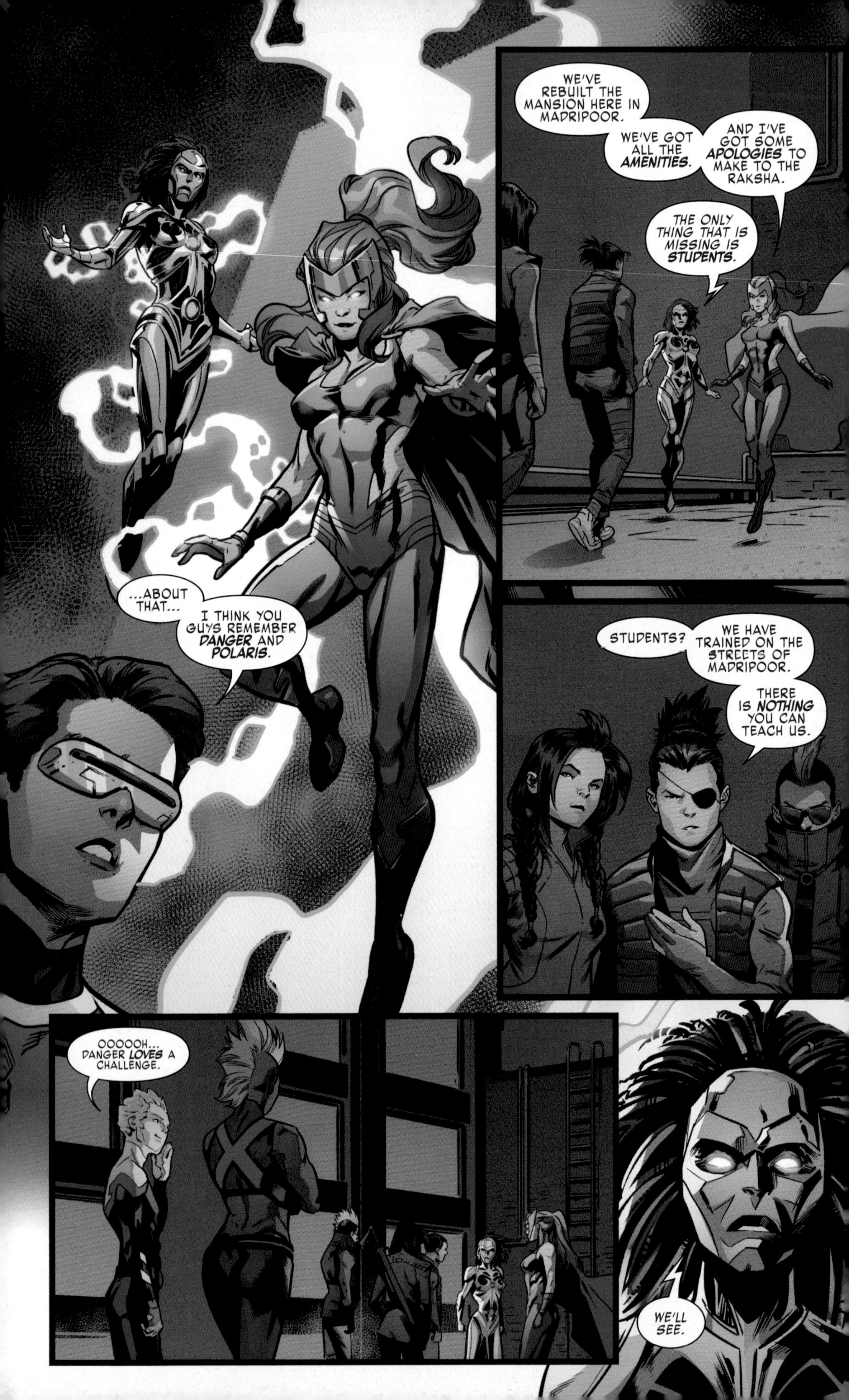
WE'VE REBUILT THE MANSION HERE IN MADRIPOOR.
WE'VE GOT ALL THE AMENITIES.
AND I'VE GOT SOME APOLOGIES TO MAKE TO THE RAKSHA.
THE ONLY THING THAT IS MISSING IS STUDENTS.
...ABOUT THAT...
I THINK YOU GUYS REMEMBER DANGER AND POLARIS.
STUDENTS?
WE HAVE TRAINED ON THE STREETS OF MADRIPOOR.
THERE IS NOTHING YOU CAN TEACH US.
OOOOOH... DANGER LOVES A CHALLENGE.
WE'LL SEE.

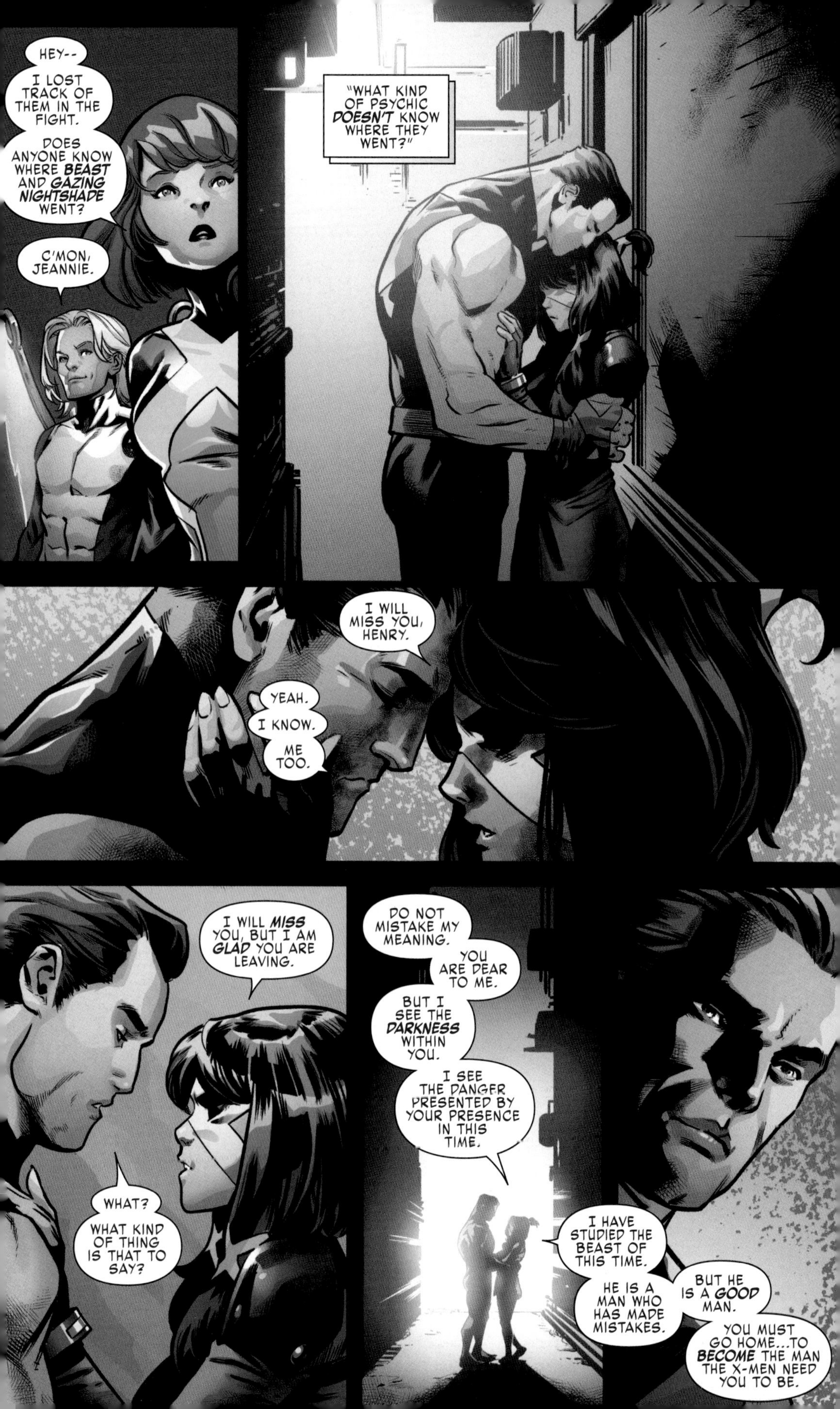
HEY--
I LOST TRACK OF THEM IN THE FIGHT.
DOES ANYONE KNOW WHERE BEAST AND GAZING NIGHTSHADE WENT?
C'MON, JEANNIE.
"WHAT KIND OF PSYCHIC DOESN'T KNOW WHERE THEY WENT?"
I WILL MISS YOU, HENRY.
YEAH.
I KNOW.
ME TOO.
I WILL MISS YOU, BUT I AM GLAD YOU ARE LEAVING.
WHAT? WHAT KIND OF THING IS THAT TO SAY?
DO NOT MISTAKE MY MEANING.
YOU ARE DEAR TO ME.
BUT I SEE THE DARKNESS WITHIN YOU.
I SEE THE DANGER PRESENTED BY YOUR PRESENCE IN THIS TIME.
I HAVE STUDIED THE BEAST OF THIS TIME.
HE IS A MAN WHO HAS MADE MISTAKES.
BUT HE IS A GOOD MAN.
YOU MUST GO HOME...TO BECOME THE MAN THE X-MEN NEED YOU TO BE.

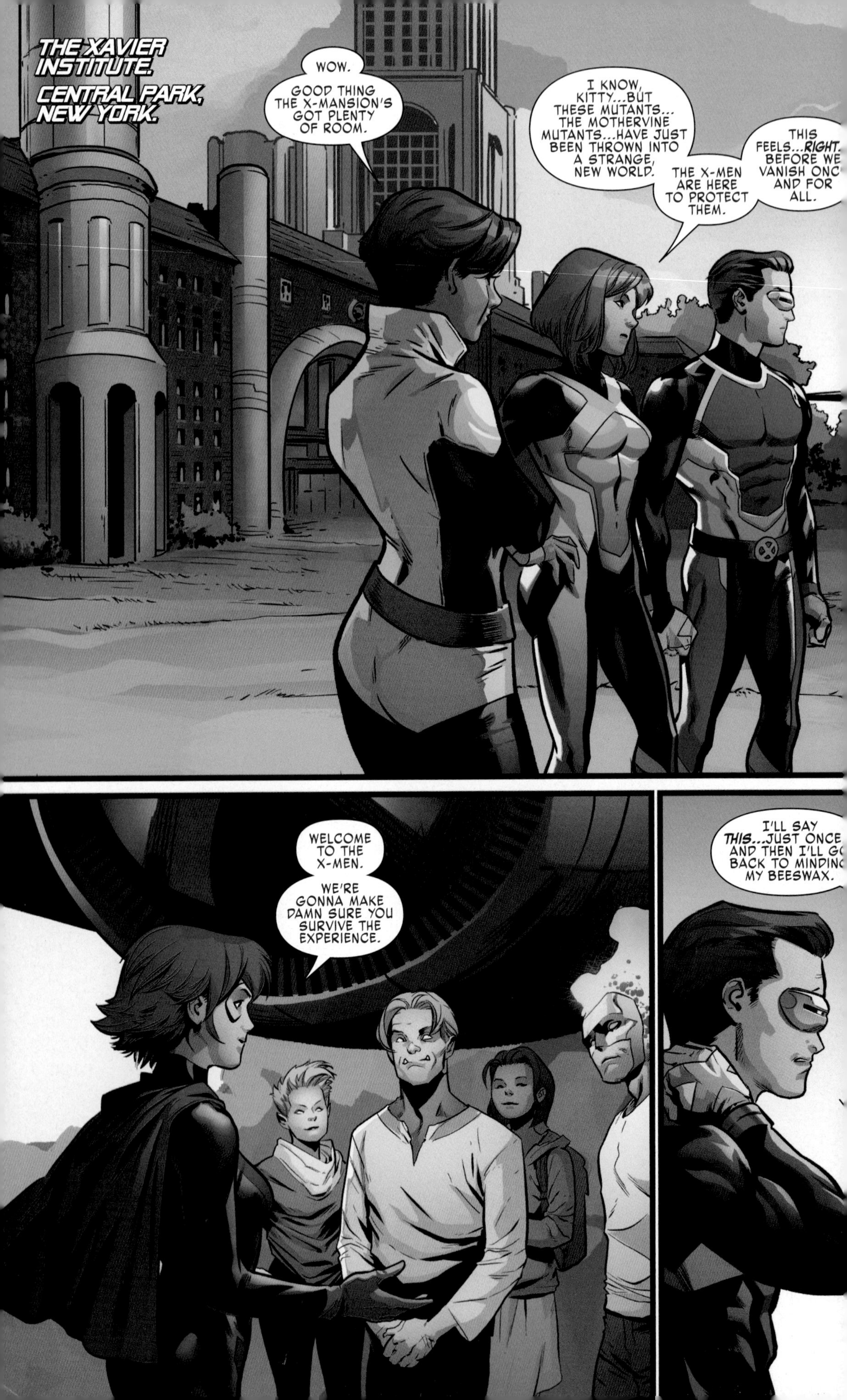
THE XAVIER INSTITUTE.
CENTRAL PARK, NEW YORK.
WOW.
GOOD THING THE X-MANSION'S GOT PLENTY OF ROOM.
I KNOW, KITTY...BUT THESE MUTANTS... THE MOTHERVINE MUTANTS...HAVE JUST BEEN THROWN INTO A STRANGE, NEW WORLD.
THE X-MEN ARE HERE TO PROTECT THEM.
THIS FEELS...RIGHT. BEFORE WE VANISH ONC AND FOR ALL.
WELCOME TO THE X-MEN.
WE'RE GONNA MAKE DAMN SURE YOU SURVIVE THE EXPERIENCE.
I'LL SAY THIS...JUST ONCE AND THEN I'LL GO BACK TO MINDING MY BEESWAX.

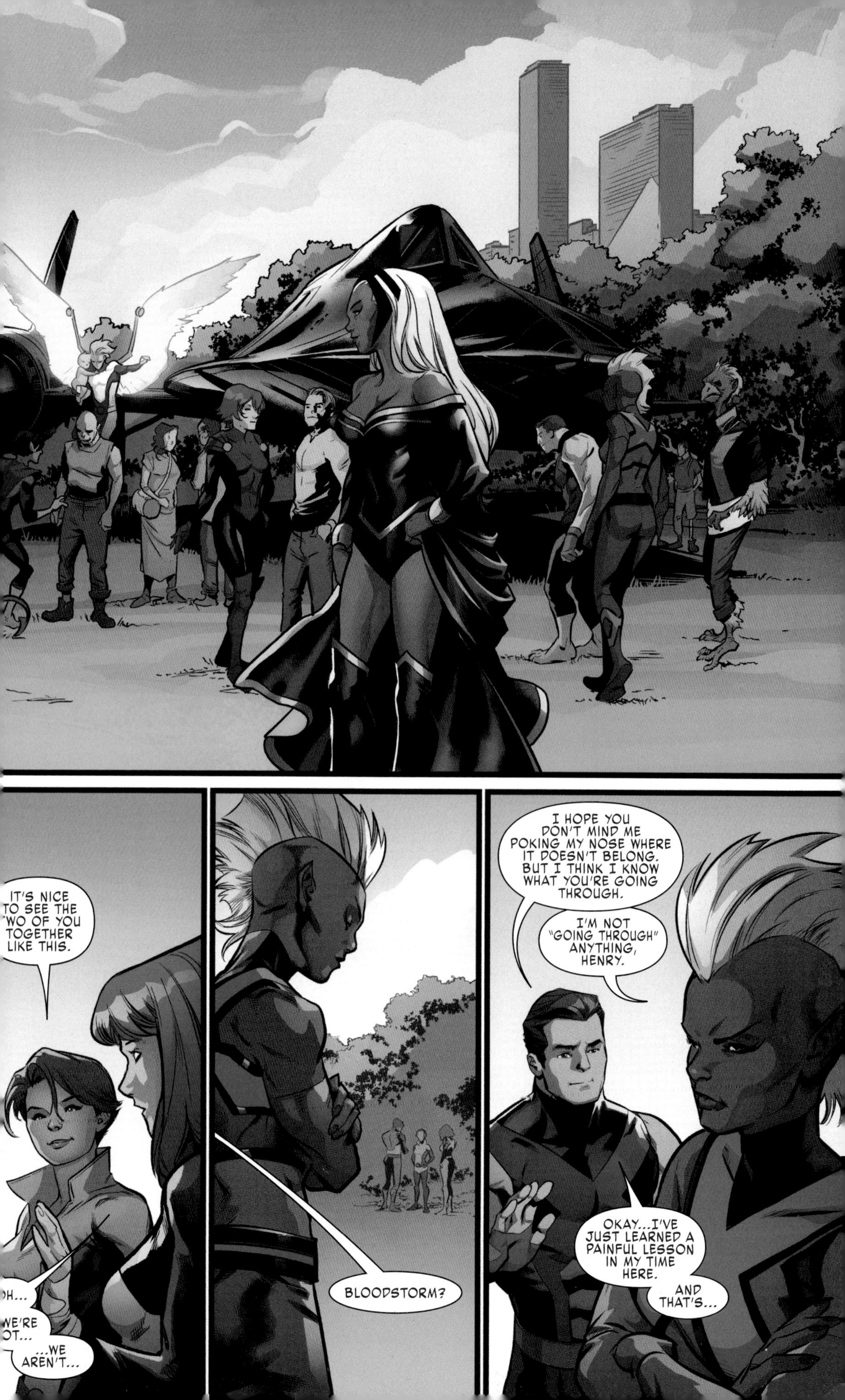
IT'S NICE TO SEE THE TWO OF YOU TOGETHER LIKE THIS.
OH... WE'RE NOT...
...WE AREN'T...
BLOODSTORM?
I HOPE YOU DON'T MIND ME POKING MY NOSE WHERE IT DOESN'T BELONG. BUT I THINK I KNOW WHAT YOU'RE GOING THROUGH.
I'M NOT "GOING THROUGH" ANYTHING, HENRY.
OKAY...I'VE JUST LEARNED A PAINFUL LESSON IN MY TIME HERE.
AND THAT'S...

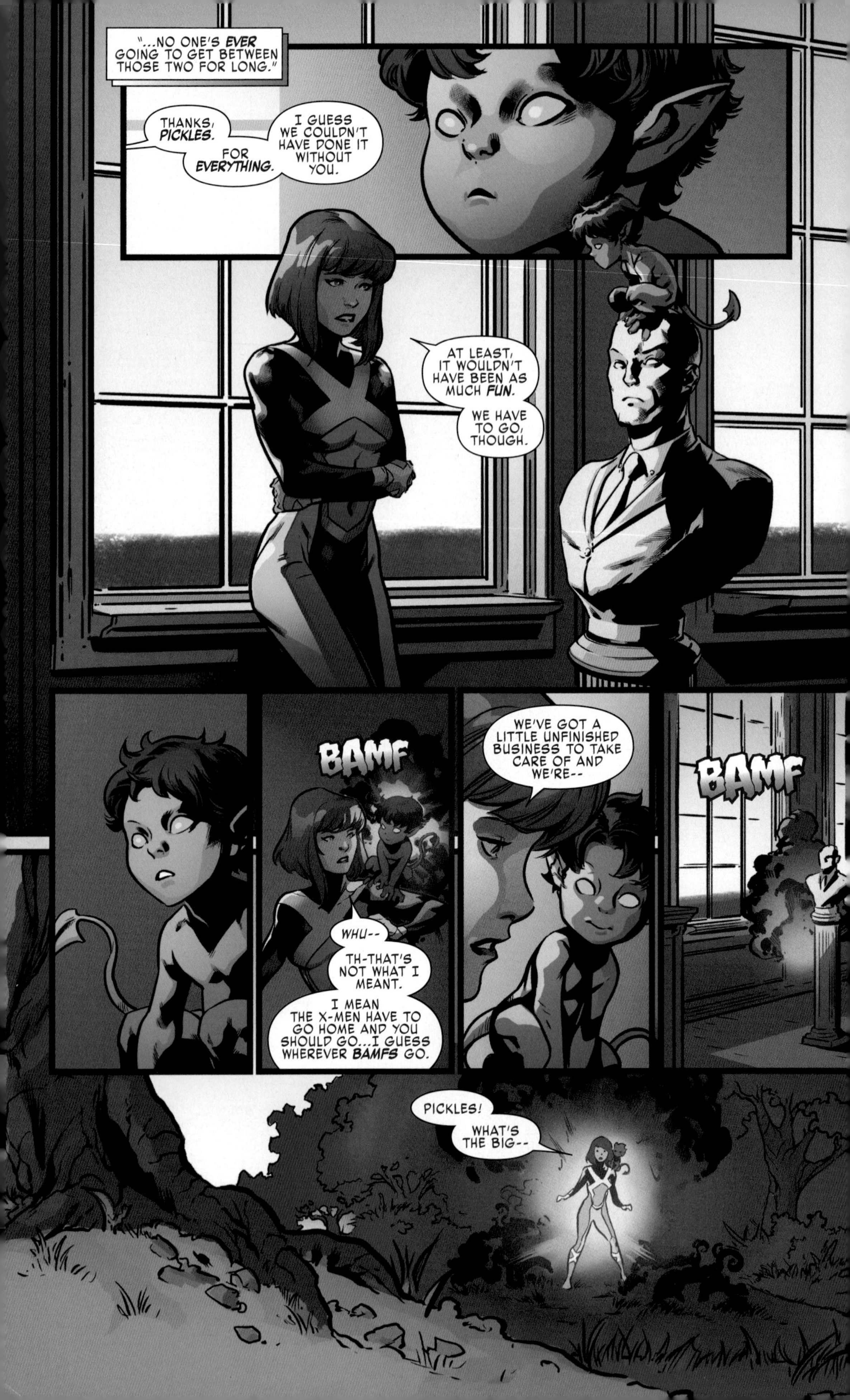
"...NO ONE'S EVER GOING TO GET BETWEEN THOSE TWO FOR LONG."
THANKS, PICKLES.
FOR EVERYTHING.
I GUESS WE COULDN'T HAVE DONE IT WITHOUT YOU.
AT LEAST, IT WOULDN'T HAVE BEEN AS MUCH FUN.
WE HAVE TO GO, THOUGH.
BAMF
WHU--
TH-THAT'S NOT WHAT I MEANT.
I MEAN THE X-MEN HAVE TO GO HOME AND YOU SHOULD GO...I GUESS WHEREVER BAMFS GO.
WE'VE GOT A LITTLE UNFINISHED BUSINESS TO TAKE CARE OF AND WE'RE--
BAMF
PICKLES!
WHAT'S THE BIG--

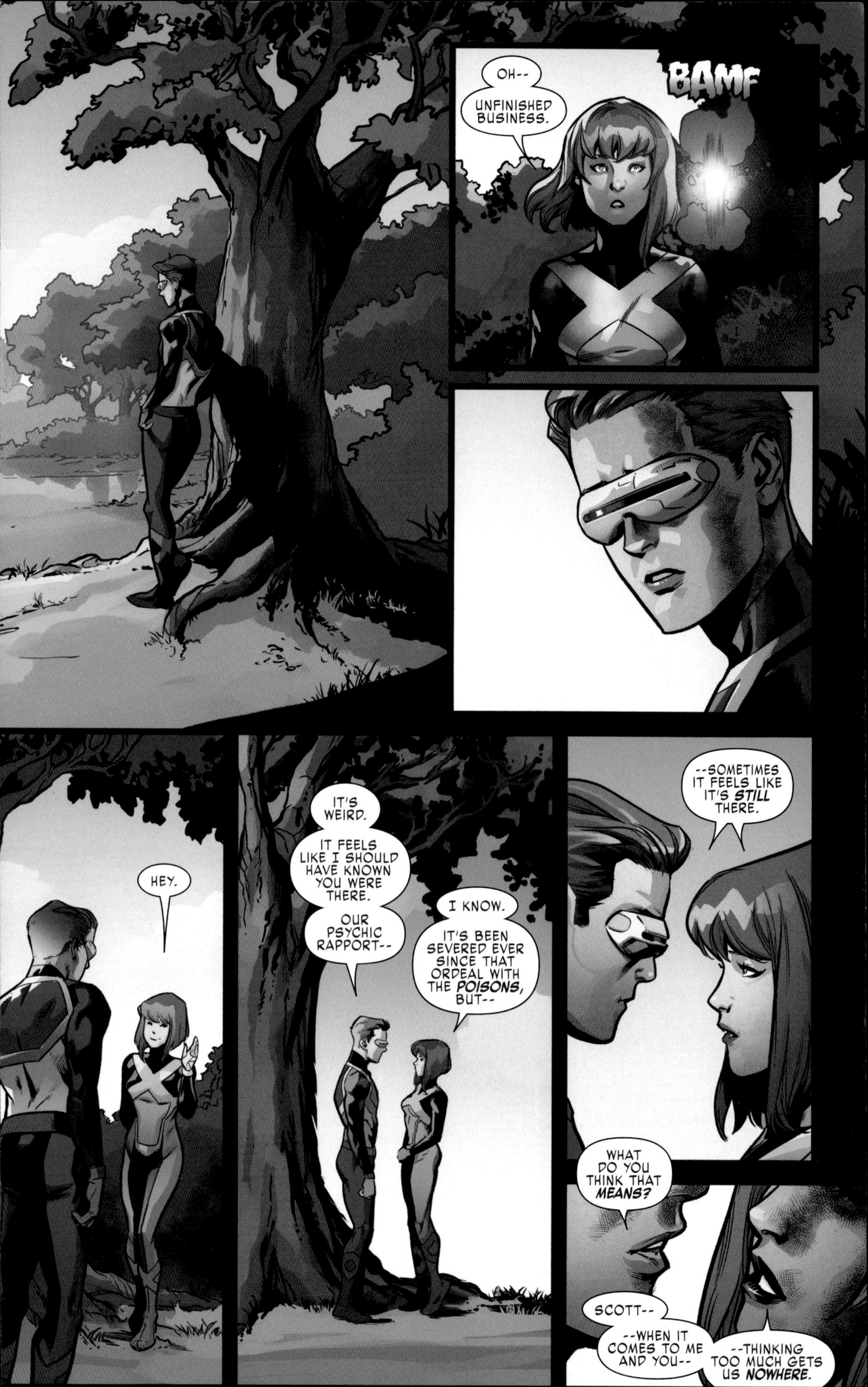
OH--
UNFINISHED BUSINESS.
BAMF
HEY.
IT'S WEIRD.
IT FEELS LIKE I SHOULD HAVE KNOWN YOU WERE THERE.
OUR PSYCHIC RAPPORT--
I KNOW.
IT'S BEEN SEVERED EVER SINCE THAT ORDEAL WITH THE *POISONS*, BUT--
--SOMETIMES IT FEELS LIKE IT'S *STILL* THERE.
WHAT DO YOU THINK THAT *MEANS?*
SCOTT--
--WHEN IT COMES TO ME AND YOU--
--THINKING TOO MUCH GETS US *NOWHERE*.

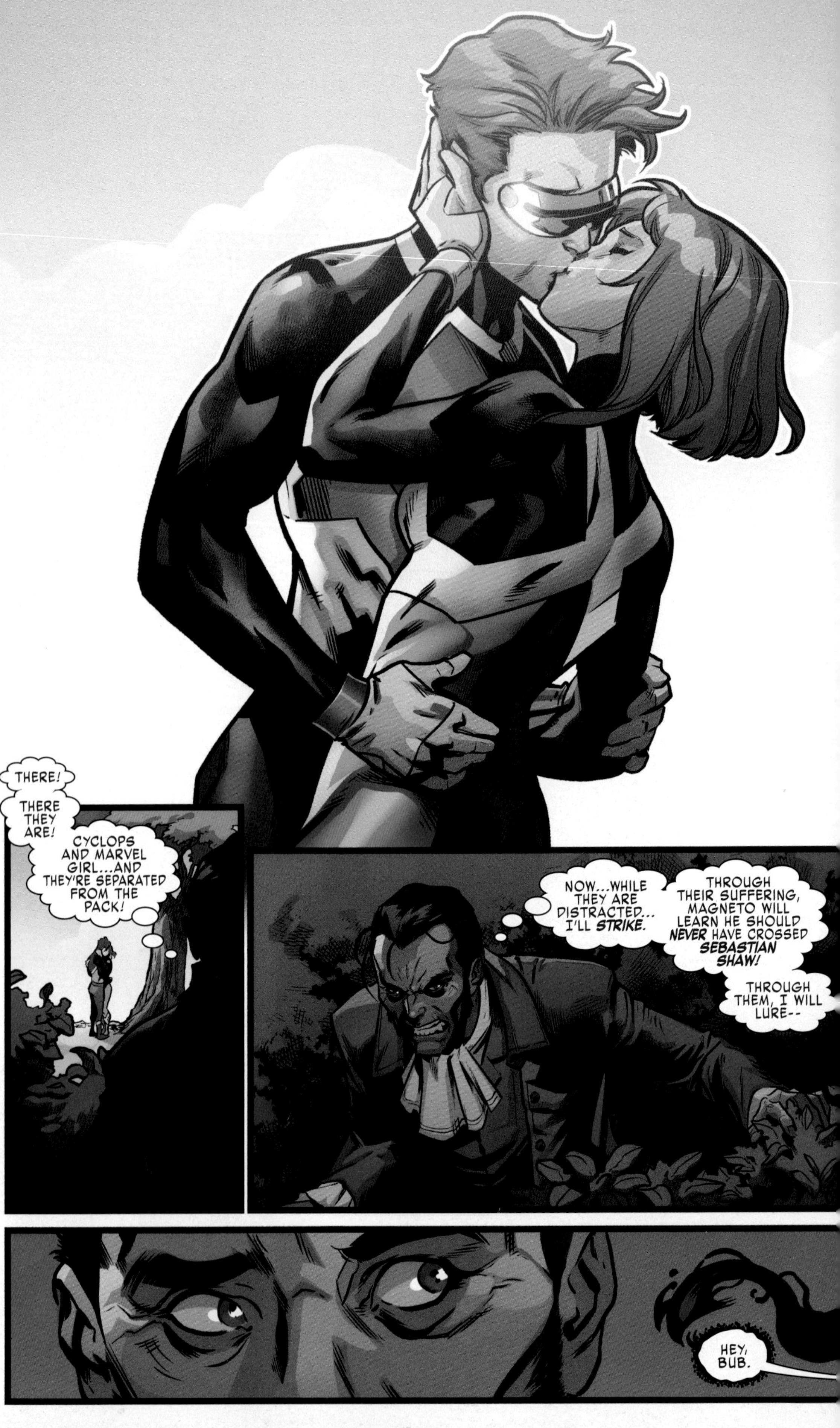
THERE!
THERE THEY ARE!
CYCLOPS AND MARVEL GIRL...AND THEY'RE SEPARATED FROM THE PACK!
NOW...WHILE THEY ARE DISTRACTED... I'LL STRIKE.
THROUGH THEIR SUFFERING, MAGNETO WILL LEARN HE SHOULD NEVER HAVE CROSSED SEBASTIAN SHAW!
THROUGH THEM, I WILL LURE--
HEY, BUB.

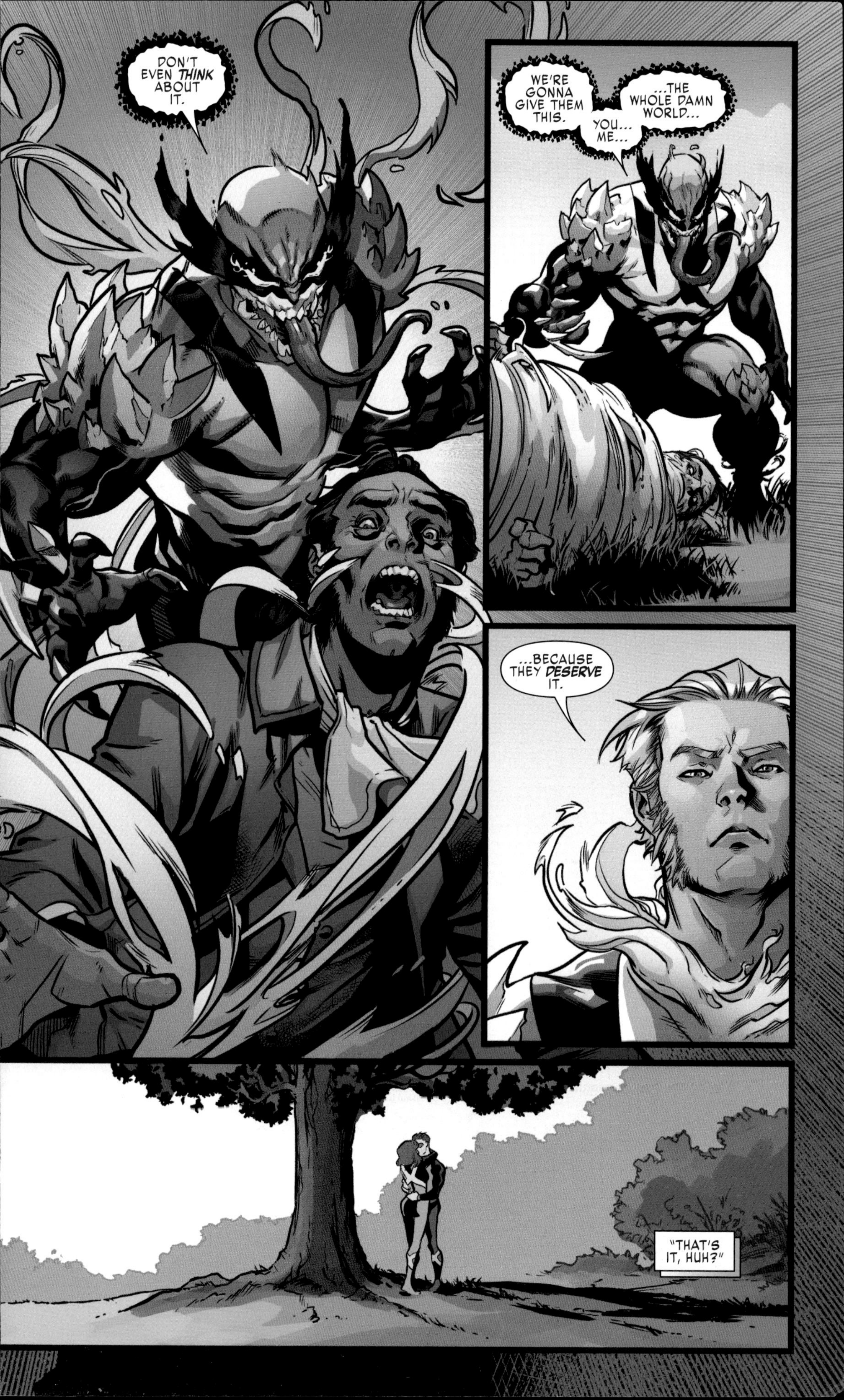
DON'T EVEN *THINK* ABOUT IT.
WE'RE GONNA GIVE THEM THIS.
YOU... ME...
...THE WHOLE DAMN WORLD...
...BECAUSE THEY *DESERVE* IT.
"THAT'S IT, HUH?"

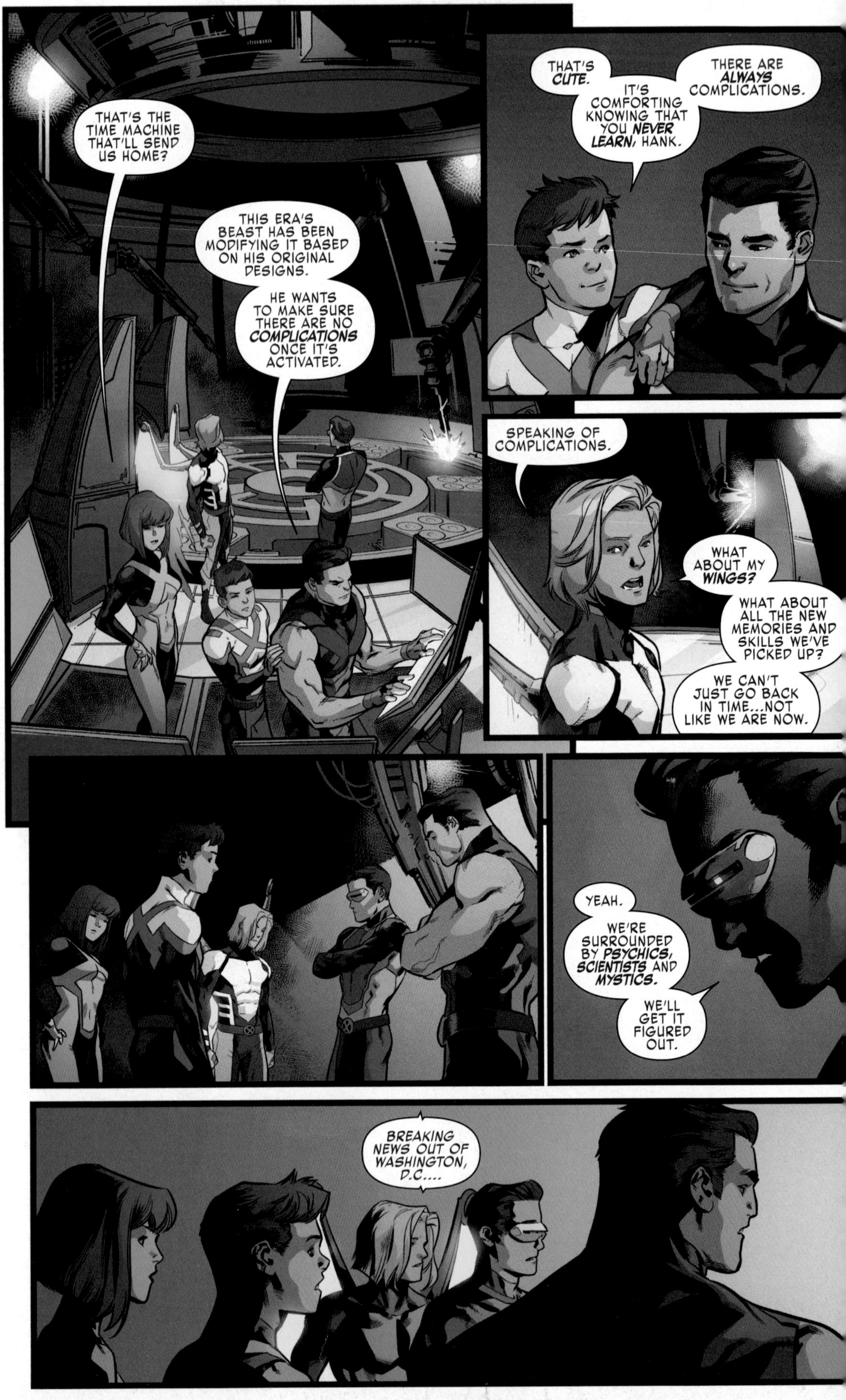

THAT'S THE TIME MACHINE THAT'LL SEND US HOME?
THIS ERA'S BEAST HAS BEEN MODIFYING IT BASED ON HIS ORIGINAL DESIGNS.
HE WANTS TO MAKE SURE THERE ARE NO COMPLICATIONS ONCE IT'S ACTIVATED.
THAT'S CUTE.
IT'S COMFORTING KNOWING THAT YOU NEVER LEARN, HANK.
THERE ARE ALWAYS COMPLICATIONS.
SPEAKING OF COMPLICATIONS.
WHAT ABOUT MY WINGS?
WHAT ABOUT ALL THE NEW MEMORIES AND SKILLS WE'VE PICKED UP?
WE CAN'T JUST GO BACK IN TIME...NOT LIKE WE ARE NOW.
YEAH.
WE'RE SURROUNDED BY PSYCHICS, SCIENTISTS AND MYSTICS.
WE'LL GET IT FIGURED OUT.
BREAKING NEWS OUT OF WASHINGTON, D.C....

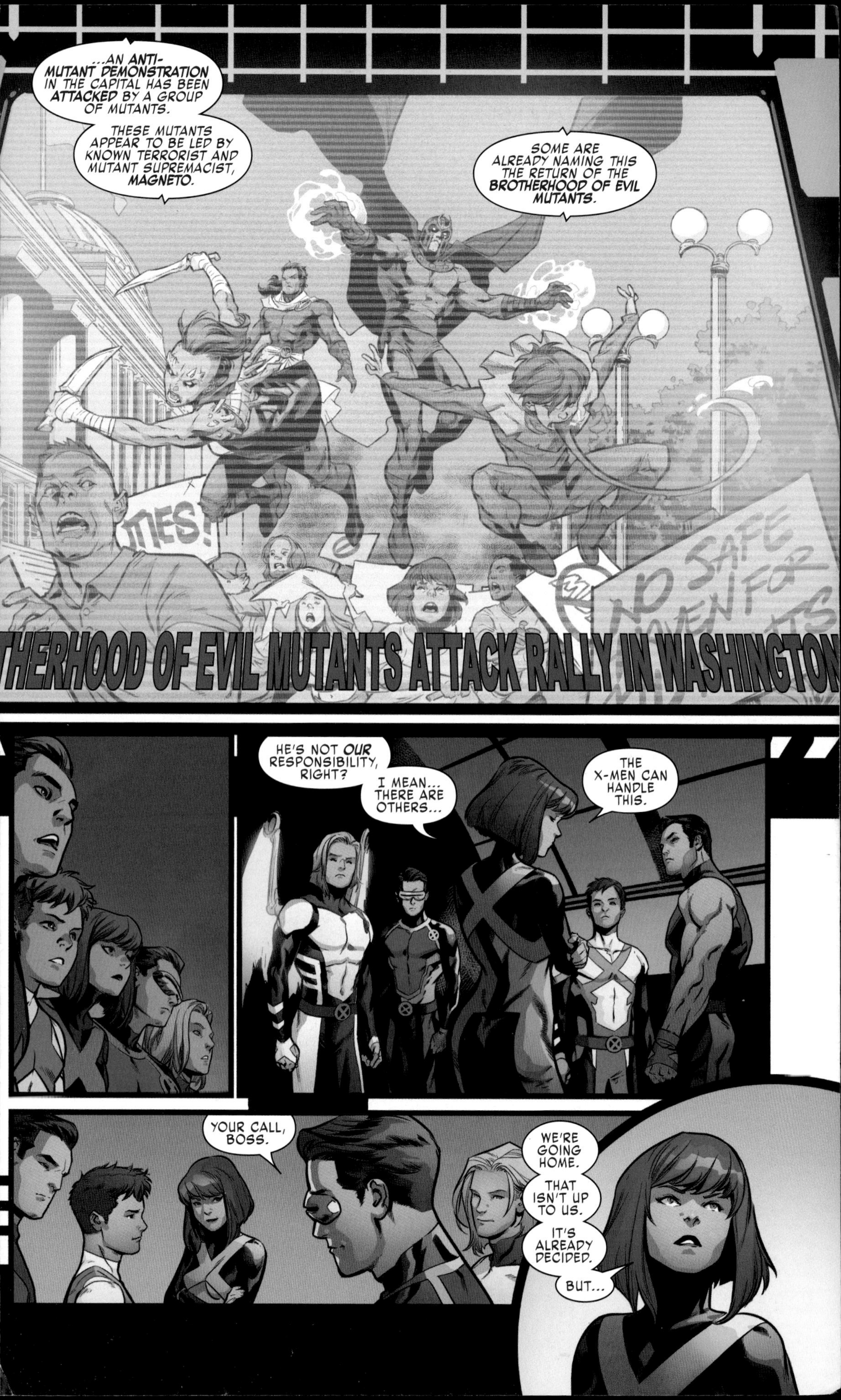
...AN ANTI-MUTANT DEMONSTRATION IN THE CAPITAL HAS BEEN ATTACKED BY A GROUP OF MUTANTS.
THESE MUTANTS APPEAR TO BE LED BY KNOWN TERRORIST AND MUTANT SUPREMACIST, MAGNETO.
SOME ARE ALREADY NAMING THIS THE RETURN OF THE BROTHERHOOD OF EVIL MUTANTS.
THERHOOD OF EVIL MUTANTS ATTACK RALLY IN WASHINGTON
HE'S NOT OUR RESPONSIBILITY, RIGHT?
I MEAN... THERE ARE OTHERS...
THE X-MEN CAN HANDLE THIS.
YOUR CALL, BOSS.
WE'RE GOING HOME.
THAT ISN'T UP TO US.
IT'S ALREADY DECIDED.
BUT...

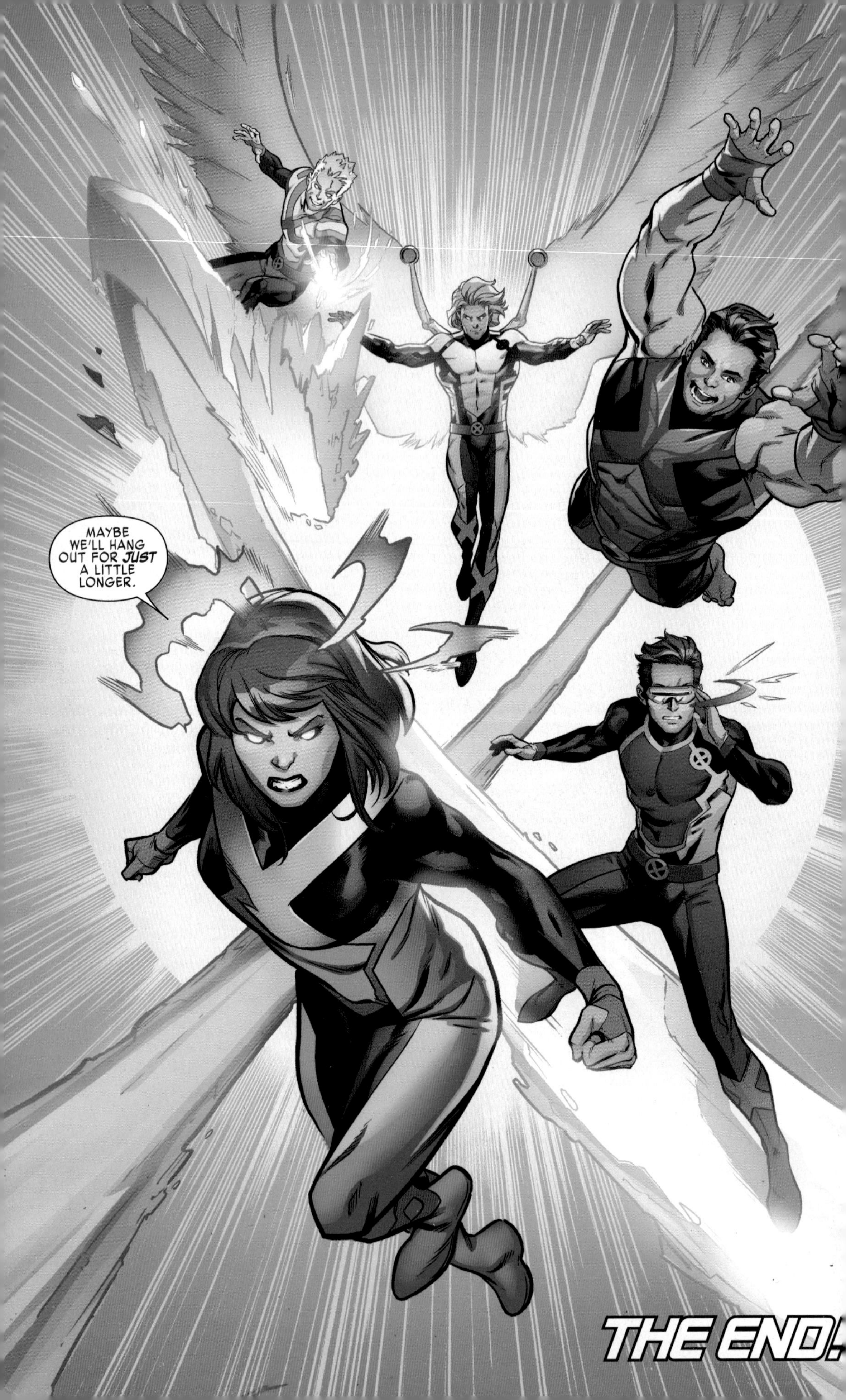
MAYBE WE'LL HANG OUT FOR *JUST* A LITTLE LONGER.
THE END!